Armageddon Insurance

The New Cold War History

Odd Arne Westad, *editor*

This series focuses on new interpretations of the Cold War era made possible by the opening of Soviet, East European, Chinese, and other archives. Books in the series based on multilingual and multiarchival research incorporate interdisciplinary insights and new conceptual frameworks that place historical scholarship in a broad, international context.

A complete list of books published in The New Cold War History is available at www.uncpress.org.

Armageddon Insurance
Civil Defense in the United States
and Soviet Union, 1945–1991

....

EDWARD M. GEIST

The University of North Carolina Press   Chapel Hill

© 2019 The University of North Carolina Press
All rights reserved
Set in Charis by Westchester Publishing Services
Manufactured in the United States of America

The University of North Carolina Press has been a member of the
Green Press Initiative since 2003.

Library of Congress Cataloging-in-Publication Data
Names: Geist, Edward, author.
Title: Armageddon insurance : civil defense in the United States and Soviet
 Union, 1945–1991 / Edward M. Geist.
Other titles: Civil defense in the United States and Soviet Union, 1945–1991 |
 New Cold War history.
Description: Chapel Hill : University of North Carolina Press, [2019] | Series:
 The new Cold War history | Includes bibliographical references and index.
Identifiers: LCCN 2018018512| ISBN 9781469645247 (cloth : alk. paper) |
 ISBN 9781469645254 (pbk : alk. paper) | ISBN 9781469645261 (ebook)
Subjects: LCSH: Civil defense—United States—History—20th century. |
 Civil defense—Soviet Union—History—20th century. | Cold War.
Classification: LCC UA926 .G45 2019 | DDC 363.350947/09047—dc23
 LC record available at https://lccn.loc.gov/2018018512

Cover illustrations: Top, detail of *Action Following the Signal "Chemical
Attack"* poster; bottom, detail of *Nuclear Weapons* poster (author's personal
collection).

Small portions of chapters two through five were previously published as
"Was There a Real 'Mineshaft Gap'? Bomb Shelters in the USSR, 1945–62,"
Journal of Cold War Studies 14, no. 2 (2012): 3–28. Used here with permission.

To my dissertation advisor, Donald J. Raleigh

Contents

Acknowledgments, xi

Introduction, 1
Propaganda, Mobilization, and Survival

1 Inauspicious Beginnings, 17

2 The Window of Survivability, 53

3 The "Oh My God!" Phase, 97

4 The Real Mineshaft Gap, 138

5 Strategy for Survival, 189

Conclusion, 240
Insurance Forgone

Notes, 255

Bibliography, 295

Index, 315

Illustrations and Tables

Illustrations

Nagasaki tunnel shelters, 18

Herbert Block decries underdevelopment of civil defense (late 1950), 50

Herbert Block on civil defense appropriations (August 1951), 61

Herbert Block on civil defense (September 1953), 109

Estimated effectiveness of OCD fallout shelter system, 1966, 160

Oak Ridge fallout shelter and evacuation map, 1973, 183

April 1982 political cartoon illustrated the absurdities of Reagan's CRP plan, 215

Tables

February 1959 shelter plan of Frunze district, Moscow, 92

Evolution of shelter plans of Ukrainian SSR, 1962–66, 177

Estimated effectiveness of alternative civil defense programs considered by the U.S. Department of Defense, 1977, 205

Acknowledgments

Much like surviving nuclear war, writing a book is much easier with a supportive community. My fascination with civil defense dates back to my childhood in Oak Ridge, Tennessee. I began my studies of U.S. and Soviet civil defense as an undergraduate at the College of William and Mary, where I received advice and encouragement from Fred Corney and Tsuyoshi Hasegawa. I am particularly indebted to my graduate advisor Donald J. Raleigh for his patience and guidance over the course of my studies at the University of North Carolina, without which I would definitely not be where I am today. I am also grateful to Michael Hunt, whose advice and recommendations proved invaluable during and after graduate school.

Generous funding from the United States Department of Education (Fulbright-Hays) and the American Council of Learned Societies allowed me to live and work in Moscow, Washington, and Kiev, enabling the research that became this book. My fellow researchers in Moscow deserve my gratitude for their support following my mother's tragic death during my stay there. After completing my doctoral work I returned to Washington as a Stanton Nuclear Security Fellow in RAND's Arlington office. I began drafting this book in my final months as a Stanton Fellow, so the Frank R. Stanton Foundation contributed to this project as well. In the course of these travails I met some wonderful friends and colleagues working on topics related to civil defense, including Frank Blazich and Alex Wellerstein. My fellow Oak Ridger Carl Willis instigated our adventures in Chernobyl and Semipalatinsk that not only informed my research but made my life much more exciting.

This work is what it is because of the willingness of several archivists and librarians who went above and beyond the call of duty to provide me with the materials I needed. One of the bibliographic consultants at the Russian National Library brought me the drawer from the military department's internal subject matter catalog for civil defense books published prior to 1960, guiding me to countless sources of whose existence I would otherwise have been entirely unaware. An archivist at the Central State Archive of Moscow Oblast' bent her employer's rules and permitted researchers unlimited photography. I also benefited from the willingness of the National Archives in College Park to allow me access to materials that had not yet been sorted or indexed by the archivists.

As the fortunate beneficiary of a postdoc at Stanford's Center for International Security and Cooperation funded by the John D. and Catherine T. MacArthur Foundation, I had the opportunity to devote my full attention to developing this book in 2014–15. Lynn Eden deserves my thanks for her role in bringing me to Stanford. My mentor David Holloway shared his immense knowledge of Soviet nuclear history and his wise counsel as I developed the book. My CISAC colleagues read parts of the manuscript and provided constructive criticism. James Cameron and Bart Bernstein pointed me to some crucial sources I never would have found otherwise. This book also benefited from the feedback and attention of UNC Press, including the four anonymous peer reviewers. I would also like to thank the RAND Corporation not just for providing me with the requisite flexibility to bring this project to fruition, but also for allowing this historian to become his subject matter. The views expressed in this book are solely my own and not those of the RAND Corporation or its clients.

Armageddon Insurance

Introduction
Propaganda, Mobilization, and Survival

This time when the sirens went off, it was not a test. At 11:41 A.M. on July 30, 1957, Soviet air defense informed city governments in Ukraine that it had detected two-engine enemy jet bombers approaching Soviet airspace from over the Black Sea. As the aircraft were then west of Sevastopol, they would reach the industrial centers of eastern Ukraine within a few hours. Believing that this alarming development might be the opening salvo of World War III, civil defense sprung into action. Following the orders of the Ministry of Defense, at 12:50 P.M. civil defense issued an official air raid warning in the Ukrainian city of Dnepropetrovsk.

The inhabitants of Dnepropetrovsk did not know how to react to the wailing alarms. Owing to equipment shortages, only some parts of the city had sirens. Furthermore, not all factories relayed the signal to their employees, and the wired radios many Soviet citizens depended on for information failed to repeat the signal. Workers remained at their posts while other city residents generally did little in reaction to the warnings that nuclear attack might be imminent.

At 1:30 P.M. civil defense issued an all-clear signal, as the "enemy jet bombers" had landed at a Soviet air base in Zaporozhia at 1:03 P.M. As it turned out, these aircraft were actually a group of six Soviet IL-28 bombers, misidentified by Soviet radar because they returned across the border without official clearance.[1]

Although Soviet officials did their best to forget about this embarrassing case of mistaken identity, it dramatically illustrates that they feared that civil defense was something that they might actually need. The government of the Union of Soviet Socialist Republics (USSR) believed that nuclear attack could come at any time, and, at a moment when it mistakenly believed that war might be under way, it attempted to protect its population using civil defense. On the other side of the Iron Curtain, its U.S. counterpart thought along similar lines. On the morning of May 5, 1955, "the United States Air Force was unable to identify a squadron of bombers flying over the Pacific Ocean," seemingly en route to central California. "For a few minutes, the situation was as it would have been in the case of an impending attack including the fact that no one involved in the warning system was certain whether or not an attack was about to occur." Perturbed officials gave "an order . . . to sound the alert warning sirens for a probable attack," which went off in Berkeley and Oakland. Yet as in Ukraine a few years later, the "enemy bombers" were soon discovered to be friendly craft. "It took the Air Force only a few minutes to identify the bomb squadron as an American one. All was back to normal in approximately ten minutes."[2]

What Is Civil Defense?

Civil defense is the use of measures such as shelter and evacuation to reduce damage to life and property caused by enemy attack or other disaster. The definition of civil defense in both of the superpowers evolved as the Cold War progressed, owing only in part to the increasing number and yield of nuclear weapons. At first, civil defense concerned itself only with the consequences of enemy air attack, lacking any institutional mandate to prepare for natural or technological disasters. Over time, however, civil defense devoted more attention to these emergencies and, by 1991, both American and Soviet civil defense expanded their purview to preparations to survive and mitigate the effects not only of nuclear war but also of industrial accidents, extreme weather events, and natural disasters such as earthquakes. As a result, civil defense came to be known by different names—as "emergency management" in English, and *grazhdanskaia zashchita* (civil protection) in Russian.

In both of the superpowers, however, civil defense was more than a concept; it was an institution—and these institutions strove to act in what they considered their own self-interest. Cold War civil defense comprised multiple components that shifted in accordance with its changing institutional missions. At a bare minimum these consisted of administration, mobilization, and training efforts, but they often also included the design and construction of bomb shelters, the development of evacuation plans, and the stockpiling of supplies. In addition, civil defense intersected with other aspects of war planning, such as economic mobilization and ensuring continuity of government after a nuclear attack. However, these only intermittently fell within the direct purview of Soviet or American civil defense because of numerous shifts in administrative boundaries. Even as other areas of the nuclear strategic postures of the United States and the USSR became more similar, their civil defense efforts increasingly diverged.

Scope and Methodology

To compare the superpowers' civil defense efforts, this book provides the first historical study of the USSR's civil defense program during the Cold War.[3] Although many archival documents about Soviet civil defense remain unavailable, the Russian and Ukrainian governments have released materials that address such topics as the Soviet leaders' decision-making process about civil defense, the amount budgeted for the program, and their opinion of its usefulness.[4] These sources reveal a considerably more complicated picture than the assessments produced by Western defense specialists during the Cold War. Neither an impotent "paper program" maintained for propaganda purposes nor a scheme to attain a strategic advantage over the West, the USSR's civil defense was an earnest attempt to maintain hope that the Soviet state could survive a nuclear attack in some form, however hobbled.

This book also offers a comparative institutional history of Soviet civil defense with its American counterpart. While this institutional focus marks a departure from recent scholarship about U.S. civil defense, which tends to focus on various facets of the program's history rather than the organization itself, it revives a rich tradition. Institutional histories produced by American civil defense advocates, the earliest studies of the topic, first emerged in the late 1940s and predominated for nearly forty years. Their authors, often themselves civil defense employees, sought to explain the failure of U.S. civil defense to attract sufficient political support and find ways to change this.[5] Starting in the 1980s, anxieties about the arms race inspired a new generation of scholars to scrutinize civil defense with a more critical eye.[6] Some accounts portrayed civil defense as a quintessential example of American Cold War nuclear mendacity, seeking to use it to critique past and present defense policy. Another group of historians published studies in the 2000s investigating how civil defense reflected postwar American culture.[7]

This account differs from earlier works on U.S. civil defense in both its institutional focus and its comparative approach, as well as its use of previously unexamined sources. Most of the records of U.S. civil defense agencies held in the National Archives remain uncataloged because of a lack of funding and personnel. I was fortunate enough to gain access to some of these materials, which offer an intimate portrait of the internal dynamics of these organizations and the personalities that ran them.

This book aims to hew as closely as possible to the archival record as it tracks the institutional history of U.S. and Soviet civil defense. To ascertain the motivations of the leaders of the superpowers' civil defense programs, this book pays particular attention to what the available documents indicate about these figures and their priorities. The picture that emerges of these individuals is sometimes deeply unflattering, but they seem not to have been guilty of the mendacity that both their contemporaries and latter-day scholars sometimes accused them of. To assess the goals and objectives of civil defense, I emphasize the budgetary history of the programs, as the minutiae of congressional negotiations and Politburo meetings did much to determine the course of the two nations' civil defense efforts.

A lack of accessible documents forced me to neglect certain topics. Foremost among these is continuity-of-government planning, an enterprise closely related to civil defense but one that remains highly classified in both the United States and the former USSR. The dearth of accessible Soviet documents on this subject dashed my hopes to include it in my comparative analysis. To my great surprise, I found very few references to continuity-of-government planning in the Soviet civil defense documents I saw, even for Moscow. Where I had expected to uncover elaborate plans to spirit the Soviet elite to safety if nuclear war threatened, or at least an emphasis on ensuring the continued functioning of state organs within Soviet civil defense plans, I saw little evidence for either. While the Soviet Union was rumored to have developed wildly elaborate continuity-of-government arrangements, without better documentation, I cannot reach a judgment about their accuracy. At the very least, the apparent lack of coordination between Soviet civil defense and continuity-of-government planning suggests that the latter did not live up to its formidable reputation.

In other areas, particularly popular culture, the profound differences between American and Soviet society forestall meaningful comparative analysis. In contrast to its officially sanctioned efforts to extoll the benefits of civilian nuclear energy, the USSR had very little "atomic culture" of the sort scholars such as Spencer Weart and Paul Boyer ably studied in the U.S. context.[8] While in America tales of atomic war flooded pulp magazines and movie screens shortly after Hiroshima, censors saw to it that ordinary Soviet citizens remained ignorant of what a mushroom cloud looked like until 1954. Bolshevik leaders considered the question of whether nuclear war could destroy the Soviet experiment, or even the implication that the USSR might not be strong enough to prevent another world war, to be so ideologically fraught that they strongly discouraged the production of novels and films exploring the topic of nuclear war. As a consequence, there are only isolated examples of Soviet "atomic culture," mostly from the 1980s.

I take pains to discuss these in detail, but they are insufficient to sustain a chronological comparison with the countless responses to the nuclear dilemma found in U.S. popular culture. Similarly, the lack of public opinion research in the USSR leaves me without any Soviet counterpart to the numerous public opinion surveys carried out by U.S. civil defense authorities between the 1950s and 1980s. Reports sent to party authorities and anecdotal evidence, however, strongly suggest that civil defense was as unpopular among Soviet citizens as it was among their counterparts in the capitalist world.

Explaining the Failure of Civil Defense

In the view of U.S. and Soviet civil defense officials, their own programs were failures. Neither U.S. nor Soviet civil defense ever concluded that it had achieved a substantial operational capability to protect its people from the effects of nuclear war. While the ambitions of U.S. civil defense remained stillborn owing to a lack of presidential enthusiasm and staunch congressional opposition, Soviet civil defense had a very limited estimate of what it could accomplish despite comparatively lavish funding. In private, U.S. and Soviet civil defense officials regularly expressed their frustrations with their inability to secure sufficient resources for a credible civil defense effort, and they spent decades searching for some way to bolster their meager base of political and popular support.

The great mystery of Cold War civil defense is that the superpowers rejected it for reasons that do not make much rational sense. Economic, strategic, and technical arguments have all been made against the possibility of civil defense in nuclear war and offered as explanations for U.S. and Soviet civil defense policies, but evidence for their historical influence is mixed at best. Economic arguments against civil defense investment were influential among political elites on both sides of the Iron Curtain, but it turns out that many opponents of civil defense who claimed such motivations eagerly supported strategically and technically dubious investments in nuclear weapons. Senator Henry Jackson of Washington, whose opposition crippled the U.S. public fallout shelter program in the mid-1960s, stands out as a notable example of this. While claiming to oppose civil defense for reasons of "economy," he fought tooth and nail to advocate for antiballistic missile (ABM) systems that would cost much more than the shelters, even though Pentagon studies had determined these systems would not work but the shelters would.

President Kennedy expressed his bewilderment with the congressional opposition to civil defense at a meeting a few months after the Cuban Missile Crisis. "On the one hand, they're talking about having all these atomic weapons. On the other hand, they don't want to take even the slightest trouble to protect the American population, yet they expect us to fire these weapons off." Kennedy felt a personal obligation to try to build a workable civil defense, despite the skepticism of much of his own cabinet: "We've got to have a program," he insisted. "I'd rather take the political burden [of pushing for higher civil defense spending] than I would of making, in effect, that we've abandoned this program."[9] In 1976, secretary of state Henry Kissinger expressed a similar sentiment during a discussion of the USSR's civil defense program. "It is an incongruous situation for a country to plan for nuclear war and not to save its society," he emphasized.[10] Yet both the United States and, to a lesser extent, its communist rival placed themselves in this "incongruous situation" for the bulk of the Cold War.

Furthermore, despite their prominence in latter-day scholarly accounts, strategic arguments against civil defense seem to have played a relatively little role in its failure to attain its institutional goals. In the West, many critics argued that any kind of defense against nuclear attack, including civil defense, would signal aggression to Moscow and increase the chances of war. Yet these objections do not seem to have been decisive in congressional debates on the topic, and both the Carter and Reagan administrations endorsed stronger civil defense policy despite the *objections*. Soviet theorists conceptualized nuclear strategy in different terms, and the USSR's accession to the ABM Treaty in 1972, which many Western observers interpreted as a sign that the Kremlin accepted the principle of mutual vulnerability, coincided with the historical apex of that nation's civil defense spending.

Moreover, both Moscow and Washington were so inept at inferring and interpreting each other's civil defense policies that these failed to serve as a meaningful strategic signal. Some Western analysts in the 1970s misconstrued the Soviet civil defense program as a major contributor to the USSR's strategic strength and warned shrilly that this supposed "mineshaft gap" jeopardized American security.[11] When these paranoid analyses contending that Soviet civil defense served as the foundation of an aggressive "war survival strategy" found their way back into the USSR in the late 1970s, Soviet civil defense officials reacted with a mixture of offense and bewilderment.[12] Even though the USSR's civil defense put that of the United States to shame, the biggest "mineshaft gap" of all was between the ambitions of civil defense officials on both sides of the Iron Curtain, who dreamed of creating programs that could plausibly work, and their inability to convince political elites to pay for them.

At their boldest, Soviet and U.S. civil defense attempted to reshape nuclear strategy and even the arms race itself to suit their institutional goals. At the beginning of the 1960s, Soviet civil defense officers appropriated foreign strategic theories to justify why the USSR needed to resuscitate its then-moribund program. Their success convincing military officials to incorporate civil defense into the USSR's nuclear strategy placed the program on the trajectory that carried it to its 1970s peak. In the United States, in the mid-1960s assistant secretary of defense for civil defense Steuart L. Pittman argued that civil defense should be considered a form of arms control. He suggested that cooperation with the Soviet Union on civil defense, beginning with technical exchanges and possibly building up to steps such as the mutual elimination of megaton-range weapons on humanitarian grounds, could not just make war less destructive if it occurred, but make it less likely in the first place.

Nor do U.S. and Soviet leaders seem to have rejected civil defense because scientists told them it was physically impossible. This outcome resulted not only from a lack of technical consensus among scientists in either country as to whether nuclear war was survivable, but also from disagreement about what form an enemy attack would take. The technical viability of civil defense depends on the nature of the nuclear threats it is designed to defend against. Not all nuclear wars are the same. The sole historical example of a nuclear war was both survived and won. In its final days World War II was a nuclear war—one from which the United States emerged entirely victorious and one from which Japan recovered. The technical case for civil defense grew increasingly tenuous as the yield, and particularly the number, of weapons on each side increased, but there were still reasons to believe that it might make a significant difference in the number of survivors— particularly if the adversary refrained from attacking populations per se. Even in the 1980s a lively scientific debate continued on the subject.[13]

The only way to know for sure whether civil defense can really make a meaningful difference in surviving nuclear war is by actually fighting one— at which point it is already too late. We cannot rule out the possibility that a nuclear war could produce unforeseen effects that would render any attempt to survive it hopeless. This is a very good reason not to fight a nuclear war, and not to use the threat of nuclear war as an instrument of foreign policy. It is not, however, a compelling rationale to forgo preparations to survive nuclear war so long as the possibility of such a conflict exists. The choices made by American and Soviet leaders do not reflect much appreciation of this principle.

The history of the superpowers' civil defense efforts reveals a disturbing parallel between them: both the Soviet and the American governments were willing to risk the destruction of civilization, yet saw comparatively little reason to try to save it if they came to blows. Engaged in what Thomas Schelling dubbed "competition in risk taking," neither Washington nor Moscow hesitated to gamble with its own survival, much less that of others.[14] If the scientific case for civil defense is flimsy, then the argument for hazarding a nuclear apocalypse over relatively minor political disagreements is considerably more so. That the world escaped the Cold War nuclear competition without a conflagration is not evidence this wager was a safe bet. As more information has come to light about how close the two blocs almost came to war in 1962 and 1983, more and more scholars have come to the conclusion that luck, rather than wisdom, accounts for our survival.

The contradiction between the U.S. and Soviet embrace of nuclear weapons as the solution to their security problems and their unwillingness to take reasonable precautions to protect their citizens from nuclear attack speaks volumes about the two societies' conflicted relationships with the threat of nuclear war. This book employs the institutional histories of the two states' civil defense programs to explore how the two societies, different as they were, came to this contradictory position.

The American Contract State versus the Soviet Garrison State

A specter haunted America in the early years of the Cold War—the specter of the garrison state. This terrifying menace threatened to destroy the things the United States was defending—liberty, democracy, and free enterprise—in order to save them from their nefarious communist enemy. To deter or defeat Stalin and his multitudinous hordes, America needed to be strong, but how could it accomplish this without adopting at least some of its enemy's methods and undermining its cherished values from within? The Truman administration, Congress, and the American public struggled with this vexing question and ultimately settled on an imperfect compromise: a contract state could not mobilize societal resources as extensively as the Soviet command economy but made only limited interventions into national life.[15] U.S. and Soviet civil defense emerged and evolved in the context of the competition between the American contract state and the USSR's garrison state.

American sociologist Harold Lasswell introduced the term "garrison state" during the Second World War to describe how the trends seen in the various belligerent societies would play out in coming decades. Communist, fascist, and democratic states alike would converge into defense-oriented military technocracies dominated by "specialists on violence." Compelled by life-or-death competition with its like-minded peers, the garrison state would employ whatever means available to maximize its fighting effectiveness, including domestic coercion, propaganda, and wholesale social engineering. Lasswell himself regarded Hitler's Germany and Stalin's Soviet Union as merely transitional forms on the path to such dystopias. In his vision, the shape of the garrison state would be determined by the nature of modern warfare, rather than by ideology. Liberal and communist ideals alike would bow to the demands of defense.[16]

Fortunately, Lasswell's nightmare vision never fully materialized in either superpower. Cold War Americans self-consciously rejected moving too far toward a garrison state, even while they accepted a degree of peacetime mobilization unprecedented in U.S. history.[17] The Soviet Union, meanwhile, resembled a garrison state much more closely than its capitalist rival, but it differed from Lasswell's ideal type in that the Soviet military always remained firmly subjugated to Communist Party authority. Soviet leaders such as Stalin and Khrushchev repeatedly took steps to marginalize the military to neutralize perceived threats to their power, some of which seriously compromised the USSR's ability to defend itself.[18] The Soviet Union was a garrison state only insofar as the party found it desirable.

The Soviet Union therefore constituted what I term a "party-garrison state." The party-garrison state emerged as the result of a process initiated by the Communist Party in the 1920s to consolidate its domestic authority and defend the country from potential foreign intervention. The party-garrison state aimed to maximize the military's potential to defend the Communist Party and its revolutionary project, rather than protecting Soviet territory or population per se. In fact, it was oriented at countering domestic threats as much as foreign threats. Consistent with the Bolsheviks' collectivist mentality, the lives of individuals—even Communist Party members—were not regarded as particularly important relative to the interests of the party-state. A key distinction between the party-garrison state and Lasswell's ideal type was the critical importance of ideology. Instead of withering away in the way he envisioned, both it and the Communist Party continued to dominate as long as they remained viable, and once they were no longer so, the entire garrison state collapsed along with them.

Despite this deviation, the USSR was a garrison state in the sense that it evinced many of the traits Lasswell perceived in the 1940s. The Soviet Union oriented an extraordinary fraction of its planned economy to defense even in peacetime. The command economy could reallocate resources in ways a market economy could not, enabling the USSR to become a superpower despite its comparatively weak technical and economic base.[19] The Soviet Union also maintained a large standing army composed mostly of conscripts, which was envisioned as the nucleus of an absolutely immense mobilized force in wartime.[20] While the country's system of universal conscription targeted only men, all citizens were required to undergo both military and civil defense training in the course of their schooling. The Soviet government sustained this extraordinary degree of mobilization from the 1930s until the final phases of its existence.[21]

In an insightful 1992 article, political scientist Aaron L. Friedberg argued that the United States did not become a garrison state during the Cold War because the structure of its domestic institutions limited the ability of the central government to impose its will on the country as a whole. In contrast to the "strong" Soviet state, which could (and did) impose its will on the entire USSR by coercive means, he classifies the Cold War United States as a "weak contract" state, which "extracted money and manpower for military purposes, but it did so at levels lower than those Lasswell had anticipated and certainly far lower than came to be common during the same period in the Soviet Union." This system emerged over the course of the first decade of the Cold War. "The three distinguishing characteristics of the contract state," Friedberg holds, were "its constrained extractive scale (the fact that it did not tax and conscript even more heavily than it did), its limited directive scope (the fact that it concentrated on procuring arms and research rather than directing overall national economic development), and its reliance on the contract mechanism to harness private resources to national purposes."[22]

The U.S. and Soviet civil defense programs during the Cold War offer an excellent test case to compare and contrast the workings of the American contract state with the Soviet party-garrison state. Several scholars, most extensively Andrew D. Grossman, have argued that the U.S. civil defense program demonstrates that the American Cold War contract state was a sham, mere cover for a coercive "civic garrison state."[23] Grossman and others charge that the Truman administration architected the civil defense program "as instruments of social control, the primary objective of which was to prevent the American public from becoming so terrified over the effects of nuclear weapons as to erode the domestic political consensus for postwar grand strategy."[24] A close examination of the failures of U.S. civil defense to actualize its desired policies, however, demonstrates that domestic pressure groups were able to stymie almost all of its initiatives—a telltale symptom that the United States was a "weak" state after all. Rather than a dire conspiracy to militarize American life, civil defense helps illustrate how the American Cold War consensus converged on an inconsistent cluster of policies that seems to have undermined the nation's security by unintentionally signaling an extremely aggressive posture to the USSR.

Soviet civil defense, meanwhile, exemplifies the peculiarities and limitations of the party-garrison state. States are only "strong" or "weak" relative to one another, and their ability to overcome domestic pressure groups is inevitably greater in some areas than others. The USSR aspired to be a totalitarian state in which the party transformed every aspect of life to construct an ideal communist society, but its actual power to enact positive change was always far more circumscribed than it would like. While it aimed to "engineer human souls" and remake its citizens into "new Soviet people," in the 1950s the CPSU struggled to get local authorities to stop using bomb shelters as root cellars so they might be available for use in case of surprise attack. For all its willingness to utilize coercive instruments to achieve its goals, the Soviet party-garrison state often stumbled in its ill-fated quest for domestic and international security.

Civil defense is a necessary condition for a nuclear age garrison state, but not a sufficient one. The weakness of civil defense was merely one of the many reasons that the United States failed to become a garrison state during the Cold War, while the comparatively extensive Soviet program merely contributed to the party-garrison state.

Mobilization and Survival

Was civil defense intended to shape people's minds rather than save their lives? The extreme difficulty of surviving nuclear attack led many people in both superpowers to ridicule their government's civil defense efforts. In both countries, people repeated popular jokes mocking civil defense. For instance, Americans quipped, "What do you do when you see the flash? You put your head between your legs and kiss your ass goodbye." In the USSR, people told a slightly more complicated version of the same joke: "What do you do when you hear the air raid sirens? You wrap yourself in a sheet and crawl slowly to the cemetery. Why slowly? So as not to inspire panic."[25] Civil defense never enjoyed widespread popularity or support from the inhabitants of either the United States or the Soviet Union. That civil defense during the Cold War became the object of widespread popular derision has led many to assume that it could never have been sincerely embraced by anyone.

It turns out that U.S. and Soviet civil defense officials were deadly serious about protecting citizens from nuclear attack, but both countries' civil defense propaganda sometimes served other, sometimes unrelated, purposes. American and Soviet civil defense alike produced propaganda intended to condition individuals' perceptions about both their own state and the enemy. Following Soviet nomenclature, I term this ideological and political socialization of citizens *agitation*. In both superpowers, civil defense propaganda attempted to convince citizens of the existence of an enemy threat and of their own government's determination to protect its people. At times, civil defense propaganda served a purpose other than its ostensible one, such as consolidating popular support for Stalin's policies in the late 1920s or giving an outlet to Americans' patriotic impulses in the months after Pearl Harbor. Yet this is not to say that civil defense was a sham. The cynicism of Cold War civil defense has been exaggerated because while it had a propaganda function, this was complemented in both superpowers by earnest efforts to create civil defense programs that could meaningfully protect citizens by means of shelter or evacuation. Much of the time these activities were operationally and institutionally distinct from public information campaigns. This book aims to explore how the complicated relationship between the practical and agitational aspects of civil defense evolved in each superpower.

In the United States, the "serious" work of civil defense largely consisted of developing the technical and conceptual foundation for a program that could shield at least a fraction of the American people from a Soviet nuclear attack. Civil defense officials understood that such an effort would be extraordinarily expensive and economically disruptive, and that it might run counter to the country's traditions, but many of them earnestly believed that it was an essential insurance policy against a nuclear attack emanating from the USSR. They devoted most of their time and effort to convincing the American people and government—particularly Congress—to support the realization of their ambitions. For most of the Cold War, U.S. civil defense propaganda was subordinate to this goal—that is, it sought to mobilize citizens to support the political project of a greatly expanded civil defense effort, rather than to survive nuclear war per se. While this objective served the institutional interests of civil defense, it was not mendacious in the way it may appear in retrospect. A civil defense program with any hope of working would require immense public investment, and this funding could be secured only with the support of a broad political consensus. In the view of civil defense officials, convincing ordinary citizens of the possibility and necessity of such a program was an essential prerequisite to saving the country from an enemy attack they genuinely feared.

At times, U.S. civil defense propaganda had a different goal: placating civil defense enthusiasts to conserve resources for other national priorities. President Dwight Eisenhower was never warm on civil defense, and his administration propounded several dubious approaches to protecting the public, namely, tactical evacuation (evacuating cities in the few hours between the detection of Soviet bombers and their arrival at their targets) in the mid-1950s and home fallout shelters in the late 1950s. Tactical evacuation and home shelters made individual citizens responsible for their own survival, avoiding costly federal investments the president found distasteful. Eisenhower would likely have eschewed even these token efforts had it not been for pressure from influential members of Congress such as Estes Kefauver and Chet Holifield, who pressed for the kind of shelter programs sought by civil defense officials. The relative lack of influential political proponents of civil defense among U.S. politicians after the mid-1960s reduced the need to maintain a nominal program for political reasons, allowing civil defense to slip into relative obscurity until the 1980s.

U.S. civil defense propaganda never produced satisfactory results for the agencies that produced it. While the civil defense media campaign waged by the Federal Civil Defense Administration in the early 1950s may have played a key role in convincing American citizens that the Soviet Union could attack the continental United States with nuclear weapons, this propaganda did not have the hoped-for effect of producing widespread political support for increased civil defense spending. In the Eisenhower years, attempts to promote relatively inexpensive civil defense programs that passed most costs onto individual citizens received a Bronx cheer from both civil defense advocates and critics, who saw these efforts as either hopelessly inadequate or pointless (or both). The poorly conducted effort to promote evacuation programs in the Reagan era became a lightning rod for critics of that president's defense policies, who ridiculed the administration by highlighting its dubious claims that dispersing Americans into the countryside when war appeared imminent could save most of them in a nuclear attack.

The "agitational" and "practical" aspects of civil defense took on a considerably different relationship in the Soviet Union. In the 1920s, civil defense propaganda played a nontrivial role in the political struggle that ended with Joseph Stalin's consolidation of power. In the mid-1920s the Soviet Union was riven by a struggle for power after the death of Vladimir Lenin and had yet to establish the mechanisms of mass mobilization that would define its later history. In 1927, a breakdown of relations with Western powers led to a "war scare" that both Stalin and his rivals attempted to leverage for their own benefit. The "war scare" included the first efforts to carry out mass civil defense training in the Soviet Union, but these sought to achieve domestic political goals rather than protect citizens from enemy air attack. In fact, the USSR established a civil defense program only in 1932. While the USSR never quite became the type of "garrison state" feared by American social scientists in the 1940s, during World War II and its aftermath it was arguably the most thoroughly militarized society in modern history. Once Stalinism was fully established in the 1930s, the Bolshevik regime possessed a comprehensive system of economic, political, and social controls that placed the country in a state of permanent mobilization. Stalin's consolidation of power rendered political persuasion and the placation of powerful dissenters, the "non-practical" goals of U.S. civil defense propaganda, largely irrelevant.

Soviet civil defense propaganda still served political and ideological objectives, albeit distinctively Soviet ones. Promoting civil defense helped reinforce official narratives of omnipresent foreign threats to the USSR, which in turn justified policies that constrained citizens' freedom and standard of living. Civil defense also reinforced the Soviet government's claims to care for its people's well-being. Soviet propaganda sometimes exaggerated the ability of the country's civil defense to protect citizens—for instance, by implying that enough shelters existed for all city dwellers. Soviet leaders were desperate to project an image of strength to both domestic and foreign audiences. Claiming that the country could withstand nuclear war served this end, but it also drew attention to an undesirable ideological contradiction: if the USSR was really so powerful, why could it not prevent the West from destroying Soviet cities with atomic bombs? Admitting that civil defense might be necessary was itself an admission of weakness. Disagreement about this issue extended to the highest levels of the Communist Party leadership, with individuals such as Anastas Mikoian (the second-most influential figure in the country in the late 1950s) arguing that civil defense was a waste of money and that the country should seek security elsewhere. Critics such as Mikoian ultimately lost this argument, and the USSR invested billions of rubles in civil defense during the tenure of Leonid Brezhnev (1964–82).

The USSR's attempts to create a civil defense against nuclear attack were driven by Soviet leaders' acute sense of their own vulnerability. Until the late 1960s Soviet nuclear forces lagged behind those of the United States both quantitatively and qualitatively. Moreover, even after achieving numerical parity with the U.S. nuclear arsenal, Soviet military analysts were pessimistic that much of their strategic forces would survive an American preemptive strike. Soviet leaders, as it turns out, refused to accept the concept of "Mutual Assured Destruction" not because they seriously believed that they could win a nuclear war but because they lacked confidence they could deny victory to the Americans. The devastation of the Soviet Union seemed a near certainty, but the Soviet military's own analyses indicated that too little of its retaliatory forces might survive to destroy America in turn.[26] That the U.S. military continued to seek the ability to destroy Soviet strategic forces even after secretary of defense Robert S. McNamara articulated the "Assured Destruction" doctrine in the mid-1960s further stoked Soviet anxieties. In Soviet eyes, the United States appeared to be a devious and determined adversary—one that could plausibly threaten to start a nuclear war.[27]

Relatively confident that preparations for an American preemptive attack could be detected in advance, the USSR planned its civil defense on the assumption that there would be days or weeks of warning. A combination of evacuation and shelters would protect at least some fraction of the country's population from nuclear attack. Declassified documents contradict claims made by Western analysts in the 1970s that the Soviet Union thought its civil defense would allow it to "win" a nuclear war. Instead, Soviet civil defense was a desperation measure that the USSR's rulers had relatively little faith in, but feared they might need anyway. In short, it was "Armageddon insurance."

Organization of the Book

This work is organized to follow the Soviet and U.S. civil defense organizations' evolving technical and strategic conception of nuclear war throughout the Cold War period (1945–91). Chapter 1 clarifies the reasons why neither the United States nor the Soviet Union embarked on a civil defense program addressing nuclear weapons until 1950 and 1953, respectively. Domestic political calculations, rather than skepticism about the technical feasibility of passive defenses against the atomic bomb, caused this delay.

The second chapter focuses on the period during the 1950s when American and Soviet civil defense planned for a nuclear war fought using a limited number of low-yield nuclear weapons delivered by vulnerable subsonic manned bombers. In contrast to a conflict waged with thousands of high-yield thermonuclear weapons carried by impossible-to-intercept ballistic missiles, which became possible a decade later, planners had good reason to believe that such a war would be not merely survivable but winnable—and both Washington and Moscow expected civil defense to help win it.

The third chapter describes how civil defense planners adjusted to the qualitatively new nuclear threat that materialized with the introduction of thermonuclear weapons and ballistic missiles during the mid-1950s. Furiously rapid developments in both nuclear weapons and researchers' understanding of them compelled Soviet and U.S. civil defense alike to consider alternative tactics to protect civilians.

The fourth chapter investigates the diverging courses of U.S. and Soviet civil defense from the early 1960s to the mid-1970s. While Kennedy's effort to create a nationwide system of fallout shelters failed in the face of insurmountable congressional opposition, the USSR invested increasing resources in both bomb shelters and ambitious plans to evacuate urban populations to the countryside.

The final chapter reveals for the first time the extent to which Soviet civil defense efforts influenced U.S. defense policy during the late Cold War and the strange resulting intersection between civil defense and nuclear strategy. Convinced that the USSR could use its civil defense for strategic leverage, the Carter and Reagan administrations endorsed an ill-conceived policy of "crisis relocation" as their counterparts in the USSR lost their faith in the ability of their program to secure the survival of the Soviet state.

1 Inauspicious Beginnings

At about 7 A.M. on August 6, 1945, air raid sirens in the city of Hiroshima, Japan, alerted citizens of the need to take cover. They streamed into bomb shelters throughout the city. Erected after American air raids on Japan began in earnest the previous year, these shelters were largely primitive, earth-covered structures. The residents of Hiroshima, however, did not remain in them for long: a single weather plane flew over the city and promptly departed. Leaving the shelters, the people of Hiroshima set out about their usual routine.

The alert seemed to be just another of the countless false alarms that encouraged a blasé attitude toward the air raid signals. At 8 A.M. radar identified a small group of American B-29s approaching Hiroshima. Japanese air defense assumed that this was likely a reconnaissance mission. Japanese radio issued an all-clear signal while simultaneously advising residents to seek shelter if B-29s appeared over the city. Yet only a few residents of Hiroshima heeded the warning and returned to their shelters as the B-29s approached. Many of them did not live to regret this decision. One of the B-29s, the *Enola Gay*, carried a payload consisting of a single atomic bomb. This previously untested weapon exploded 1,900 feet above the city center at 8:15 A.M., while most of Hiroshima's residents went about their daily business.[1] As a result, about 70,000 people perished instantly. Although the shelters immediately below the point where the bomb detonated collapsed due to the shock wave, those over half a mile from the epicenter experienced no damage.[2]

Events unfolded similarly in Nagasaki on August 9. An air raid alert sounded about 7:50 A.M., but air defense issued an all clear around 8:30 A.M. At 10:53 spotters sighted two B-29s, but, apparently assuming that this was also a reconnaissance mission, they did not order another air raid alert. At 11:02, one of the B-29s released an atomic bomb, which detonated over an industrial section of the city. The failure to signal workers and residents of Nagasaki to take cover meant that most of them were not in shelters at the time of the explosion.

As the United States Strategic Bombing Survey (USSBS) found in its postwar study of the effects of the atomic bombings, those residents lucky

Tunnel shelters in Nagasaki. According to the United States Strategic Bombing Survey, "All the occupants back from the entrances survived even in those tunnels almost directly under the explosion. Those not in direct line with the entrance were uninjured." National Archives.

enough to be in shelters at the time of the explosion fared remarkably well. In Nagasaki, 400 people who took cover in hillside tunnel shelters survived—despite their location being close to ground zero. As the USSBS report noted, "The shelters consisted of rough tunnels dug horizontally into the sides of hills with crude, earth-filled blast walls protecting the entrances. The blast walls were blown in but all the occupants back from the entrances survived even in those tunnels almost directly under the explosion. Those not in direct line with the entrance were uninjured." Tragically, these shelters could have accommodated many more people: "The tunnels had a capacity of roughly 100,000 persons. Had the proper alarm been sounded, and these tunnel shelters been filled to capacity, the loss of life in Nagasaki would have been substantially lower."[3] On the basis of Japan's experience with atomic bombing, the *Bulletin of the Atomic Scientists* reported in

August 1946 that "without question, shelters can protect those who get to them against anything but a direct hit."[4] Despite widespread consensus that civil defense against nuclear weapons was possible, throughout the late 1940s the United States conducted only limited preliminary research into shelter design and planning, even as the Truman administration contemplated the creation of a comprehensive civil defense program to combat the hypothetical Soviet nuclear threat. This oversight had dire, far-reaching consequences for the future of American civil defense.

While American observers expressed their optimism about the possibility of civil defense against the new weapon, the leader of their communist adversaries proclaimed that his citizens were not even afraid of it. Stalin had declared that the atomic bomb might frighten a "weak-nerved" people but that the Soviet people were nothing of the sort. Acknowledging the colossal threat the ballooning American nuclear arsenal posed to Soviet cities therefore risked contradicting official ideology. Until late 1953, the Soviet leadership had failed to order civil defense to prepare for an atomic attack, and, as a result, the USSR's civil defense organization, Mestnaia protivovozdushnaia oborona (Local Anti-Air Defense, or MPVO), had no authority to move into this new, politically sensitive field. Even within its own highly classified internal documentation, which often bore only limited resemblance to its public propaganda, MPVO planned for a war without nuclear weapons. This did not change even after the Soviet Union tested its own atomic bomb and ended the American nuclear monopoly in 1949.

While civil defense might seem like an ideal vehicle for propaganda and agitation, neither the United States nor the Soviet Union exploited much of its potential for these purposes in the opening years of the Cold War. This oversight is particularly puzzling given that each country had an extensive history of employing civil defense for domestic policy goals only indirectly related to its ostensible goal of protecting civilians from enemy air attack. In the 1920s and 1930s civil defense played a significant role in the Stalinist regime's efforts to erect the party-garrison state. For years before the Bolsheviks established a formal civil defense program, Soviet "voluntary" organizations carried out civil defense propaganda campaigns emphasizing the immediacy of foreign threats to the USSR. During WWII, the U.S. Office of Civilian Defense recognized the unlikelihood of significant Axis bombings of the U.S. mainland and self-consciously crafted itself as a useful outlet for Americans' patriotic impulses. Yet neither U.S. nor Soviet propagandists exploited civil defense this way in the late 1940s. Menacing citizens with the possibility of atomic attack could help justify the many sacrifices needed to prepare for confrontation with the other superpower, but it also posed political and ideological risks in both countries that seem to have dissuaded most government officials who might have been tempted to resort to this rhetorical strategy. In the United States, some influential pundits warned that civil defense might be the harbinger of the dreaded garrison state, kneecapping the efforts of civil defense proponents to get a program off the ground and contributing to its ultimate institutional weakness once it was established. The Soviet Union had no need to use civil defense to erect a garrison state because it already *was* one, but Generalissimo Stalin's peculiar ideological pronouncements about the bomb made it treacherous for his propagandists to proclaim that U.S. nuclear attack posed an existential threat to the Soviet experiment.

Skepticism about the feasibility of civil defense against nuclear weapons played little role in the two superpowers' delayed pursuit of it. Instead, domestic political calculations—and in the Soviet case, dictator Joseph Stalin's dismissive attitude about the military utility of the new weapons—forestalled prompt action to upgrade civil defense for the atomic age.

In contrast with Stalin's regime, which stubbornly discounted the enemy nuclear threat, the administration of President Harry Truman (1945-53) ultimately grew convinced of the necessity of civil defense owing to an unfounded fear that a Soviet nuclear attack might be imminent. Political compromises including legislation delegating civil defense responsibility to state and local governments and a dubious appointment to head the new Federal Civil Defense Administration (FCDA), however, laid a shaky foundation for future civil defense efforts.

The Beginnings of Civil Defense

The first glimmers of civil defense appeared in the nineteenth century, when armies constructed "bomb-proof shelters" to protect servicemen and ammunition from enemy artillery fire. These "bomb-proofs" saw use in major conflicts of the period including the War of 1812 (1812-15), the Crimean War (1853-56), and the American Civil War (1861-65). For instance, during the Siege of Sevastopol in 1854-55, the Russian army constructed a "bomb-proof" garrison capable of housing 20,000-25,000 men, as well as other protective structures.[5] During the American Civil War, civilians also took shelter in "bomb-proofs."[6] The 1864 book *My Cave Life in Vicksburg* described the experiences of Confederate civilians as they cowered in their "caves"—earthwork shelters built to shield Vicksburg's residents from Union artillery fire during the 1863 siege of the city.[7]

The development of dirigibles and airplanes introduced the possibility that shelters might be needed for protection against air-dropped bombs, as well as artillery shells. At the turn of the twentieth century, inventors and science fiction writers foresaw the potential of aircraft, in conjunction with advanced weapons, to devastate civilian populations. H. G. Wells's 1914 novel *The World Set Free* portrayed a war of the 1950s in which "atomic bombs" dropped by hand from monoplanes eradicated entire cities, resulting in a political and cultural revolution.[8] While not the first tale to foresee an "atomic" threat to civilization, Wells's novel introduced the concept of a city-destroying "atomic bomb" delivered by plane—a vision realized in 1945.[9]

Following the outbreak of World War I in August 1914, air attack against civilians became a reality. Starting in 1915, German airships began making raids against English cities, inspiring the introduction of civil defense measures such as shelters. German Zeppelin attacks during WWI proved largely of propaganda value owing to the inflammability and fragility of these craft, but toward the end of the war, more effective heavy bomber aircraft supplanted them. The German bomber threat during World War I culminated in the appearance of the first bomb shelters in Russia, but America's cities escaped the war unmenaced by German air attack. The possibility that the Germans would use their bombers against cities in western Russia, particularly Petrograd, inspired the infant Soviet government to take steps to create civil defense measures for civilians against aircraft.[10] Mercifully, the February 1918 conclusion of the Treaty of Brest-Litovsk between the Russian Soviet Federative Socialist Republic and Germany saved Petrograd from the increasingly effective German air threat. Wilhelmine Germany also hoped to carry the air war to American cities. At the conclusion of the war in November 1918, the Zeppelin factory was putting finishing touches on the L 72—an enormous airship designed for the purpose of bombing New York City.[11] After the war, the American popular press duly reported that the armistice had spared New York from a Thanksgiving Zeppelin attack.[12] Foreign aircraft would not threaten the United States for another twenty-three years.

Civil Defense and the Origins of the Party-Garrison State

In early 1927, Soviet newspapers declared that war with the West was imminent. Party officials warned that this conflict was "inevitable" and pressed for rapid mobilization to defend the country from the armies of militarily and technologically superior states. The precise impetus for this sudden alarm remains unclear. Soviet leaders had initially hoped that the Locarno Treaties concluded by the Western powers with Germany in late 1925 would improve the USSR's international position, but over the course of 1926 they grew increasingly concerned that these countries would decide to adjust eastern European borders at the USSR's expense.[13] In May 1927 British police raided the London offices of the Soviet Union's trade organization in the United Kingdom, the All-Russian Co-operative Society (ARCOS).[14] While British intelligence had suspected correctly that ARCOS operated as a front for Soviet espionage activity, the mundane materials captured in the raid fell far short of what they expected. Even though no one was charged or even arrested for espionage or subversion as a result of the raid, it still led the Conservative Baldwin government to sever diplomatic relations, which Kremlin leaders interpreted as a possible indicator of impending war.[15]

Traditional Western historiography dismissed the 1927 war scare as a cynical fabrication concocted by Stalin to marginalize his political enemies, but more recent scholarship has diverged from this interpretation. Stalin's rivals for power, such as Grigory Zinoviev, also invoked the war scare in the struggle for influence, so there was no clear-cut difference of opinion on the subject between the different factions in the Communist Party in 1927.[16] Indeed, Stalin himself asserted that his comrades overrated the chances of war.[17] The real question was the extent to which high-ranking party leaders believed that there was real threat of an imminent Western attack, as official propaganda constantly reiterated, or if they thought that a war was likely but still years in the future. Stalin seems to have fallen into the latter category, as he remarked at the time, "War is inevitable—that much is incontestable. But does that mean it can't be put off a few years? No, it doesn't. That leads to a solution: delay the war against the USSR either until the moment when revolution breaks out in the West, or until the moment when imperialism receives stronger blows from the colonized countries (China and India)."[18]

In the bellicist worldview of Soviet leaders in the late 1920s, the omnipresent state of war emergency demanded extreme domestic policy solutions. Once Stalin crushed both Zinoviev's Left and Nikolai Bukharin's Right

Opposition, he and his allies went ahead with these policies, including crash industrialization, the collectivization of agriculture, the brutal repression of perceived domestic enemies, and a cultural revolution. While communist leaders had motivations other than supplying a modern army, their words and actions reflected a conviction that the need to defend the revolution militarily justified their chosen means. As Stalin put it in 1931, "We are fifty or a hundred years behind the advanced countries. We must make good this distance in ten years. Either we do it, or they will crush us."[19]

Even before Stalin consolidated his power in the late 1920s, such fears inspired the Bolshevik regime to begin cultivating both human and technical resources for the future defense of the Soviet Union. Ravaged by years of incessant warfare, the USSR lacked the industry, technology, and trained personnel to compete with the militaries of potential enemies such as Great Britain. Leading communists perceived these deficiencies as critical weaknesses, inspiring them to begin organizing popular movements in the hope of overcoming them. On March 8, 1923, they instigated the launch of the Obshchestvo druzei Vozdushnogo Flota (Association of Friends of the Air Force, or ODVF), which aimed to popularize aviation by harnessing popular enthusiasm. Attracting 2.5 million members by 1925, the ODVF tempted young Soviet citizens with the prospect of becoming part of the exciting new world of aviation. While visions of technical triumph or aerial adventure surely tempted many of those who joined, the ODVF also emphasized the military aspect of its mission. One of its slogans asserted that "without victory in the air, there is no victory on the ground!"[20]

In addition to the aircraft possessed by their capitalist rivals, communist leaders also feared and coveted the chemical weapons these craft might carry. On May 19, 1924, they founded the Dobrovol'noe obshchestvo druzei khimicheskoi oborony i khimicheskoi promyshlennosti (Voluntary Society of Friends of Chemical Defense and the Chemical Industry, known as DOBROKhIM). DOBROKhIM aimed to further the development of the USSR's chemical industry, improve Soviet agriculture through the increased use of chemicals, and prepare the population for defense against chemical attack. The Soviet leadership placed immense importance on these seemingly mundane tasks, as evidenced by the involvement of the foremost figures in the USSR's military and secret police on DOBROKhIM's central committee. People's commissars of defense Mikhail Frunze (who died under suspicious circumstances in 1925) and Kliment Voroshilov (Stalin's handpicked successor for Frunze, who held the post from 1925 until 1934), as well as secret police head Felix Dzerzhinskii, personally oversaw the affairs of DOBROKhIM. Touting the slogan "Mass defense against gases is the task of a laboring people!," DOBROKhIM propaganda portrayed the consequences of a capitalist gas attack in dire terms, assuring readers that the imperialists would not hesitate to assault Soviet civilians with chemical and possibly biological weapons.[21]

Within a few years, the Kremlin merged three popular organizations devoted to the development of Soviet defense industries and military capabilities into a single entity that bore responsibility for all civil defense training. The ODVF and DOBROKhIM merged to become AVIAKhIM in May 1925 under the leadership of Aleksei Rykov. An "Old Bolshevik" who had been a prominent communist since the late 1890s and Lenin's successor as chair of the Council of People's Commissars, Rykov attracted the jealousy of the increasingly powerful Stalin, who gradually pushed him out of positions of power and had him executed for spurious treason charges in 1938 after the last of the infamous Moscow show trials. In January 1927, AVIAKhIM merged with a third organization, the Obshchestvo sodeistviia oborone (Society for Assistance to Defense, or OSO).[22] The OSO descended from an earlier body called the Voenno-nauchnoe obshchestvo (Military Science Society) and focused on cultivating defense-related skills such as marksmanship among Soviet youth. Now known as OSOAVIAKhIM and retaining Rykov as chief, the combined society pursued the aims of its three forebears. Rykov commented in July 1927 that "every Soviet worker should be able to use a rifle, should know how to defend himself against gas warfare, and should know what he can do to strengthen the military power of his state both during the period of preparations [for war] as well as during the defense of the Soviet state."[23] The eclectic combination of fund-raising, aviation, shooting sports, military training, and civil defense drills set the precedent OSOAVIAKhIM followed for decades to come.

Whether or not party leaders believed their own rhetoric about the war scare, their pronouncements sparked genuine anxiety among the population. In January 1927, before the ARCOS affair, Rykov, Bukharin, and Voroshilov (one of Stalin's closest associates) all gave speeches declaring that war could occur before autumn or even "within days." This led to hoarding and panic buying that deepened the country's ongoing supply problems and economic crisis.[24] Parts of the Soviet population hostile to the Communist Party greeted news of the possible war with enthusiasm. The secret police compiled reports for the party leaders detailing how these internal enemies, such as *kulaks* (prosperous peasants), hoped Western invasion would dislodge the hated communists from power.[25]

The Soviet government did not respond to the war scare by mobilizing the country for an imminent war, because even if it wished to it lacked the means of doing so. When the Red Army reviewed its capabilities in the aftermath of the Russian Civil War, its officers were horrified to discover that its ability to fight an industrialized great power such as Great Britain was effectively nonexistent. In an era of increasingly mechanized warfare, the Soviet Union lacked the industrial base required to mass-produce the tanks, airplanes, and poison gases military theorists expected the next war would be fought with.[26] Nor would these machines fight on their own: the conflict would be a mass war, with millions of men under arms and the entire rear mobilized to support them.

OSOAVIAKhIM, and therefore civil defense, played a central role in the media blitz that accompanied the 1927 war scare, but its campaign was not about military preparedness training or civil defense per se. Because the USSR did not establish a civil defense agency until 1932, there was no active civil defense program for OSOAVIAKhIM to promote, and as a voluntary society with a few million members it was woefully inadequate to substitute one on its own. As historian Kenneth D. Slepyan observed, the aim of the propaganda campaign was really "to spark the transformation of society by frightening it." The desired transformation was both material, in the form of industrialization, and mental, in the form of the eradication of "backwardness."[27] By cultivating a generation of enthusiastic young communists with the requisite martial mentality, OSOAVIAKhIM and the party could create the human foundation for the material and psychological transformation of the USSR into a modern military power capable of defending the revolutionary project from any enemy—the party-garrison state.

In the late 1920s the party-garrison state remained aspirational, as the Soviet Union was in the process of establishing the command economy and mechanisms of social control that would define most of its later history. Historians disagree as to whether the 1927 war scare directly sparked the foundation of the USSR's military-industrial complex or if it emerged only toward the end of the first Five-Year Plan.[28] In any case, the specific characteristics of the party-garrison state resulted from the historical context in which Stalin and his associates established it. In particular, the party-garrison state was organized to fight a specific type of war: industrial, mechanized combat between huge conscript land armies. In the 1920s this was a prescient vision for the future of warfare, and the Soviet Union managed to secure victory in the war it ultimately fought. But the party-garrison state was not designed to prepare the state for a nuclear war, nor was it well adapted to the long-term competition it waged with the United States in the postwar period.

Even though the 1927 civil defense propaganda campaign primarily existed to use foreign threats as a means of achieving domestic policy goals, OSOAVIAKhIM did attempt to carry out earnest public education and training efforts. In some cases, these seem to have been counterproductive for the larger goals of the campaign, as they called too much attention to the extreme weakness of the infant Soviet Union. For years prior to 1927, OSOAVIAKhIM and its predecessors had been circulating lurid descriptions of how bourgeois powers would use air power and chemical weapons to attack the Soviet interior. A 1925 Soviet book on defense against chemical weapons explained how the class logic of future wars against the USSR dictated that capitalist powers would attempt a crippling chemical weapons strike against Soviet cities at the immediate opening of hostilities. Bourgeois nations would need to prevent Soviet armies from mobilizing because a long war would risk the outbreak of socialist revolution in their own countries— and they would do so with a devastating poison gas attack on administrative and industrial centers.[29] Another 1925 brochure charged that bourgeois laboratories were hard at work creating weapons that could "transform an enormous city into an eerie graveyard of humanity in mere hours."[30] Local OSOAVIAKhIM committees reported that such portrayals "instilled a feeling of defenselessness in the population," undermining the intended message that the USSR could and would be defended.[31] The more mundane military training carried out by OSOAVIAKhIM in the 1920s seems to have been unsatisfactory owing to an utter inadequacy of instructors, training materials, and equipment.

Despite its eager establishment of "volunteer" civil defense organizations, the Soviet Union launched a formal civil defense program only in the 1930s. During the late 1920s Soviet military researchers investigated bomb shelter design, publishing their findings in a series of technical manuals.[32] In 1930 Narkomkhoz (The People's Commissariat of Industry) of the RSFSR (Russian Soviet Federative Socialist Republic) issued the first regulations for bomb shelter design.[33] On October 4, 1932, the Soviet government established the MPVO under the auspices of the Workers' and Peasants' Red Army.[34] Shortly thereafter bomb shelter construction for civilians began on a small scale that continued throughout the prewar period.

During the 1930s OSOAVIAKhIM's training exercises and propaganda campaigns became an integral part of the Soviet Union's emerging Stalinist culture.[35] While Rykov lost his position as head of the organization in

1931 because of his association with Nikolai Bukharin and other critics of Stalin's crash industrialization policies, OSOAVIAKhIM's esteem with the Kremlin grew as concerns about foreign military attack mounted.[36] After the 1932 formation of MPVO, public training and propaganda remained the sole province of the "voluntary" OSOAVIAKhIM. In the early 1930s OSOAVIAKhIM initiated a program to train civilians to respond to air and chemical attacks dubbed Gotov k protivovozdushnoi i protivokhimicheskoi oborone (Ready for Anti-Air and Anti-Chemical Defense, or Gotov k PVKhO). Students and workers throughout the Soviet Union, after theoretical study, moved on to practical drills, including the fitting and use of actual gas masks. Those who excelled in these drills could receive an elaborate badge that decorated the jackets of many aspiring young Stalinists during the 1930s. By August 1935, over 580,000 Soviet citizens had earned this honor.[37]

Civil defense constituted merely one goal of OSOAVIAKhIM: the Stalinist regime held numerous other objectives for the organization as it faced the formidable task of preparing the population for the looming war against Nazi Germany. The organization harnessed popular interest in technology and the ideological enthusiasm of Soviet young people for the needs of the USSR's defense. In addition to civil defense training, OSOAVIAKhIM taught Soviet youth to handle firearms with propaganda calling on them to emulate the supposed sharpshooting feats of Stalin's crony Kliment Voroshilov and instructed others about the mechanics of modern military hardware such as tanks, while a lucky few learned to pilot aircraft. The Kremlin sought to use OSOAVIAKhIM to keep the Soviet population apprised of the rapid evolution of military technology, on occasion even ordering the organization to prepare to respond to weapons that did not yet exist. Concerned about potential developments in bacteriological warfare, in 1938 the Council of People's Commissars decreed that OSOAVIAKhIM form three units for combating bubonic plague and four to confront tularemia (a zoonotic bacterium well suited to use as a biological weapon). Compared with the overall population of the Soviet Union, however, OSOAVIAKhIM remained relatively small, with about seven million members as of April 1938.[38]

Meanwhile, in the United States, bomb shelters and civil defense received little attention during the 1920s and 1930s. The atmosphere of isolationism, in addition to the presumed inability of hostile aircraft to reach America, led to general complacency about antiair defenses. After the outbreak of war in Europe in September 1939, however, Americans began taking a greater interest in civil defense, and popular articles on the subject began appearing in newspapers and magazines. Americans saw in the London Blitz a vision of their own potential future. In contrast to the USSR's long-standing program to prepare its citizens to survive air attack, the United Kingdom had inaugurated an equivalent effort only with the passage of the Air Raid Precaution Act in December 1937. Britain's new "Civil Defence" struggled heroically to overcome this late start and establish effective defenses for British urbanites in the face of aggressive German air raids.[39] Enterprising Americans imagined more proactive ways the United States might shelter its citizens. For example, a May 1941 *Popular Mechanics* article, "Averting Death from the Skies," described a proposal by Emil Bie, a New York Board of Transportation engineer, to use sand to convert New York City's shallow subway system into shelters for three and a half million people, and provided illustrations of fanciful bombproof skyscrapers.[40] A few months later, World War II made civil defense a much more immediate concern in both the United States and the Soviet Union.

Soviet Civil Defense in WWII

Stalin's USSR erected the party-garrison state at almost inconceivable human and material cost because the Bolsheviks feared that foreign invaders would inevitably attempt to drive them from power. Time proved them right, and the party-garrison state fulfilled its purpose: the Soviet Union emerged from World War II more powerful than ever before. Yet at the moment it was most needed, the party-garrison state almost failed. Serious cracks emerged in the military campaigns following the 1939 Molotov-Ribbentrop Pact, when Stalin dispatched the Red Army to annex neighboring territories and extend his country's strategic buffer. In contrast to the seemingly unstoppable triumphs of Hitler's Wehrmacht, the Red Army showed numerous inadequacies in its campaigns in Poland and the Baltic Republics, and the Finns managed to fight it to a humiliating truce in the Winter War. Soviet officials scrambled to address these problems, and their efforts in 1940–41 resulted in the transfer of the MPVO from the Red Army, which had more immediate concerns, to the NKVD (Ministry of Internal Affairs), where it remained in the postwar period.[41]

The German invasion of June 22, 1941, put the party-garrison state, and therefore the MPVO and OSOAVIAKhIM, to the ultimate test. On July 2 of that year, the Council of People's Commissars issued a resolution ordering OSOAVIAKhIM to instruct every Soviet citizen from the ages of eight to sixty in antiair and antichemical defense. Building on its prewar efforts, the organization made rapid progress. In Moscow alone, OSOAVIAKhIM trained

1,340,600 residents during 1941. Young and old inhabitants of the USSR learned not only how to administer basic first aid and use a gas mask, but also how to douse incendiary bombs and clear the rubble of collapsed buildings.[42] By the end of the war, over ninety-eight million individuals had passed the organization's basic civil defense training. Over 2.5 million underwent the more advanced courses required of the MPVO's "self-defense groups" charged with protecting apartment buildings and places of work. During the early years of the war, the enemy forced Soviet citizens to put their OSOAVIAKhIM civil defense training to practical use. Unlike their Nazi rivals, Stalin and the rest of the Soviet leadership found their prewar civil defense training so satisfactory that they saw no need to overhaul its content during the war, instead merely expanding it enormously.[43] OSOAVIAKhIM itself grew from a depleted 6,786,000 in 1942 to over sixteen million in 1945.[44] On the whole, the Soviet government considered OSOAVIAKhIM's prewar and wartime mobilization efforts so successful that it retained many aspects of them for decades to come.

After the Axis invasion, the MPVO initiated a crash program to provide more bomb shelters by structurally reinforcing the basements of existing buildings. As no comprehensive regulations for this task existed, the MPVO rushed an improvised manual into publication.[45] During the war, the MPVO used these regulations to convert thousands of basements into shelters. In wartime Moscow, the MPVO possessed about 1,500 gas shelters, 6,215 blast shelters, and space to shelter about 530,000 people in the metro. Altogether, these shelters could protect about 1.5 million Muscovites.[46] In 1943, the People's Commissariat of Construction issued a modernized set of shelter design regulations for "shelters of the second category," which encompassed most civilian shelters. In accordance with the new specifications, these shelters were supposed to accommodate no more than one hundred people, be located as close as possible to the populations they served, and possess blast doors, ventilation systems, running water, plumbing, and first-aid stations.[47]

Compared with cities such as Dresden, Tokyo, and London, where tens of thousands of civilians perished as a result of bombing raids during the war, Moscow and other Soviet urban centers escaped airborne attacks relatively unscathed. In large measure this was not because of the MPVO's efforts to defend the USSR's cities, but rather because strategic bombing against the Soviet Union was not a major Axis priority. Nazi leaders launched their war of conquest with the aim of capturing Soviet urban centers relatively intact and repopulating them with ethnic Germans, so they planned their campaigns accordingly. While Nazi extermination squads roamed the captured territories targeting Jews and communists for immediate execution, Hitler's government settled on a plan of intentionally starving the bulk of the USSR's population.[48] The case of Leningrad offers a tragic example of how these policies operated in practice. Over one million Soviet soldiers and civilians perished during the 872-day siege of the city, but only a few thousand of that unfortunate multitude were victims of bombs dropped from Axis aircraft. Instead, the vast majority of them died of hunger or disease.

German bombing of Soviet urban centers was quite modest, compared with the scale of U.S. and British bombing of German cities. During the war, Axis aircraft dropped 1,611 high explosive and over 100,000 incendiary bombs on Moscow. These attacks failed to knock a single Moscow factory out of action, which is not that surprising given that larger quantities of bombs were dropped during some individual Allied bombing raids on cities such as Dresden and Tokyo. According to official statistics, only a total of 1,235 people died in all Axis air raids on the Soviet capital, and a further 5,406 suffered injuries.[49] As a result, the Soviet Union probably overestimated the effectiveness of its civil defense system. Significantly, the nonuse of chemical and biological weapons during the war appears to have led the MPVO to downplay earlier concerns about these threats, as well as the new atomic threat, in the postwar period.

American Civil Defense in WWII

Complacent that geography would protect the United States from enemy air attack, Americans gave little thought to the problem of civil defense during the interwar period. Only the outbreak of war in Europe in September 1939 spurred Washington into action. On May 25, 1940, President Franklin Roosevelt signed an executive order creating the Office of Emergency Management within the Executive Office of the President, which in time spawned many of the numerous agencies that organized America's war mobilization effort.[50] Meanwhile, German bombing of the United Kingdom elicited concerns from local government officials that their cities might become Hitler's next target, most notably mayor Fiorello La Guardia of New York. Under La Guardia's leadership, these officials pressured the Roosevelt administration to create an organization to facilitate the defense of American cities against air attack. Caving in to pressure from the mayor, on May 20, 1941, President Roosevelt signed an executive order transforming the Division of State and Local Cooperation within the Office of Emergency

Management into the Office of Civilian Defense (OCD). Furthermore, Roosevelt appointed La Guardia director of the OCD, a responsibility he took on without salary and while remaining mayor of America's largest city.[51]

The division of the nascent OCD into two operating divisions reflects the self-contradictory institutional mission that quickly wrecked its credibility once the United States entered the war. The first of these divisions, the Civilian Protective Branch, concerned itself with shelters, blackouts, and other "protective" measures. The second, the Civilian War Services Branch, promoted community activities including salvage, housing, health, nutrition, and morale building.[52] Local civil defense organizations followed the same division into these two branches. La Guardia elected to make local government, rather than state government, the primary basis of the civil defense organization, snubbing state authorities in the process and causing considerable administrative confusion.[53] Furthermore, La Guardia neglected the mission of the Civilian War Services Branch, dismissing its activities as "sissy stuff." Exasperated with this obstinacy, the Budget Bureau resorted to a threat to withhold all funds from the OCD until La Guardia relented. In September 1941, La Guardia appointed First Lady Eleanor Roosevelt assistant director in charge of the Civilian War Services Branch. Assistant Director Roosevelt proceeded to seek out unorthodox appointees, including film actor Melvyn Douglas and professional dancer Mayris Chaney to manage its activities. These choices attracted disastrous negative publicity to the OCD. Press critics uncharitably dubbed the personnel of the Civilian War Services Branch as "strip-tease artists," "leeches," and "piccolo players," while members of Congress charged that Douglas's "leftist leanings" were making the OCD "a pink tea party."[54] The OCD never recovered from the resulting blow to its prestige.[55]

Following the United States' entry into the war after the Japanese attack on Pearl Harbor, President Roosevelt decided that the OCD required a full-time director in light of the office's increased workload and La Guardia's primary responsibilities as mayor of New York City. In January 1942, Roosevelt appointed James M. Landis, dean of the Harvard Law School, as special assistant to administer the OCD's day-to-day affairs. The following month La Guardia resigned, after which Landis took over as director. Soon Eleanor Roosevelt resigned as well, leaving the OCD bereft of the colorful personalities that made its early history so turbulent.[56] Roosevelt's April 1942 executive order formally investing Landis as OCD head streamlined the agency, retaining some of the tasks of the Civilian War Services Branch but eliminating the goal of "maintaining morale."[57] Under Landis's leadership, the OCD moved to overcome the damaged reputation it garnered under La Guardia, but by mid-1943, Landis himself recommended to President Roosevelt that the OCD be abolished and its responsibilities passed on to other agencies.[58]

After a brief outburst of public anxiety about an imminent Axis air attack following Pearl Harbor, Americans soon realized that the probability that German or Japanese bombers would appear in their skies was remote. As well as rendering the OCD's efforts to protect American cities from enemy bombing irrelevant, the failure of the Axis to menace the United States by air engendered skepticism about civil defense efforts that endured well into the postwar era. Although the OCD enlisted millions of volunteers to participate in its programs, they had little to do. At its peak, the Citizens' Defense Corps, assembled by the OCD's Protective Services Branch, comprised about ten million volunteers, of whom over 8,570,000 possessed definite duty assignments.[59] Factories produced millions of helmets, armbands, and lapel pins to outfit a small army of air raid wardens, who soon became objects of mirth and even ridicule. As James Landis remarked after the war, "There's a limit to the business of being an air raid warden, particularly when no bombs are dropping."[60] The association between civil defense and wasted effort proved a persistent bugbear to Landis's Cold War successors.

Landis resigned from the OCD in August 1943 and suggested the transfer of the OCD's protective services to the War Department. The War Department, however, increasingly considered civil defense a distraction from the ongoing war effort, and convinced the president to retain the agency. This respite hardly stemmed the ongoing collapse in morale among OCD personnel, as the agency muddled along and increasingly curtailed its operations in expectation of its own imminent elimination.[61] Shortly after the surrender of Nazi Germany in May 1945, Roosevelt's successor Harry Truman signed an executive order stipulating that the OCD be abolished effective June 30. Most of the state and local organizations ceased operations shortly thereafter, although the legislation enabling them remained in effect in a number of states.[62]

Civilian Defense Becomes "Civil Defense"

After the war ended, both the American and Soviet governments eagerly sought information about the effects of the atomic bombings at Hiroshima and Nagasaki. Following the attacks the Soviet embassy in Tokyo seized the opportunity to send investigators to the two bombed cities. Soviet observers beat their American counterparts to Hiroshima by a matter of weeks, with the first two reaching the city on August 16, 1945.[63] A larger Soviet fact-finding mission arrived in Hiroshima in mid-September to take photographs and interview eyewitnesses of the bombing. A separate group, including a cinematographer, traveled to Nagasaki to investigate the effects of the bombings there.[64]

The report ultimately forwarded to Stalin and a few other senior Soviet leaders in November 1945 downplayed the power of the atomic bomb. Soviet ambassador to Japan Iakov Malik asserted that Japanese press "exaggerated" the bomb's destructive force and the duration of its effects to justify Tokyo's surrender. "Japanese popular opinion picks up these media portrayals, distorts them, and sometimes reduces them to absurdities," he claimed, particularly with regard to the effects of radiation.[65] On the train ride back from Nagasaki, the Soviet investigators by chance shared a compartment with Dr. David Willcutts, medical officer of the U.S. Navy's Fifth Fleet, who reinforced their dismissive attitude toward the new weapons. Insisting that tales of radiation hazards persisting in Hiroshima and Nagasaki for days after the bombings had no basis in fact, he reassured the Soviets that the Japanese "strongly overstate the effectiveness of the atomic bomb."[66]

Investigators under the auspices of the USSBS followed the Soviet observers. Among the Americans visiting Hiroshima and Nagasaki was lieutenant colonel Barnet W. Beers, who would become the Pentagon's civil defense chief.[67] The efficacy of shelters and civil defense greatly interested the USSBS, as it sought to determine the effectiveness of strategic bombing efforts in fulfilling U.S. war aims. On the basis of the Japanese experience, it concluded that shelters were efficacious against nuclear weapons. Despite these optimistic conclusions, however, for political and ideological reasons both the United States and the Soviet Union hesitated to adapt their civil defense programs to face the atomic threat.

In the United States after the end of World War II, civil defense passed out of the public eye even as anxiety about the new atomic bomb gripped American public discourse. Advocates of the international control of atomic energy strove to popularize the belief that no practical defense against nuclear weapons existed, and that therefore an atomic war would mean the likely demise of civilization.[68] Meanwhile, the American military began pondering the questions of how the next war might be fought and what role civil defense might play in it. These inquiries began even before the atomic bomb became public knowledge. On August 4, two days before the atomic bombing of Hiroshima, the Office of the Provost Marshal General received orders to study the problem of civil defense in light of wartime experience and make recommendations regarding how it might best be administrated in the future. Under the direction of Barnet W. Beers, personnel from the Provost Marshal General Office crafted a bold new vision of civil defense for the atomic age.[69]

Beers's team, as well as other figures in the War Department, concluded unanimously that the Office of Civilian Defense was a woefully inadequate model for a postwar program. Their report, completed in April 1946, identified three basic flaws in the agency: its lack of advance planning, its discombobulated and inconsistent command structure, and the inclusion of tasks unrelated to civil defense within its mandate.[70] They envisioned postwar civil defense as a strong federal program managed by the War Department General Staff that would make use of a national shelter policy, evacuation, industrial dispersal, mass training, and other expensive and potentially disruptive measures to protect civilians and economic resources from enemy air attack.[71] To mark their definitive break with the past, Beers's group dumped the term "civilian defense" because they considered it too tainted by the dubious legacy of the OCD. Admiring the businesslike effectiveness of the UK's wartime program, they Americanized the British "civil defence" into "civil defense," coining the name soon adopted by the postwar program.[72]

The Stalinist Way of War

While Beers and his team developed their schemes to create an effective civil defense against atomic bombs, the Soviet government went to increasing lengths to learn more about the effects of the new weapons. With only a smattering of theoretical data and no devices of its own, the Kremlin schemed to make the most of the imminent U.S. nuclear test at Bikini Atoll, planned for the summer of 1946. In February, Soviet officials eagerly sought an invitation for representatives from the USSR to observe the test.[73] Three months later, the United States notified Moscow that it would invite two representatives of the Soviet government and one from the Soviet press. Aiming to make the most of the U.S. test to learn about the effects of nuclear explosions on ships, the USSR chose a naval engineer who worked as an editor for the Soviet navy's newspaper as its "press" representative, while sending two physicists—D. B. Skobel'tsyn and M. G. Meshcheriakov—as the other two observers. Upon his return to the Soviet Union, Meshcheriakov penned an extensive description of the tests ultimately forwarded to Stalin himself.[74]

Meshcheriakov's experiences in the Pacific convinced him of two things: that the Americans had no intention of accepting international control of nuclear weapons, and that therefore the Soviet Union needed to begin developing means of defending against the new bombs as quickly as possible. In April 1947, the physicist wrote a letter pressing these two points to the odious secret police chief Lavrentii Beria, who oversaw the USSR's nuclear program. From what he saw during the Bikini tests, Meshcheriakov asserted that "the Americans are probably developing a service for the waging of atomic war within their military." But while the American tests convinced him that the United States might launch a nuclear attack against his country, they left him with little doubt that civil defense could help mitigate its effects. Meshcheriakov opined to Beria that "as soon as possible we must begin training specialists in our military technical schools who, if it proves necessary, could organize an anti-atomic defense service for major population centers and strategic targets."[75]

Meshcheriakov's proposal fell on deaf ears. Prior to 1953, the subject of the effects of nuclear weapons and defense against them remained taboo not just in the Soviet public press but also within the government. Despite widespread awareness that American war plans centered on a massive attack on the USSR using nuclear weapons, Stalin obstructed proposals from the leaders of his nuclear weapons program to begin preparing the military and society to face the effects of such an onslaught. Available documents contain no evidence that the Soviet Union possessed a plan as to what to do if the United States attacked Soviet military or civilian targets with nuclear weapons until 1951 at least, and maybe not until after Stalin's death.

Other well-informed figures within the Soviet atomic project concurred with Meshcheriakov that the failure to consider the problem of defense against atomic weapons jeopardized Soviet security. On December 17, 1947, Boris Vannikov, the head of the First Main Directorate (the ambiguously named organization set up in 1945 to manage the USSR's efforts to build its own atomic bombs), drafted a letter to Stalin about his concerns that the introduction of nuclear weapons "posed new problems in the field of defense organization," especially in light of the qualitatively new issue of radiation. On the basis of Western publications, Vannikov outlined the destructive effects of the atomic bomb, including the blast wave, thermal effects, and radiation. He further noted that the intensely radioactive waste resulting from nuclear bomb production might be weaponized as well. "At present, the development of defensive measures against damaging radiation effects demands intensive research and preparatory efforts within military organizations," warned Vannikov. The discovery of atomic energy, he argued, "requires a reassessment of many aspects of military affairs, industrial development, and related undertakings." In light of the inevitable disorganization of both the front and the rear that would follow a nuclear attack, "it is essential to prepare for it now," Vannikov emphasized. Moreover, he asserted that "the Americans, possessing military nuclear materials, are concerned above all others with the questions of defense against atomic weapons." He supported his claim with an overview of American research efforts during the 1946 nuclear tests at Bikini Atoll.[76]

To catch up with and overtake the United States in the critical field of defense against nuclear weapons, Vannikov presented Stalin with several concrete proposals. The Ministry of the Armed Forces would train military personnel and investigate the wartime implications of nuclear energy. The Ministry of Internal Affairs, meanwhile, would prepare civil defense to do the same for the Soviet civilian population. Finally, Gosplan (the USSR's centralized economic planning authority) "or some other body at the government's discretion" would study the problems of industrial dispersal and civilian construction. Vannikov envisioned the creation of a new organization within the Ministry of the Armed Forces to direct antiatomic defense efforts, comprehensive studies undertaken at military research institutions, and the training of military personnel at all levels to face the novel hazards created by the atomic bomb.[77]

Instead of going directly to Stalin for approval, Vannikov's letter traveled through the Special Committee under the Council of Ministers, which filtered all information about the nuclear weapons program sent to the dictator. A meeting on January 12, 1948, headed by Lavrentii Beria and chair of the Council of Ministers Georgii Malenkov and attended by various leaders of the Soviet atomic program, addressed the issues raised by Vannikov's proposal. The Special Committee commanded Vannikov, nuclear physicist Igor Kurchatov, and three of its other members to draft a letter to Stalin within the next five days in regard to Vannikov's proposal. This missive would both describe the work in nuclear defenses going on in militaries outside the USSR and propose that the Soviet Union undertake similar efforts under the direction of the Ministry of the Armed Forces, suggesting specific measures it should take to protect the country from nuclear attack.[78] Clearly, Beria agreed with Vannikov that the Soviet military could no longer remain in the dark about the American atomic threat, and that the USSR should prepare to confront the deadly cargo that Washington's bombers might deliver to Soviet cities.

But the final letter that the Special Committee forwarded to Stalin on March 5, 1948, eliminated many of Vannikov's urgent proposals. Beria retained Vannikov's analysis of American research into nuclear defense, and the letter informed Stalin that "in light of the great destructive power of atomic bombs the Americans are paying special attention to the dispersal of industry, military installations, and the populations of large cities." It made four recommendations for Soviet policy: first, that the defense of the country against nuclear weapons be made the responsibility of the Ministry of the Armed Forces; second, that a Special Division within the General Staff of that ministry be created for the leadership and management of this work; third, that the laboratories and institutes of the armed services undertake research to develop means of defending the country against atomic attack; and finally, that military schools and academies train personnel in atomic specializations, including military physicists, radiochemists, engineers, and medics. Beria struck Vannikov's suggestion that Gosplan undertake studies of the dispersal of new industrial and urban construction with the participation of the Ministry of the Armed Forces, eliminating any mention of civil defense. Vannikov's main thrust—that the Ministry of the Armed Forces begin studying the nuclear defense problem—remained, but where Vannikov envisioned training military personnel "at all levels" in antiatomic defense, as well as taking meaningful steps to prepare both the military and the civilian population for atomic war, the letter sent to Stalin refrained from stating just how significant these efforts would be.[79]

Beria probably watered down Vannikov's original vision in an attempt to avoid offending Stalin by acknowledging the threat the U.S. atomic monopoly posed to the Soviet Union. The draft of the letter developed by the five members of the Special Committee including Kurchatov and Vannikov retained the proposal to have Gosplan begin research into civil defense problems.[80] If Beria himself objected to the essence of Vannikov's ideas, he could easily have tabled them at the outset rather than sending them to his temperamental, suspicious boss. Unfortunately, what Vannikov suggested necessitated widening the exposure of Soviet citizens to information about nuclear weapons, as well as contradicting Stalin's insistent belief that the bomb posed no immediate threat to Soviet security. As Beria managed the Soviet atomic project and served as its direct intermediary with Stalin, he occupied the best position to anticipate the dictator's attitude toward the letter. The version Beria crafted struck a middle ground, retaining the possibility of undertaking the most important aspects of Vannikov's nuclear defense scheme while minimizing the risk of inciting Stalin's wrath. With luck, Stalin would approve a resolution allowing the Ministry of the Armed Forces to initiate a program in the immediate term that could lay the groundwork for future defense readiness, and Stalin's position would become more flexible once the USSR broke the atomic monopoly. Within a few years, the Red Army would have the weapons, doctrine, and trained personnel to respond to an American atomic attack on the Soviet Union.

The outcome of the letter revealed the limits of the party-garrison state's power to override the will of its architect, Joseph Stalin. Stalin apparently approved the creation of a version of Vannikov's proposed Special Division within the Ministry of the Armed Forces, but it remained a small, secretive organization incapable of shaking Soviet defense policy out of its dogmatic lethargy, much less preparing it to fight a nuclear war.[81] The Special Division undertook research efforts during early Soviet nuclear tests to examine the effects of the atomic bomb on military and civilian equipment, but its findings remained secret to all but a fraction of the Soviet General Staff and the leadership of the Soviet nuclear weapons project. Soviet espionage efforts enlisted spies such as Klaus Fuchs to forward information about nuclear weapons effects to Moscow, but these gleanings suffered the same fate.[82] Within Stalin's military, what little discussion of the consequences of the atomic bomb that took place occurred in secret. Memoir literature attests that the Soviet General Staff received a report on the A-bomb in 1948, and select military personnel viewed a film of A-bomb tests in 1951 followed by a short lecture on the topic.[83] Still, the bulk of even high-ranking Soviet officers remained ignorant of the new nuclear reality.

Civil Defense and the American Cold War Contract State

The haphazard process through which the United States established its civil defense program during the Truman administration illustrates that its federal system was a weak contract state. Restricted to suboptimal approaches by the strictures of federalism, the architects of U.S. civil defense policy were compelled to erect a system whose utter inadequacy for the challenges of nuclear war was more apparent to them than anyone. They persisted, however, because they genuinely feared that nuclear war would become a reality and believed a weak program would be better than nothing.

While Stalin forestalled Vannikov's proposal to begin preparing the USSR's civil defense to face nuclear attack, civil defense became the subject of a tug-of-war between various agencies of the United States government. After an attempt by the War Department to tackle the subject in

1946–47, defense secretary James Forrestal established the Office of Civilian Defense Planning within the National Security Resources Board. A recently formed organization established by President Truman, the NSRB sought to lay the groundwork of the economic and societal mobilization for the next major war. To run the OCDP, Forrestal tapped Bell Telephone executive Russell J. Hopley, who accepted the job on the condition that Colonel Beers serve as his personal assistant.[84]

Forrestal directed the OCDP to begin developing concrete plans for the establishment of an effective civil defense program, a task to which its members enthusiastically applied themselves. Concerned that state governments and Congress would refuse to approve of a civil defense system under Washington's centralized authority, the OCDP foresaw a return to the system of state and local control that led to such unimpressive results during World War II. To manage the federal civil defense effort, its report recommended the creation of an Office of Civil Defense within either the Executive Office of the President or the Office of the Secretary of Defense, preferably the latter. This document, usually called the "Hopley Report," intentionally utilized vague language because its authors expected that it would be subjected to public comment after its November 1948 publication. Unfortunately, the OCDP failed to consider the potential public response to it—an oversight that soon resulted in disastrous consequences not only for the OCDP but also for its patron Secretary Forrestal.[85]

At the time of the publication of the Hopley Report, Forrestal's political difficulties amounted to not merely the growing ire of President Truman and much of the military establishment but also the omnipresent vitriol of the odious gossip columnist and radio personality Walter Winchell. Winchell was known for both his fast-paced staccato delivery and his willingness to circulate libelous rumors to blackmail or humiliate his enemies. His newspaper columns and radio broadcasts reached tens of millions of Americans in the late 1940s. Winchell objected to Forrestal's skeptical attitude toward the foundation of the state of Israel and seized upon every opportunity to discredit him—one of which proved to be the publication of the Hopley Report. On his radio show on November 21, Winchell bombastically declared that the Hopley plan posed "the greatest internal threat to our liberty since the British burned the White House in 1814." Claiming that "this is a far more dangerous attack on your Constitution than Hitler or Stalin ever attempted," he urged "Mr. and Mrs. United States" to write their congressmen about Forrestal's civil defense menace, which, according to Winchell, threatened to suspend the Bill of Rights, silence the radio and press, eliminate the FBI, establish concentration camps, and abolish organized labor, among other horrors.[86] The next week Winchell beseeched Americans to order a copy of the Hopley Report from the Government Printing Office "and have yourselves a nightmare."[87]

Those Americans who took up Winchell's suggestion may have found their nightmares wanting, as the Hopley Report hardly contained a blueprint for converting the United States into an authoritarian dystopia. As a 1967 assessment observed, "The OCDP had planned an almost toothless organization and had provided for the most minimal extension of federal power."[88] In addition to Winchell, the only press commentary denouncing the document came from the Communist *Daily Worker*, which attacked it as an example of American militarism, and the *Christian Century*, which saw "shades of Hitler Germany" in its proposal of legal immunity for civil defense workers carrying out their duties.[89] Other publications largely endorsed the Hopley Report, even though they often expressed reservations. The *New York Times* editorial page stated that "we commend it to Congress and to all citizens as a reasonable and important document," opining that "to take action now to set up a civil defense organization would be only common prudence."[90]

Punditry aside, resistance to militarizing the American home front extended deep into the Truman administration itself. Even though the civil defense agency envisioned in the Hopley report would be insipid, it would still be in the newly established Department of Defense. But the department wanted to make civil defense someone else's problem. Not only did the U.S. military not want to use civil defense as a Trojan horse to remake the country into a garrison state, the Joint Chiefs of Staff, the navy, and the air force all now concurred that civil defense ought to be outside the Department of Defense because it might distract the agency from its primary mission. Stung by Winchell's denunciations and the mixed response to his efforts, Hopley resigned from the OCDP, and some of his associates felt that Winchell's calumny contributed to his premature death in 1949.[91] In light of the negative feedback, Forrestal decided that a civil defense agency would have to be under civilian authority, and he pushed for the statutory establishment of one within the NSRB, but distinct from the board staff. President Truman rejected Forrestal's proposal to go ahead and create a civil defense agency, and in March 1949 he transferred responsibility for civil defense to the NSRB, with the stipulation that it continue to study the topic rather than create an operational civil defense program.[92] Considering the secretary of defense increasingly politically unreliable, the president demanded Forrestal's resignation on March 28, 1949, and the former secretary of defense joined Hopley in an early grave later that year.[93]

During the months that followed, the NSRB made only minimal progress toward developing a civil defense program. The OCDP was hindered by the dysfunctional nature of the NSRB, which was engulfed in controversies about postwar defense policy. The NSRB lacked a regular chair between 1948 and 1950, leaving assistant to the president John R. Steelman to run it in an acting capacity. Some historians later charged that Truman condemned civil defense to this institutional limbo because he hoped to prevent it from becoming a significant element of national defense policy, although the NSRB's leisurely steps to outline civil defense policies for adoption by the states suggest otherwise.[94] This topic gained considerable urgency after the first Soviet nuclear test on August 29, 1949.

In contrast to U.S. nuclear tests during the 1940s, which focused their attention on merely confirming the weapons worked or determining their effect on military targets, the first Soviet nuclear test incorporated ambitious measures to explore the effects of nuclear attack on Soviet civilian construction. With years to choose and prepare the test site on the northeastern Kazakh steppe, the First Main Directorate and Soviet military had time to erect a wide array of structures. The test site featured not only a variety of Soviet industrial and residential buildings but also a bridge and 1,538 animals to test the effects of the bomb on living organisms.[95] The explosion on August 29 largely annihilated the nearby buildings. A three-story brick structure located 800 meters from the blast was demolished, yet animals in its basement remained alive. Single-story wooden buildings fared less well—fire caused by the bomb's thermal effects completely destroyed those located at 800 and 1,600 meters, and the blast wave flattened one at 1,200 meters. The blast also tore the steel bridge, located half a kilometer from the explosion, from its foundations and flung it fifty meters. Bomb shelters, however, survived even at relatively close distances. While the explosion destroyed those less than 250 meters from ground zero, those at 500 meters merely suffered "minor damage" and those beyond 700 meters basically suffered no damage at all.[96] While these results suggested that Stalin was very wrong about the atomic bomb "being something that could only frighten a weak-nerved people," they indicated that civil defense measures such as shelters could offer real protection against it.

Surprisingly, Stalin refrained from announcing his triumph, and his rival Harry Truman ended up announcing it to the world. Possibly aiming to perpetuate the official fiction that it already possessed nuclear weapons

(Soviet foreign minister Viacheslav Molotov had declared in 1947 that "the secret of the atomic bomb" had "long since ceased to be a secret"), the Kremlin made no effort to publicize the nuclear test, either at home or abroad.[97] Shortly after the USSR detonated its nuclear device at the end of August, however, American radiological surveillance detected it. On September 23 President Truman announced that Stalin now had the bomb—sparking a flurry of anxiety among Americans about the country's lack of civil defense.[98]

Truman's Civil Defense Reversal

Following Truman's announcement of the Soviet nuclear test, the administration's torpid progress on civil defense policy elicited protests from influential government figures. Massachusetts representative John F. Kennedy penned an indignant letter to the president on October 8, 1949, commenting that "in view of your recent disclosure of Russia's possession of the atomic bomb, it is shocking to find that so little progress has been made in this vital field." Although Kennedy acknowledged that "it takes months and even years to develop an adequate Civil Defense System," he expressed his view that "because of unsettled world conditions, I hope and respectfully request that you will urge those responsible for Civil Defense planning to speed up this entire program."[99] Numerous state and local government officials wrote Washington expressing similar concerns or making inquiries as to how they should go about establishing civil defense programs. On October 10, Senator Brien McMahon, chair of the Joint Committee on Atomic Energy, announced plans for congressional hearings on civil defense.[100] In an October 14 letter to President Truman, John Steelman concurred with Kennedy's concerns and asserted that "in view of the considerable degree of interest now being shown by state and local governments, and by numerous individuals and nongovernmental groups, agencies of the Federal Government are taking steps to produce as fast as possible the over-all standards and guiding criteria which civil defense planners at the state and local levels require."[101]

Despite this sense of urgency, Steelman and his subordinates were loath to take any steps that might appear to be steps toward a garrison state. In January 1950 Steelman appointed Paul J. Larsen, a bona fide atomic scientist as director of the Sandia Special Weapons Base Laboratory in Albuquerque, New Mexico, director of an expanded Civilian Mobilization Office within the NSRB. In congressional testimony, Larsen defended the NSRB's incremental approach to developing a program and even echoed Winchell's attacks on the Hopley Report with a warning that pursuing civil defense too aggressively might lead to a garrison state. Despite calls for a serious civil defense program from local officials, neither Congress nor the White House recommended pursuing one.[102] This attitude reflected the slackening of the anxieties unleashed by President Truman's announcement of the Soviet bomb test. Although the Soviet bomb and the fall of China in late 1949 represented lamentable setbacks to Washington, war still seemed remote compared with the recent crisis over Berlin. Civil defense, Truman reasoned, could wait.

The appointment of W. Stuart Symington as head of the NSRB in April 1950 greatly improved the outlook for civil defense. Even before he took over the post, Symington outed himself as an advocate of a much more aggressive civil defense policy. On June 26, Symington made a speech before the annual convention of the American Red Cross in Detroit in which he provided a comprehensive argument for the necessity of civil defense. Symington claimed that the USSR's air force was "the largest in the world in nearly all categories" and that it was "capable of delivering a surprise atomic attack against any part of the United States"—both of which would have come as surprises to Stalin.[103] In light of the existential threat posed by the Soviet atomic bomb, Symington told the audience that civil defense "could well make the difference between a serious and a fatal disaster," and it might even be "the deciding factor in our ability to get up off the floor and fight back." Approvingly citing Hopley's belief that civil defense constituted the "missing link" of America's defense, Symington reassured listeners that "this whole complex problem of civilian defense is being worked on, and it is our hope to present an over-all plan this fall."[104] Beers and his staff came to the NSRB from the Pentagon at Symington's request to help overcome various difficulties, including that of accessing classified information about nuclear weapons effects.

The second half of 1950 proved to be quite a heady time for the Truman administration, as the day before Symington gave his speech the forces of Kim Il-sung's Korean People's Army crossed the 38th parallel into South Korea, beginning the Korean War. For those in the American military and government whose views of communism resembled Symington's, the invasion of South Korea confirmed their worst fears. Reasoning that this incursion might mark the opening salvo of a communist war for world domination, they feared that Europe or America might be the next victim. More sober observers recognized that even if Stalin and Mao lacked a desire to initiate a new world war, if their nations became embroiled in the conflict on the Korean Peninsula one might erupt anyway. Over the following several months, Kim Il-sung's forces conquered nearly all of Korea, then retreated in the face of a counterattack in mid-September by the U.S.-dominated United Nations Expeditionary Force. In a serious miscalculation that ultimately cost him his career, General Douglas MacArthur invaded North Korea and approached the Chinese border, sparking the entry of the People's Republic of China into the war on October 25. Humiliated by defeats at the hands of the Chinese People's Volunteer Army, MacArthur publicly threatened to use the atomic bomb to regain the initiative for the United States.[105]

Even in the heady atmosphere of mid-1950, when many inside and outside the government earnestly believed they were witnessing the opening phase of World War III, the NSRB hesitated to establish a robust federal civil defense organization. Fearful that too much centralization would be more unacceptable to state and local governments and to Congress, Symington decided to endorse a relatively weak civil defense agency in the report the NSRB published on September 8. This was not because of a lack of advocates for a robust civil defense policy inside or outside the Truman administration. But like some other proposals to militarize the American home front, civil defense could not overcome objections that too much federal intrusion into everyday life would undermine the country's cherished traditions. For every unprecedented defense-related intervention into Americans' homes, such as the unprecedented peacetime draft established in 1947, others, such as Universal Military Training, were rejected after attracting opposition from a variety of stakeholders.[106] The weak contract state condemned civil defense to an intermediate category. Officially endorsed by the administration and Congress, it could not secure the resources to carry out much more than publicity campaigns.

Soviet Civil Defense after the War

Fears that the Korean War might spread seem to have compelled Stalin to reconsider his refusal to address the effects of nuclear weapons—albeit to little real effect. Apparently optimistic that the successful Soviet nuclear test would make Stalin more reasonable about preparing the Soviet military to face a nuclear attack, in October 1949 Beria sent a proposal to Stalin to share the results of the test with the Ministry of Defense so it could begin developing antiatomic defense measures. Stalin seems to have blocked this step, because in June 1950 Beria raised the issue again.[107] The dictator increased his estimate of the likelihood of war with the West following the outbreak of hostilities in Korea, and in late July 1950, Stalin finally gave his begrudging approval—albeit with caveats that forestalled the Soviet military from undertaking the measures Vannikov and Beria envisioned.[108] While the resulting Council of Ministers resolution allowed the transfer of data on "the destructive and damaging effects of the atomic explosion on civilian and industrial buildings, field and permanent fortifications, and the weapons of the army and navy," it directed that work on this topic be carried out not merely with the usual Bolshevik secrecy but with *konspirativnost'* (conspiratoriality).[109] This demand for secrecy forestalled the Soviet military from familiarizing more than a handful of individuals with the test findings, much less launching a serious personnel training effort. Furthermore, the resolution made no effort to make the MPVO privy to information about nuclear weapons effects, and Soviet civil defense would win access to the data only after Stalin's death. In the meantime, the MPVO and OSOAVIAKhIM continued their planning and training as though atomic bombs did not exist.

While OSOAVIAKhIM's system of societal militarization survived into the Cold War, the organization itself did not. In January 1948, the Council of Ministers divided OSOAVIAKhIM into three organizations, presumably in the belief that more focused associations would be more effective. The largest of these was the Dobrovol'noe obshchestvo sodeistviia Armii (Voluntary Society of Assistance to the Army, or DOSARM).[110] DOSARM inherited the important responsibilities of imparting skills needed for the USSR's defense to the population, including civil defense. DOSARM's all-Union soviet soon dictated that all its local organizations "sharply improve" civil defense propaganda among the Soviet population."[111]

DOSARM's civil defense propaganda effort reflected the contradictions of Stalin's American policy in that it aimed to increase popular antagonism toward the United States while entirely ignoring the possibility of a nuclear attack on the USSR. DOSARM dictated that all its local subsidiaries study civil defense. This effort, however, emphasized the same types of weapons and tactics as OSOAVIAKhIM's propaganda efforts dating back to the 1920s. Not acknowledging the existence of the atomic bomb, DOSARM materials touted blackout curtains and sand buckets as indispensable tools for confronting air attack. To ensure the quality of instruction in local groups with few members, DOSARM instituted a system of joint civil defense training drills and competitions. Stalinist culture thus made civil defense a sort of competitive sport as DOSARM propaganda celebrated the best-prepared teams' exploits in the national media. Workers from the Leningrad Mint wowed judges, taking top prize in the first national civil defense competition.[112] For every DOSARM organization demonstrating such enthusiasm for civil defense, however, countless others scraped by with the bare minimum effort required to escape criticism.

Recognizing the 1948 breakup of OSOAVIAKhIM as a mistake that failed to make popular military training more effective, in 1951 the Soviet government merged DOSARM with the other two "military-patriotic" organizations into a single institution: the Dobrovol'noe obshchestvo sodeistviia armii, aviastii, i flotu (Voluntary Organization for Assistance to the Army, Air Force, and Navy, or DOSAAF). DOSAAF's institutional interests spanned the gamut from teaching Soviet citizens to drive to sponsoring all-Union model boat races. Compared with the allure of shooting competitions or flying a plane, civil defense training faced stiff competition for the time and enthusiasm of DOSAAF members. The Kremlin aimed to make DOSAAF the centerpiece of its efforts to prepare the Soviet population for war and commanded that DOSAAF attempt to expand its membership rolls to include every adult Soviet citizen. DOSAAF readily complied, coveting not just a broader membership base but also the massive increase in its budget the membership dues of tens of millions of new enrollees promised.[113] The leadership of the organization regarded civil defense as an important aspect of its activities, but made it a lower priority than enlarging the organization's overall membership as much as possible.

During the last years of Stalin's life DOSAAF trained individuals for roles within a *gruppa samozashchity*—a "self-defense group" associated with their employer, school, or residence. According to the 1950 civil defense training manual *Gruppa samozashchity*, the self-defense group constituted "the primary formation of local anti-air defense," and therefore the work of "liquidating the consequences of air attack" fell on its members rather than uniformed government personnel.[114] Regulations stipulated the organization of at least one such self-defense group in residential buildings with over 300 residents, along with workplaces and educational institutions of up to 250 individuals.[115]

Each self-defense group comprised six or seven units: a policing and surveillance unit, a fire defense unit, a degassing unit, an emergency rescue unit, a medical unit, and a shelter unit. Facilities with large quantities of livestock, such as collective farms, might add a veterinary unit. Each unit consisted of five to seven persons with an additional two in reserve.[116] A regulation self-defense group therefore numbered a minimum of 38 individuals—a significant proportion of a school or factory with 250 people.

Although in theory the self-defense groups would do most of the work of civil defense following an enemy attack, the MPVO enjoyed only indirect influence over them. MPVO officers approved the choice of self-defense group leaders, but DOSAAF possessed direct responsibility for civil defense training and all civil defense propaganda. Local MPVO officers might or might not review the self-defense groups, and surviving records suggest they did so only intermittently.[117] The MPVO itself manifested a characteristically Stalinist penchant for secrecy, issuing few unclassified publications and leaving DOSAAF to explain civil defense to the Soviet public. DOSAAF, however, answered directly to the Kremlin rather than the MPVO General Staff, and the organization's numerous and eclectic responsibilities resulted in the neglect of civil defense by both local DOSAAF groups and its national leadership.

Civil Defense's Odd Couple: Wadsworth and Caldwell

As state and municipal authorities scrutinized the NSRB's civil defense plan, the Truman administration started taking steps to create what would become the FCDA. It did so without the assistance of Paul Larsen, who resigned and washed his hands of civil defense in September 1950. While the White House searched for a suitable candidate for civil defense administrator, James J. Wadsworth stepped in to manage the Civil Defense Office. The scion of a prominent New England family and a former Republican New York state representative, the forty-five-year-old Wadsworth garnered his position in civil defense as the consequence of sheer nepotism. His brother-in-law happened to be none other than Stuart Symington, who pointed out that while Wadsworth's postwar employment in the Economic Cooperation Administration (the agency in charge of administering the Marshall Plan) was "reasonably high on the Federal ladder," it was still a "dead-end job." Symington urged Wadsworth to seek out a place in the "Big League of Washington," where people held their positions by presidential appointment. The NSRB's Office of Civil Defense seemed a good fit for a man of Wadsworth's ambitions, despite his total unfamiliarity with civil defense, and in June 1950 he started work on what would become his "baby" for the remainder of the Truman administration.[118]

Although he never bore the title of federal civil defense administrator, Wadsworth ran the day-to-day affairs of American civil defense from late

1950 until early 1953. Upon his arrival at the Civil Defense Office, housed in a "monstrous, attic-like space" on the top floor of the Executive Office Building, Wadsworth encountered what he described in his memoirs as "a full chicken colonel, whose life-long hobby had been Civil Defense." "Barney" Beers, as everyone called him, came to Wadsworth bearing congratulations, but he "wore such a lugubrious expression," Wadsworth recalled, "that I was worried about him." It soon became apparent that Wadsworth himself elicited the colonel's worried countenance, as "he was horrified that anyone could have been elevated to the job who so sorely lacked experience!" After some frank conversation, the two men agreed that "through application and super-hard work we could squeak through, if people didn't demand too many answers too soon." Beers, whom Wadsworth characterized as "a very knowledgeable fellow as well as a great one for lightening the mood when things were grim," spent several weeks tutoring Wadsworth about the dreary subject matter of civil defense. Wadsworth proved a fortuitous choice, as he rapidly acclimated to the needs of his new job. Over the course of the summer, Wadsworth helped translate the concepts Beers championed in the NSRB civil defense plan into legislation for submission to Congress.[119] After Larsen's departure from the Civil Defense Office in September 1950, Wadsworth took over as acting director.[120]

Symington hoped that his brother-in-law might assume the mantle of civil defense administrator, but political considerations dictated otherwise. Wadsworth's affiliation with the Republican Party posed a serious obstacle, especially given that his earlier work with the Economic Cooperation Administration and the Air Transport Association lacked prestige. The transparent nepotism behind Wadsworth's hiring also drew sharp fire. Wadsworth attracted the acid tongue of gossip columnist and radio personality Drew Pearson, who characterized the acting director as "an amiable Teddy Bear of 50, whose only credits were that [he] had an important father and an important brother-in-law, and no record worth looking at."[121] In addition to Wadsworth's real or imagined shortcomings, the political difficulties facing the increasingly embattled President Truman also called for a different choice. These problems resulted from the growing contradictions within the Democratic Party between liberal New Dealers and conservative segregationist Southern Democrats, who formed a short-lived breakaway "Dixiecrat" party in 1948. In a gambit to retain the fickle loyalties of Southern Democrats without compromising too much of his progressive domestic agenda, Truman decided to distribute some plum appointments to prominent Southerners, including the position of civil defense administrator. On December 1, President Truman announced Millard F. Caldwell Jr., the former governor of Florida, as his nominee for the post.[122]

Although he lacked any background in civil defense, Caldwell possessed several attributes that appeared to be potential assets for a civil defense administrator—as well as some horrific liabilities. Born in Knoxville, Tennessee, in 1897, Caldwell started a law practice in Florida in 1925 but soon became involved in local politics, working his way up to serve as a representative for Florida in Congress from 1933 until 1941. The tragic death of Caldwell's son in a traffic accident in 1940 while living in Washington resulted in a profound distaste for the capital and his decision not to stand for reelection. Caldwell returned to Florida, where he became governor in 1945.[123] In that post Caldwell established a record of strong opposition to federal intervention into civil rights issues, proposing a devious scheme whereby various Southern state governments could pool their resources to create regional segregated colleges for African Americans, circumventing Supreme Court decisions demanding "separate but equal" funding.[124] Much more ominously, early in his term as governor, Caldwell refused to remove a sheriff involved in a terrible lynching incident in October 1945, using the excuse that he did not care to "interfere with the performance of duty by local officials."[125] Caldwell tried to redefine the lynching as an ordinary murder—a tactic that met with nationwide protests not only from the African American press but also from *Time* and *Collier's*. Having warned the latter magazine in advance not to publish its scathing editorial about him, the governor sued *Collier's* for libel and won an award of $237,000, which he donated to the segregated African-American Florida Agriculture and Mechanical College to disprove the magazine's calumny against his racial views.[126]

This colorful history failed to dissuade Truman from appointing Caldwell civil defense administrator, not only because doing so would assuage Southern Democrats but also because in a small way Truman owed his victory in the 1948 election to the ex-governor. Caldwell's reluctant support of Truman in 1948 helped prevent Florida's electoral votes from going to Dixiecrat candidate Strom Thurmond, allowing the president to accomplish his dramatic upset victory.[127] Although his demonstrated loyalty to Truman probably served as Caldwell's main qualification for his post, supporters rationalized that Caldwell's background in Congress and as chair of the National Governors' Conference in 1946 and 1947 indicated readiness to fulfill both the legislative and organizational demands of the nascent FCDA.[128] While the NAACP mounted a protest campaign asserting that Caldwell's record on race issues disqualified him for the post, no one pointed out that the closest

"Dont Go To Any Bother ··· I'd Rather Just Drop In"

Herbert Block decries underdevelopment of civil defense. A 1950 Herblock Cartoon, © The Herb Block Foundation.

thing to expertise in civil defense or nuclear weapons that he possessed was his service as an army artillerist during World War I.[129]

On the same day that he appointed Caldwell civil defense administrator, President Truman signed Executive Order 10186, establishing the FCDA within the Executive Office of the President.[130] Caldwell arrived to take charge of a rapidly expanding organization growing from the nucleus of the NSRB Civil Defense Office. Only Colonel Beers possessed more than a few months of experience in civil defense, and he imparted his arcane knowledge to Caldwell as he had to Wadsworth. In Wadsworth's memoirs, the deputy administrator characterized his new boss as "a very able citizen" and recalled that "we hit it off perfectly from the start," despite the dramatic contrast between the tall, perfectly coiffed Southern Democrat Caldwell and the balding, stocky blueblood Yankee Republican Wadsworth.[131]

The new FCDA faced challenges great and small as it chased its goal of preparing America's civilian population to face a Soviet nuclear attack. In the months immediately following the signing of Truman's executive order, the FCDA pursued three principal aims. First, Wadsworth labored to facilitate speedy congressional action on the Civil Defense Act of 1950, which would provide a standing legal basis for the FCDA. Based on the model legislation included in the NSRB civil defense plan, the new law passed both houses with minimal opposition on January 2, 1951, and President Truman signed it into law on January 12.[132] Second, the appointment of Caldwell as civil defense administrator required congressional approval. At Caldwell's nomination hearing in the Senate Armed Services Committee on January 15, only one witness appeared besides the ex-governor: Clarence Mitchell of the NAACP, who argued that Caldwell was an unfit candidate because of his "prejudice against colored citizens." Caldwell disputed Mitchell's criticism, but defended his refusal to address his constituents with an honorific such as "Mr." or "Mrs." on official mail as he "reserved the right to address any person in such manner as I please, and in accordance with my own views."[133] Apparently the Senate Armed Services Committee approved of this sentiment, as it voted unanimously to confirm Caldwell's nomination—as did the Senate itself the next day.[134] The final task of the FCDA—eliciting congressional and popular support for its ambitious civil defense program—would prove far more difficult.

Conclusion

In the early 1950s, both the United States and the Soviet Union came to regret their tardiness in developing civil defense against atomic weapons. Struck by a sudden sense of urgency about the possibility of nuclear war, American and Soviet observers concurred that their governments had squandered an irreplaceable opportunity during the 1940s to lay the groundwork for an effective civil defense effort. Eugene Rabinowitch, the editor of the *Bulletin of the Atomic Scientists*, lamented shortly after the outbreak of the conflict in Korea that "we have wasted five precious years." Rabinowitch, a previous advocate of the internationalization of atomic energy converted to the cause of civil defense by the prevailing circumstances, worried that the uninspiring recent history of civil defense would continue to haunt future efforts. "An immense gap remains," feared Rabinowitch, between the "extent of the national catastrophe which an atomic attack may produce five years hence . . . and the parochial organization which is being planned to deal with it. It seems as if planning starts with what can be done without too much expenditure and what can be done without too much dislocation of peacetime city life," he worried, "rather than with a realistic estimate of the dimensions of the problem."[135] A few years later, Soviet defense minister Nikolai Bulganin and minister of medium machine-building (i.e., the nuclear industry) Viacheslav Malyshev found their country even less prepared to tackle the challenge of civil defense. In September 1953 they wrote to Georgii Malenkov, Stalin's successor as party secretary, that the Ministry of Internal Affairs had done "absolutely nothing about the defense of the population, cities, and industrial centers against atomic weapons." They attributed this deplorable situation to "excessive secrecy" and proposed urgent measures to rectify it as quickly as possible.[136]

In part, both the United States and the Soviet Union hesitated to create civil defense programs addressing nuclear weapons because they considered it unnecessary, but the underlying cause for these delays was the limitations of their respective states. Individuals from both countries boasting substantial firsthand experience with the effects of nuclear weapons, such as Beers and Meshcheriakov, stood at the forefront of those calling for aggressive civil defense efforts. The leaders of the two superpowers, however, saw little reason to act on such warnings until the early 1950s. The Truman administration hoped that the American nuclear monopoly would last long enough that the politically fraught decision about civil defense could be delayed for the immediate future. The dubious legacy of the United States' civil defense effort during World War II, furthermore, substantially increased the political and cultural obstacles facing a revived program. Some Americans feared that a robust civil defense effort would be a step toward the dreaded garrison state, helping encourage the weak program institutionalized as the FCDA. Stalin, meanwhile, evidently believed his own rhetoric that the "strong-nerved" Soviet people need not fear the atomic bomb, blocking initiatives from his advisors to upgrade the party-garrison state for the nuclear age. As it turned out, the party was the weak link in the party-garrison state, and when the party was dysfunctional, as it was in the late Stalin era, it could not act to defend itself. The repeated efforts of Meshcheriakov, Vannikov, and finally Beria himself could not convince the obstinate dictator to reconsider his utter refusal to acknowledge the physical hazards posed by nuclear weapons, even to his own military. Only Stalin's death in March 1953 enabled his successors to begin addressing the possibility of nuclear war in earnest. Both superpowers would soon learn, however, that the political and institutional obstacles to the creation of a viable civil defense program were even steeper than the physical ones.

2 The Window of Survivability

Addressing the American citizenry at 3:15 P.M. on August 22, 1953, the president warned that "our homeland is under threat of immediate attack. A cold-blooded unscrupulous enemy seeks to plunge us into another war." This ruthless foe was the USSR, whose growing menace to the United States had finally erupted into an unprovoked assault. Dwight Eisenhower continued that "at this moment Russian bombers are penetrating our air defenses" and that, despite the best efforts of interceptors to shoot down the attacking aircraft, "many of the enemy planes will get through to drop bombs on their targets. Vigilance and readiness are now the price of our safety and freedom." Informing citizens that "our civil defense forces are now in action," Eisenhower intoned confidently, "I know that every American is ready and prepared to protect himself as best he can if his community is attacked. I know that every American is ready to give aid to his neighbor. In this hour of trial we must not give way to fear. We must stand together in calm strength, ready to cope with this attack. This is the hour of supreme trial. So help us, God."[1]

Despite the valiant efforts of the military to destroy the Soviet invaders, atomic bombs soon began exploding over American cities. At 5:02, Eisenhower announced that "our nation has just been attacked by a cold-blooded, ruthless enemy—Soviet Russia. Russian planes have dropped bombs on 16 American cities. This unprovoked attack has killed and injured American citizens and destroyed American property." In the aftermath of this tragedy, the president gave listeners reason for hope: "Our civil defense forces are meeting their test in this our hour of trial and need." Most importantly, Eisenhower implored citizens to resist an enemy even more dire than the A-bomb: panic. "Do not panic and do not be misled by reports of mass destruction or of dishonorable surrender," he warned.[2]

Not content merely demolishing America's metropolitan centers with atomic bombs, the forces of godless communism utilized all the tools at their disposal, including chemical, biological, and psychological warfare. Enemy agents undertook aggressive actions to undermine American morale, such as circulating a false report that President Eisenhower was missing and presumed dead after the destruction of the nation's capital. The boldest of the communist subversives went so far as to make a radio broadcast proclaiming himself the "governor of the United Soviets of America." Broadcaster Edward R. Murrow reassured listeners that "this agent is now in jail," and beseeched that loyal Americans rapidly report any of his comrades to the authorities.[3]

Federal civil defense administrator Val Peterson believed that civil defense had saved the United States from defeat in the atomic war despite the deaths of millions of Americans. "The estimated total of dead and injured is 7,000,000," bemoaned Peterson, but he added optimistically that "we can all thank God that the all-out effort of the enemy to crush us with a sudden unprovoked and dastardly attack has failed." Although Peterson admitted that casualty figures were "tragically high," they were "proportionately low in view of the type of attack and population density in the cities struck," as "they would have been far heavier if our CD forces and volunteers had not acted so well and so swiftly."[4] Meanwhile, the United States promptly retaliated against the Soviet attack. Chairman of the Joint Chiefs of Staff admiral Arthur W. Radford stated that, while the military shot down only 125 of the 400 Soviet Tu-4 bombers before they dropped their bombs, Americans could console themselves that "aircraft of the Strategic Air Command have successfully penetrated the Soviet homeland. Military and industrial targets at strategically located points throughout Russia have been attacked. At the moment I can't say more than that the retaliatory force of our Strategic Air Command bombers has been released upon the enemy."[5] Presumably, this would be the first step toward American victory in World War III.

The Public Affairs division of the Federal Civil Defense Administration invented the Soviet attack of August 22, 1953, as part of "Operation Tryout," a test exercise investigating how the United States government would communicate with its citizenry in the context of a nuclear strike. Scripted in painstaking detail, Operation Tryout simulated the transmission of reports about the developing atomic war via America's radio networks and wire services. The FCDA considered Operation Tryout a great success, concluding that it had done "a highly creditable job."[6]

Intended for circulation within only the government and part of the media, Operation Tryout embodied the FCDA's hopes for how civil defense would function after it realized its ambitions to prepare the American people to survive nuclear war. In Operation Tryout, events unfolded according to the FCDA's plans, allowing civil defense to limit damage to American lives and property while simultaneously thwarting the Red assault on American morale. The FCDA considered the nuclear war envisioned in the exercise a realistic near-term possibility, even though its leaders recognized that without better training and more resources, civil defense could do little to blunt the impact of a Soviet attack.

During the early 1950s, both U.S. and Soviet civil defense planned for a nuclear war fought using a limited number of low-yield nuclear weapons delivered by vulnerable subsonic manned bombers. In contrast to a conflict waged with thousands of high-yield thermonuclear weapons carried by impossible-to-intercept ballistic missiles, which became possible a decade later, planners had good reason to believe that such a war would be not merely survivable but winnable—and both Washington and Moscow expected civil defense to help win it.

But despite the relatively manageable challenges facing civil defense at the time, compared with those of a few years later, for institutional and cultural reasons neither the American weak contract state nor the Soviet party-garrison state made much progress toward viable civil defense programs. In the United States, the FCDA sought a multibillion-dollar shelter construction program, with the support of the Truman administration, but congressional opposition led by fiscal conservatives condemned it to oblivion. Convinced that the lack of political support for its programs stemmed from public ignorance of the nuclear threat, the agency developed an ill-fated propaganda campaign that intentionally sought to stoke individuals' fear of nuclear war in the theory that this would translate into political support for the FCDA's shelter-building efforts. The Soviet Union, meanwhile, resuscitated its wartime shelter-building effort and launched an ambitious training campaign in the mid-1950s, but faced both economic and ideological obstacles to developing a robust civil defense. Soviet civil defense initially pursued a program premised on the same sort of war envisioned by the FCDA a few years earlier, but Stalin's declaration that the atomic bomb was "only something that might frighten a weak-nerved people" set a precedent of downplaying the hazards posed by nuclear weapons that left a problematic ideological legacy for his political heirs.

"Shoes without Soles": Truman's Stillborn Public Shelter System

The shelters envisioned by American civil defense during the Truman administration differed from the fallout shelters proposed later in that they were intended to protect occupants from only the blast and prompt radiation effects of nuclear weapons. Citizens would expect to spend mere hours inside these blast shelters, unlike fallout shelters, which typically offered minimal or no blast resistance and demanded weeks of continuous occupancy. Both U.S. and Soviet civil defense envisioned that urban residents would stream into these shelters upon hearing air raid sirens warning of approaching enemy bombers. Citizens would remain in the shelters only until the air raid concluded, after which they would emerge to assist in civil defense rescue and recovery efforts. Initially, civil defense hoped that suitable space would be found in existing basements to shelter much of the population. All that would be required would be to identify the shelter areas with signs; otherwise, they would be the same basements as they were in civilian life. Some basements might require structural reinforcement, but otherwise they would remain basements with signs on them. Finally, the remainder of the population would take cover in a number of dedicated freestanding shelters, potentially constructed to serve a practical peacetime role such as a parking garage.

Under Truman the FCDA sought billions in shelter funding for two reasons. First, the FCDA, like the Truman administration generally and much of the American public, regarded Soviet nuclear attack as an imminent threat. The FCDA had a statutory mandate under the Civil Defense Act of 1950 to create a civil defense that would allow the United States to withstand nuclear war. By 1951 Harry Truman no longer hesitated to request billions for defense programs. The second reason why the FCDA eagerly solicited shelter funding did not contradict the first, but was more self-serving. Simply put, the billions of dollars required to build a comprehensive system of blast shelters in American cities would have made the FCDA one of the wealthiest and most powerful agencies in the federal government. Dispensing millions in federal largesse every year, the FCDA would be courted by local and state governments, as well as congressional representatives, in search of lucrative matching funds. Besides their belief that creating a system of shelters for America's major cities represented their patriotic and humanitarian duty, the men and women of the FCDA had every incentive to chase increased federal funding. Internal FCDA records reveal a portrait of an agency ambitious to acquire resources commensurate with the ultimate challenge—surviving nuclear war—and desperately frustrated with its inability to overcome the political hurdles preventing it from doing so. Far from seeking to lull Americans into a false sense of security, as some scholars have asserted, FCDA propaganda sought to alarm citizens into demanding a robust civil defense that would translate into massively increased civil defense spending—particularly for shelters.[7]

The lack of hard data on which to base a shelter program did not restrain the ambitions of American civil defense planners. To resolve the many critical questions fundamental to planning a major U.S. shelter effort, the NSRB (and subsequently the FCDA) partnered with other government agencies, including the Atomic Energy Commission (AEC) and the Census Bureau, to provide assistance. Despite the unavailability of reliable figures for how many shelters would be needed and how much they would cost, the NSRB—and after December 1, 1950, the FCDA—actively pursued an ambitious shelter program. The September 1950 NSRB civil defense plan promised that, while providing shelter protection for all Americans was "financially impossible," a public shelter program would serve the United States' "critical target areas." To fulfill this task "economically," this program would make use of existing structures wherever possible.[8] As early as November 29, 1950, however, the NSRB budget specified an expenditure of $2.25 billion between 1951 and 1954 on bomb shelters. The federal budget would provide $1.125 billion of this total, and matching funds from states would provide the other half. The NSRB assumed, on the basis of conjecture, that fifteen million Americans in critical target areas would "require shelter not now available."[9] The FCDA planned to distribute these matching funds to states on the basis of their population living in "critical target areas."[10]

Predictably, the prospect of the availability of so large a sum of federal money, in addition to the ongoing hysteria about the possibility of a Soviet nuclear attack, aroused the interest of state and local governments. Even before the passage of the Civil Defense Act of 1950, governors and mayors began seeking information from the FCDA about how they could receive shelter money.[11] The dance for funds also went the other way. Federal civil defense administrator Millard Caldwell encouraged state governors, senators, and other officials to motivate their legislatures to budget millions for shelter construction in the coming year.[12]

With billions of dollars seemingly in the offing, private firms jumped at the chance to get into the shelter business. Dozens of architects, contractors, and construction firms contacted the government in search of shelter work or information on how to construct shelters. Some sought contracts for the construction of public shelters, while others hoped to profit by selling private shelters to a fearful populace. Leisurehouse Incorporated, of Wichita, Kansas, wrote the Research Division of the FCDA about efforts to develop "prefabricated Ra-Dome shelters." These were to be sold in both a "family" model and a "communal-industrial" model, the latter of which could serve in peacetime as space for recreational activities including "ping-pong" and "horseshoe pitching." A photograph of a model of the proposed shelter, revealing its bizarre, half-buried design, was enclosed. Leisurehouse expressed hope that government matching funds and financing would be available for the construction of these shelters.[13]

One enthusiastic and enterprising businessman in New York City, Alfred H. Bergman, vice president and director of sales of the Presscrete Company, made the construction of bomb shelters his personal crusade, writing countless letters to government officials urging a crash program of shelter building. In a January 26, 1951, letter to Millard Caldwell, Bergman lamented that "what is being done here [in New York City], if it reflects what is being done in the rest of the country, will certainly spell C-A-T-A-S-T-R-O-P-H-E and D-E-F-E-A-T for the United States," and "it is horrible to realize that we are headed for the worst war in our history and Business As Usual. God Help us if we don't wake up soon." Bergman enclosed a letter he had written to the majority leader of the City Council of New York in which he urged passage of a law stipulating that all property owners be ordered to construct bomb shelters. While Bergman's obsession with the prospect of Soviet nuclear attack may have been genuine, he had fiscal motives too. He sought to market shelters of his own design that, he promised, could protect the residents of the city for a mere forty to sixty dollars a person. He grumbled that, given the lack of government interest, "American lives apparently aren't worth $40 apiece."[14]

Although the FCDA made a remarkable effort to carry on a polite correspondence with private concerns such as Leisurehouse and Presscrete, its internal correspondence reveals a high degree of exasperation with what seem to have been a small army of technically uninformed profiteers. While the FCDA generally refused to analyze shelter designs for private firms, it studied a few for institutional purposes and generally found them seriously wanting. For instance, on December 12, 1950, Maryland Concrete Products sent its proposed family shelter design to the NSRB for review, requesting government approval prior to putting the shelter on the market. The FCDA Office of the Chief of Engineers drew up a list of twenty-five faults in the proposed shelter, concluding that "this design appears to have many undesirable features and to be wasteful of material."[15]

In fact, as of early 1951 the FCDA had almost no enthusiasm for the home shelter trend. Intent on creating a public shelter system capable of accommodating millions of Americans, civil defense planners sought to downplay private shelters. A February 1951 FCDA memorandum charged that "privately built shelters outside of critical areas represent an improper and unpatriotic effort, inasmuch as their construction subtracts from the national security resources and makes it just that much more difficult for other persons who *really do need* shelters to have them." This democratic spirit suffused the FCDA's shelter planning: "Luxury types of shelters (e.g. with built-in bars, rumpus rooms, and unnecessarily expensive air conditioning features which it would not be feasible to provide in communal shelters) are, to say the least, in exceedingly bad taste for any individual to build." Also in "bad taste," according to the memorandum, was "the building of very expensive types of shelters in order to afford a few fortunate persons a markedly higher degree of protection than the average citizen could possibly hope he will be able to get in the public shelters. In times such as these it does not lead to better feeling to have any citizen's safety determined too importantly merely by the size of his wallet."[16]

Besides an idealistic belief that Americans in target areas deserved effective shelter regardless of their socioeconomic status, the FCDA also hoped to avoid committing construction resources inefficiently in light of the perceived need to mobilize the United States' economy for a world war with the communist bloc. The hope to economize on critical defense materials such as cement suffused FCDA shelter planning: "Crowded communal shelters afford very considerably cheaper protection per occupant than conventional, room-type, outdoor family shelters ordinarily would do," explained the memorandum, so "the FCDA should, therefore, not encourage outdoor private shelters except where the private shelters are of especially inexpensive types." On the whole, Caldwell's FCDA conceived of shelters not as a personal responsibility but as an integral part of the nation's defense complex: "a bomb shelter is provided for (or permitted to) the individual simply on the basis of his protection by it being of more benefit to the national situation than can be had by similar expenditures on other measures (and *not* by virtue of any imagined right of the individual)," concluded the memorandum.[17]

In early 1951, FCDA officials assumed that Congress would soon appropriate the requisite matching funds to begin shelter construction. In a February 28, 1951, letter to the mayor of Detroit, Millard Caldwell assured him that "funds should be available to us in the next six to eight weeks."[18] The House Appropriations Committee, however, did not cooperate with the plans of the Truman administration and the FCDA. On April 6, 1951, the Appropriations Committee reviewed the FCDA budget request in the Third Supplemental Appropriations Bill, finding much for which it did not care. Dismissing the FCDA's plans as "nebulous," the committee reduced the

FCDA's $403 million budget request to $186,750,000 and "hinted strongly that the agency should restrain itself," according to the *Washington Post*.[19] Shelters formed the single largest item in the budget request, totaling $250 million of the $403 million. The committee reduced this to $75 million, stating in its report that "sufficient funding is available to enable a start to be made on a survey of existing facilities and where possible to strengthen them to serve as shelter areas. Unless proper control is maintained over the funds available for this work there is nothing to prevent money from being expended without desirable results and at an astronomical cost to the government."[20] Paltry as these sums were, the actual appropriation in the final bill that emerged from the reconciliation process proved far stingier. Reducing the overall total from $186,750,000 to a paltry $32 million, it left the FCDA without any funds to begin shelter construction.[21] The U.S. budgetary process proved a linchpin of the weak contract state.

This setback did not discourage the FCDA from again requesting $250 million for shelter construction in fiscal year 1952. In August 1951, the House Appropriations Committee eviscerated the FCDA budget a second time, complaining that "the committee, in its report accompanying the Third Supplemental Appropriations Bill, 1951, recommended a civil defense concept based on the training and education of the general public in matters of self-protection and the coordination of the civil defense efforts of the various states and municipalities." Notwithstanding that this vision was neither commensurate with the challenges of nuclear war nor in agreement with the language in the Federal Civil Defense Act of 1950, the committee whined that "the plans and estimates submitted to the committee in justification of the appropriation request do not reflect this concept."[22] In practice the committee possessed the prerogative to set the nation's civil defense policy however it saw fit, and it refused to appropriate funds for any aspect of the FCDA's programs that it found disagreeable, whittling the agency's ambitious plans down to a mere propaganda effort. The Appropriations Committee showed even less enthusiasm for shelters than it had a few months earlier. "The estimate of $250,000,000 for protective facilities is denied," declared the report. "Testimony received by the committee failed to disclose either the need for a shelter program as contemplated by the estimates or adequate plans for the expenditure of funds."[23]

Predictably, congressional refusal to appropriate more than a pittance for civil defense, and particularly its failure to budget anything for shelters, infuriated FCDA officials. Millard Caldwell grumbled that "trying to have civil defense without shelters is like having shoes without soles."[24] In a

"I'll Be Glad To Lend You My Sickle"

Herbert Block on civil defense appropriations. A 1951 Herblock Cartoon, © The Herb Block Foundation.

letter to Governor Frank J. Lausche of Ohio, Caldwell charged that "if our funds are unduly limited, there will be a needless number of casualties if an attack occurs. Congress must assume that risk."[25]

Shocked by this unforeseen development, the leaders of the FCDA decided that lackluster political support for civil defense resulted from widespread underappreciation of the possibility of imminent nuclear attack. Caldwell asserted that "the action of the House is undoubtedly due in large part to the general public apathy to civil defense. The most vicious menace in America today is the shocking apathy of the American people to their danger from enemy attack." The federal civil defense administrator declared that "in the interest of our people and the free world we cannot surrender to this apathy, despite what is done or is not done by the Congress."[26] James Wadsworth told reporters that "the people of this country are not aware generally of the dangers of enemy attack. They are not aware that they desperately need to know how to save their own skins."[27] In accordance with this outlook, Caldwell's FCDA undertook a propaganda program to combat public "apathy" while simultaneously continuing its efforts to create the large public shelter system it considered an essential component of civil defense. The front page of the May 1951 issue of the FCDA's official newsletter, *Civil Defense Alert*, simultaneously bore the headlines "Leaders Plan Campaign against Public Apathy" and "Standards and Specifications for Air-Raid Shelters Are Based on Extensive Study and Research."[28]

In defense of the House Appropriations Committee and its chair, Missouri Democrat Clarence Cannon, FCDA records support the committee's accusation that the FCDA lacked "adequate plans" to spend the requested $250 million for shelters. As of 1951, the requisite technical knowledge to construct a bomb shelter to survive a nuclear explosion was not yet available, rendering realistic shelter planning impossible. The FCDA produced its cost estimates for constructing shelters before completing even its preliminary shelter design studies. Despite the FCDA's eagerness to request federal money, it proved hesitant to publish technical manuals on shelter surveying and design that it did not consider accurate.[29] While this choice reflects positively on the FCDA's commitment to creating an effective civil defense for Americans, it made it extraordinarily difficult to convince skeptics that the FCDA would spend shelter funding responsibly.

Working in concert with the AEC, the FCDA developed its shelter designs by testing the structures in actual nuclear explosions. Unfortunately, the FCDA's shelter designs did not always withstand the effects of nuclear weapons as well as envisioned. Furthermore, the FCDA lacked sufficient opportunity to do all the tests it needed to. As a result, all of the shelter design manuals appeared months or years later than scheduled, and some contained caveats revealing the limits of the FCDA's knowledge.[30] In some instances, nuclear testing demonstrated that the FCDA's shelter designs were simply inadequate. The minutes of the January 16, 1952, FCDA assistant administrators' meeting noted "the home-type shelter manual was ready for issuance but that several of the recommended designs do not tie in with the results of the recent atomic tests." Despite this setback, the FCDA manuals division proposed to complete a version of the home shelter manual, which it had originally hoped to release in late 1951, "within 60 days."[31] Ultimately, it took another year of research to satisfy the FCDA that the home shelter manual was ready. In fact, the FCDA released the manual to the public only in mid-1953, after nuclear tests in Nevada demonstrated the viability of the proposed shelter designs.[32]

While the FCDA failed to instruct individuals how to construct private shelters to survive nuclear war, its efforts to create a public shelter system began to bear fruit. Unfortunately, this harvest consisted of basements with signs on them. Despite the fact that Congress refused to appropriate the sums requested by the FCDA for shelter construction, some eager state and city civil defense organizations went ahead with shelter surveying and marking. These efforts did not always meet with FCDA approval. In November 1952, the FCDA's Monthly Field Report lamented that "many local CD programs are reluctant to start shelter programs because of the expense, manpower, and paperwork involved." The report noted that "some organizations have been forced into action by local chambers of commerce or civic groups, but often the action taken is limited to looking over some major buildings in the business district and posting shelter signs without much regard to shelter class or suitability."[33] One major municipality guilty of this misdeed was Boston. Discouraged by the complexity of the official government procedure, city officials began marking shelter spaces without it. The FCDA found that, as of January 1952, "the city of Boston has surveyed 360 buildings and has selected and marked shelters, however, many of the shelters would not meet FCDA standards."[34]

Other cities proved more willing to follow the FCDA's lead in shelter development. Philadelphia, in particular, made an enthusiastic push for shelters. In January 1952, the FCDA's Monthly Field Report stated approvingly that "Philadelphia's shelter survey is over 50% complete, covering buildings in 2,042 blocks that normally house 235,031 persons. It is estimated that the survey has cost $150,000 to date. Shelter signs have been procured but have not been posted." In Washington, D.C., civil defense had completed only a fraction of its survey but had begun to post shelter signs in federal buildings and located shelters meeting FCDA criteria for a significant proportion of the population in the surveyed area. Other cities discovered, however, that they lacked buildings that met the demands set by the FCDA for shelter. East St. Louis "abandoned its shelter survey after finding that only five buildings could qualify under FCDA's shelter criteria." New Orleans surveyed thirty-three buildings but found that none of them could serve as a first-class shelter.[35] As a result of such setbacks, public shelter surveys sputtered in much of the country, but in certain areas they forged ahead with considerable enthusiasm. Denver, Colorado, for instance, expanded its shelter survey to include industrial plants, and the board of education requested a shelter survey of all public schools in the area.[36] Colorado civil defense posted shelter signs in the statehouse indicating where to cower in case of nuclear attack.[37] The extent of state and local government support determined the success of the shelter survey program in any given locale.

On the whole, however, it managed to have only a limited impact before it became a victim of the changing political climate.

Salesmen for Armageddon Insurance

In the tempestuous debate after 1945 regarding how a postwar U.S. civil defense program ought to be organized, the problem of how to mobilize the population to participate in civil defense received relatively little attention. In late 1950, it appeared that Americans might support a revived civil defense effort with relatively little prompting. The ongoing war scare resulting from the Soviet atomic bomb test and the Korean War made the threat of atomic attack seem frighteningly imminent to many Americans, inspiring a vocal minority to clamor loudly for survival preparations. Politicians such as John F. Kennedy and scientists such as Ralph Lapp bemoaned the weakness of the nation's civil defense efforts, and throughout 1950 magazines and newspapers published numerous pieces about civil defense. The problem facing the FCDA appeared to be harnessing an untapped pool of public enthusiasm, rather than convincing the public to support its programs. In a few short months, this assessment proved highly overoptimistic.

Following its creation in December 1950, the FCDA inherited the propaganda program of the NSRB Civil Defense Office, which as of the beginning of 1951 boasted a single major product—a pamphlet titled *Survival under Atomic Attack*—but it had already established collaborative relationships with print and broadcast media to publicize civil defense. While running the Civil Defense Office as acting director, James J. Wadsworth had collaborated on a CBS television program titled "Primer for Survival," and with the rapid development of the civil defense program, television networks sought out both administrator Millard Caldwell and Wadsworth for interviews.[38] The hosts of these programs felt little inclination to criticize the FCDA's ambitious civil defense proposals. At the suggestion of the White House, in late January 1951 Caldwell and Wadsworth appeared on *Battle Report*, a "semi-official" program on NBC hosted by the same John Steelman who ran the NSRB in 1949.[39] In February, they gave interviews to Lawrence Spivak on *Meet the Press* and to Eleanor Roosevelt on *Mrs. Roosevelt Meets the Public*.[40]

To gauge the likely public reception of their programs, civil defense officials turned to public opinion surveys. In April 1950, the Civil Defense Office began discussions with the University of Michigan Survey Research

Center about a civil defense public opinion survey, and with Symington's support the NSRB formally approved the project early in the summer.[41] That fall, investigators from the Survey Research Center canvassed eleven major American cities, questioning citizens from all walks of life about their attitudes regarding civil defense. Only a small fraction of the people interviewed supported the civil defense measures the FCDA hoped to sell to Congress: a memo to Wadsworth noted that "the replies to the question on shelters indicate that only 14% believe that shelters should be built *now*." The survey concluded that these undesirable attitudes appeared to be symptoms of a larger problem that the FCDA would need to address: "The surprising number that admit partial or complete ignorance about the effects of atomic bombing shows the enormity of the educational task before us, and in this connection is the frank admission of 23% that they wish to escape talk about the atomic bomb."[42]

To overcome the obstacles posed by the discomfort many Americans felt even thinking about nuclear weapons, the FCDA turned to psychology, which appeared to offer solutions to Americans' unhealthy attitudes toward atomic attack. Research on the subject began in 1949, when psychologist Irving L. Janis of Yale University began his studies of the psychological aspects of civil defense. In the summer of 1950, the *Bulletin of the Atomic Scientists* published excerpts from his RAND Corporation report on the subject. In this piece Janis drew on interviews of survivors of Allied bombing raids on Germany and Japan to investigate whether individual and group behavior during air attacks would lead to mass panic. Although he admitted that after nuclear attack "the mere sight of the dead and dying will produce a terrifying effect upon almost everyone in the area of disaster," Janis found reason for optimism, as "to the extent that the public is informed about ways and means of coping with the dangers and trained to participate in civil defense, disruptive fear reactions will be minimized." Janis argued that civil defense offered a cure for nuclear anxiety, as "the adequacy of civil defense preparations designed to increase the physical safety of the population have a direct bearing on the emotional impact of an atomic disaster." Building a functioning civil defense, in conjunction with an "educational program for the general public," promised Janis, would imbue the populace with "realistic expectations" as well as "counteracting feelings of helplessness when the danger becomes imminent."[43]

Civil defense authorities and social scientists alike considered feelings as dangerous as atomic explosions. In his 1951 book *Air War and Emotional Stress*, Janis explained that "it is generally recognized that if at some future time large-scale A-bomb attacks are launched against the United States, the psychological impact upon the American people might prove to be as shattering as the physical devastation." Moreover, "long before any wartime disaster occurs, there may be a high degree of psychological vulnerability to the A-bomb threat," as during an international crisis increasing recognition that "our cities may be destroyed and millions of Americans may be killed" could "arouse intense emotional reactions."[44] Citing a survey carried out of ordinary citizens in the summer of 1950, Janis noted that "almost all the respondents explicitly denied that they felt any anxiety about the possible danger of A-bomb attacks," and that "so long as this highly optimistic belief persists, a certain amount of public indifference toward civil defense is to be expected."[45] The respondents' (accurate) perception that a Soviet nuclear threat remained years in the future gave them confidence that civil defense could be delayed for the time being, but Janis commented hopefully that "the interview material suggests that communications which call attention to the magnitude of the danger would be effective in evoking heightened awareness of the need for civil defense," including "popular magazine articles, newspaper features, radio and television programs, movies, free pamphlets, and other mass media."[46]

To sell America on the idea of civil defense, therefore, the FCDA first needed to challenge citizens' apathy about the imminence of the threat. Just as the Lambert Pharmaceutical Company famously convinced Americans of the menace of a disease called "halitosis" in order to sell its cure in the form of Listerine, the FCDA sought to convince the people of the United States that Soviet aircraft might drop atomic bombs on their cities at any moment in order to sell civil defense. Following FCDA planning assumptions about the form a future nuclear war would take, *Air War and Emotional Stress* outlined a "number of speculative suggestions about possible solutions" to this worrisome challenge, with the caveat that "some of these involve controversial issues on which little agreement will be found among social scientists until further research has been done."[47] In particular, Janis warned that "in order to avoid extreme reactions of anticipatory anxiety, it is probably essential to bring about a stepwise increase in awareness of the reality and proximity of the bomb threat, before the danger appears to be actually at hand." Otherwise, a "sense of futility might spread throughout the entire nation, handicapping the entire civil defense program."[48] In its haste, however, the FCDA decided it could not wait, and its propaganda informed Americans that atomic bombs might fall on their cities at any moment.

Civil Defense and the "Behavioral Sciences"

While developing its civil defense propaganda, the FCDA turned to the prevailing paradigm in American social science—behavioralism, which sought to break down disciplinary barriers in an attempt to create a generalized theory of human behavior.[49] Although this ambitious intellectual project largely collapsed during the late 1950s, it wielded enormous influence in American defense policy circles during the opening years of the Cold War. Behavioralists struck a utilitarian middle ground between the stifling empiricism of behaviorism, which denied the importance of subjective experience, and the collectivist social analyses of the United States' communist enemies. Behavioralism comprised a number of competing theories about the origins of human behavior, but all agreed that individuals provided the basis of human societies. One highly influential school among behavioral scientists, which historian Ron Robin dubs the "sociological variant," argued that "fundamental social factors, such as membership in primary groups and social networks," determined human behavior. Defined as "cohesive and autonomous clusters of individuals governed by an informal codex of rules regulating the behavior of members," primary groups included street gangs and military units, as well as families and neighborhoods. In contrast with prevailing sociological models, which contended that primary groups ceased to play a critical role in modern societies, these behavioralists believed such social networks continued to serve as the basis of human behavior.[50]

The influence of the sociological variant of behavioralism reached the zenith at the moment the FCDA launched its initial publicity and recruiting efforts. Riding high from the meteoric impact of the 1949 book *The American Soldier*, which utilized this framework to explain the behavior of U.S. servicemen during World War II, behavioral theory found favor in think tanks such as RAND, where Janis pursued his civil defense research, as well as among philanthropic foundations such as the Ford Foundation, which established a lavishly funded behavioral sciences division in 1951.[51] Americans promptly applied behavioralist theory to their perceived defense needs, such as understanding the psychological motivations of the communist enemy for the purposes of psychological warfare and deprogramming. Distinctively, the sociological variant of behavioralism insisted that ideological considerations played almost no role in human motivation. *The American Soldier*, for instance, argued on the basis of its surveys that American soldiers "exhibited weak to nonexistent political commitments" and that they would even momentarily accept "any plausibly worded statement of the interpretation of the war." The authors maintained that loyalty to their primary groups, in this case their combat units, motivated soldiers to express loyalty to the American government and its war aims, rather than an ideological commitment to democracy or freedom. Equitably ascribing the same logic to America's Nazi and communist enemies, behavioralists contended that, despite appearances to the contrary, ideology played a negligible role in their motivations as well.[52] These scientists did not limit their inquiries to those in uniform: behavioralists also insisted that loyalty to primary groups explained Americans' party affiliations and voting in presidential elections.[53]

The publicity campaign the FCDA launched in 1951 provided an irresistible opportunity to subject the American public to a practical test of behavioralist theories. Following the planning assumptions about a possible nuclear attack underlying its massive public shelter proposals, the FCDA utilized the precepts of behavioralism to construct a narrative of nuclear survival that would make the greatest psychological impact on the population, motivating them to become enthusiastic proponents of and participants in civil defense. If ideology played no role in Americans' motivations, appeals to patriotism could be discarded. So too could denunciations of the threat of communism, since presumably Americans dreaded the Red menace only because the other people they cared about did too. Instead, FCDA propagandists attempted to shock citizens out of their apathy by repeatedly insisting that the atomic bomb posed an existential threat to their primary groups—their communities, neighborhoods, and particularly their families. Reasoning that Americans would clamor for civil defense once they became convinced that atomic bombs threatened to kill their loved ones, the FCDA made the nuclear family the centerpiece of its narrative of nuclear survival. This narrative, circulated extensively in print, radio, and other media, featured prominently in the most famous example of civil defense propaganda in American history—the 1951 educational children's film *Duck and Cover*. The development process and lamentable fate of *Duck and Cover* illustrate how the FCDA attempted to implement its sweeping ambitions to shape the American psyche, and how these efforts swiftly ran aground.

The Short and Disastrous Career of *Duck and Cover*

In the minds of many Americans, *Duck and Cover* remains synonymous with civil defense, thanks to both its wide exposure in its 1950s heyday and its afterlife as the object of antinuclear satire in the 1980s. Starring an anthropomorphic, bow tie–wearing turtle named Bert who urges children to "duck and cover" in order to survive nuclear explosions, the film proved irresistible to the makers of the 1982 documentary *The Atomic Cafe*, who selectively edited it to make an ironic mockery of the Reagan administration's defense policies.[54] Rescued from decades of obscurity, *Duck and Cover* came to symbolize everything wrong with both the nuclear arms race in general and civil defense in particular. More generally, *Duck and Cover* became emblematic of American culture of the 1950s, and generations born long after that decade often assume that the film epitomizes the paranoia and gullibility of Americans in the era of McCarthyism and cars with tailfins. Needless to say, this legacy differed markedly from that the makers of *Duck and Cover* envisioned for their film.

Duck and Cover began as merely one of the lengthy list of propaganda films the FCDA drew up while planning the media blitz it hoped would convert the American public into civil defense believers. The first of these, *Survival under Atomic Attack*, loosely adapted the pamphlet of the same name and premiered in March 1951, shortly after Congress voted down the FCDA's budget request. The *Civil Defense Alert* proudly announced that this one-reeler would be the first of ten such films, with such exciting titles as "Preparing Your Home against Atomic Attack" and "What You Should Know about Biological Warfare." The list of planned releases included the nondescript "Civil Defense for Schools," which eventually became *Duck and Cover*.[55]

Owing to budgetary and personnel limitations, the FCDA delegated the task of creating many of its planned publicity materials to outside firms. The FCDA Public Affairs Division sought to get maximum propaganda value for minimum government investment by allowing firms to make the desired films on their own budget and retain the royalties from their distribution. The implemented arrangement incorporated three tiers: the FCDA, the film distributor Castle Films, and production companies such as United World Films, Teletran, and Archer Productions, which made *Duck and Cover*. While the FCDA stipulated the content of the films and collaborated heavily in their development, *Duck and Cover* demonstrates how the production companies exercised considerable discretion in crafting their products. Outsourcing production and distribution offered two advantages to the FCDA. Doing so allowed the FCDA to take advantage of existing studios and the talents of experienced filmmakers and to offload costs onto the production companies. As Wadsworth boasted at the Motion Picture Association of

America on the premiere of *Survival under Atomic Attack*, "The picture was produced at the cost of not a single cent to the Government and people of the United States." According to the deputy administrator, United World Films made the film because of a "genuine desire to serve their country in the organization of civil defense," but the makers of the FCDA's films also coveted the more tangible rewards they received in the form of revenue from the sale and rental of prints.[56]

Unfazed by the risks attendant to making civil defense films for the government at their own expense, some film producers actively pursued work with the FCDA—including Archer Productions. Archer Productions boasted a short but successful history producing capitalist America's domestic propaganda—advertising. The firm's staff of "hidden persuaders" stood at the cutting edge of their field, concentrating on the burgeoning business of producing television commercials. With the number of American households owning television receivers swelling rapidly in the early 1950s, television commercials promised to become the primary means for reaching potential buyers; but Archer Productions aimed even higher: it sought to transition to a full-fledged television studio producing series for sale to network broadcasters. Pursuing this lofty ambition, the firm craved the national publicity that participating in the emerging FCDA propaganda campaign might provide. On a tip from the president of United World Films, in April 1951 vice president Leo Langlois of Archer Productions approached civil defense authorities about the possibility of making one or more of the films. To get the film "Civil Defense for Schools," which Archer particularly wanted, the FCDA coerced it into agreeing to produce another film, *Our Cities Must Fight*. Langlois elicited the services of his old friend Ray J. Mauer of the Campbell-Ewald advertising agency to write the scripts for the films. A copywriter with no background as a screenwriter, Mauer eagerly took on the novel task of scripting the civil defense films.[57]

At the time when the FCDA and Archer Productions set out to make "Civil Defense for Schools," anxieties about atomic attack ran so high among some school administrators and teachers that they had begun civil defense training and drills without federal guidance, sometimes with grotesque results. Probably the most extreme of these were initiatives in several areas of the United States in 1950 to promote the tattooing of schoolchildren under their left arm with their blood type, on the assumption that this would help in the treatment of the victims of an atomic attack. Particularly common in

Indiana, these efforts seem to have continued in a few places into the mid-1950s but never received active FCDA endorsement.[58]

The film's content remained undecided at the time Archer Productions and the FCDA Public Affairs Division began their collaboration, so the FCDA and Archer Productions arranged a conference with the National Education Association to get feedback from professional educators.[59] Head of the FCDA motion picture branch Howard R. H. Johnson, Langlois, and Mauer sat and listened to twenty-odd teachers discuss their ideas and experiences regarding how to instruct children about civil defense. After a slow start, a woman with a proper British accent set the ball rolling with an utterance that would echo across America: "We have duck and cover drills in our school." The coiner of this phrase, Helen Seth-Smith, was an English expatriate and assistant headmistress of the Potomac School in McLean, Virginia. Johnson, Langlois, and Mauer simultaneously latched onto "duck and cover" as the centerpiece of their new film, and Mauer set about drafting a preliminary script.[60]

Although Seth-Smith contributed a name to "duck and cover," she did not invent the concept. Credit for the tactic of ducking and covering to minimize the chances of injury or death during an atomic attack belonged to residents of Hiroshima and Nagasaki who serendipitously happened upon it. As Janis elaborated, "A substantial proportion of the respondents in Hiroshima and Nagasaki reported having reacted immediately to the intense flash alone, as though it were a well-known danger signal," despite their total unfamiliarity with nuclear weapons. "A number of them said that they voluntarily ducked down or 'hit the dirt' as soon as the flash occurred and had already reached the prone position before the blast swept over them," and "the prompt action proved to be of a highly adaptive character in that it minimized exposure to the secondary heat and blast waves, preventing burns and concussive blows."[61] "These findings," asserted Janis, "suggest that casualties in an A-bomb attack might be reduced if the population has been well-prepared in advance to react appropriately to the flash of the explosion."[62] The proponents of such training measures hardly considered them foolproof: the *Army Medical Bulletin* estimated in a 1948 article that under optimal circumstances it might reduce deaths in an atomic attack by 20 percent.[63] Unlike shelters or coordinated evacuation plans, however, instructing Americans to "hit the dirt" and cover their faces when they saw the flash of an atomic bomb could be implemented swiftly and at negligible expense to the government, which appealed to civil defense planners struggling to win congressional support for costlier measures. Both the brochure and the film of *Survival under Atomic Attack* prominently touted the "duck and cover" tactic, even though it remained nameless.

To make "ducking and covering" appeal more to America's schoolchildren, Mauer decided to incorporate an animated protagonist—"Bert the Turtle." Finnish ex-Disney animator Lars Calonius, founder of Archer Productions and brother-in-law of Langlois, envisioned Bert as a tortoise with a predilection for bipedal locomotion wearing a stiff, old-fashioned collar and bow tie, along with a steel helmet like those sported by air raid wardens during World War II. Tormented by a mischievous firecracker-wielding monkey (presumably a simian proxy for the United States' communist enemies), Bert swiftly retreated to the safety of his shell. Calonius's whimsical sketches excited the FCDA.[64] To populate the live-action part of the film, Mauer introduced three children featuring the names of his real-life offspring: Tony, Paul, and Patty, who demonstrated the survival tactics civil defense recommended. With FCDA approval of Bert and the script, Archer Productions set out to produce the film in a manner commensurate with its limited budget.[65]

Since the FCDA provided no funding to make *Duck and Cover*, the filmmakers took advantage of free labor and shooting locations. The superintendent of New York City's public schools approved the use of P.S. 152 in Astoria, Queens, for filming the school scenes of the film, and its pupils and teachers served as uncredited actors and actresses. Leo Langlois's son played "Tony," the boy who leapt from his bicycle to duck and cover in the adjacent gutter on witnessing the atomic flash. Mauer appeared as a civil defense official, helping his son-by-proxy get out of the gutter and dust himself off. Cameraman Drummond Drury filmed all these scenes with a silent 35mm camera, with voiceovers added later. In addition to saving precious dollars, these expedients incorporated the makers of *Duck and Cover* into its vision of nuclear war. As realized, the film literally and figuratively portrays members of the Langlois and Mauer families "ducking and covering" to survive the atomic bomb.[66]

Regarding the soundtrack of *Duck and Cover* as more important than its cast, Archer Productions took advantage of the professional talent it used in its television commercials to ensure a polished-sounding final product. Character actor Robert Middleton provided his comforting television-pitchman voice for the film's narration. Another character actor, Carl Ritchey, read Bert's single line of dialogue in a tone more befitting a cartoon character: "Remember what to do, friends. Now tell me right out loud. What are you supposed to do when you see the flash?"[67] Most importantly, Bert needed an infectious theme song to drive his point home. Langlois commissioned the duo of Leo Carr and Leon Corday, writers of the immortal car commercial jingle "See the U. S. A. in Your Chevrolet," to work their magic on civil defense.[68] Jazz singer Dave Lambert sang the resulting lyrics, which began "There once was a turtle by the name of Bert / And Bert the Turtle was very alert / When danger threatened him he never got hurt / He knew just what to do!"

The final product of this collaborative effort thrilled the FCDA, which set about promoting Bert. To maximize exposure of the dapper turtle, the FCDA printed three million copies of a sixteen-page illustrated booklet, "Duck and Cover," drawn by Calonius. Not content with this step, the FCDA Audio-Visual Division developed a radio program based on "Duck and Cover," which ran just under fifteen minutes in length and was distributed to radio stations nationwide in the form of a 16" 33 rpm record.[69] Bert burst onto an unsuspecting public in January 1952, when the *Civil Defense Alert* breathlessly announced that "the nation's youngsters will soon be playing a new game called 'Duck and Cover' and their teacher will be a turtle." The film, radio program, and booklets would all be available soon, it promised.[70] The public premiere of *Duck and Cover* took place in the nation's capital on January 7, 1952. On January 24, the FCDA screened the film for educators in Manhattan, and on February 23, a television station in New York City broadcast Bert's antics for the edification of the viewing public. Not to be outdone, Archer Productions took dramatic steps to promote its creation. Milton Mohr, the firm's publicity guru, dreamed up such ideas as making a life-size cardboard cutout of Bert to pose next to celebrities. *Duck and Cover* boasted numerous firsts, according to its makers: "It is the first motion picture using the atomic bomb as the subject to be slanted toward children"; the first to receive the endorsement of the National Education Association, the FCDA, and New York State Civil Defense; "and above all, the first film about the atomic bomb in which no atomic explosion is seen."[71]

In their zeal to strike a balance between inculcating awareness among children of the prospect that a Soviet bomber might destroy their city at any moment and unnecessarily frightening them, the makers of *Duck and Cover* made compromises that resulted in a surreal portrayal of the nuclear dilemma. Archer Productions rationalized its curious choices with the excuse that "it is obvious that this subject had to be broached with the utmost delicacy so that children would not be shocked or alarmed." In keeping with the dictates of behavioralist theory, the film eschewed all mentions of ideology. Terms such as "capitalism," "communism," "freedom," "democracy," "America," "Soviet," and "Russia" found no place in the narration. Instead, the threat came from the atomic bomb, which an unspecified "enemy" might "use against us." The only villain portrayed in the film was the antisocial monkey who menaces Bert with a firecracker. As Archer's promotional materials indicated, the film then explained "that being alerted and trained for an atomic explosion is no different than training firemen to do their jobs or teaching children how to cross streets at the proper section and proper lights."[72] To instruct children about how to know the atomic bomb when they saw it without portraying an atomic explosion, the filmmakers struck upon the idea of portraying the "flash" in the live-action sequences only, while relegating blast effects to Bert's Kafkaesque animated world, where they reduced a tree and several houses to smoldering ruins. Taking mercy on both Bert and America's schoolchildren, however, no mushroom cloud appeared in the film to shock or alarm them.[73]

The absence of such disturbing imagery likely offered scant comfort for the film's youthful audience, as the flash proved an omnipresent threat to the hapless people portrayed in it. As Patty's teacher explained, atomic bombing could come either with or without warning. If warning alarms sounded, children needed to make their way to the nearest safe place—optimally, they could just follow the "S-signs" to the as-yet-conjectural shelters that the FCDA still hoped to convince Congress to fund. Perhaps the continuing dearth of such shelters mattered little, as the film implied that warning was not a luxury that the unnamed enemy would provide. Both the city and the country, warned the narrator, needed to be aware that the flash might come at any moment. Children might be studying in their classrooms, strolling down a city street, or bicycling when the atom bomb struck. Rural America offered no refuge, as the film portrayed a man leaping from his tractor to duck and cover upon glimpsing the horrifying luminescence.[74]

Duck and Cover implied that America's youth would confront the flash with the assistance of their primary groups, whether their classmates or their families. "Older children were purposely used as actors to demonstrate the duck and cover method so effectively employed by the turtle," explained Mohr's promotional text, "for the simple reason that children will more readily emulate an older child than a teacher or adult demonstrator."[75] In the film, "older boys" explained the technique for their younger classmates. Reflecting America's slowly liberalizing racial norms, *Duck and Cover* included both black and white children, with at least one African American face in almost every shot of the well-dressed pupils. The American family appeared in the shape of a white middle-class couple with a son and daughter, enjoying a pleasant barbecue picnic. Alarmed by the flash, they promptly ducked and covered, quivering together in fear beneath their picnic blanket along with their jar of Gulden mustard.[76]

Duck and Cover employed a standard psychological gambit of American advertising by inculcating a specific anxiety (the fear of nuclear explosions) to motivate viewers to take action to alleviate that anxiety—learning to "duck and cover" as well as participating in civil defense more generally. Archer Productions and the FCDA aimed not to create a sedative to soothe children's fears of nuclear war, but rather to create a carefully constructed piece of fearmongering propaganda that harnessed the latest social science theories to sell civil defense the same way Madison Avenue marketed deodorant and chrome-laden automobiles. While manipulative, *Duck and Cover* was not dishonest. Even though self-interest motivated both the FCDA and Archer Productions, they earnestly believed both in the threat of nuclear war and that the kind of public education exemplified by the film could make a meaningful, if limited, dent in the number of deaths from an atomic attack. Privately, FCDA officials recognized that much more expensive and disruptive measures would be essential to achieve more than a token reduction in the death toll resulting from a nuclear strike. *Duck and Cover* indirectly served this goal with its portrayal of public shelters, as well as by raising public anxieties about nuclear attack—fears that might translate into increased political support for civil defense. The same psychopolitical strategy undergirded countless other examples of FCDA propaganda, including its other films and the "Alert America" Convoy that premiered along with *Duck and Cover*.[77]

Within a few months of Bert's debut, events started going seriously awry for both Archer Productions and the FCDA. Archer executives took pains to milk their civil defense work for free publicity, hoping that it would boost their public profile as their firm made the precarious transition from advertising agency to television producer. Archer invested a large sum to purchase and soundproof a soundstage, but in May 1952 actor Raymond Massey withdrew from Archer's first planned television series, *American Almanac*, which resulted in the withdrawal of the firm's financial backers and its rapid bankruptcy. The FCDA purchased the rights to *Duck and Cover* for $13,000 and continued to use Bert to promote civil defense in print, radio, and film forms.[78] The scaly mascot's best efforts proved to be of little avail, however, as the error of the assumptions behind *Duck and Cover* and the rest of the FCDA's publicity campaign grew increasingly apparent.

Ironically, the most damning critique of FCDA propaganda efforts emerged from a research effort initiated and sponsored by the agency. The FCDA launched Project East River in 1951 with the objective of gaining insight into the problems facing the faltering civil defense effort. A body of qualified experts from outside the FCDA undertook a comprehensive review of prevailing policies in a variety of areas, not the least of which was "information and training," delivering their final report on September 5, 1952. Although Project East River agreed that a functional civil defense would require far more funding than the FCDA received from Congress, it made numerous damning criticisms of the FCDA's policy mistakes, particularly in the propaganda field. As part 9 of the *Report of Project East River* explained, "In many respects, the investigations and studies of the Panel on Public Information and Training have been discouraging. In no other phase of the civil defense program are there more difficulties and resistance to be overcome." Despite all the FCDA's efforts, "civil defense is not a popular subject. People do not wish to be bothered nor do they want to think about it."[79] The challenges facing civil defense appeared so steep, the authors opined, as to inspire "reasonable doubt that the desired public education program can ever be satisfactorily carried out."[80]

The *Report of Project East River* found much to criticize about the FCDA's public information campaigns: "With the advent of the Korean difficulties, it appeared that the civil defense structure of the nation should be brought to a state of readiness at the earliest possible moment to meet an immediate threat." Convinced that Soviet attack might be imminent, state and federal civil defense "jumped into the business of recruiting workers and leaders before the organizational structure and training programs were ready. As a result, relatively few volunteers were recruited," and "many volunteers were quickly disillusioned."[81] Moreover, the desperate sense of urgency caused the FCDA to market civil defense in terms that failed to generate the hoped-for upswell of public support. "Thus far, the major appeal has been on the likelihood and imminence of attack. The country, now in its second year of major civil defense effort, has not responded to the continuous campaign stressing the need for civil defense."[82] Even in September 1952, the failure of the narrative of nuclear war exemplified by *Duck and Cover* and other FCDA propaganda seemed obvious. "As the appeal has not led to durable results, new ways must be found for establishing a sounder basis for civil defense needs and participation," charged the report.[83]

On the basis of the sociological surveys conducted by the University of Michigan for the FCDA, the *Report of Project East River* diagnosed the problem facing civil defense as public complacency. The surveys indicated that FCDA publicity efforts impacted public opinion, albeit not in the manner their designers hoped. The authors conceded that "the information programs of the Federal Civil Defense Administration and some of the state and local organizations have been effective in acquainting the public with basic civil defense data." Unlike in 1950, "two out of every three people have a generally accurate idea of what civil defense is," but "the public is still not accurately informed of the effects of the atomic bomb," which the authors attributed in part to the obsessive secrecy the government applied to information about nuclear weapons.[84] Eschewing the notion that skepticism about the feasibility of civil defense undermined public support, the *Report of Project East River* argued that the "major barrier to involvement and activity in civil defense is the feeling that 'it can't happen here' or 'to my family' or 'to my city.' This belief is tied to one that the country will not be attacked, or, if attacked, the military could prevent the attacking force from getting through and causing any serious damage." Faith in America's military strength posed a growing problem for civil defense planners: "The idea that the military can perform this miracle is on the increase and is held by the majority of the population—by both those who feel that war is quite probable and those who discount the chances of war."[85]

In light of these failures, the *Report of Project East River* recommended both undermining perceptions that "the United States is completely impregnable" and emphasizing that civil defense could become a "deterrent to possible enemy action."[86] With regard to Americans' paranoia about the effects of nuclear weapons, the authors also suggested that "a program should be undertaken and intensified to correct the beliefs in exaggerated effects of atomic radiation."[87] Most centrally, civil defense needed to abandon the rhetorical logic behind all of its previous propaganda efforts. "The current civil defense effort has been based essentially on fear of atomic attack," it noted, but "such an approach does not sustain continued interest and support."[88] To better achieve this goal, "the public should be informed that there is a continuing possibility of an attack upon the United States but the emphasis should not be on its likelihood or imminence but rather on the results of such an attack."[89] Repudiating most existing civil defense propaganda, of course, necessitated that "the total publication and training aids program of the Federal Civil Defense Administration should be thoroughly reviewed."[90] A mere nine months after its triumphant release, the

Report of Project East River recommended that the FCDA dump *Duck and Cover.*

Within a few short years, the FCDA attempted to consign the film to the Orwellian "memory hole." The second page of the 1956 FCDA film catalog listed most of the films released in 1951–52 as "obsolete," explaining that rapid progress in weapons technology necessitated the constant reassessment of "public information materials" in order to "insure that they reflect current civil defense practice and policies." The FCDA requested that all copies of *Duck and Cover*, along with the other films, be returned to the FCDA's Motion Picture Branch, presumably so that they could be destroyed.[91] Adding insult to injury, Millard Caldwell's successor as federal civil defense administrator, Val Peterson, even invoked the phrase "duck and cover" to implicitly mock the policies of the previous administration.[92]

The failure of the FCDA's efforts to win popular and congressional support swiftly depleted the morale of the administrator, who soon began begging President Truman to accept his resignation. Fortunately, this limited the opportunities for the former governor to stain federal civil defense policy with his prejudice. Millard Caldwell's unapologetic racism attracted withering criticism not merely from the NAACP but also from subsequent historians of American civil defense, several of whom claim the FCDA instituted racist policies at his behest.[93] The historical record, however, fails to justify these interpretations of Caldwell's influence at the FCDA, albeit for reasons deeply unflattering to the photogenic Floridian. Caldwell's background as an outspoken proponent of segregation both before and after his foray into civil defense attests to the authenticity of his racism, but he played little role in either the formulation of FCDA policy or the administration of its day-to-day affairs. In fact, he often could not be bothered to come to the FCDA's offices. As Wadsworth recalled decades later, Caldwell hated the capital and "every so often the Governor would go back to Florida for a few days, just to get the taste of Washington out of his mouth."[94]

In Caldwell's absence, Wadsworth stepped in to serve as de facto civil defense administrator. In the heady months in early 1951 when the FCDA made ready to present its ambitious plans to Congress, Caldwell eagerly took to his role as the agency's public figurehead, making numerous radio and television appearances. When Congress dashed the FCDA's hopes again and again that year, Washington and civil defense lost their allure for Caldwell, and his disappearances to Florida became more frequent. In his memoirs, Wadsworth charitably attributed Caldwell's flagging work ethic to how his agency came to function with "clock-like precision," but in actuality the

FCDA had failed miserably in its primary policy objectives, and its staff suffered from sharply flagging morale. In February 1952, Caldwell asked the president to relieve him of his post, but as the *New York Times* reported, Truman persuaded Caldwell to stay until a replacement could be found.[95] As it turned out, few men coveted Caldwell's job. Truman solicited air force general Carl Spaatz, former governor Preston Lane of Maryland, and former governor Roy Turner of Oklahoma, all of whom declined. By the summer, newspapers were launching attacks on Caldwell. "Mr. Caldwell, who is paid $17,500 a year, spends only a few days a month in his Washington office," reported one excoriating article, which quoted Wadsworth as saying that "he doesn't spend enough time here and he knows it. He's not very happy."[96] The arrangement suited Wadsworth, however, who ran the FCDA in the meantime and submitted decisions for Caldwell's signature when necessary.[97] "Civil Defense really was my baby from the beginning," Wadsworth later confessed.[98]

After a summer of not going to the office and hoping that President Truman would find someone willing to take over his job, Caldwell was finally provided an opportunity to escape with the defeat of Democratic presidential candidate Adlai Stevenson in the 1952 election. Disinclined to remain in his post, Caldwell wasted no time in sending his resignation notice to Truman. On November 8, the *New York Times* announced that Caldwell was "the first of Truman's official family to quit."[99] In the interim, the Republican Wadsworth became acting administrator, with the expectation that he would become President-elect Eisenhower's full administrator in the new year. Wadsworth asked his Yale classmate Henry Cabot Lodge Jr. to approach Eisenhower about this prospect, only to have Lodge return with a different proposal. In light of Wadsworth's record as assistant administrator, Lodge asked, "Why should such a sterling character be wasted on civil defense?" Instead, Lodge proposed that Wadsworth come to New York with him to become deputy ambassador to the United Nations, revealing that Eisenhower and John Foster Dulles had already approved of the idea. Stunned, Wadsworth accepted and left the FCDA for greener pastures, leaving the troubled legacy of his civil defense policies for others to overcome.[100]

Uncle Joe Digs In

In many respects, the stillborn American shelter program closely resembled the USSR's realized shelter efforts in the late 1940s and early 1950s. Growing tensions with the United States resulted in a revival of Soviet civil defense efforts in 1947. Along with a return to mass civil defense training exercises, the MPVO began building a few new shelters, as well as maintaining existing shelters in a state where they could be rapidly put into service in case of war. This task proved complex, as these "shelters" often took surprising forms and served unorthodox peacetime uses. The wartime improvised basement shelter construction policy resulted in an array of structures that usually bore scant resemblance to the orderly, well-equipped ones described in Soviet civil defense manuals.

A comprehensive registry of the shelters in Moscow's Frunze district compiled in 1952 illustrates the reality of Soviet bomb shelters in the years leading up to Stalin's death in 1953. Moscow possessed thousands of bomb shelters in the mid-1950s, but many of these "shelters" were little more than glorified basements. Despite its location near the center of Moscow, the MPVO apparently constructed few shelters in the Frunze district prior to the outbreak of war in 1941. Most of the hundreds of shelters in this part of the city dated to 1941 and 1942, with a handful built both prior to the war and following it. The majority of these shelters consisted of basements in residential, educational, and industrial buildings, some over fifty years old, either judged structurally adequate for shelter service or reinforced to withstand bombing. Few of these shelters possessed blast doors, and fewer still boasted ventilation equipment. Regulations allowed that ventilators could remain dismantled in peacetime.[101] Given the desperate shortage of built space in the urban USSR, these shelters were used in peacetime in a wide variety of ways: as root cellars, coal cellars, industrial equipment storage, *krasnye ugolki* (red corners, essentially local points for popularizing communist propaganda), offices, or even housing.[102] Regulations stipulated that the shelters be available for occupancy within twenty-four to seventy-two hours of the declaration of a "threatening situation."

Typical of these shelters was that found under a prerevolutionary building at no. 4 Vesnina Street. Built in 1942, this basement had a floor area of 62 square meters and a volume of 122 cubic meters. According to its documentation, the shelter could accommodate ninety people. But during peacetime the shelter served as storage for dry vegetables; civil defense promised that these comestibles could be cleared out within a day if the need arose. The MPVO noted that while this shelter was technically supposed to possess a number of hermetically sealed blast doors, as of mid-1952 it had none.[103]

Shelters under construction in the housing sector during the early 1950s generally still followed the wartime pattern, except for boasting slightly better equipment. For instance, during the 1952 shelter census the Frunze district MPVO staff converted a basement at 31 Pliushchikha Street into a bomb shelter. This building, built as upscale apartments in 1912, possessed a seventy-five-square meter basement, which in the MPVO's view provided sufficient space to shelter 136 people. As of 1952, the basement served as storage space for a bookstore. While this shelter possessed blast doors, it lacked ventilation equipment.[104] The MPVO undertook surveys to find basements suitable for conversion to shelters in existing buildings, mapping out promising basements and taking thorough measurements.[105] New construction sometimes contained shelters as well, but the MPVO reserved the most sophisticated shelters for its own personnel, as well as critical workers at important factories. Declassified documents reveal that the bulk of money expended on shelters in the 1950s funded relatively sophisticated shelters in the industrial sector, rather than those in residential buildings.

Despite the fact that the MPVO maintained thousands of shelters in Moscow alone, and thousands more throughout other Soviet cities, ordinary citizens and foreign observers remained only dimly aware of them due to obsessive secrecy. The MPVO classified even the most mundane information about shelters, including their locations, capacity, and specifications. Local MPVO staffs dutifully stamped all their reports and routine correspondence "secret" or "top secret." Generally the shelters lacked signs indicating their location, for in theory the MPVO would post signs when war seemed imminent and Moscow declared a "threatening situation" alert. Furthermore, given the crude nature of many of the shelters, ordinary citizens could hardly be expected to recognize them as shelters per se. Often these "shelters" looked like basements full of celery roots, books, or factory equipment, because, excepting the MPVO's paper trail, this was precisely what they were. Finally, secrecy regulations forbade MPVO employees from discussing shelters in public. In December 1954, the Moscow civil defense staff circulated an order blasting employees for "incidents of weakened vigilance in everyday work," such as telephone conversations divulging state secrets regarding shelter construction and nascent antiatomic defense measures. More troublesome, some employees held such discussions while traveling in service vehicles or on public transport, or while in cafeterias "in the presence of persons having no relationship to the civil defense service." The city civil defense staff demanded greater vigilance from all workers, ordering the implementation of new security measures for preventing the divulgence of state secrets.[106]

The shelters the MPVO built from scratch necessarily stood out more than the converted basements did. Certain priority facilities—particularly those that lacked suitable basements for use as shelters—received "freestanding shelters." Unlike basement shelters, these earth-covered structures could be recognized for what they were even by an untrained eye. Furthermore, freestanding shelters proved the most costly individual item in the MPVO budget. During the 1950s these shelters generally cost several hundred thousand rubles apiece to construct, with some large examples exceeding 300,000 rubles. Their construction also posed larger challenges than that of the basement shelters owing to their greater cost in money and materials. For instance, during 1953 the civil defense staff of the city of Liubino, near Moscow, worked to complete a new freestanding shelter at the station of the Moscow-Kursk-Donbassk railroad, as well as to modernize two existing freestanding shelters at the station. Along with the construction of a storage building for civil defense equipment and the conversion of an existing structure into a shelter, the MPVO in 1953 budgeted 235,000 rubles for these tasks.[107] Yet the unavailability of an essential type of metal pipe and blast doors delayed construction of the new freestanding shelter.[108] Indeed, as of December 1953 three of the shelters at the station still lacked doors, which MPVO officers attributed to the failure of the Moscow Metal-Stamping Factory to fill the order on time.[109] Civil defense records reveal that the MPVO spent an inordinate amount of time and effort attempting to overcome such challenges in shelter construction.

A Belated Beginning

While the men and women of the FCDA failed to bring the American people around to their cause, their Soviet counterparts in the MPVO continued to ignore the existence of the nuclear threat. So long as Stalin lived, civil defense policy followed the same line it had before and during World War II. The dictator's demise on March 5, 1953, inaugurated a reconsideration of civil defense, along with numerous other Stalinist dogmas. The "collective leadership" that succeeded Stalin broke the monopoly on information about nuclear weapons within the Soviet government previously held by the Special Committee. The collusion of the other remaining members of the Presidium (as the CPSU Politburo was called between 1952 and 1966) to remove Beria from power and his subsequent execution eliminated the figure who previously micromanaged the Soviet nuclear complex as his personal empire. Georgii Malenkov, the only surviving Presidium member possessing extensive experience with the Special Committee, inherited Stalin's post as chair of the Council of Ministers.

On July 21, 1953, Malenkov directed Nikolai Bulganin, the minister of defense, and Viacheslav Malyshev, the post-Beria manager of the USSR's nuclear weapons complex, to develop a proposal for "the defense of the Soviet Army and population from atomic bombs" over the course of the next month.[110] On September 25, Bulganin and Malyshev reported that because of the extreme secrecy measures applied to all information about the Soviet atomic project, the MPVO had done "absolutely nothing" to study the problem of defending Soviet cities from nuclear explosions. They suggested that the Ministry of Internal Affairs redress this oversight in short order, developing a plan by February 1954 to defend "the most important administrative and industrial centers," publishing manuals and instructions by March, and initiating the training of MPVO staff by April. Furthermore, the ministers urged that the MPVO reorganize its leadership structure and its central scientific research laboratory to facilitate these ambitions.[111]

Convinced that Stalin's obstinate refusal to confront the possible effects of a nuclear attack on the USSR had been a terrible mistake, the Council of Ministers passed a resolution on September 29 ordering the Ministry of Internal Affairs (MVD) to initiate planning to defend the Soviet population from nuclear weapons.[112] Largely following Bulganin and Malyshev's proposal, the resolution dictated that the MPVO, in conjunction with the Ministry of Health, develop a manual for the populace on defense against atomic weapons, but publish it only with the approval of the Council of Ministers. The resolution also required that the MVD update its norms for the design and construction of civilian and industrial buildings "taking into account the demands of defense against atomic weaponry" by May 1, 1954. Finally, the resolution called for the MVD to cooperate with the Ministry of Defense and the Ministry of Health on an ambitious complex of measures to facilitate the defense of the Soviet military and population from nuclear attack, with coordinated efforts to develop new techniques and equipment as well as train personnel.[113]

The task of developing the new civil defense policy fell to the MPVO General Staff, which adapted its existing institutional traditions to the nuclear age. Fulfilling the Council of Ministers resolution, in mid-1954 it produced two documents outlining how the MPVO aimed to confront the atomic threat. The first, *Rukovodstvo po podgotovke krupnykh naselennykh punktov i ob"ektov narodnogo khoziaistva k zashchite ot vozdeistviiakh atomnogo oruzhiia* (Instructions regarding the preparation of major population and industrial centers against effects of atomic weapons), outlines the effects of nuclear weapons and the means of defense against them for the MPVO's own workers, who like most other Soviet citizens enjoyed no previous familiarity with these topics. The second, *Pamiatka naseleniiu po zashchite ot atomnogo oruzhiia* (Handbook for the population regarding defense against atomic weapons), did the same for lay readers in the form of a small pamphlet similar to *Survival under Atomic Attack*. Together, these documents provide invaluable insights into both how the Soviet government envisioned a future nuclear war and what it wanted its citizens to think about it.

The *Rukovodstvo* asserts that the United States would employ nuclear weapons to destroy and demoralize the civilian population, reduce the USSR's military-industrial potential, and cause the breakdown of the country's government. Specifying major political and industrial centers along with train depots, power stations, and ports as likely targets for America's nuclear arsenal, it also warns that the bourgeois enemies of communism might contaminate lesser targets using radioactive materials.[114] Civil defense could only lessen, rather than eliminate, the consequences of such an attack: "Only with the punctual fulfillment of all the requirements stipulated in this *Rukovodstvo* will the significant reduction of the losses resulting from atomic weapons be possible."[115] Fortunately, the MPVO expected that the machinations of the USSR's foes could be detected in advance (as did the rest of the Soviet government in its planning for nuclear war). When circumstances necessitated it, the government of the USSR would issue the *Ugrozhaemoe polozhenie* (threatening situation) alert. After hearing this signal, citizens would ready bomb shelters, make blackout preparations, and evacuate part of the population in addition to cultural treasures. To defend themselves, Soviet citizens would rely on the same "self-defense groups" they had in the past, although the MPVO expected that communities near likely target areas would assist evacuees and the injured.[116] A combination of shelters and evacuation would protect the population from the bomb, and after it fell they would cooperate under government direction to minimize casualties, repair damage, and maintain the Soviet war effort until victory.[117]

In addition to establishing a narrative of nuclear war for planning purposes, the *Rukovodstvo* also provides instructions on how to acclimatize the Soviet population to the nuclear threat. According to the authors,

"The preparation of the population for anti-atomic defense should instill a firm belief in the possibility of defense against the effects of atomic weapons." The *Pamiatka* would always serve as the basis for instruction of the population and MPVO personnel regarding the new weapons. Primary responsibility for this task fell to DOSAAF, which would incorporate these topics into its "Gotov k PVKhO" program, as well as organize training efforts for the rest of the Soviet population.[118] According to the *Rukovodstvo*, after training, citizens would know not only the MPVO's signals and how to conduct themselves during the "Threatening Situation" and in the aftermath of atomic attack, but also basic first aid, the use of shelters and gas masks, and how to decontaminate clothes, household goods, and buildings.[119]

The *Pamiatka* presents these topics for lay readers in its brief thirty pages. Opening with declarations of the peace-loving essence of Soviet foreign policy, it insists that "reactionary circles in the capitalist countries" hoped to use nuclear weapons against the USSR as they had against the peaceful populations of Hiroshima and Nagasaki. Fortunately for Soviet citizens, "it can be assuredly said that there are available effective means of defense against these weapons, just as there are against any other." After a brief description of the physical basis of atomic energy, the manual introduces Soviet readers to an image of a mushroom cloud—an icon of the atomic age utterly novel to them thanks to Stalinist censorship.[120] The conclusion of the pamphlet echoes Stalin's position on the military significance of the bomb:

> Every Soviet citizen should remember that atomic and other weapons of mass destruction are incapable of determining the outcome of a war by themselves, and that the result of a war, if it is launched against our motherland and the people's democracies, will be determined by the people of those states, armed with the latest technology and masterfully employing it, people of strong mind certain of the rightness of their cause, possessing a strong and reliable rear.
>
> While successfully building a communist society, Soviet people will be vigilant toward the provocations of the enemies of the Soviet Union and will reliably defend their beloved motherland.

True Soviet patriots would pay heed to civil defense, as "the fulfillment of the demands made by this handbook of every citizen will enable the further strengthening of the Union of Soviet Socialist Republics as well as providing defense against atomic weapons."[121]

Unfortunately for the MPVO, DOSAAF paid little heed to preparing for the weighty responsibilities the *Rukovodstvo* and the *Pamiatka* assigned to it. Although this choice came back to haunt the organization's leaders, prior to mid-1955 the matter did not seem to be particularly pressing as the Council of Ministers had not ordered DOSAAF to take decisive action on it. For the time being, DOSAAF merely published a series of articles about atomic energy and atomic weapons in its magazine *Voennye znaniia* (Military Knowledge) with titles such as "Atomic Energy," "Characteristics of the Atomic Explosion," and "Means and Measures of Anti-Atomic Defense."[122]

An atmosphere of uncertainty pervaded Soviet media discussions of nuclear weapons after the death of Stalin, owing to the legacy of Stalinist censorship, the rapid evolution of weapons technology, and, most importantly, an open conflict between different members of the leadership on the issue. A series of increasingly ominous comments appeared in the Soviet press about the nuclear danger in late 1953 and early 1954. They culminated in Malenkov's declaration in a March 12, 1954, speech that, in light of "modern methods of warfare," a new world war would result in "the ruin of world civilization."[123] Interpreting Malenkov's statement as a signal of a shift in the Kremlin orthodoxy, both Soviet radio and fellow travelers in the West parroted the sentiment that thermonuclear war would end human civilization. Malenkov's outlook found less favor with his comrades in the Presidium, who compelled him to repudiate it in a speech before the Supreme Soviet on April 26 and declare that such a conflict would destroy only world capitalism.[124] Although Malenkov's reversal informed Soviet citizens that his previous position was unacceptable, they still awaited clear directions on what they ought to say instead. With official policy on nuclear weapons in constant flux, DOSAAF and other Soviet institutions felt safer biding their time rather than acting on their own initiative and taking the risk of promulgating incorrect dogma about the politically fraught topic of nuclear war.[125]

The Soviet public understandably found this state of affairs confusing. One month, *Pravda* declared nuclear war unsurvivable, and the next, it reversed its position. In contrast to a few years earlier, Soviet presses published a few translations of foreign fiction addressing nuclear themes, but added editorial comments apprising readers of the authors' ideological improprieties. The editorial postscript to the 1954 Soviet edition of Icelandic author Halldor Laxness's 1948 novel *Atómstöðin* (The atom station), for instance, warns that "naturally, the Soviet reader cannot agree with his pessimistic portrayal, typical of bourgeois literature, of the death of world culture as a consequence of atomic war," but excuses this error because Laxness employed it in conjunction with "an ironic subtext" and therefore it ought not be taken literally.[126] Reports of citizens' bewilderment soon began reaching the Kremlin. A list of "typical questions posed by workers to Party lecturers and agitators" sent to the Communist Party Central Committee at the end of June 1955 included several biting inquiries about the government's nuclear policies. "Can human, animal, and plant life survive at the site of an atomic explosion, and after how much time has passed?" wondered one concerned Soviet citizen. Another came to a comforting hypothesis for the government's slow progress on civil defense: "Why is our anti-atomic defense propaganda carried out so poorly? Is it because we're absolutely sure that there won't be an atomic war?"[127]

On June 29, 1955, the Council of Ministers passed resolution No. 1207-686, "On the Means of Increasing the Readiness of the MPVO for the Defense of the Population and Industry against Atomic Weapons."[128] This directive began the process of implementing the policies outlined by the MPVO in its *Rukovodstvo* the previous year, not the least of which was that DOSAAF initiate a campaign to train the Soviet population in antiatomic defense. Seeing no time to waste, the Presidium ordered that DOSAAF begin this vital work immediately—despite the fact that it had not made preliminary preparations such as developing class plans, lectures, posters, films, or textbooks. DOSAAF scrambled to create these as quickly as possible, but they would not be ready until after the new year. With nothing but the *Pamiatka*, science popularizer Ivan Naumenko's book *Atomnaia energiia i ee ispolzovanie* (Atomic energy and its applications), the *Voennye znaniia* articles, and a handful of other sources, republic, oblast, and local DOSAAF organizations conceived their own instructional plans as a desperation measure to fulfill the Presidium's resolution.[129] DOSAAF organizations also utilized the assistance of the Knowledge Society, the Komsomol, and MPVO personnel in these efforts. Although plans varied considerably from place to place, they generally consisted of a twenty-hour course to prepare instructors and a ten-hour course for ordinary adult citizens.

Owing to these handicaps, the results of the first antiatomic defense campaign proved underwhelming. General Pavel Belov, the head of DOSAAF, confessed in a 1956 report to the Communist Party Central Committee that "the DOSAAF Central Committee has undergone severe criticism for the fact that it failed to punctually provide local organizations with literature, posters, and textbooks on the topic of anti-atomic defense."[130] The absence of these meant that the areas of the Soviet Union that began training instructors and ordinary citizens in 1955, such as Moscow and Leningrad, probably suffered from inferior practical results. The civil defense campaign made especially poor progress in the USSR's Baltic republics, where few of the inhabitants spoke Russian and many viewed the Moscow government with suspicion. In early 1956, the DOSAAF Presidium noted with disgust that in Estonia its organizations outside Tallinn had made essentially no effort to start training either instructors or the general public. Among numerous other sins, the Estonians often made participation in antiatomic defense training voluntary, in contravention of regulations.[131]

After the campaign ended in 1956, however, DOSAAF declared that it had been a success. Official statistics stated that, over the course of eighteen months, 92.5 million adult Soviet citizens received instruction in antiatomic defense, which constituted 90.2 percent of the government's planning target. DOSAAF trained approximately 1.2 million instructors, who organized around three million separate classes.[132] On close inspection, these figures exhibited typical Soviet inflation, as some local DOSAAF organizations and local authorities skimped on instruction, exaggerated the number of people in their training classes, or simply lied about their results. In one extreme case, the "Arsenal" factory in Kiev reported to Moscow that it had trained all its employees in antiatomic defense, when in fact no classes on the subject had been organized there.[133]

Soviet civil defense propaganda presented only a hazy narrative of what form the future war would take. Soviet civil defense manuals and films never described a specific scenario in which civil defense might become necessary. Instead, they emphasized three general characteristics the future war would possess. First, the USSR's main antagonist would be the United States in conjunction with its West European allies. Second, these nations would begin the war, but there would likely be a period of days or weeks of warning prior to nuclear attacks on the USSR. Third, the Soviet Union would win the war, thanks to both its military might and the unbreakable will of its people. Soviet civil defense propaganda also avoided making promises about how effective measures such as shelter and evacuation would be for protecting the population. The dire images of ruined cities that illustrated Soviet civil defense manuals and posters, in conjunction with the USSR's terrible losses in WWII, hardly suggested that the country would escape a future war without massive casualties.[134] For the most part, the narrative of nuclear conflict in Soviet civil defense propaganda of the 1950s reflected the party leadership's outlook on the topic, even its ideological distortions.

Unlike its American counterpart, Soviet civil defense did not need its propaganda to justify either its specific policies or its existence to the public at large. Where the FCDA hoped to coax the American people to lend their support to its ambitious civil defense program, in the USSR the Presidium had already decided to lavish funding on the MPVO in the same resolutions ordering DOSAAF to train every Soviet citizen to survive nuclear war. As a result, Soviet civil defense propaganda focused largely on technical concerns, rather than political and ideological ones. The party did not need civil defense to justify establishing a garrison state, because the USSR already was one. DOSAAF and its predecessors possessed decades of experience molding citizens into diligent defenders of the Soviet experiment. Civil defense merely reiterated these long-standing themes of Soviet propaganda in the new context of the nuclear age.

The fact that the Presidium set civil defense policy prevented the MPVO from fine-tuning propaganda to better fit its institutional needs and forestalled prompt adaptation to rapid advances in weapons technology. More powerful bombs and faster, more survivable delivery systems challenged the assumptions made in the Presidium's 1955 and 1956 resolutions and popularized by civil defense propaganda, but the MPVO could not simply update its policies to account for the growing American threat. Another problem arose from the fact that DOSAAF, rather than the MPVO itself, developed and distributed most civil defense propaganda. Not only were DOSAAF's institutional interests quite distinct from those of the MPVO, but DOSAAF carried out its civil defense campaigns incompetently. Although in some localities DOSAAF organizations enlisted the help of local MPVO staffs to ensure quality civil defense training, in others they simply ignored civil defense training or abetted the falsification of reports to the center regarding the progress of the ten- and twenty-two-hour campaigns.[135] Handcuffed by these institutional strictures, the MPVO could not readily adapt to the new reality of thermonuclear weapons, managing this transition only after its reorganization as Grazhdanskaia Oborona (Civil Defense) in 1961. The MPVO's only consolation was that the absence of open discussion about civil defense in the USSR shielded the organization from public criticism for these failings. Their counterparts in the FCDA, meanwhile, saw their erstwhile allies make public defections following the revelation of the hazards posed by thermonuclear weapons.

Although the plans presented in DOSAAF's civil defense propaganda assumed that nuclear attack would occur only after a warning period, the leaders of the Soviet Union were not blind to the possibility that this view might be overly optimistic. Refusing to discount the prospect of surprise attack, the Presidium's June 1955 orders stipulated that all existing bomb shelters be "liberated" from their mundane peacetime uses so that they could be ready for immediate occupancy at any time. The real-world opportunity cost of this step must have been immense, given the large number of shelters and the wide range of their everyday roles. It rapidly became an enormous headache for local MPVO staffs charged with carrying it out. For instance, in Podol'sk, a city of about 110,000 people south of Moscow, the order went out on September 5, 1955, for all existing shelters to be vacated by October 1. As of January 1, 1956, the MPVO reported that seventy-five of eighty shelters in the city and fifteen of sixteen shelters at industrial sites were emptied.[136] As of a year later, however, the MPVO still had not freed up the last shelters, which continued to serve as storage space, repair shops, and offices.[137] At the same time, the MPVO undertook a program of modernizing existing shelters by expanding shelter construction. In 1955 Podol'sk added eighteen shelters in new housing construction and converted two basements for use as shelters—an increase of shelters in the housing sector of 30 percent over the previous year.[138] The next year the city added a further fifteen shelters.[139]

In spite of the costs and difficulties imposed by the Presidium's June 1955 civil defense orders, in April 1956 this body instituted even greater demands on the MPVO.[140] According to a new *Postanovlenie po MPVO* (Order Regarding Local Anti-Air Defense), civil defense now needed to plan for attack from biological as well as chemical and nuclear weapons. A new twenty-two-hour course would train every Soviet adult in defense against all these weapons of mass destruction. On June 15, 1956, the Council of Ministers supplemented the new order with new regulations regarding shelter construction, placing greater demands on the protective capabilities of shelters, rendering existing shelters obsolete while making new shelters more expensive.[141] Furthermore, the realities of the arms race necessitated the construction of shelters in areas of the country where they had been unnecessary during World War II. As a result of the Presidium's 1955 and 1956 orders about civil defense, the Soviet Union undertook an extremely expensive program of shelter construction during the late 1950s—an expenditure whose wisdom some men in the Kremlin soon came to doubt.

The lackluster results of the 1955–56 civil defense training campaign did not forestall the Presidium from laying the groundwork for an even more ambitious civil defense training campaign before the completion of the first. The April 1956 *Postanovlenie* stipulated that DOSAAF prepare to conduct a second, twenty-two-hour civil defense training course that would incorporate nuclear, chemical, and biological weapons. The new campaign would begin when the previous one ended at the beginning of 1957 and continue for two years. This time DOSAAF made advance preparations. When the twenty-two-hour training course began, DOSAAF already possessed colorful posters and films illustrating the horrible deaths Soviet citizens might experience in the next war due to weapons of mass destruction. Moreover, the new campaign emphasized hands-on training exercises, including the use of gas chambers and a nausea-inducing poison gas for gas mask training. In 1958, thirty million citizens underwent this extreme exercise, although in many places it could not be conducted due to a lack of resources.[142]

The MPVO's public propaganda did not accurately reflect the assumptions about nuclear war it used in its internal planning. This propaganda exaggerated the abilities of the MPVO to shelter and alert people, but simultaneously disguised the fact that the MPVO's thinking was sometimes much more advanced than implied in films, posters, and manuals. For instance, despite the fact that the *Rukovodstvo* characterized evacuation as an important civil defense measure in 1954, civil defense manuals did not begin discussing this measure in the context of defense against nuclear weapons until 1958.[143] The earliest manuals describing the effects of nuclear weapons gave the impression that Soviet cities possessed adequate shelters for the entire urban population that would serve as the basis of Soviet civil defense against nuclear attack.[144] A 1957 manual on bomb shelters states that "the provision of a sufficient quantity of shelters" provided Soviet citizens with protection from nuclear attack.[145] In reality, even the targets for shelter construction fell far short of this. In Podol'sk, for instance, regulations called for shelters adequate for only 20 percent of the city's population.[146]

Even this moderate target outstripped the actual capacity of the shelters existing in Soviet cities. The February 1959 sheltering plan for the population of Moscow's Frunze district reveals the yawning gulf between the aspirations of civil defense and its actual resources.

"Dispersed" in the table indicates the number of people who would be left without shelter during an attack. In case of a surprise attack, with only twenty to thirty minutes to take cover following the detection of enemy bombers and missiles, 140,000 of the Frunze district's 215,000 inhabitants would find themselves in this unenviable category. Given additional warning time, the MPVO planned to take steps to increase shelter space by upgrading

February 1959 shelter plan of Frunze district, Moscow

	20- to 30-minute warning	24-hour warning	48-hour warning	72-hour warning
Population in need of shelter	215,000	177,900	137,800	135,700
Population sheltered in metro	42,000	59,900	59,900	59,900
Population in shelters with ventilators and filters	8,300 [58][a]	8,400 [58]	19,400 [135]	37,800 [242]
Population in shelters without ventilators and filters	20,600 [143]	22,000 [153]	11,000 [76]	n/a
Population in shelters meeting anti-atomic defense requirements	9,600 [67]	9,600 [67]	9,600 [67]	9,600 [67]
Population in shelters not meeting anti-atomic defense requirements	19,300 [134]	20,800 [144]	20,800 [144]	25,200 [175]
Population in new construction	3,600 [25]	3,600 [25]	3,600 [25]	n/a
Population in basements	800 [6]	800 [6]	800 [6]	n/a
Population in dugout shelters	n/a	5,600 [141]	10,800 [271]	15,200 [379]
TOTAL	75,300	100,300	105,500	109,900
"Dispersed"	139,700	77,600	32,300	25,800

Source: TsGAMO, f. 6880 op.2 d. 764 ll. 42–43.
[a] Bracketed figures indicate number of shelters.

existing shelters, rapidly completing shelters under construction, and building hundreds of earthwork shelters, as well as evacuating as much of the population as possible. Even so, after three days the plan envisioned 25,800 people in the Frunze district without shelter. Despite the availability of the metro, Moscow's shelter base could not accommodate most of the population. The situation in smaller Soviet cities mirrored that in Moscow—for instance, according to regulations, Podol'sk should have possessed 187 shelters with 28,800 spaces at the beginning of 1957, but it had only 113 shelters with 14,767 spaces as of that date.[147] In cities across the USSR, the MPVO scrambled to construct more shelters while rapid urban population growth raised the number needed ever higher.[148]

It appears that shelter building consumed an inordinate amount of the MPVO's time, money, and manpower in the 1950s. Under MPVO regulations, ministries responsible for various industries determined which of their plants were most critical, and therefore favored for shelter construction funding. These ministries budgeted funds for construction of shelters at their plants themselves, rather than being funded from the MPVO budget like shelters in residential buildings. This arrangement led to absurd results, such as some candy factories receiving more civil defense investment than military avionics plants.[149]

MPVO officers supervised the shelter design and construction process, spending a great deal of effort attempting to persuade factory managers to fulfill their obligations regarding civil defense. The reluctance of these managers to participate in civil defense is unsurprising, given that the MPVO's demands did nothing to benefit the factories' bottom line. A Soviet factory's primary goal was to fulfill, and hopefully overfulfill, production targets state planners set for it. Civil defense worked against this imperative by demanding that factories devote time, material, and manpower to measures such as building shelters that, according to the 1955 Presidium orders, could not be put to any kind of peacetime use. Although factories received funding from their respective ministries for shelter construction, shelters cost more than mere rubles. Factory managers had to expend their personal political and economic capital—known as *blat* (pull) in Russian—to get materials and labor to construct the shelters, and predictably they preferred to reserve this resource for items that would help fulfill their production targets.

The case of shelter construction illustrates how the ostensibly totalitarian Soviet party-garrison state struggled to carry out its own demands in practice due to contradictory incentives and systematic dysfunction. In 1958 numerous factories, schools, and research institutes in the Frunze district received stern reprobations for their failure to complete bomb shelters.[150] Some brazen managers felt comfortable ignoring or countermanding the MPVO's orders.[151] The fact that the MPVO had few punitive measures other than persuading local state and party organs to intervene on their behalf surely contributed to its difficulties in this arena.[152]

The Soviet Union expended a considerable amount of money on bomb shelter construction in the 1950s. The cost of individual shelters varied enormously, from mere tens of thousands of rubles for converting a small

The Window of Survivability   93

basement for shelter use to well over 300,000 rubles for the largest, most elaborate freestanding shelters. The total expenditure for these structures reached imposing levels by contemporary Soviet standards. Podol'sk, for instance, had an annual civil defense construction budget averaging well over 1 million rubles throughout the late 1950s.[153] Most districts of Moscow also expended millions of rubles a year for shelters.[154] Given that the government budgeted at least 9.6 billion rubles for shelter construction during the Seven-Year Plan (1959–65), it appears that Soviet investment in bomb shelters during the late 1950s was on the order of about 1 billion rubles a year.[155] This was no mean sum, as official statistics stated that capital outlay for all types of construction in the USSR in 1955 totaled 93.5 billion rubles.[156] The percentage of the defense budget devoted to civil defense in the Soviet Union was probably about ten times greater than in the United States.[157]

Conclusion

For all their differences, the FCDA and the MPVO shared a common assumption: that a nuclear war could be survived and won. This belief suited their institutional interests, but it also echoed expert opinion prior to the introduction of thermonuclear weapons. The effects observed in the atomic bombings in Japan and in the U.S. and Soviet nuclear tests, troubling as they were, led scientists on both sides of the Iron Curtain to conclude that civil defense measures such as shelters and evacuation could significantly reduce the human consequences of nuclear war. The relatively limited number of nuclear bombs available, as well as the limitations of contemporary delivery systems, also encouraged hopes that nuclear wars would remain small and relatively manageable. Until the late 1950s, subsonic manned bombers remained the predominant means of delivering nuclear weapons, and these craft were highly vulnerable to defenses including jet interceptors, antiaircraft guns, and surface-to-air missiles. During the Truman years the FCDA planned for a nuclear attack consisting of mere dozens of relatively low-yield fission weapons. While FCDA officials still expected such an assault to result in millions of casualties even if its civil defense plans worked as intended, the experiences of the Second World War gave them confidence that it could be overcome. Their Soviet counterparts appear to have reasoned along similar lines.

Even in the face of an apparently surmountable nuclear threat, however, both the FCDA and the MPVO failed to realize their ambitious schemes to protect the U.S. and Soviet populations from nuclear attack. In the United

States, the FCDA faced intractable opposition from a Congress and population rightly skeptical that the USSR posed an imminent nuclear threat. Indifferent leadership and a series of political and media miscalculations helped ensure that the FCDA's grandiose shelter plans remained a pipe dream. While the support of the Soviet Union's authoritarian government allowed the MPVO to make more progress on building shelters than the FCDA and compelled millions of Soviet citizens to attend mandatory civil defense training courses, the MPVO's concrete achievements paled in comparison to its goals. Handicapped by its late start and beset by widespread popular and official apathy, powerful party officials increasingly doubted the wisdom of investing in the MPVO's costly civil defense plans.[158]

The history of U.S. and Soviet civil defense during the opening years of the Cold War demonstrates the limited ability of both the U.S. weak contract state and the Soviet party-garrison state to make good-quality defense decisions. The United States contemplated civil defense for the wrong reason—namely, the fear of an unprovoked Soviet attack that Moscow had neither the inclination nor the ability to carry out—but rejected it for reasons that were similarly dubious. Congress possessed an inescapable influence in the U.S. political system to shape the civil defense program, but the way it wielded this power resulted in incoherent policies. Congress both passed a law demanding the creation of a functioning civil defense against nuclear attack and then refused to fund it. Meanwhile, the USSR's party-garrison state failed to respond effectively to the emergence of a real existential threat to the Soviet experiment. Even after Stalin's death allowed Soviet civil defense to begin addressing nuclear weapons in earnest, party leaders denied the MPVO of both the material resources and the ideological freedoms it needed to address the Western nuclear threat. The ideological risks of admitting that the Soviet state might not be able to defend itself inhibited efforts to improve the country's defense capability. As a consequence, the Soviet party-garrison state failed on its own terms.

As it happened, both the FCDA and the MPVO squandered the brief "window of survivability," as technological progress qualitatively changed the nature of nuclear war as the 1950s progressed. Fearful of the prospect that their enemy was pursuing thermonuclear weapons, which might be thousands of times more powerful than existing fission bombs, both superpowers aggressively sought this new technology. In August 1953, the USSR detonated its first deliverable thermonuclear weapon in Kazakhstan, and in March 1954 the United States followed with tests of its own, more advanced "two-stage" designs in the Pacific. In a fateful incident that boded ill for the fortunes of civil defense, one of the U.S. tests created massive unanticipated radioactive fallout, necessitating the evacuation of a nearby island and causing an international incident when the deadly residue contaminated a Japanese fishing vessel. Despite the vigorous efforts of the U.S. AEC to keep this embarrassing incident veiled in secrecy, by early 1955 Washington found itself forced to admit that the new weapons created huge amounts of radioactive fallout that could contaminate immense areas.

Although some scientists in both countries feared (or hoped) that "hydrogen bombs" might require immense resources to produce or otherwise prove impractical, unfortunately the new weapons turned out to be so simple and cheap to build that they could be stockpiled in immense quantities. Advancements in nuclear technology facilitated expanded production of uranium and plutonium, and improved weapons designs allowed bombs to use smaller quantities of these scarce materials. As a result, by the late 1950s a thermonuclear bomb with a yield equivalent to millions of tons of TNT cost less to build than the primitive fission weapons of a decade earlier, even though the new weapons were hundreds of times more powerful. Both the United States and the Soviet Union constructed huge numbers of the new bombs, qualitatively transforming the nature of the nuclear conflagration civil defense needed to plan for. Instead of a war fought using dozens or hundreds of kiloton-range bombs, now a superpower conflict could result in thousands of multimegaton detonations, with unpredictable effects on people and the environment. Over the coming decade, both U.S. and Soviet civil defense struggled to adjust to this ominous new reality.

3   The "Oh My God!" Phase

"It is impossible to deny," asserted Comrade Malyshev, "that an immense threat of the destruction of all life on earth looms over humanity." What had impelled this change of heart on the part of the minister of medium machine-building, who stood at the apex of the USSR's nuclear weapons complex? According to an April 1954 article manuscript penned for Malyshev by Igor Kurchatov and other preeminent Soviet nuclear scientists, the recognition of the ecological hazards posed by the new thermonuclear bomb necessitated this reappraisal of the nuclear dilemma. The contamination of Japanese fishermen by the U.S. hydrogen bomb test on March 1 of that year merely hinted at the terrible potential of these weapons for absolute destruction. "The rate of production of nuclear explosives is such that they will be sufficient to render the surface of the earth unsuitable for life within a few years," it warned, adding further that according to unspecified "calculations," the "explosions of about one hundred large hydrogen bombs could have this result."[1]

Why did Malyshev, the same man who drafted the proposal that Soviet civil defense begin preparing for a nuclear war less than a year before, suddenly reverse his views about the survivability of nuclear war? While the alarming destructiveness of thermonuclear weapons surely played a role, the whims of Malyshev's political patron Georgii Malenkov seem to have provided the main impetus. Malenkov, who appeared to be the USSR's most powerful politician after the execution of Lavrentii Beria, made a series of public statements in late 1953 and early 1954 that culminated in a declaration that thermonuclear war would result "in the demise of civilization." The other members of the post-Stalin "collective leadership," however, united in opposition to Malenkov's stark reversal of previous Soviet dogma about the impact of nuclear war.[2] Compelling Malenkov to recant his views publicly, the Kremlin declared that a nuclear conflagration would result in the demise of capitalism, while socialism would emerge triumphant if not unscathed. The MPVO, meanwhile, adapted to this political controversy by ignoring it. Ordered in 1953 to plan for a conflict fought using relatively simple fission weapons, the organization embarked on an ambitious campaign to build bomb shelters and train the Soviet population for civil defense while simply disregarding the ideologically fraught proposition that thermonuclear weapons threatened the survival of the Soviet regime.

U.S. civil defense, meanwhile, experienced profound soul-searching after the hydrogen bomb tests in 1954 showed that the new weapons created an immense "fallout" hazard that might subject areas hundreds of miles away from the blasts to lethal radiation hazards. Fallout turned some of civil defense's most enthusiastic promoters into critics almost overnight. On January 19, 1955, Phillip Wylie, author of the pro–civil defense novel *Tomorrow!*, wrote a letter to Edward B. Lyman, the FCDA's director of public affairs, turning down an invitation to visit the agency's new headquarters in Battle Creek, Michigan.[3] "It isn't that I'm reluctant to come to Battle Creek," explained Wylie, "but that I have a strong feeling that enemy weapons are becoming of such a nature as to preclude any sane or useful effort toward 'civil defense.'" Wylie explained that his sudden change of opinion resulted from "the problem of 'fall-out' as it relates to the big Hydrogen bomb," which in his view made the then-current FCDA policy of evacuating cities "preposterous" and "a waste of human time." He continued that "the ecological dangers following the use of such weapons seems of greater import to me than any other problem." Wylie ended on the less-than-upbeat note that "if I can figure out a way whereby I think I can help you again you can be sure I will volunteer."[4]

Lyman replied to Wylie expressing how well the FCDA understood his state of mind. At "any other time I would have been deeply discouraged at such lines from the author of *Tomorrow!*," he wrote. "But I can sympathize with your feelings because I went through very much the same thing not so many months ago. So did almost everyone else here with 'Q' clearance." Lyman explained that "just about everyone who goes through a briefing on this horrible subject comes out of the room in a state of shock we have come to call the 'Oh My God!' phase." The FCDA, however, refused to be cowed by the scale of the thermonuclear threat. "Perhaps the reason we came out of it is that we're paid to find answers to these things, not give up because they seem too big to get our minds around," mused Lyman. "If we give up, what happens to the country?"

The solution, Lyman argued, was to "make a fresh start and go at it one step at a time." The old paradigms needed to be abandoned: "We have been telling the guy in the street that it was *his* life Civil Defense was going to save. Someone else might get killed, but *he* wouldn't. Subconsciously, I suppose, we were hoping to save everybody, even while we were preparing with the other hand for the greatest mass casualties in history." Now all that could be hoped for was marginally improving the survival rate: "We have to discipline our minds to thinking in terms of percentages. If by taking a certain measure we can save an additional one or two percent," reasoned Lyman, "there will be that many more people to help rebuild America." He concluded that the FCDA had a duty to overcome the fallout problem no matter what: "What we have to concentrate on is not how much of America may be lost but how much of it can be saved, and how we can rebuild what is left into a living nation. Believe me, Phil, the problem can be made manageable. It *has* to be!"[5]

Neither the U.S. weak contract state nor the Soviet party-garrison state proved to be up to the task of making the hydrogen bomb "manageable." Institutional imperatives compelled both U.S. and Soviet civil defense to rebound aggressively to the "Oh My God!" phase. Protecting the population from nuclear fallout stood to be colossally expensive, giving civil defense officials ample incentive to press their respective governments to attempt it. While compelled by domestic political considerations to promote civil defense measures that they knew to be of minimal effectiveness to the public, the leaders of American and Soviet civil defense led clandestine campaigns to garner the countless billions they calculated an effective civil defense would cost. In both superpowers, this strategy backfired. Hemmed in by the Eisenhower administration's desire for fiscal constraint, the FCDA publicly endorsed home fallout shelters, but its officials argued privately that the new threat demanded a colossally expensive shelter program, and increasingly clashed with the White House over civil defense policy. Eventually losing patience with these demands, Eisenhower shook up the FCDA's leadership and merged it with the Office of Defense Mobilization to create the Office of Civil and Defense Mobilization (OCDM), with a smaller budget than the FCDA had alone. In the USSR, the thermonuclear threat briefly produced an even greater effect on the political fortunes of civil defense. While declassified Soviet civil defense publications indicate that its analysts remained well informed of Western publications about fallout, the organization could not reshape its program without party approval—and at the time, prominent communists were voicing doubts about whether a more ambitious civil defense program was either possible or desirable. The increasing influence of such skeptics convinced premier Nikita Khrushchev to order the near-total cancellation of the entire Soviet civil defense program at the end of 1959.[6]

The Unenviable Trajectory of U.S. Civil Defense

President Eisenhower was frustrated. His choice for federal civil defense administrator, Val Peterson, increasingly advocated policies contrary to the wishes of the White House. The former governor of Nebraska, Peterson proved his loyalty during Eisenhower's 1952 campaign for the presidency, and had been rewarded with his post as chief of the FCDA. At first, Peterson had taken steps to curtail the excesses of the previous administration's civil defense policy, denouncing Truman's proposed program of blast shelters as a ruinously expensive boondoggle. Instead, Peterson endorsed a policy of evacuating American cities in the few hours between the detection of an ongoing Soviet attack and the arrival of enemy bombers at their targets, even though the air force had yet to complete the radar systems that could detect such an attack reliably and the FCDA had yet to conduct the research to confirm that the swift evacuation of urban centers could be made feasible. Despite these pitfalls, "tactical evacuation" had the advantage of low upfront costs, which appealed to the economy-minded Eisenhower. Within less than a year, however, Peterson began advocating privately for the same kind of costly public shelter program the FCDA sought during the Truman years. Analysts within the FCDA convinced him both that the tactical evacuation policy was unlikely ever to be of more than limited effectiveness, and that the USSR might develop intercontinental ballistic missiles (ICBMs) much sooner than most people in Washington imagined.[7]

Dwight D. Eisenhower's accession to the presidency in 1953 had crushed the FCDA's efforts to create a public blast shelter system. Peterson made clear that he (and, implicitly, the new administration) regarded his predecessor's public shelter efforts as disastrously misguided. At a March 19, 1953, press conference, Peterson said, "I think civil defense got off to a bad start by talking about billions of dollars for underground shelters. That frightened the taxpayers and it frightened Congress. It was poorly conceived because it was too expensive." Peterson did not write off shelters altogether, however: "I believe very strongly in shelters, but they should be economically feasible. A lean-to shelter in the basement is excellent." In response to this suggestion, a reporter pointed out that houses in California generally lacked basements. Peterson replied that "nothing is better than a trench."[8] Echoing this sentiment, in June 1953 Peterson congratulated the House Appropriations Committee for its refusal to fund the previous administration's shelter scheme, ostensibly because "the vast improvement in the destructive power of nuclear weapons could turn such public shelters into death traps in our large cities."⁹

In a marked reversal from previous policy, Peterson's FCDA launched an effort to encourage Americans to construct home shelters at their own expense. Finally publishing its long-delayed home shelter manual, the FCDA embarked on an effort to drum up support for these crude structures. In Los Angeles, civil defense displayed the mannequins that "survived" the atomic test at Yucca Flats to promote home shelters to gawking visitors.¹⁰ But it appears that civil defense employees did not regard the home shelter policy with much enthusiasm. Home shelters could not escape their inherently inegalitarian nature, as America's poor lacked basements in which to build shelters, or yards in which to dig trenches. Home shelters offered no protection to America's vulnerable urban cores, which the FCDA considered the prime target for enemy attack. Home shelters offered only one "advantage": their low cost to the government, which appealed to the budget-conscious Eisenhower administration. The FCDA, meanwhile, benefited little from the promotion of home shelters. The home shelter concept did not increase the fiscal or political resources available to the organization, and was contrary to the FCDA's statutory mission to create a workable civil defense. Despite the clear lack of White House approval, some FCDA employees continued to lobby for a system of public shelters.¹¹

Within months of becoming civil defense administrator, Val Peterson joined them. He confessed while testifying before Congress in 1956 that "if I have committed any errors in civil defense it may have been that I was too frugal in my first year or so in the agency," which he attributed to "the greatest consideration and care for the money of the taxpayers." Yet "from that time on," he emphasized, "you will find in every utterance I have made . . . I have spoken out very frankly and bluntly and candidly about the needs in this area."¹²

Although Peterson only hinted at these views in public, he made himself increasingly obnoxious in National Security Council meetings with his advocacy. In a February 1954 NSC meeting, Peterson argued that the results of the 1952 "Ivy Mike" thermonuclear weapons test in the Pacific should be publicized to "scare the American people out of their indifference" and develop popular support for civil defense, eliciting an angry response from the president. Eisenhower opposed any attempt to bolster the fortunes of civil defense by "scaring people to death."¹³ Moreover, Peterson demonstrated a tendency to voice uncomfortable truths that upset Eisenhower. At another NSC meeting a few weeks earlier, the civil defense administrator had observed that "if we had a major attack, dictatorship is the answer you have to come to, even if you couldn't talk about it." Objecting that under such circumstances "we would be beyond the point of keeping the nation together," the president suggested that rather than contemplating such unpleasant eventualities, the NSC should "think in terms of possibly 25 or 30 cities being shellacked."[14]

The recognition of the colossal fallout problem posed by the new thermonuclear weapons emboldened Peterson to propose astonishingly ambitious civil defense programs to the NSC. The disastrous outcome of the Castle Bravo H-bomb test in March 1954, which inadvertently irradiated both unlucky Marshall Islanders and Japanese fishermen, revealed that the new weapons could create lethal radiation hazards over expanses thousands of square miles in size. Although the FCDA responded publicly with an insipid media campaign urging suburban Americans to construct their own home fallout shelters, within the secretive confines of the NSC its officials urged that the new reality demanded an extremely expensive system of public fallout or blast shelters—preferably both.

The emergence of powerful allies in Congress suggested that the FCDA could expect the necessary political support to overcome the president's opposition. In 1955, Senator Estes Kefauver of Tennessee held hearings on the perceived inadequacies of the Eisenhower administration's civil defense policies, followed by even more extensive hearings sponsored by representative Chet Holifield of California the next year. These hearings placed Peterson and other FCDA officials in the curious position of having to defend policies they themselves disdained to politicians who favored the aggressive shelter campaigns they sought privately. Major general Otto J. Nelson charged that the FCDA's programs were ineffectual because neither the Eisenhower administration nor Congress was willing to contemplate the kind of program that might work, but "this is not to be admitted publicly but instead an ineffectual phantom program is to be set up with appropriate individuals and agencies to serve as scapegoats."[15] Much to the surprise of the committee members, Peterson readily agreed to the substance of Nelson's assertion. Civil defense for thermonuclear war, he emphasized, could not be developed on a shoestring budget: without the requisite resources, planning remained "academic."[16]

In response to Holifield's assertions that the FCDA had failed in its moral and statutory responsibilities by not presenting Congress with a serious shelter construction proposal, Peterson reiterated multiple times that after the fate of Caldwell's requests for shelter funding, he planned to present one to

Congress only when he was armed with sufficient research to justify its cost and effectiveness estimates.[17] The former governor stated that "I am personally in favor of the construction of shelters and would like to see the government do everything it can to stimulate it," but that until the FCDA's ongoing survival studies were completed, he was "dubious about going before the Appropriations Committee."[18] Furthermore, he intimated that the reason he had not been more aggressive in promoting policies he clearly favored lay in resistance from the White House and the NSC. Questioned by Holifield and director of investigations Herbert Roback as to why he "felt inhibited making recommendations to Congress," Peterson emphasized that "I make my recommendations to the Congress through the proper channels of Government as does anyone who is part of the administration," and that "this committee is not necessarily those channels."[19] Hinting how weary he was of defending the woefully inadequate measures the FCDA promoted due to its anemic funding, the civil defense administrator informed Holifield that "I have contempt for anybody who attempts to minimize the sheer destructiveness and death and desolation that will befall mankind if these weapons are dropped."[20] Peterson elaborated,

> I personally believe that if you kill from 10 to 25 million Americans and injure another 10 to 25 million Americans, all of which is possible, I do not believe you will use money in the United States. . . . We will eat gruel made of wheat cooked as it comes out of the fields and corn parched, and animals slaughtered as we catch them before the radioactivity destroys them. When we talk about clothing we are not talking about suits any more and collars and neckties; we are talking about anything to cover the human body. . . . If this kind of war occurs, life is going to be stark, elemental, brutal, filthy, and miserable.[21]

Perceiving the interest of Kefauver and Holifield as a sign that political fortunes had turned in favor of civil defense, the FCDA hatched multiple plans to persuade the president and the NSC to fund a massive public shelter effort. In mid-August 1956 Peterson presented the NSC with a proposal to spend over $13 billion on a federally financed shelter program. Anticipating success, the FCDA in October forwarded a budget request to the Bureau of the Budget that included more than $1 billion over the next two years for bomb shelters.[22] In December, Peterson and his agency had the audacity to submit an even more costly $30 billion shelter proposal to the NSC. Making his case on the basis of studies carried out by the Stanford Research Institute, Peterson argued that only a massive investment in public shelters could possibly protect Americans from a Soviet nuclear attack.[23] Thirty billion dollars was an astonishingly large sum—even the Interstate Highway System approved earlier that year was predicted to cost a mere $25 billion—but a few months later, the Holifield Committee endorsed a national shelter program costing between $20 and $40 billion.[24] In early 1957, Eisenhower faced a revolt by civil defense advocates determined to win support for a civil defense effort commensurate with the hazards posed by thermonuclear weapons, and his own appointee for federal civil defense administrator was one of its ringleaders.

The president ultimately quelled this rebellion by disposing of both Peterson and his increasingly disobedient agency. Eisenhower appointed Peterson ambassador to Denmark—the post the Nebraskan had originally hoped for in 1953, and one from which he could not agitate for tens of billions in increased government spending.[25] In August 1957 Leo Hoegh, the recently defeated former governor of Iowa, replaced him as head of the FCDA. Disappointingly, Hoegh proved little more "loyal" than Peterson on the shelter problem, informing the NSC that a fallout shelter system costing $20 billion or more would be a wise investment that "might save fifty million American lives."[26] Institutional reforms, however, soon deprived Hoegh of the opportunity to defy the administration on shelter policy. In July 1958, Eisenhower killed two birds with one stone by merging the FCDA with the Office of Defense Mobilization, another bothersome relic of the Truman administration whose mission of mobilizing the U.S. economy for a war with the USSR conveniently overlapped with that of civil defense. This step created the appearance of decisive action to appease civil defense advocates in Congress while reducing the ability of civil defense officials to advocate for increased funding. While in theory the OCDM bore greater responsibilities than the FCDA had, and enjoyed the cabinet agency status that the FCDA had lacked, its budget was considerably smaller.[27]

The Eisenhower administration defied expert opinion by disregarding calls for a more ambitious civil defense policy. To examine the merits of Peterson's shelter proposals, Eisenhower assembled the Gaither Committee, an eclectic group of scientists, policymakers, and industrialists headed by attorney and RAND Corporation cofounder Horace Gaither. If Eisenhower hoped the committee would demolish the case for federal spending on blast and fallout shelters, he was sorely disappointed, as the recommendations in its late 1957 final report exceeded those of both Peterson and the Holifield Committee. It called for $25 billion for fallout shelters, $10 billion for equipment, and potentially an additional $20–$30 billion for blast shelters.[28] Similar recommendations emerged from the RAND Corporation, the National Academy of Sciences, and a panel chaired by Republican New York governor Nelson Rockefeller.[29]

The fate of the FCDA's shelter proposals exemplifies how the American weak contract state made decisions for political rather than strategic reasons, and how ethically dubious those reasons sometimes were. Eisenhower and his administration rejected civil defense not because they believed that their scientists were wrong about its feasibility or that deterrence was infallible, but because of the threat it posed to offensive armament programs. At a November 7, 1957, NSC meeting, Eisenhower, secretary of state John Foster Dulles, and the remainder of that august body considered the findings of the Gaither Report. While Leo Hoegh, representing the FCDA, upheld the merits of shelters, his arguments and those of the Gaither Report did not impress Dulles and the remainder of the NSC. Dulles worried that a major shelter effort might make North Atlantic Treaty Organization (NATO) allies fear that the United States was preparing for war. Other NSC members argued that it might be difficult to maintain both an offensive and a defensive mood in the population, and that the United States should stand by its policy of retaliation. Tellingly, they noted that the military would be unenthusiastic about a shelter program competing with the armed forces for funding.[30] Ultimately, the government pursued all of the recommendations of the Gaither Report unrelated to civil defense, including large investments in offensive armaments (especially missiles) that stoked the arms race and helped precipitate the nuclear near misses of the early 1960s—the crises over Berlin and Cuba.[31]

The chastened Hoegh found himself compelled to go along with the administration's impotent new "national shelter plan," which was really just an excuse to feign some kind of activity to appease congressional civil defense advocates while limiting federal investment. Announced on May 7, 1958, this policy "placed joint responsibility for fallout protection on the Federal Government and the American people." This meant that the federal government encouraged Americans to build fallout shelters for themselves: "There will be no massive federally-financed shelter construction program," the policy declared. Instead, the five-point program emphasized continued research, including shelter surveys on a sampling basis, and the construction of a series of prototype shelters "to stimulate State, local government, and private investment in fallout shelters."[32] It seems Eisenhower

The "Oh My God!" Phase 105

was perfectly happy with public shelters—so long as their construction costs did not come out of the federal budget. In practice, however, the policy became a publicity effort to convince Americans to build their own home fallout shelters. Later that year, a new manual, *The Family Fallout Shelter*, explained how to do so.[33]

Flirting with Tactical Evacuation

During the mid-1950s, both American and Soviet civil defense seized on the tactic of evacuation to help protect their citizens from nuclear attack, only to discover it offered no easy alternative to the ruinously expensive prospect of building bomb shelters for urban residents. FCDA evacuation planning exercises revealed unpleasant social and cultural rifts and posed formidable logistical challenges. In the Soviet Union, civil defense planners determined that their limited transportation resources would necessitate leaving many urban residents in target areas even with days of warning. Advancing weapons technology and the overwhelming expense of blast shelters, however, compelled both nations to rely more, rather than less, on evacuation for civil defense as the decades passed. Unfortunately, evacuation could plausibly protect citizens only under certain circumstances—necessitating that governments declare that the enemy would conform their attack to the assumptions in civil defense plans.

Evacuation for civil defense can be divided into three types: postattack, tactical, and strategic, each of which requires different technical capabilities and logistical planning. Postattack evacuation consists of survivors departing the area of a nuclear explosion after it occurs. Many survivors would be injured and require medical treatment, and the radiation and fire hazards in the zone of destruction would threaten the lives of anyone who remained as well as pose obstacles to the survivors' escape. Postattack evacuation did not represent a substitute for sheltering, but it remained essential for maximizing the number of survivors, so both American and Soviet civil defense planned for it.

Tactical evacuation consists of the movement of populations out of probable target areas between the detection of imminent enemy attack and when the bombs arrive at their destinations. Such a goal places extreme demands on both the means of detecting the enemy attack to provide sufficient warning time and the transportation conveying evacuees out of the presumed target areas. During the Cold War, only the United States in the mid-1950s appeared briefly to meet these two requirements. Thanks to its advantageous geographic position, the construction of early-warning radars in the Canadian arctic and off America's coasts, and the slowness of early Soviet intercontinental delivery systems, there existed reason to hope that American cities would enjoy several hours between the detection of Soviet bombers and their arrival. America's well-developed road network and high rate of private car ownership suggested that this period would be sufficient to evacuate the nation's urban cores. The USSR possessed neither of these advantages, as its location relative to enemy bases and inadequate radar cover meant that, even before the introduction of ballistic missiles and supersonic bombers, many of its cities might receive mere minutes of warning. As a result, Soviet civil defense never pursued tactical evacuation, instead betting on strategic evacuation.

Strategic evacuation aimed to avoid the pitfalls of tactical evacuation by shifting populations out of probable target areas in anticipation of enemy attack, rather than waiting for it to begin. In principle, strategic evacuation could protect the population better than either tactical evacuation or a blast shelter system. With days or weeks of warning, expedient measures such as additional shelter space could be developed in host areas. Therefore, under optimal circumstances strategic evacuation might save everyone, as long as the war failed to precipitate an ecological apocalypse. Despite its seductive potential, strategic evacuation still raised imposing challenges—most importantly, when it should be called and why. Evacuating major cities would obviously result in serious economic dislocation and could not continue indefinitely, so the decision to launch a strategic evacuation could not be taken lightly. What sort of enemy actions might trigger a strategic evacuation? Other than the obvious one of the enemy's strategic evacuation of its own cities, no examples came to mind. Strategic evacuation also required enemy cooperation to work. Opponents could attempt to neutralize the benefits of strategic evacuation by retargeting their weapons to the areas hosting the evacuees, or by attacking during the evacuation. American and Soviet strategic theorists downplayed these concerns, arguing that rational actors would not take these courses of action. Even if self-interest could be counted on to keep the enemy from spitefully foiling one's civil defense plans, strategic evacuation still posed a colossal logistical challenge. In light of the radiological hazards caused by thermonuclear weapons, the evacuees would all require fallout shelter—in addition to food, clothing, sanitation, and countless other needs. For all its promise, strategic evacuation offered no easy solution to the challenge of civil defense in nuclear war.

During the Truman administration the FCDA explicitly rejected evacuation as a civil defense technique because of the weakness of radar coverage of the continental United States, its beliefs about the nature of the Soviet threat, and the perceived psychological hazards of evacuation. Prior to the mid-1950s, American radar could not reliably detect an ongoing attack, giving rise to the fear that citizens might learn of a Soviet attack only when the first atomic bombs began exploding over American cities. The Pentagon believed that the Soviet leadership would not hesitate to launch a clandestine nuclear attack if it appeared advantageous, leading to the assumption that civil defense could not depend on more than a few minutes of advance warning, if that—jeopardizing the effectiveness of any kind of civil defense measure, including sheltering. To help patch the holes in the country's defenses, the United States Air Force in 1950 created the Ground Observer Corps, an organization of civilian volunteers armed with binoculars manning observation posts and scanning the skies for Soviet bombers.[34] In 1952, the *Report of Project East River* fingered the weakness of America's radar network and air defense capabilities as a critical obstacle to implementing an effective civil defense policy.[35]

Some observers held that evacuation would be an inadvisable idea under any circumstances. Figures such as Phillip Wylie argued forcefully that evacuating America's cities would inculcate a defeatist mentality. In a September 19, 1950, letter to Stuart Symington, Wylie claimed that to allow the American people to believe they might be evacuated would risk a nationwide panic like that evoked by Orson Welles's 1938 *War of the Worlds* radio broadcast. "So long as people assume they are expected to evacuate, as now, the prospect will be alarming and stultifying and in any atomic emergency, they will try to flee en masse." The "cardinal fact behind civil defense," he asserted, must be that "the people must stick to their 'guns' no matter what happens," in order to maintain wartime production and "evoke courage."[36] The leadership of the FCDA concurred with Wylie's assessment, and in 1951 they contracted Archer Productions to produce *Our Cities Must Fight*, a short film informing Americans that evacuating their cities during an atomic war would be "desertion" and "something pretty close to treason."[37]

Those Americans who closely followed their government's civil defense propaganda likely found the sudden policy reversal on evacuation after Val Peterson's 1953 takeover of the FCDA confusing. Initially Peterson echoed his predecessors' line on the matter, declaring in a March 8, 1953, interview on *Meet the Press* that "the enemy would win the war if we evacuated our cities in event of attack," yet within a few months evacuation became the

"It Looks Darling"

Herbert Block on civil defense. A 1953 Herblock Cartoon, © The Herb Block Foundation.

basis of the FCDA's entire civil defense effort.[38] Where earlier the FCDA blasted evacuation as tantamount to handing victory to the Kremlin, by August 1953 Peterson had made an about-face. In an interview on *Crossfire* on August 12, Elmer Davis asked Peterson, "For people living in a city, isn't it a good idea to stay put, if they can?," to which the federal civil defense administrator replied, "I don't think so." Peterson admitted that "that was our first concept in civil defense, and it is still our official concept," but that "assuming the Air Force can give us increased warning time, I am inclined to think that what we must do to preserve American lives" is to "learn how to evacuate these cities." To master this new art, he continued, "we must have trials," assuring Davis that "it is not so hopeless as it sounds. I am inclined to think that people would find that they could walk eight to ten miles, which would take them to comparative safety." Motivated Americans, Peterson believed, could speedwalk their way to survival: "I am sure they could walk eight to ten miles in under two hours under compulsion of atomic attack."[39] Peterson reiterated his support for tactical evacuation in a *Newsweek* interview while also endorsing strategic evacuation of "children, the aged, and helpless people." He confided, however, that at present the FCDA lacked both evacuation plans and sufficient warning time to put such plans into effect, and that therefore "what we have in the way of civil defense is still inadequate and very spotty."[40]

Peterson readily admitted that his agency's tactical evacuation plans remained far from operational readiness and that they could probably never be implemented successfully in some cities. He confessed in an April 1954 radio address that "there are a few cities—New York, San Francisco, and New Orleans are three obvious ones—where effective evacuation within any reasonable warning time would be extremely difficult." Peterson optimistically held that these examples would prove to be the exception rather than the rule. The FCDA found the results of its early tactical evacuation drills heartening. "Operation Walkout," which cleared part of Spokane, Washington, had been "a sobering success," declared Washington State civil defense director Daniel E. Barbey.[41] "Operation Scat" in Mobile, Alabama, garnered similar accolades from civil defense authorities. The FCDA staged increasingly ambitious civil defense evacuation drills, culminating in efforts such as "Operation Exit" in June 1955, in which South Bend, Indiana, evacuated 400 city blocks, including "the entire downtown business area, a major segment of the industrial area, and a portion of the residential area," with a total population of about 50,000, in a period of forty-three minutes.[42] Although close inspection reveals serious shortcomings in these exercises, in retrospect the degree of cooperation and conformity displayed by citizens in obedience to inconvenient civil defense drills seems incredible. Civil defense authorities concluded that, for many cities, tactical evacuation would be a practical possibility with a few hours of warning time.[43] But Peterson acknowledged that future improvements in weapons technology might render tactical evacuation obsolete. In October 1953, Peterson stated in a radio interview that with "the introduction of intercontinental ballistic missiles carrying atomic warheads—if and when that comes, in fifteen or twenty-five years—we might be forced to go into the business of building shelters in America." Emphasizing that "we are not proposing that today," Peterson expressed his hope that with increased warning time, evacuation could serve as a practical means of defending American urban dwellers against atomic attack.[44]

The FCDA's propaganda promoting tactical evacuation revealed the troubling socioeconomic inequalities simmering beneath optimistic portrayals of Americans cooperating courteously for survival, as well as reminding citizens that evacuation might not allow them to escape atomic attack unscathed. A 1955 FCDA brochure titled "4 Wheels to Survival: Your Car and Civil Defense" advised Americans to "keep your car in good mechanical condition" and "keep your gas tank at least half-full at all times," as doing so might "spell the difference between life and death for you and your family." Motorists could take comfort in the fact that "tests under an actual atomic explosion in Nevada proved that modern cars . . . give a degree of protection against blast, heat, and radiation." The pamphlet suggested that an automobile would be the ideal postatomic domicile for Americans: "Shelter in an unexpected blast is a bonus you get from your car. More importantly, your car provides a small movable house. You can get away in it—then live, eat, and sleep in it in almost any climactic conditions, if necessary, until a civil defense emergency is ended." Of course, a well-maintained car remained above the reach of many, so the FCDA beseeched motorists to "pick up walking evacuees, if you have room."[45] The agency refrained from patronizing carless Americans with a leaflet titled "2 Feet to Survival: Your Legs and Civil Defense." Tactical evacuation, like the FCDA home shelter program, gave the well-to-do a better shot at survival than their less fortunate counterparts.

In addition to appealing to Americans' love affair with their automobiles, the FCDA also resorted to outright fearmongering to promote tactical evacuation. The agency circulated an elaborate press kit to city civil defense organizations outlining a detailed model publicity campaign. The FCDA suggested that promotional efforts begin weeks in advance and enlist the assistance not merely of city officials but also of local social organizations and businesses. Public-spirited local advertisers, it hoped, would pay for ads with taglines such as "It isn't far from the death zone to survival—walk out quickly and calmly," or more self-interested businesses might seek to boost sales with statements such as "In a real attack an empty gas tank could cost you your life! Keep your tank filled with [brand name gasoline]." Another "tremendously effective method of publicizing the urgency in this test evacuation," recommended the FCDA, would be to "arrange with the commanding officer of an Air Force base or with a Civil air service at your local airport to fly over the city the day before the test and drop a leaflet such as the one shown on this page." The illustrated leaflet featured the outline of a bomb containing the words "If this had been a bomb, you would be DEAD."[46]

Examples such as these exemplify how the leaders of U.S. civil defense outsourced their agencies' public relations efforts, and as a result, the absurdities of civil defense propaganda provide much less insight into their goals than is often assumed. The archival record reveals that Millard Caldwell and Val Peterson spent most of their time cultivating support for more ambitious civil defense programs in the executive and legislative branches, leaving the Public Affairs Office to develop publicity campaigns as it saw fit on the basis of vague, generalized instructions. Herald Kirn, the OCDM's director of audio-visual planning from 1958 to 1961, recalled that "there was no real pressure from higher ups. There were agency policies which we followed as part of the overall program. We did work fairly independently, following those policies."[47]

The bewildered response of Americans to the accidental sounding of air raid sirens in the 1950s demonstrated that years of civil defense propaganda had failed to inculcate the intended responses. The May 5, 1955, incident in Oakland, California, was merely one of a chain of such cases. During the early Cold War these incidents were relatively common, and they occurred for many reasons. In Washington, D.C., a telephone company maintenance error caused the sirens to sound on November 25, 1958. Most egregiously of all, on September 22, 1959, an irresponsible fire commissioner in Chicago sounded the sirens to celebrate the first American League victory by the White Sox in forty years. Social scientists studying the lessons of these incidents came away distressed that citizens did not respond to the signals the way civil defense had instructed them to. As a 1961 study remarked, "For a civil defense air raid warning to serve its purpose, the signal must be so powerful, the response so conditioned, or so ensured by some organizational apparatus, that protective behavior follows from the signal without environmental reinforcement."[48] Its authors concluded that "hearing the warning siren alone is totally inadequate," as "protective action was taken only by a rather small percentage of the population of each city sampled": only 2 percent of those surveyed in Chicago, for instance. Instead, "what people do, in fact, upon hearing the siren, is to seek additional information," and "the majority of the persons sampled turned to unofficial, informal, and, in terms of civil defense criteria, incorrect sources" to find it.[49] That Americans did not internalize the message of civil defense propaganda bothered the researchers far less than that they did not do what they had been told to: "A sound civil defense policy does not necessitate converting the whole population into true believers," they rationalized, but "it requires reaching and directing them through social organization."[50]

Counterintuitively, civil defense played little role in the greatest federal infrastructure program of the Eisenhower era—the Interstate Highway System. Eisenhower's enthusiasm for highways was a rare departure from his usual skepticism for increased domestic spending, but fiscal conservatives felt that the bill could be justified only if the new interstates would somehow contribute to national defense. Civil defense failed to harness this opportunity to further its goals despite the best efforts of the FCDA and its congressional allies. During the lengthy process that resulted in the passage of the Federal Highway Act of 1956, FCDA officials and civil defense advocates aimed to shape the nascent interstate system to help facilitate urban evacuations. They complained that the versions of the bill being considered lacked an explicit linkage between the needs of civil defense and federal investments in highways and managed to have language to this effect added to draft versions of the act.[51] But the consensus decision-making process of the weak contract state did not favor civil defense even in this seemingly auspicious instance. When Eisenhower signed the final bill into law in June 1956, however, the sole reference to civil defense it contained was an isolated statement that "it is hereby declared to be in the national interest to accelerate the construction of the Federal-aid highway systems, including the Interstate System, since many of such highways . . . are inadequate to meet the needs of local and interstate commerce, the national and the civil defense."[52]

Evacuating Soviet Spaces

Evacuation proved even more challenging for the Soviet party-garrison state than for the United States. Soviet civil defense authorities disagreed as to the role evacuation ought to play in their plans to protect citizens from nuclear weapons, and the extent to which their early efforts to develop "anti-atomic defense measures" relied on evacuation remains unclear. Russian historian A. V. Gusev states that the Council of Ministers' June 1955 resolution "On the Means of Increasing the Readiness of the MPVO for the Defense of the Population and Industry against Atomic Weapons" made evacuation, rather than shelters, the fundamental basis of Soviet civil defense planning, but the 1954 *Rukovodstvo* stated that evacuation of "the population and cultural treasures" was envisioned only "for the most significant industrial and administrative centers."[53] Archival records indicate that the MPVO's initial civil defense efforts for nuclear war neglected evacuation planning, and that evacuation grew in importance only during the late 1950s to become the centerpiece of Soviet civil defense efforts after the program's reorganization in 1961. A 1956 article in the MPVO's classified internal journal *Informatsionnyi sbornik MPVO* (Collected Information of the MPVO) suggests that some MPVO officers at that time believed that evacuation offered the best method for civil defense against nuclear weapons, and that the MPVO General Staff felt the need to disabuse them of this view. "The role of shelters in circumstances of a nuclear attack has been underestimated in a number of cases," it editorializes. "The opinion that the problem of the defense of the population can be solved only by means of dispersal is unquestionably incorrect, as even following the largest possible evacuation no less than 50 percent of the population will remain in the cities, and will have to be sheltered." The article concludes that, "therefore, opinions to the effect that shelter-building is inadvisable are, to some extent, harmful."[54]

In contrast to Soviet evacuation efforts during World War II, the MPVO's postwar plans aimed to continue production during an extended period of strategic warning rather than to prevent critical industrial resources from falling into enemy hands. Therefore, where in 1941 the Soviet government evacuated factories and their workers away from the front, in the late 1950s evacuation plans called for keeping factories fully staffed and moving only the nonworking population. The MPVO General Staff recognized the probable result of such a policy—that the critical workers would "self-evacuate" to follow their families, threatening the Kremlin's goal of keeping defense industries functioning during a crisis period. To stem this problem, the *Rukovodstvo* recommended that "children and seniors with able-bodied family members engaged in production or in city institutions ought to be evacuated [to areas] in the vicinity of the city."[55]

The MPVO's evacuation planning proceeded slowly at first because of the need for cooperation from other government agencies. For example, the Podol'sk MPVO staff's plan for 1956 assigned two of its officers to "prepare materials for examination by the city government regarding evacuation during the special period of children, the nonworking population and transportable hospital patients" during the first quarter of that year. The following quarter, the MPVO would help Podol'sk establish a city evacuation commission. In the third quarter of 1956, the Podol'sk MPVO staff would dispatch its officers and members of the evacuation commission to the areas around Podol'sk to determine where to send the city's evacuees and then develop a detailed evacuation plan.[56] In 1957 the city conducted a small evacuation drill, setting up a model collection point that registered arriving members of the population, after which motorized vehicles carried them out of Podol'sk.[57] Evacuation planning continued to be a sideline for the Podol'sk MPVO staff, however, and even several years later the evacuation plan remained unusable. As of November 1959, the Podol'sk MPVO admitted in a report to the commander of the Moscow oblast's MPVO that its evacuation plans were unworkable, albeit for reasons beyond their control. As examples of the "isolated inadequacies" of the evacuation plan, the report notes that "due to the additional seizure of a number of facilities in the Podol'sk region for the needs of the Ministry of Defense the problem of where to host displaced persons is not completely resolved," and that the Soviet Army's plans to commandeer vehicles during a mobilization would also leave the MPVO without means of transporting evacuees out of the city.[58]

An important motivation behind the MPVO's limited emphasis on evacuation stemmed from its leaders' doubt that they would actually enjoy strategic warning before a nuclear attack. For instance, as of January 1959, Podol'sk planned that, even after evacuation, 73,000 of the city's 140,000 residents would remain and require shelter. The city possessed shelters with space for only about 17,000 people, with additional basements the MPVO estimated sufficient for 5,700 people. The city's shelter plan, however, included a line item that foresaw the "dispersal" of 120,000 people in "naturally occurring shelters and out of the city" if attack came without advance warning.[59] Podol'sk officials took this prospect seriously, readying electric sirens to alert the population of surprise attack within a period of two to three minutes.[60] Public MPVO propaganda downplayed or disregarded the possibility that a nuclear war might begin without a period of advance warning, likely due to the organization's recognition of its near impotence to protect the population under such circumstances. Paradoxically, the MPVO also hesitated to denote the existence of its evacuation plans publicly until 1958, giving the impression that Soviet civil defense plans placed a greater reliance on shelters than they actually did.[61] A reluctance to discuss evacuation during civil defense training threatened the MPVO's ability to initiate an evacuation during a crisis period, but it avoided discussion of a topic liable to incite alarm among the population—a benefit the Soviet government may have considered worth the trade-off.

The MPVO's evacuation plans reached the apex of their ambition and complexity for the USSR's capital, as the 1959 evacuation plans for Moscow's Kirov district exemplify. Unlike Podol'sk, which planned to evacuate residents a short distance to the area immediately surrounding the city, the Kirov district drew up an elaborate scheme to convey its evacuees to Stavropol Krai in the Northern Caucasus. One hundred thirty-six thousand people lived in the Kirov district in early 1959, of whom 4,100 would be mobilized into the Red Army in case of war, 83,600 would remain in

Moscow, and 48,700 would evacuate.[62] The Kirov district Evacuation Commission designated twenty-seven separate collection points to gather the evacuees over two days. Most of the evacuees would take regional trains from Paveletskii Train Station to the city of Stupino south of Moscow, where they would board long-distance trains to Stavropol Krai.[63] The need for a stopover in Stupino introduced complications to Kirov district's evacuation efforts, as the Stupino city government tarried in developing its plans for the reception and distribution of the evacuees. The government of Kirov district wrote to the Moscow Evacuation Commission in January 1959 complaining that its multiple requests for this information had gone unanswered. Its letter demanded that Stupino rectify this problem promptly, as the district evacuation plan was already overdue but could not be completed without Stupino's input.[64] The Kirov district Evacuation Commission expected that the evacuees would reach their destinations in the Caucasus only after a period of five to nine days, necessitating extensive preparation to meet their needs for food and medical care.[65] Stores in Moscow would prepare rations for the evacuees prior to their departure, and the MPVO trade service bore responsibility for their distribution.[66]

Upon their arrival in the Caucasus the evacuees would become the responsibility of local authorities, although the Kirov district Evacuation Commission planned to send some of its officials to the evacuation zones to oversee preparations for the Muscovites' arrival.[67] Kirov district's evacuation plans, unlike Podol'sk's, violated the MPVO General Staff's 1954 recommendation that evacuees remain close to their families. The specific exigencies of Moscow discouraged keeping the capital's evacuees nearby. With all but the smallest cities in the densely populated Moscow oblast evacuating their populations into the surrounding countryside, the area would already be overrun with evacuees even without the addition of millions of Muscovites. Furthermore, the children and seniors of Kirov district would be far safer in the Caucasus than anywhere in the Moscow area, with its proliferation of attractive administrative and industrial targets for American nuclear bombs.

The Fallout Menace Emerges

When the USSR tested its first thermonuclear weapon in August 1953, the leaders of the FCDA joined other U.S. government officials in downplaying the importance of this development. Although the United States had already tested a thermonuclear device in the Pacific the previous year, it was a massive, impractical apparatus that could never be carried by an airplane; the Soviet weapon, however, might be small enough to be deliverable.[68] But its relatively low yield—400 kilotons—encouraged U.S. authorities, desperate to avoid being scapegoated for falling behind in the arms race, to dismiss it as something less than a "true" superbomb.[69] Peterson echoed these voices: in an April 1954 radio address, he informed citizens that "the first thing to bear in mind is that, in terms of civil defense planning, the H-bomb is nothing new." According to Peterson, "The H-bomb simply creates a bigger problem for us, not a different kind of problem. It is one that we Americans can lick if we keep our heads and plan realistically." Realism, seemingly, consisted in large measure of continuing previous FCDA policy: "everything which we . . . have taught for three years about community organization and family preparedness is still good." At the same time, Peterson disowned one infamous civil defense slogan: "Nevertheless—and this is important—let nobody get the idea that a policy of 'duck and cover' is our only answer to the H-bomb. That would be plain ridiculous." For the time being, the administrator emphasized that evacuation provided the best possible protection against Soviet thermonuclear weapons.[70]

On March 1, 1954, the United States tested a thermonuclear bomb at Bikini Atoll in the South Pacific. Over twenty times as powerful as the Soviet thermonuclear test in Kazakhstan the previous year, the colossal explosion obliterated much of the coral atoll, whose irradiated remains soon began to descend downwind. Three hours after the test, this radioactive dust began falling on the deck of the Japanese fishing vessel *Lucky Dragon*, seventy-two miles from Bikini Atoll. Soon its crew fell ill with radiation poisoning, and one of them ultimately died. This fallout also victimized the unlucky inhabitants of Rongelap Atoll, seventy-five miles from Bikini. Blanketed with fallout, the islanders suffered symptoms of radiation poisoning, and three days after the test, the United States government evacuated them from their homes.[71] The Atomic Energy Commission, however, hoped to minimize the public relations consequences of this fallout disaster.

While the AEC claimed that the unpredicted consequences of the test at Bikini resulted from a change in wind direction and that the bomb tested at a much higher yield than expected, it had actually dismissed the possibility of fallout hazards due to its own carelessness. Little local fallout had been observed in the 1952 Ivy Mike test, convincing AEC and military scientists that its radioactive remnants had been trapped in the stratosphere. In actuality they had neglected to place instruments in the isolated part of the Pacific where its fallout had descended. They convinced themselves that the ambitious test series planned for 1954 could be conducted at the much less remote Bikini Atoll, assuming that nearby inhabited islands and ships would be safe from significant contamination.[72] Because the dire consequences of the test at Bikini took officials entirely by surprise, the events on the *Lucky Dragon* and Rongelap created a public relations nightmare. The AEC attempted to extricate itself via denial and obfuscation, including blaming the incident on the coincidental fact that the device had worked "too well." Unfortunately for Val Peterson and the FCDA, the AEC's attempts to elude culpability for its mistakes worked to discredit civil defense.

As of the end of April 1954, when Val Peterson claimed that the hydrogen bomb did not pose any qualitatively new challenges to civil defense, the FCDA actually remained unaware of the hazards of fallout from thermonuclear weapons. At first, the AEC refrained from apprising Peterson and his underlings of its embarrassing radioactive contamination gaffe. That summer, however, the AEC saw fit to brief civil defense officials with security clearances on the events in the Pacific. Presented with charts of the 7,000-square-mile fallout area, the new reality stunned FCDA leaders. Despite the AEC's revelation, the FCDA could not take meaningful action to address the fallout threat. Not only did the AEC refuse to provide civil defense with all the available technical information about fallout, but its classification procedures forbade the FCDA from sharing what it did know with anyone without a security clearance, including most FCDA employees.[73] Thus paralyzed, the FCDA had no choice but to remain silent on the fallout problem.

Aiming to help the FCDA overcome this crippling secrecy, nuclear physicist and enthusiastic civil defense advocate Ralph Lapp came to the rescue with a November 1954 article in the *Bulletin of the Atomic Scientists*. On the basis of Japanese sources, unclassified scientific literature, and his own calculations, Lapp concluded that "the Federal Civil Defense Administration must be permitted access to classified data about fall-out. Furthermore, the agency must be able to translate these data or 'sanitize' them so that a realistic picture of the radioactive hazard can be given to the American people."[74] Under increasing public pressure, the AEC finally relented in early 1955. On February 9, 1955, the FCDA issued Advisory Bulletin No. 179, "Residual Radiation in Relation to Civil Defense," which declared that "the shelter program is no longer a city and reception area program; it is a general program, as almost no area is free from some threat from fallout contamination."[75] In September 1955 the FCDA published a technical bulletin describing the construction of shelters to protect against fallout. Thus the "fallout shelter" entered the American stage.

The design requirements for fallout shelters differ radically from those for the blast shelters built by the MPVO and proposed by the FCDA in the early 1950s. To protect against a nuclear weapon, a blast shelter (*ubezhishche* in Russian) at a minimum needs to provide protection against blast, thermal impulse, and penetrating radiation. Owing to their low yields, early nuclear weapons produced only limited amounts of fallout, particularly when airburst in the manner civil defense planners expected. As envisioned by the FCDA and the MPVO, their blast shelters needed to facilitate only short-term occupancy. The possibility of a firestorm, as occurred at Hiroshima, inspired the FCDA to encourage shelter occupants to leave as soon as possible after an attack.[76] Fallout shelters, by contrast, needed to protect against only one hazard—radiation produced by fission products created in a nuclear explosion. While the average half-life of these fission products is measured in hours, they produce intense penetrating gamma radiation that can be shielded only with a great deal of mass. Furthermore, the nature of the fallout hazard dictates that shelter occupants may not be able to leave their shelters for weeks, and that they may have to spend most of their time in shelters for months.

Home Fallout Shelters: An Unloved Compromise

The Eisenhower administration seems to have foisted the home fallout shelter policy on the newly founded OCDM. The FCDA's 1957 draft of the shelter section of the National Plan for Civil and Defense Mobilization shows that, even late that year, civil defense hoped to make a federally financed shelter program part of America's defense policy.[77] In all likelihood no one despised the 1950s effort to sell home fallout shelters to the public as an effective civil defense measure more than the beleaguered employees of the FCDA and the OCDM. Benjamin Taylor, acting director of the FCDA's Engineering Office, Technical Advisory Services, expressed this frustration during his testimony before the Holifield Committee in 1956. Asked by Holifield whether he "took the position now" that "to have the shelter we need in this country, you cannot have it on the scale required except with Federal funds?," Taylor replied affirmatively and added, "We have made a valiant effort to get shelter going on the pay-for-it-yourself and do-it-yourself basis; and, as I say, it has not met with much success."[78] The home shelter policy not only failed to serve the institutional interests of civil defense but also actively undermined them by making their organization and civil defense look absurd. The policy found few supporters; one major exception was the 1959 Governors' Conference, which passed a resolution based on the fallout shelter policy developed under the direction of Governor Nelson Rockefeller for the state of New York. This proposal would have required private citizens to build their own fallout shelters—effectively making Eisenhower's home shelter policy compulsory. Simultaneously, however, it envisioned federal "financial support and inducements" to encourage shelter construction, much like the shelter policy ultimately implemented in Switzerland.[79] But because of a lack of legislative support, this proposal, like so many other shelter proposals, went nowhere.

Numerous historians have examined the phenomenon of the home fallout shelter and its resonance in American culture.[80] They note that, while Americans generally failed to heed the call of the government to construct home fallout shelters, these shelters still became the topic of widespread public controversy.[81] As Kenneth D. Rose colorfully put it, "Shelters quickly produced their own fallout, attracting a torrent of criticism and making them popular objects of vilification."[82] Private home fallout shelters inevitably suffered from numerous flaws. First, they could not escape their fundamentally classist nature. The poor could not afford the several hundred dollars' worth of materials required, and they usually lacked basements or backyards in which they could construct such shelters. With the intrinsic economic bias came an associated racial bias. Second, the home fallout shelter policy favored certain regions and localities over others. Houses with basements, for instance, were far more amenable to the construction of fallout shelters—yet most houses in the southern part of the country lacked basements. Furthermore, the home shelter policy offered no prospect of survival to urban dwellers. The introduction of ICBMs resulted in the abandonment of evacuation planning by American civil defense, writing off city residents. Finally, home shelters offered only limited protection to those who went so far as to build them. In sum, private home shelters had little to recommend them, even as a propaganda measure.

The home fallout shelter policy exemplifies the pathological outcomes that sometimes resulted from the contradictions in the American weak contract state. Neither the critics nor the advocates of civil defense supported it. The critics of civil defense rejected the home shelter policy because it was weak, and because of their opposition to all civil defense measures. Civil defense supporters, meanwhile, typically advocated costly programs including fallout shelter, blast shelter, and preattack evacuation if circumstances allowed it.[83] Herman Kahn, perhaps the most famous American advocate of civil defense, described what he characterized as an "adequate" civil defense in his 1960 book *On Thermonuclear War*. Costing a total of $200 billion, the plan foresaw $80 billion of that spent on personnel shelters and $30 billion on industrial shelters. As envisioned in the book, this system would be built up over a period of years at an average annual cost of around $10 billion. According to Kahn, "With the addition of a competent active offense and defense system, the civil defense system probably cannot be destroyed without the attacker using weapons which either are or come perilously close to being Doomsday Machines."[84] Although none of them advocated a shelter program as aggressive as Kahn's, civil defense advocates in the political sphere, such as Chet Holifield, Nelson Rockefeller, and John F. Kennedy, envisioned considerable government-led and government-supported shelter construction efforts. As it happened, one of those men was soon to move into the White House.

Taking Aid and Comfort from the Enemy

To give weight to their pleas for costly civil defense programs, both U.S. and Soviet civil defense increasingly turned to the activities of their enemy counterparts during the mid-1950s. The prospect of a real-life "mineshaft gap," they hoped, would compel political leaders to match the real or imagined civil defense investments of their adversary. To facilitate this goal, both organizations cultivated accounts of enemy civil defense, manipulating available information to lend support to favored policy outcomes.

Alarmist interpretations of enemy civil defense emerged as soon as both the United States and the Soviet Union began civil defense programs. Issued on April 30, 1952, National Intelligence Estimate NIE-60, "Civil Defense in the USSR," examines the MPVO on the basis of published Soviet sources and reconnaissance available to the CIA at that date. "We believe that the USSR must already be given a substantial civil defense capability, probably greater than that of any other major country except perhaps the UK," wrote the authors, implying that the MPVO's program indeed outpaced that of the cash-starved FCDA. Some aspects of Soviet civil defense flabbergasted the American spymasters, however; despite the fact that it appeared "well-planned and organized," they noticed that "it is not clear from available evidence that the USSR is making any specific preparations for civil defense against atomic weapons."[85] Rationalizing that "preparations are underway which contribute indirectly to Soviet readiness for such attacks," the authors erroneously postulated that "it is probable that the USSR is preparing for atomic defense in its broader civil defense measures." NIE-60 speculates about the Kremlin's rationale for keeping these imaginary preparations to survive nuclear war secret, suggesting that "one motive for such minimizing might be to reduce the possibility of panic immediately preceding or during atomic attacks."[86] Contrary to the fears of many in the FCDA and Strategic Air Command, the CIA saw little reason to interpret the Kremlin's activities as evidence of a crash program integral to a Soviet design to launch an atomic war against the United States as soon as possible: "Although the civil defense system appears capable of rapid expansion in event of an emergency, there is no evidence of preparations which would indicate an expectation of early hostilities," concludes the report.[87]

Stalin's propagandists also found rhetorical uses for the FCDA's activities. In a bombastic 1952 propaganda work titled *American Imperialism: The Bitterest Enemy of the Peoples*, author V. Korionov homed in on the civil defense propaganda issued by the FCDA as proof that the Americans hoped to spark a new world war. Korionov denounced the efforts of American civil defense to issue dog tags to schoolchildren in order to identify their bodies in case of atomic war, characterizing these, along with the infamous "duck and cover" air raid drills of American civil defense, as a naked attempt not merely "to undermine pupils' capacity for independent thought" but also to "inculcate an ideology of slavish submission."[88] Along with the similar menace to impressionable young minds posed by comic books, another target of the author, *American Imperialism* charges that U.S. civil defense threatened world peace, reiterating well-established Stalinist dogma that militarist "warmongers" threatened the outbreak of a new war.

The CPSU Presidium's 1953 decision to initiate civil defense planning for atomic attack inspired the Soviet government to investigate foreign civil defense efforts more thoroughly. This policy shift, however, did not forestall Soviet observers from retaining their earlier conviction that American civil defense served primarily as a means of inculcating "atomic psychosis" and deluding the populace into accepting their government's unjustifiable hostility toward the USSR, rather than as a logical hedge against a possible Soviet nuclear attack. Soviet writers maintained that their own civil defense, in contrast, was obviously entirely innocent and reasonable in light of the American threat.

Shortly after the Presidium made its about-face on civil defense policy in 1953, American civil defense embarked on an annual national civil defense exercise known as "Operation Alert." Trumpeted in both print and broadcast media and involving federal, state, and local government officials, along with trial evacuations of some urban populations, a propaganda exercise of this scale could not avoid attracting the attention of the Soviet Union. Operation Alert 1955 was the subject of an article in the winter 1956 issue of Soviet civil defense's classified journal, which declares unequivocally that "the goal of this campaign constituted an attempt by the ruling circles of the U.S. to convince Americans to believe in the possibility of an air attack on the United States."[89] The Soviet report notes that Operation Alert hardly proved the robustness of American civil defense, stating that "the exercises demonstrated the unreadiness of the country in the field of civil defense" and reporting that the Senate Armed Services Committee had determined that "at present the U.S. is not in the condition to handle the consequences of a nuclear attack."[90] This conclusion hardly reassured the article's author, as he saw the goal of American civil defense not as defense against the USSR's nuclear arsenal but rather as a means of justifying aggressive imperialistic policies and inculcating a "military psychosis" among the American population. The occurrence of a number of protests against Operation Alert in cities such as New York, however, struck him as a hopeful sign that Washington's militaristic policies found little support among the American people.[91]

MPVO officials quickly seized on Operation Alert as a means of convincing the Communist Party to justify greater investment in its own civil defense. In a report about Operation Alert 56 circulated to the Ukrainian Communist Party Central Committee, the assistant head of Ukrainian civil defense claimed that the 1956 exercise had been more successful than the one the previous year. Furthermore, while echoing earlier assertions that a major goal of the exercises was promulgating "military hysteria," the author argued that Operation Alert sought to "increase the effectiveness of the American system of civil defense in case of the possible enemy use of weapons of mass destruction."[92] Aiming to legitimize MPVO policies, the author implied that the FCDA's evacuation plans followed the same general principles as those envisioned by Soviet civil defense. "According to the leaders of [American] civil defense, research has revealed that the best way to reduce civilian casualties during atomic attack is the evacuation of cities into safe areas, where the part of the population not directly connected with production would relocate in advance," states the report, giving the misleading impression that the FCDA envisioned a policy of strategic evacuation with critical workers remaining in cities, instead of its actual

The "Oh My God!" Phase 123

policy of tactical evacuation.[93] In addition to this attempt to justify MPVO evacuation planning, the author also took advantage of the ongoing debate in the United States about the relative merits of shelters and evacuation to support Soviet spending on bomb shelters, pointing out that a congressional committee had denounced the FCDA's policy of evacuation as inadequate and instead urged the construction of a multibillion-dollar system of blast shelters to protect urban residents.[94] The implicit message of this report was clear: the Communist Party should support the MPVO's ambitious and costly program to develop shelters in Soviet cities, lest a real "mineshaft gap" emerge between the two superpowers.

During the late 1950s, the MPVO produced several assessments of American civil defense efforts for its staff advancing similar arguments. In 1956 the MPVO's classified journal featured an article by V. Sinitsyn, "Civil Defense of the USA," describing the FCDA's organization and activities. Sinitsyn concluded that "the measures ongoing in the U.S. civil defense system constitute one of the elements of a preparatory plan for a new world war undertaken by American reactionary circles. It should be kept in mind that the imperialists of the United States of America utilize these measures to maintain high profits and as a means of inculcating war psychosis."[95] While the CIA pieced together information about enemy civil defense from returned German prisoners of war, Western visitors to the USSR, and snippets of information from the Soviet published sources, the MPVO merely needed to follow the American press to remain apprised of enemy civil defense. Two MPVO officers, R. A. Bakanov and S. Dzharylglasov, wrote a classified 1959 book, *Civil Defense of the USA*, describing the FCDA on the basis of its publications from 1950 to 1955. Drawing primarily on sources including the FCDA's annual reports, the NSRB civil defense plan, and pamphlets such as "What You Should Know about Radiological Warfare," the authors outlined how American civil defense operated in theory.[96] Bakanov and Dzharylglasov warned readers that "these measures are not enacted equally everywhere," as "the degree of civil defense readiness varies greatly in different states." The introduction explains that, owing to the "propagandistic character" of FCDA publications in which "wishes are sometimes substituted for facts," their portrayal of American civil defense downplayed its failings.[97] The volume, however, never clarifies the extent of this problem and implies better implementation of FCDA regulations than really existed. *Civil Defense of the USA* reveals that Soviet analysts assumed American civil defense resembled the professionalized, if still dysfunctional, MPVO more closely than it actually did.

As their Soviet counterparts pondered the activities of the FCDA, analysts in the United States investigated Soviet civil defense activity. A 1958 CIA report included photographs of a bomb shelter under construction in Kiev, noting that the USSR's civil defense program represented "the expenditure of considerable sums in construction and training." Refusing to issue a firm conclusion on the goals of Soviet civil defense, CIA analysts repeated their earlier verdict that what was known about the program showed no signs of a plan to start a nuclear war at some future date.[98]

In 1959, the Holifield Committee issued a report, *Civil Defense in Western Europe and the Soviet Union*, providing one of the first publicly available assessments of Soviet civil defense in the West. Seeking rationales for its long-standing desire for more vigorous civil defense preparations in the United States, the committee seized on the potential strategic implications of the Soviet program. "At the present time the United States lacks the means to protect its people in the event of nuclear war, and Soviet strategists cannot be unaware of our nakedness in civil defense," it cautioned. Finding that "the Soviet Union has developed a substantial civil defense program," the committee noted that "whether Soviet leaders believe their preparedness in this area is sufficient to tip the 'delicate balance of terror' in their favor is not known at the present time." Certain aspects of the MPVO's planning confirmed the Holifield Committee's dire suspicions about Soviet intentions: "Significantly, Soviet civil defense planning seems to be less concerned with warning time than do NATO or American defense authorities." Clearly, this meant that the Kremlin planned to start a nuclear war at its convenience, as "the 'alert' sounded by an aggressor to his own people has a vastly different strategic significance than the 'alert' sounded in the defending nation after an attack has been launched."[99]

Meanwhile, at RAND Corporation in California, a sovietologist named Leon Gouré embarked on a lengthy career studying Soviet civil defense. Gouré's early life not only prepared him for his future as America's premier expert on this topic, but also gave him ample personal reason to distrust the Soviet regime. Gouré was born in Moscow in 1922, and his Menshevik father took his family into exile in 1923, initially settling in Berlin. Gouré's Jewish heritage necessitated another departure following Adolf Hitler's ascension to power in 1933—this time to Paris, where he lived until German forces overran the city in 1940. Shortly after his arrival in Hoboken, New Jersey, the eighteen-year-old Gouré enlisted in the United States Army, receiving expedited U.S. citizenship in the process. After taking part in the Battle of the Bulge, he served in counterintelligence, where his fluency in

Russian, French, and German proved indispensable. His formative years inculcated an antipathy toward the Soviet Union that strongly colored Gouré's subsequent work. After the war, Gouré attended New York University, graduating in 1947, and then completed a master's degree at Columbia in 1949. Gouré joined RAND's office in the nation's capital in 1954 and transferred to its branch in Santa Monica in 1959, where he rubbed shoulders with Albert Wohlstetter, Herman Kahn, and other prominent nuclear strategic theorists. There, Gouré embarked on the study of Soviet civil defense that would define his subsequent career.[100] In 1961 he completed a lengthy report on the subject, and in 1962 published it in book form as *Civil Defense in the Soviet Union*.[101]

In his book, Gouré selectively interpreted available information about Soviet civil defense to correspond with the strategic theories of his RAND colleagues. The author explained in his preface that "the purpose of this book is solely to acquaint the reader with civil defense activities in the Soviet Union and with some of the attitudes and views behind them," and that therefore "no comparisons have been made between the Soviet system and similar Western programs." Clarifying that it was not his intention "to argue for or against such a program for the United States," Gouré insisted his study merely aimed to "understand the motivations and intentions" of Soviet leaders.[102] "Any suggestion that the Soviet civil defense program may be intended primarily as reassurance to a worried population, or as an adjunct of Soviet propaganda about alleged Western aggressive plans," wrote Gouré, "is contradicted by the very complexity and costliness of the program." Hypothesizing that "the relatively inexpensive construction of fallout shelters" would serve those purposes, he reasoned that "if the Soviet leadership is willing to make such a large effort, it must mean that its concern is not primarily with public morale, but that it regards civil defense as a significant contribution to the Soviet defense posture and as essential to the country's survival in case of war."[103]

Assuming that Kremlin leaders sought to best the United States at every turn, Gouré echoed Herman Kahn's fears that Soviet civil defense might become an instrument of coercion. Emphasizing the program's reliance on strategic warning, he charged that Soviet leaders might "decide to exploit their civil defense capability for some political purpose" and that "they may be more inclined than they would be otherwise to take certain risks in limited crises." Gouré suggested the ominous possibility that in a future crisis the USSR might issue the "threatening situation" alert "either to underscore the extreme seriousness of the situation and thus strengthen the leadership's negotiatory position or to reinforce the Soviet deterrence posture in an effort to dissuade the enemy from resorting to military action." Given the appeal of such a maneuver and seeing "no technical obstacle" to it, Gouré proposed that "one reason why the Soviet leaders have thus far refrained from it" was "the obvious risk" that it would provoke American retaliation. In the future, however, he worried that "the Soviet leaders might not be afraid of the possible provocative effect of a 'threatening situation' alert," especially if they were convinced that the USSR "had achieved military preponderance over the West."[104] Confirming his long-standing suspicions of Soviet intentions, Gouré concluded that Soviet civil defense still posed a credible threat to U.S. strategic interests, even though it "evidently has many shortcomings and certain obsolete features."[105]

Ironically, both *Civil Defense of the USA* and *Civil Defense in the Soviet Union* were utterly outdated at the time of their publication owing to organizational shifts in American and Soviet civil defense. Bakanov and Dzharylglasov's book neglects developments after 1955, when the FCDA still emphasized tactical evacuation and its efforts to address the fallout problem remained in their infancy. The Eisenhower administration dismantled the FCDA in 1958, creating the OCDM in its stead, and introduced a policy of emphasizing home fallout shelters. Gouré, meanwhile, failed to ascertain the temporary victory of civil defense opponents in the Soviet government between 1959 and 1961. Far from the continuous, well-organized program portrayed by Gouré, when *Civil Defense in the Soviet Union* emerged from the presses in 1962, Soviet civil defense possessed almost no operational capability because of organizational changes and near-total personnel turnover. Both Gouré and his Soviet counterparts, however, had similar goals: to use the enemy's preparations to survive nuclear war as justification for their policy preferences.

The Near Demise of Soviet Civil Defense

By the late 1950s, some high-ranking members of the Soviet political elite clearly believed that money spent on civil defense would be better spent elsewhere. Georgi Malenkov famously lost his power struggle with Nikita Khrushchev owing, in part, to his claim that the Soviet Union could not survive a thermonuclear war.[106] Although Malenkov was no longer part of the Presidium after 1957, one increasingly prominent member of that body shared his disbelief in the survivability of nuclear war. Anastas Mikoian, who became Khrushchev's closest political ally after 1957, considered civil defense unworkable and a waste of resources. During World War II, Mikoian had obstinately refused to retreat to a bomb shelter during German bombing raids, preferring to remain at his desk.[107] In the late 1950s, Mikoian made a habit of expressing his views regarding the unworkability of bomb shelters in thermonuclear war during his many visits abroad promoting Soviet trade. For instance, during his 1959 visit to the United States, Mikoian told a group of reporters that against thermonuclear weapons, shelters were useless except as a means of psychological consolation against the nuclear threat.[108] After watching films of nuclear weapons tests, Mikoian was quoted in an August 1960 CIA report as remarking, "Why should I support billions for bomb shelters?" In February 1959, Nikita Khrushchev commented to the Norwegian ambassador that the Council of Ministers had discussed the question of bomb shelters and had become convinced that "nothing could be done."[109] Although this statement suggests that by early 1959 Khrushchev had already decided that bomb shelters were a fool's bargain, shelter construction continued until the end of that year, when the axe fell.

Much like their counterparts in the Eisenhower administration, the leaders of the Soviet Union in the 1950s experienced cognitive dissonance about the threat to their nation resulting from the introduction of thermonuclear weapons. Both superpowers' strategic postures evolved organically from ad hoc measures adopted in response to the rapid developments in weapons technology. In 1955 the Soviet government declared that a thermonuclear war would end with the destruction of capitalism and the global triumph of socialism, despite the Presidium's recognition of the extreme vulnerability of the Soviet Union to nuclear attack. The ambitious goals embodied in the Presidium's resolutions on civil defense between 1953 and 1955 reflected its members' anxieties about the prospect of an American attack on the USSR. Following the Soviet Union's successful test of its R-7 ICBM in 1957 and its dramatic launch of Sputnik in October, Soviet premier Nikita Khrushchev hoped that the USSR's lead in missile technology would elicit respect from the United States and compel the capitalist powers to accommodate Soviet interests. Unfortunately for the USSR, Sputnik inspired a new wave of American paranoia about the possibility of a Soviet nuclear attack, along with fears of a "missile gap," but Khrushchev continued to hope that the USSR's newfound strength would help lessen Cold War tensions.

Apparently believing that his 1959 visit to the United States and an upcoming diplomatic summit would reduce Cold War tensions and the nuclear threat, Khrushchev and his comrades felt that they could do without civil defense. Deciding that the MPVO's shelter construction budget would be better spent in other areas, on December 30, 1959, the Presidium forbade further construction of bomb shelters, released existing shelters for civilian uses, and fired all but a skeleton staff of civil defense workers. Without personnel or funding, the USSR's civil defense system essentially ceased to function, except for DOSAAF's training efforts.[110] In April 1960, the Presidium developed a plan reallocating 9.6 billion rubles that had been earmarked for shelter construction to build housing, hospitals, and other public works.[111]

Envisioning the Worst

Georgii Malenkov himself theorized that thermonuclear war might "destroy civilization," but might it have still more dire consequences—an ecological apocalypse that could threaten the survival of the human species? Although speculation that nuclear war might have such results burst into the public discourse immediately after Hiroshima, the discovery of the fallout hazard from new megaton-range thermonuclear weapons gave such notions renewed legitimacy. Although the obsessive secrecy surrounding nuclear weapons in both superpowers denied the general public most technical data about the effects of nuclear weapons, the simple fact was that scientists lacked the requisite knowledge to answer this question. Both the United States and the USSR conducted their early thermonuclear weapons tests without preparations to gather data about the impact of radioactive fallout on the local environment, and in any case the science of ecology remained in its infancy. In the absence of authoritative information, many citizens—including former civil defense proponents such as Phillip Wylie—quickly came to assume the worst.

Writers in the West soon began producing narratives that embodied the prevailing atmosphere of nuclear doom. Even authors who believed that thermonuclear war might result in the extinction of the human race shared prevailing pessimism about the motives and rationality of the communist enemy. Nevil Shute's wildly popular 1957 novel *On the Beach*, for instance, portrays the slow death of the Southern Hemisphere owing to encroaching fallout from a nuclear war that the Soviet and Chinese communists launched against each other using genocidal cobalt bombs, with the intent of exterminating each other's populations.[112] Novelist Pat Frank's *Alas, Babylon*, first published in 1959, describes an unprovoked attack by the Soviet Union on the United States and its allies.[113] Writer Walter Miller's *A Canticle for*

Leibowitz, originally published as a series of science fiction stories beginning in 1955, implied even more pessimistically that the mere availability of nuclear weapons would make their use inevitable. Set millennia in the future, after a nuclear war reduced civilization to a new dark age, the novel concludes when humanity rediscovers atomic weapons and eventually fights another war, which Miller's monk protagonists escape by fleeing Earth in a starship.[114]

Although few of these novels portray civil defense in a flattering light, not all of their authors believed civil defense was impossible in a thermonuclear war. In his 1987 study of fictional portrayals of nuclear war, Paul Brians comments that "civil defense as a truly effective protection against nuclear war is seldom taken seriously."[115] Owing to increasing awareness of the hazards of fallout, most authors lost their enthusiasm for civil defense after the mid-1950s, like Wylie, and those that did not hesitated to laud it in their works. *Alas, Babylon*, for instance, dramatically portrayed the failures of civil defense following the Soviet attack on the United States. Panicked evacuees pick the novel's Florida setting clean of necessities, only to fall victim later to radiation poisoning, social breakdown, or starvation. The novel's omniscient narrator asserts that "this chaos did not result from a breakdown in Civil Defense. It was simply that Civil Defense, as a realistic buffer against thermonuclear war, did not exist."[116] Some critics have assumed Frank considered civil defense impossible and wrote his novel to emphasize this point, but in fact he was a civil defense enthusiast who published the nonfiction book *How to Survive the H-Bomb and Why* in 1962 and even briefly worked for the Office of Civil Defense during the Kennedy administration.[117] Like many civil defense advocates of the late 1950s, Frank directed his critique not at civil defense in general but rather at the Eisenhower administration's ineffective civil defense policies, and he approved of Kennedy's more vigorous efforts.

While a few works, such as *On the Beach* and author Helen Clarkson's 1959 *The Last Day: A Novel of the Day After Tomorrow*, horrified readers with the slow death of every human being by radiation poisoning, most others focused on the plight of survivors.[118] Brians noted disapprovingly that "one might suppose that the authors of these works would frequently have been pacifists, but such is not the case." Instead, "almost every work realistically depicting nuclear war justifies either retaliation, armed resistance to invasion, or ruthless violence against fellow citizens in the aftermath of nuclear attack." In many cases, nuclear war served merely as a plot device for establishing "a new dark age" allowing "free reign for neobarbarian violence."[119]

During the late 1950s American studios produced film and television programs that embodied prevailing cultural anxieties about the possibility that nuclear war would precipitate the end of civilization. In 1960, *Playhouse 90* adapted *Alas, Babylon* for television, incongruously ruining the original message of the novel with major plot changes that altered the focus of the story from survival and fortitude to marital strife.[120] In 1959 United Artists adapted *On the Beach* as a motion picture directed by Stanley Kramer and starring Gregory Peck.[121] Peck even attended a special premiere of the film in Moscow on December 17 of that year. Around 1,000 Soviet filmmakers and cultural officials attended the private screening. Although these viewers received the film with warm applause, they "expressed doubt that it would be shown to the general public" of the USSR, and this prognostication proved accurate.[122]

By the early 1960s favorable portrayals of civil defense became vanishingly rare in the American media. The embarrassing public defection of former civil defense advocates such as Philip Wylie, along with the untimely death of Pat Frank, left American civil defense officials without any recognizable authors or filmmakers loyal to their cause.[123] Meanwhile, films and novels such as *Doctor Strangelove* and *On the Beach* made plans to survive nuclear war the object of mockery and fear. The remainder of the Cold War passed without a single notable example of an American novel or film intended to bolster civil defense.

Unlike their counterparts in the United States, Soviet citizens during the early Cold War received only a smattering of fictional narratives about nuclear warfare. This ideologically fraught topic not only revealed fissures within the party but also threatened Khrushchev's official policy of "Peaceful Coexistence." Soviet leaders from Stalin until Gorbachev promised their people that Soviet military would probably keep the bourgeois menace at bay, and even if it did not the USSR could and would emerge triumphant. After Malenkov's forced repudiation of his claim that nuclear war would "wreck civilization," the Communist Party avoided public discussion of nuclear apocalypse, even though prominent party members such as Anastas Mikoian privately doubted that nuclear war would be survivable or winnable.[124] Official equivocation on the subject left even prominent citizens confused about whether the party line was that nuclear war would be avoided or that it would be survived. Deferring to common sense, many presumed the former. Soviet writers and filmmakers, however, implicitly understood that the topic of nuclear war could be addressed only indirectly.

In the 1950s, some Soviet authors and screenwriters adapted to the nuclear age by simply inserting nuclear themes into well-established stock socialist realist plots. This process began before Stalin's death with the 1951 publication of author Valentin Ivanov's *Energiia podvlastna nam!* (We control the power!), a thriller in which American agents plot to assassinate Soviet nuclear scientists and incite a new world war by destroying the Energy Institute with an experimental miniaturized A-bomb. Former Nazi scientist Otto Julius Hagar expresses his desire to "test" the new weapon on communist territory and begin a war with the USSR "this year." His American colleague Thomas McNeil replies with a suggestion to kill two birds with one stone: "It is our duty to extend our hegemony over the entire world. A good war will be a veritable holiday for us, and we will kill many people." By smuggling a "slow-acting portable atomic bomb" into the Energy Institute, the bourgeois schemers could reduce it to "a zone of nuclear decay" while simultaneously "complicating the international situation and possibly unleashing a conflict." The novel concludes when the communists detect the plot at the last moment, allowing them to defuse the bomb.[125]

As nuclear energy moved increasingly from the realm of science fiction to fact in the 1950s, it became subject matter for straightforward socialist realist potboilers with no pretensions to futurism. Author Ivan Tsatsulin's 1958 thriller *Atomnaia krepost'* (Atomic fortress), for instance, followed the pursuit and successful capture of capitalist agents sent into Soviet territory to investigate a giant uranium deposit at the behest of William Price, monopolist and "uranium king." Upholding the official line on the probable outcome of a war between the United States and the Soviet Union, as well as the tradition of portraying Americans as fascist sympathizers or accomplices of the Nazis, Price describes the secret history of collaboration between American monopolists and Hitler. He rues Hitler's defeat and declares Harry Truman a war criminal for the atomic bombings of Japan—not on account of the civilian casualties but rather because it revealed the secret of the atomic bomb, which ought to have been saved for a preventive war against the USSR. Thanks to Truman's stupidity, the "uranium king" lost his cherished hopes of destroying the Soviet Union: "We will lose the war," he concludes sadly.[126]

All these Soviet tales emphasize the immorality of American society and the bankruptcy of Washington's defense policies, but none of them actually portray either a nuclear war or similar technological apocalypse. A few such scenarios reached Soviet citizens in the mid-1950s from foreign sources such as the 1954 translation of Icelandic author Halldor Laxness's *Atómstöðin*.[127] Few Soviet authors dared broach the subject directly, with the result that, even in the 1980s, some American scholars of Soviet fiction remained totally unaware of any works that did so.[128] While government censorship forestalled any Soviet novelist from penning a novel resembling On the Beach or The Last Day, as with so many other taboo subjects, Soviet writers found clever workarounds to address the topic of nuclear war indirectly, such as setting their tales in outer space.[129]

Author Ivan Efremov's landmark 1957 novel *Tumannost' Andromedy* (Andromeda nebula) not merely inaugurated a new era in Soviet science fiction with its compelling portrayal of a utopian communist future, but also introduced millions of Soviet readers to a vision of a civilization snuffed out by nuclear energy. At the opening of the novel, the crew of the starship *Tantra* completes their mission to determine the fate of the planet Zirda. This world, like Earth, was one of thousands across the galaxy that communicated with other species via the "Great Circle," a transgalactic network of civilizations sharing information with one another at the speed of light. Perplexed by the cessation of transmissions from Zirda, the Great Circle requests that Earth, as the nearest planet capable of interstellar travel, mount an expedition to determine its fate. Upon arrival the humans discover that everything on the planet is dead, excepting black poppies that now cover the landscape. A probe launched from the *Tantra* reveals that "everything was normal, with the exception of increased radioactivity." Declaring that "they killed themselves and their entire planet!," the expedition's biologist notes other civilizations had also suffered the fate of the Zirdans.[130] Dangerous experiments with "partially decayed atomic fuels" resulted in the contamination of Zirda, and the humans discover that leading Zirdan scientists warned of the possible consequences and urged that the tests stop. As had alien civilizations: "One hundred eighty years earlier the Great Circle sent a brief warning, adequate for intelligent people, but obviously the Zirdan government failed to take it seriously."[131] His mission fulfilled, the *Tantra*'s commander Erg Noor optimistically concludes that as "the planet is still intact," in future centuries, after the radioactivity decayed, humanity would return to "settle and fully populate" Zirda.[132]

Efremov's vision of the communist future also explores the legacy of nuclear arms on Earth. While humanity's home planet never suffered a disaster like that which befell Zirda, Efremov leaves unanswered the question of whether a nuclear war transpired in the conflict leading to the final destruction of capitalism. Terrestrial historians under communism repeatedly cite preparations for thermonuclear war as one of the greatest crimes committed by the last generation of capitalist leaders millennia earlier. One of the novel's main characters, Veda Kong, is a historian specializing in this unpleasant chapter of human history. Occasionally archeologists stumble upon caches of the terrible weapons of mass destruction stockpiled for these conflicts, which pose serious hazards even to the extremely technologically advanced society they inhabit.[133] They locate the legendary "Shelter of Culture," which "peoples believing themselves at the forefront of science and culture built under the threat of a terrible war," storing in it "the treasures of their civilization." So as to leave no doubt as to the American identity of its constructors, Efremov mentions that they dubbed this repository the "Den of Cool" in their language.[134] Inverting Khrushchev's famous quip that "we will bury you," Efremov's novel has the capitalists burying themselves only to be disinterred by communists in the distant future.

Efremov utilizes the contents of the Den of Cool both to mock the shallowness of American consumer culture and to critique the madness of the United States' nuclear policies. The Americans made certain to store a wide variety of their chrome-laden automobiles in the shelter, a fact that baffles the communist archeologists, as do the cases of gold and gems. "How typical of their irrational confidence in the eternal and unchanging existence of their Western civilization, their language, mores, morals, and the greatness of the so-called white man," comments one.[135] She later asserts that while the builders of the shelter aimed to protect the essence of their culture, they chose items that would be useless in actually rebuilding it. The bourgeois leadership, she argues, "must have been composed entirely of incompetents."[136] Furthermore, the shelter builders booby-trapped the most secure chamber, which Veda Kong theorizes probably contains the capitalists' deadliest weapons technology. While attempting to comprehend the mechanism locking the gigantic steel door sealing it, several of the investigators perish in a huge explosion that demolishes much of the shelter's more mundane contents.[137] Efremov implies that the United States' nuclear threats manifested directly from the contradictions within their capitalist society. Unable to see beyond their own immediate class interests, bourgeois leaders could lash out with incredible destructiveness but could not even preserve their own civilization for posterity, much less perpetuate it.

On the whole, Efremov's work offered a cautiously optimistic take on the problem of nuclear warfare. Efremov's belief that nuclear apocalypse might be avoided comes as little surprise given that he authored a utopian novel, but his enormously popular *Andromeda Nebula* played a critical role in popularizing the idea of a civilization committing suicide through nuclear irresponsibility among Soviet readers. Before Efremov, no Soviet author dared broach this sensitive topic, which threatened official narratives about the USSR's role in the Cold War. Subsequently, others followed his example and eluded censorship of their tales of nuclear disaster by situating them in unfamiliar settings. The most famous Soviet tale of nuclear war in space remains science fiction writers Boris Strugatskii and Arkadii Strugatskii's 1971 novel *Obytaemyi ostrov* (The inhabited island), which critic Vladimir Gakov wrote in 1989 "remains the clearest portrayal of atomic war in Soviet literature." In this work the Strugatskiis envision a darker, more ambiguous version of Efremov's communist spacefaring future, in which a "progressor" (a space traveler whose career consists of visiting alien civilizations and facilitating their evolution toward communism) finds himself trapped on a planet ruled by several squabbling nonsocialist governments. A nuclear war wrecked at least part of the planet, but other areas remain fully inhabitable, implying that a nuclear war could be fought, survived, and possibly won.[138]

Soviet fiction about nuclear war, like the bulk of the Kremlin's rhetoric in the Khrushchev era, dwelled on the possibility of "peaceful coexistence" with the capitalist West, rather than the necessity or possibility of defense against nuclear weapons. Soviet authors never produced an analogue of Wylie's *Tomorrow!* or Shute's *On the Beach* portraying either the success or failure of civil defense in a nuclear war. Instead, Soviet tales about the atomic threat offered a more ambiguous message. In these works only a handful of people wanted a nuclear war—the militarist circles in the bourgeois leadership of the capitalist countries, particularly the United States. In all but a handful of these narratives, the peace-loving masses or Soviet power succeed in preventing the war before it begins, therefore avoiding the need to describe what it would be like. Nuclear apocalypse might befall distant imaginary worlds such as Zirda, but humanity would escape intact, if not necessarily unscathed. In time, progress toward communism would abolish the threat of nuclear war forever.

Soviet fiction reinforced Khrushchev's hoped-for peaceful coexistence, but it failed to support the propaganda needs of the civil defense program. While the FCDA sought to instill nuclear fear in American citizens, with ample assistance from the popular media both friendly and hostile to civil defense, Soviet propaganda other than that of the MPVO generally downplayed the possibility or imminence of nuclear war. The extent to which this propaganda reflected the outlook of ordinary citizens in Khrushchev's USSR cannot be ascertained with certainty, but available evidence suggests that there was little Soviet citizens relished less than the idea of a new world war. In the mid-1950s the Kremlin aimed to harness the population's desire for peace to increase economic productivity, promising citizens that overfulfilling production plans would strengthen the USSR's defense capabilities and forestall a Western attack.[139] A 1960 survey of Soviet citizens found that 96.8 percent of respondents answered yes to the question "Will humanity avoid a new war?" Only 2.1 percent answered no, indicating that "peaceful coexistence" enjoyed overwhelming popularity among Soviet citizens.[140] Lacking belief in the possibility of nuclear war, Soviet people possessed little motivation to participate in civil defense.

Conclusion

The inability of U.S. and Soviet civil defense to rise above the "Oh My God!" moment reveals the weakness of both the American contract state and the Soviet party-garrison state. While civil defense lacked popular support in both the United States and the Soviet Union during the 1950s, the institutional reverses suffered by the two countries' civil defense organizations resulted not from mass disapproval but from the opposition of a handful of well-placed critics. Whether located in the CPSU Presidium, the House Appropriations Committee, or the NSC, these men stopped civil defense before its general unpopularity could. These figures had a variety of reasons for obstructing the FCDA and MPVO from attempting to implement civil defense programs that might be capable of mitigating the thermonuclear threat. Soviet and American leaders alike fretted about the immense cost of building bomb shelters for urban populations. Some, such as Anastas Mikoian, suspected that civil defense against the H-bomb was probably infeasible and thought that a rapprochement between Moscow and Washington was not just possible but imminent. Dwight Eisenhower and John Foster Dulles, meanwhile, were more concerned that the kind of shelter program advocated by Val Peterson would set up a "defensive mood among the population" that would undermine their administration's policy of deterring the USSR by threatening "massive retaliation" against even lesser communist provocations. Both the Eisenhower administration and Khrushchev's Presidium, however, chose the same course of action to squelch calls for stronger civil defense policy: dismantling civil defense as an institution. The United States and the Soviet Union soon came to reverse this decision, but found that their promotion of dubious civil defense policies during the 1950s cast a long shadow from which neither country's civil defense program ever fully emerged.

American civil defense during the Eisenhower years shows how the weak contract state could converge on dubious policies that lacked any real constituencies. Pressure from the White House forced the FCDA to promote measures such as tactical evacuation and home fallout shelters, which everyone, from the FCDA's own analysts to the general public, knew were hopelessly inadequate to protect the U.S. population from thermonuclear attack. Although Chet Holifield surmised correctly that a disconnect existed between official policy and the true feelings of FCDA officials, they were hardly glib about the threat of nuclear war or intent on foisting a cynical fraud on the public. Instead, they were trapped between the emerging reality of thermonuclear warfare and an administration that regarded threatening other countries with nuclear weapons a better use of money than protecting the American people from the consequences of a nuclear attack. While the leaders of U.S. civil defense preoccupied themselves with trying to cultivate political support for the kind of mass shelter program that might have some hope of effectiveness, all the American people saw was a publicity effort that seemed to trivialize the threat of nuclear war. Even decades later, popular memory of these campaigns would undermine the legitimacy of civil defense in the American popular consciousness.

The Soviet party-garrison state, meanwhile, allowed ideology, rather than technical considerations, to shape its civil defense policy, even though this undermined its military readiness. Unable to reconceptualize the assumptions of its program without the Presidium's approval, the MPVO found itself compelled to promote a program designed to address primitive nuclear weapons that were already hopelessly obsolete by the mid-1950s. As a consequence, the USSR invested considerable resources during the decade in a civil defense program with little ability, even in theory, to protect Soviet citizens from America's swelling stockpile of thermonuclear bombs. The regime's waffling on the subject of thermonuclear war confused Soviet citizens and helped inculcate a popular apathy toward the civil defense program that persisted into future decades. Unfortunately, the world was on the cusp of a period during which it appeared civil defense might be an urgent necessity.

4 The Real Mineshaft Gap

Nuclear war appeared imminent, and yet nothing was ready. After years of preparation—and in the Soviet case, billions of rubles expended on bomb shelters—neither U.S. nor Soviet civil defense was ready to protect its citizens if the crisis in Cuba went hot. In both countries, civil defense had yet to recover from the institutional setbacks of the late 1950s. Khrushchev and Eisenhower alike had bet that a nuclear war would be avoided, and curtailed civil defense spending accordingly. Lacking both trained personnel and physical resources, U.S. and Soviet civil defense officials could do little more than speculate about what they would do if they were better prepared. In the heady last days of October 1962, with civilization standing on the edge of the atomic abyss, American and Soviet civil defense were equal in their impotence.

The Soviet party-garrison state's immense investment in civil defense in the 1940s and 1950s failed to pay off during the Cuban Missile Crisis. Existing shelters were inadequate to protect the Soviet Union's growing urban population. Ukraine, for instance, possessed a total of 10,287 shelters in 1962, with space for 1,532,170 people. This number was equal to only 14.2 percent of the population of the thirty-three cities in which the shelters were located.[1] Many of the USSR's shelters were reinforced basements dating to World War II or earlier, and the few that the Soviet government constructed to survive nuclear explosions were incommensurate with the challenges posed by large, multimegaton thermonuclear weapons. The USSR's lack of a system of fallout shelters for suburban and rural residents, as well as evacuees from urban areas, meant probable death for tens of millions in case of nuclear war. A 1964 Department of Defense study calculated that, without fallout shelters for rural areas, even a small fraction of the available American nuclear arsenal could result in the deaths of half the entire population of the Soviet Union, including 97 percent of the urban population.[2] As this study discounted U.S. strategic superiority in the early 1960s, and probably underestimated deaths due to causes other than blast and fallout, had the Cuban Missile Crisis escalated into a nuclear war, the result for the USSR would likely have been even more dire than it predicted.

Unfortunately for U.S. civil defense, the shortcomings of its preparations to survive nuclear war played out publicly during the crisis in Cuba. Seeking to create a workable civil defense within the stifling constraints of the weak contract state, the Kennedy administration embarked on an effort to develop a system of community fallout shelters in existing buildings. But as shelter survey efforts began only in September 1961, no more than limited progress could be expected by October of the following year. As of October 1962, Kennedy's Office of Civil Defense (OCD) managed to complete just a pilot shelter effort.[3] On October 27, 1962, assistant secretary of defense for civil defense Steuart L. Pittman reported that nationwide the OCD had marked 796 fallout shelters capable of accommodating 640,000 people, and stocked only 112 of these shelters with supplies, totaling 170,000 spaces.[4] Without shelters or trained personnel, the OCD possessed negligible ability to respond to nuclear attack. Shortly before the conclusion of the crisis on October 28, Pittman produced a proposal to swiftly develop additional shelter space in areas in the range of the Soviet missiles in Cuba, including undertaking rapid surveys of caves and mines, encouraging individuals to construct home shelters, and marking additional shelters within one week.[5]

While both Soviet and U.S. civil defense found themselves incapable of effective action during the Cuban Missile Crisis, their fates diverged dramatically in its aftermath. Immediately after the crisis, Kennedy approved Pittman's proposal to increase the amount of space available in public shelters by lowering the minimum allowable degree of radiation shielding, enabling an acceleration of the community shelter program.[6] By 1966, shelter signs had been posted on 93,110 facilities with space to shelter 81,488,000 people—about one-third of the OCD's ultimate goal. Although congressional opposition halted the purchase of shelter supplies in 1964, the OCD had acquired supplies for sixty-three million shelter spaces. Local governments, however, had stocked supplies for only thirty-eight million in shelters due to insufficient storage space.[7] Congressional opposition crippled further development of the program, preventing completion of the community shelter system. The weak contract state effectively killed the U.S. civil defense effort. Within a few years, what little ability the OCD had developed began to degrade as equipment stockpiles aged and state and local authorities turned their attention to other matters.

Events in the Soviet Union followed a dramatically different course. After the Cuban Missile Crisis, the leaders of the USSR took decisive steps to strengthen Soviet civil defense, including its shelter system. On November 4, 1963, the Council of Ministers issued a resolution stipulating that civil defense, the Ministry of Construction, the Ministry of Defense, and the economic planning organs develop systematic regulations for bomb shelter design taking into account the effects of modern thermonuclear weapons. Issued in August 1966, these regulations inaugurated a new era in the history of Soviet bomb shelter construction.[8] During the mid-1970s, the Soviet Union invested substantial resources in these shelters, completing blast shelters for about one million occupants and fallout shelters for three to four million occupants every year.[9] By the late 1970s, the United States faced a genuine "mineshaft gap."

The divergent fates of U.S. and Soviet civil defense during the 1960s resulted from their relative success reshaping nuclear strategy for their benefit. Traditionally, both political scientists and historians presumed that civil defense bore a passive relationship to the superpowers' nuclear strategies. They hypothesized that political and military leaders selected a strategy to leverage their nuclear might for some kind of objective, and then selected a civil defense policy to match. Some accounts of civil defense, such as Dee Garrison's *Bracing for Armageddon*, argue that the failure of civil defense to achieve its institutional objectives forestalled the United States government from implementing its preferred strategic posture. The events recounted in this chapter demonstrate that this puts the cart before the horse. Not only was the historical relationship between civil defense and nuclear strategy highly arbitrary, but both U.S. and Soviet civil defense attempted to reshape their nations' nuclear strategies for their own ends. To contextualize this development, this chapter provides an overview of the development of U.S. and Soviet nuclear strategy in the 1950s and 1960s and the surprising ways U.S. and Soviet civil defense attempted to manipulate it. Their relative success in doing so offers much to explain the reason why Soviet civil defense prospered while the American program withered by the early 1970s.

Civil defense sought to intervene in the crafting of nuclear strategy in order to cultivate the institutional alliances it needed to actualize its goals. In the vicious competition for resources within the superpowers' gargantuan efforts to wage the Cold War, civil defense could prosper only with the support of other, more influential patrons. In the Soviet Union, it managed to improve its position within the party-garrison state by forming a fortuitous new relationship with the increasingly powerful Soviet military, putting civil defense on a trajectory that eventually far transcended its 1950s-era peak. Soviet civil defense officials convinced the military to integrate civil defense into the USSR's newly formulated strategy to wage nuclear war, providing a powerful impetus to fund costly civil defense efforts. In the United States, however, the best efforts of Steuart L. Pittman and the OCD failed to overcome the political and institutional obstacles blocking their goal of establishing a comprehensive system of community fallout shelters. Neither the military nor the nascent arms control community responded to overtures from Pittman to collaborate with the OCD's programs. Opposition to civil defense based on technical and strategic objections played only a secondary role in this defeat. In Congress, where the battle for civil defense was lost, the same sort of vague fiscal logic that blocked shelter programs in the 1950s remained supreme even after Pittman successfully convinced a skeptical congressional committee that the fallout shelter program was technically feasible and would not have deleterious effects on the U.S.-Soviet strategic balance. Once again, the U.S. weak contract state quashed civil defense for questionable reasons. U.S. civil defense policy made neither strategic nor technical sense to the audience that mattered most—the Soviets—and they reacted by assuming the worst.

Civil Defense and the Battle to Replace "Massive Retaliation"

America's dubious nuclear strategy during the early Cold War resulted directly from the contradictions within the weak contract state. During the immediate postwar years, America's leaders saw their growing atomic stockpile not as a means of retaliating against a nuclear attack but as an instrument to punish the Soviet Union if it attacked Western Europe. The perceived superiority of the Soviet Union's conventional forces in Eastern Europe, as well as the political and practical barriers against deploying sufficient Western troops in Europe to match them, made leaning on America's atomic superiority appear an essential solution to Washington's security dilemma. Nuclear threats were much more acceptable to ordinary Americans and congressmen than the frightening prospect of turning the United States into a garrison state to match Soviet conventional forces. As representative John C. Hinshaw of California commented in a closed meeting of the Joint Committee on Atomic Energy in April 1955, to prevent the use of the nuclear arsenal might "place the Russian army as the supreme thing, and not the atomic weapon. That would be very greatly to our disadvantage, it would seem to me, in world affairs."[10]

As the USSR developed its own nuclear stockpile the credibility of this strategy increasingly eroded, but the Eisenhower administration chose to double down on it. The United States' defense commitments to its NATO allies, along with the prohibitive cost of matching the conventional forces of the socialist bloc, inspired the economy-minded Eisenhower administration to attempt to compensate simply by raising the magnitude of nuclear threats against the USSR. As secretary of state John Foster Dulles put it in 1954, it was "not sound to become permanently committed to military expenditures so vast they lead to 'practical bankruptcy,'" but as there was "no local defense which alone will contain the mighty landpower of the Communist world," the United States must resort to "the further deterrent of massive retaliatory power" to secure its interests.[11] Dubbed "Massive Retaliation," this strategy served as an excuse for the United States Air Force to acquire a huge arsenal of ever-larger thermonuclear weapons, targeted at industrial and population centers in light of limited knowledge about the location of Soviet military bases. The logic of Massive Retaliation dictated that the United States needed to maintain superiority in strategic nuclear striking power to give its threats credibility.[12]

By the late 1950s, general acknowledgment of Massive Retaliation's worrisome shortcomings emerged within U.S. defense circles, but no agreement coalesced as to what should replace it. Drawing inspiration from game theory, some American strategic theorists examined the nuclear dilemma in terms of "mutual deterrence." Although this term came to be associated with a more specific position in the strategic debate during the 1960s, it initially referred to the recognition that overwhelming U.S. nuclear strategic superiority could not be maintained indefinitely, and that the United States should accept the inevitable prospect that it would lose the "position of strength" essential for Massive Retaliation. Instead, the superpowers would be equal enough in nuclear arms to deter one another from attack—hence, "mutual deterrence."[13] While excluding Massive Retaliation, mutual deterrence could encompass an enormous range of contrasting alternative strategies, as the subsequent arguments made by American strategists revealed.

Interservice rivalry between the branches of the United States military fed into the debate over what should replace Massive Retaliation. While earlier in the 1950s the navy concurred with the air force that only overwhelming nuclear force and strategic superiority could deter the Soviet threat, by the late 1950s some naval officers embraced the idea of "minimum" or "finite deterrence" built around a relatively survivable force of silo-based Minuteman and submarine-based Polaris missiles.[14] Untargetable by enemy offensive forces, a limited force of Polaris submarines would grant Washington a high assurance of retaliation following a Soviet attack. A considerable part of the appeal of this scheme for the navy was that it would transfer the bulk of the nuclear deterrent mission from air force bombers to navy submarines. During the late 1950s, this arrangement suffered several technical weaknesses, most importantly that the proposed technologies remained completely unproven and that the Polaris missile lacked the accuracy to attack anything smaller than an area target. Therefore the retaliation would necessarily be directed at Soviet cities. Analysts working at RAND dubbed such a policy of attacking population centers as a "countervalue" targeting strategy, as it threatened what the enemy valued. Despite these shortcomings, "countervalue" appealed intuitively to influential intellectuals and political commentators, leading Herman Kahn to characterize it in 1960 as "the layman's view."[15]

Born in 1922 to Russian Jewish immigrants, Kahn followed an unlikely path to become the United States' most notorious nuclear strategist and civil defense advocate. Failing to complete his doctorate at the California Institute of Technology, Kahn joined the staff of RAND as a physicist in 1948, ostensibly because of the proximity of its Santa Monica offices to the beach—a fact that appealed greatly to Kahn, an avid swimmer. Once at RAND, Kahn drifted from his work predicting the behavior of neutrons in thermonuclear weapons to converse with researchers studying strategic questions. In time, Kahn migrated out of physics altogether to devote his attention to investigating nuclear war. Kahn combined extreme intelligence with a congenital tendency to take contrarian positions, which he often presented using his characteristic brand of black humor. "I'm against ignorance," he once said. "I'm against sloppy, emotional thinking. I'm against fashionable thinking. I am against the whole cliché of the moment."[16] Kahn's unusually corpulent figure—he weighed over 300 pounds despite the swimming—combined with the rapid-fire theatrics that enthralled and alienated his audiences to make him among the most memorable personalities of the Cold War era.[17]

Kahn was the most visible of the strategists who argued that finite deterrence would lack credibility for the United States' need to deter a Warsaw Pact invasion of Western Europe, and he maintained that only a "counterforce" strategy targeting Soviet strategic nuclear forces could accomplish this goal. Herman Kahn's prominence in debates about nuclear strategy led both his critics and admirers to assume incorrectly that he originated the often outrageous and disquieting concepts in his presentations. Although highly original, Kahn's work drew heavily on earlier studies developed at RAND and elsewhere; and other RAND strategists, such as Albert Wohlstetter, contributed to a school of strategic thought emphasizing counterforce targeting as part of a credible deterrent force. In the late 1950s, Kahn attracted the ire of his RAND colleagues by popularizing this thinking in chart-laden presentations and congressional testimony. In 1960, Kahn compiled these materials into a massive tome he gave the Clausewitzian title *On Thermonuclear War*. To Kahn's surprise, the book became a lightning rod for critics, who considered it an apologia for nuclear war rather than the reasoned critique of the Eisenhower administration's defense policies he intended. Kahn's RAND colleagues were incensed by the negative media attention his activities attracted, as they had not intended their studies of nuclear war to be fodder for public debate. Even though those at RAND largely agreed with Kahn's endorsement of counterforce, he differed with them on the importance of civil defense and lobbied for an extremely ambitious civil defense policy. Faced with an increasingly unfriendly work environment, Kahn left RAND in 1961 to found his own think tank, the Hudson Institute, which soon began receiving multimillion dollar contracts to conduct research for the OCD and other government agencies.

In *On Thermonuclear War* Kahn employed the concept of the "doomsday machine" as a reductio ad absurdum metaphor to explain his rejection of countervalue targeting strategies. Kahn made clear that, unlike the fictitious Dr. Strangelove (whom director Stanley Kubrick based in part on Kahn), he considered doomsday machines a terrible idea. Kahn directed his concerns at the extreme use of indiscriminate force embodied by the doomsday machine: "Even though it maximizes the probability that deterrence will work (including minimizing the problem of accidents or miscalculations)," he argued, "one must still examine the consequences of a failure. In this case a failure kills too many people and it kills them automatically."[18] Highlighting parallels between the brutality of the doomsday machine and prevailing strategic paradigms, Kahn contended that these "could imply that either some of the weapons systems currently being proposed are also unacceptable, or that the way we talk about these weapons systems is wrong—very likely both." Although Kahn's criticism fell primarily on Massive Retaliation, he believed that a "finite" deterrent that relied on a similar threat to kill people indiscriminately in response to a major or minor provocation would suffer similar drawbacks, while also giving the Kremlin the opportunity to subject the West to nuclear blackmail.

In addition to fearing the prospect that an inflexible strategic doctrine might result in the senseless extermination of tens of millions of people, Kahn also worried that without the ability to threaten Soviet strategic forces, the United States would lack the leverage it might need in an international crisis. "Will the Soviets find the threat of U.S. retaliation credible?" asked Kahn, who thought that finite deterrence would prove unconvincing to Moscow as "one would not think that the Soviets could believe that the U.S. would willingly commit suicide" in the defense of its European allies.[19] To overcome the contradiction between the strategic consequences of nuclear weapons and Washington's defense commitments, Kahn maintained that the nation needed to retain the ability to blunt a possible Soviet attack through strikes against enemy strategic forces, active defenses, retaliatory threats, and civil defense.[20] In Kahn's view, American strategic forces required "at least enough capability to launch a first strike in the kind of tense situation that would result from an outrageous Soviet provocation, so as to induce uncertainty in the enemy as to whether it would not be safer to attack us directly than to provoke us," in combination with "enough of a retaliatory capability to make this direct attack unattractive." Finally, there should be enough civil defense and other means of limiting damage "so that if a war occurs anyway—perhaps as a result of accident or miscalculation—the nation will continue and unnecessary death and destruction will not occur."[21]

Herman Kahn provided both humanitarian and strategic rationales for a robust civil defense program. Calculating on the basis of RAND studies that a well-funded civil defense system could reduce civilian casualties and economic damage immensely even against a Soviet attack directed against populations, Kahn argued loudly that the United States needed civil defense as insurance in case deterrence failed. Kahn contradicted himself as to whether civil defense possessed much strategic significance. Even within the pages of *On Thermonuclear War* he asserted that "in terms of getting along with the [Soviet Union], the whole purpose of the system is to allow the U.S. to take much firmer positions," while stating elsewhere that "except for increasing our ability to withstand . . . postattack blackmail tactics," the deterrent value of civil defense "is so small compared to the role the strictly military deterrence plays that it seems proper to ignore it."[22] Either way, Kahn dismissed the notion that any but the largest civil defense programs would provoke the enemy and invite preemptive attack. "Instituting the civil defense program itself," he claimed, "is (logically or illogically) no more provocative than most current recommendations for reducing our vulnerability."[23]

In opposition to Kahn, proponents of finite deterrence and its associated emphasis on countervalue targeting included many advocates of arms control, who hoped it would restrain the growth of nuclear arsenals and serve as a first step on the road to disarmament. Jerome Wiesner, a prominent professor at the Massachusetts Institute of Technology and head of John F. Kennedy's Science Advisory Committee, made some of the most influential arguments for this position. Although he hoped that arms control would ultimately result in the elimination of nuclear arsenals, Wiesner considered finite deterrence a possible first step toward this objective. "While a system of mutual deterrence is less attractive in many ways than a properly safeguarded total disarmament," he wrote in 1960, "it may be somewhat easier to achieve and could be regarded as a transient phase on the way toward the goal of total disarmament." Wiesner based his "mutual deterrence" on "the premise that it is now possible, or soon will be possible, to create offensive weapons systems sufficiently invulnerable to enemy attack by almost any practically achievable force." Reasoning that "if each side has a similarly protected and invulnerable force, there will be no opportunity and therefore no incentive to build up a so-called counter-force capability," Wiesner concluded that "in this situation, an attack is deterred by the certain knowledge that it will be followed by a devastating reply."[24]

In a widely read 1964 *Scientific American* article, Wiesner and Herbert F. York, former chief science advisor to Dwight Eisenhower, argued that as part of a finite deterrence strategy, the United States should forgo both missile defense and civil defense. Pushing primarily for the retention and strengthening of the 1963 Partial Test Ban Treaty, Wiesner and York suggested that to demonstrate to the enemy that the United States held no aggressive intentions toward the Soviet Union, and to make clear it employed a war-deterring strategic posture with countervalue targeting, Washington ought to embrace vulnerability to Soviet retaliation by eschewing the development of both antiballistic missile (ABM) defenses and civil defense. In their view, "Soviet military planners would be compelled to consider a massive civilian-shelter program as portending a first strike against them." The effectiveness of a civil defense program could not be calculated, they asserted, because "such calculations always involve predictions about the form of the attack, but as the form is unknowable the calculations are nonsensical." Furthermore, they contended that the serious pursuit of civil defense would inevitably reduce American society to a dystopian garrison state, as "there is no logical termination to the line of reasoning that begins with belief in the usefulness of fallout shelters; the logic of this attempt to solve the problem of national security leads to a diverging series of ever more grotesque measures," including the "live-in and work-in blast shelter." They maintained pessimistically that "if the arms race continues and resumes its former accelerating tempo, 1984 is more than a date on the calendar 20 years hence."[25]

Counterforce advocates such as Herman Kahn recognized the many appealing features of a finite deterrence posture, but argued that it suffered shortcomings rendering it inadequate for the United States' security needs. "This Finite Deterrence position has many things in its favor," Kahn acknowledged, as "only a finite force is required" and it "seems compatible with all kinds of measures for arms control," as well as "the Soviet desire to prevent inspection of their country." Since "the position is obviously non-aggressive and defensive," Kahn recognized that it offered hope to rein in the arms race and "abolish the use of nuclear force" for practical intents and purposes, even though nuclear war would remain a technical possibility. Finite deterrence advocates' objections to active and passive defenses, however, struck Kahn as both nonsensical and hypocritical. Kahn saw a contradiction between their belief that any attempt to protect population through these measures would be destabilizing since it "reduced the amount of terror in the balance of terror" and their embrace of the idea of limiting armaments, which he argued would have an equivalent effect.[26] Kahn charged, furthermore, that when examined in light of America's commitment to defend its allies, the case for finite deterrence fell apart. "Those who advocated pure Finite Deterrence tended to ignore or deemphasize the postwar history in which U.S. strategic arms had been procured in the early 1950's less for the direct defense of the U.S. than for the defense of Europe and Asia at a time when the Soviets seemed to be threatening these two areas," he noted. Finite deterrence, meanwhile, "promised to accelerate the spread of nuclear weapons in spite of its emphasis on arms control purposes," because "the European nations would no longer have an American strategic nuclear guarantee and would be faced with becoming a battleground—either conventional or nuclear. It also seemed quite clear that the same problem would eventually arise in Asia."[27]

In the late 1950s and early 1960s, events in Europe seemed to bear out Kahn's concerns that the waning credibility of the American commitment to defend its allies encouraged nuclear proliferation. The United Kingdom tested its own bomb in 1952, with France following suit in 1960. Numerous other nations seriously considered nuclear weapons programs, including West Germany, leading to arguments from the U.S. State Department that the United States needed to introduce some kind of nuclear sharing arrangement with its NATO allies to stem the tide.[28] The spread of nuclear weapons eroded the ability of the United States to set the agenda for the defense of the capitalist West, and a world with a large number of nuclear states threatened to increase the likelihood of nuclear war.

After John F. Kennedy moved into the White House in early 1961, his administration sought to modernize Eisenhower's stagnant doctrine of Massive Retaliation by utilizing some of the ideas proposed by strategic theorists such as Kahn. Defense secretary Robert S. McNamara initially embraced the idea of controlled counterforce targeting. In conjunction with the OCD's shelter program and the possible Nike-X ABM defense, McNamara hoped that the Pentagon could maintain a credible defense umbrella for its NATO allies while discouraging further nuclear proliferation and limiting the damage to the United States should war break out. McNamara announced the new strategy to the representatives of America's allies at the NATO Ministerial in Athens on May 6, 1962. McNamara informed the audience of this classified speech that a nuclear war in which both superpowers restrained themselves from attacks on civilian targets might result in only one-fourth the fatalities relative to a war with attacks on both counterforce and countervalue targets.[29]

McNamara felt so taken with his Athens speech that he elected to give a redacted version of it as a commencement address at his alma mater, the University of Michigan. In what became known as the Ann Arbor speech, McNamara reassured listeners that "the Alliance has overall nuclear strength adequate to any challenge confronting it" and that "this strength not only minimizes the likelihood of major nuclear war, but it makes possible a strategy designed to preserve the fabric of our societies if war should occur." The defense secretary echoed Kahn's arguments for counterforce, charging that "relatively weak national nuclear forces with enemy cities as their targets are not likely to be sufficient to perform even the function of deterrence," as "in the event of war, the use of such a force against the cities of a major nuclear power would be tantamount to suicide." Moreover, McNamara informed the audience that "in the event of a nuclear war stemming from a major attack on the Alliance," NATO's military goal "should be the destruction of the enemy's forces, not of his civilian population." American strategic power, according to McNamara, would compel the Kremlin to respond in kind as it made it "possible for us to retain, even in the face of a massive surprise attack, sufficient reserve striking power to destroy an enemy society if driven to it. In other words, we are giving a possible opponent the strongest imaginable incentive to refrain from striking our own cities."[30]

McNamara quickly tempered his enthusiasm for counterforce when he discovered the steepness of its attendant technical and political challenges.

McNamara's strategic posture did not incorporate the more extreme features of the possible counterforce deterrents Herman Kahn described in his writings, but it envisioned an offensive force composed of manned bombers and ballistic missiles that would strike Soviet military targets, as well as a secure retaliatory force to be held in reserve, primarily Polaris submarine-launched ballistic missiles (SLBMs) in conjunction with hardened intercontinental ballistic missile (ICBM) silos surviving a Soviet preemptive strike. McNamara soon found that the former requirement emboldened the air force to demand an ever-increasing quantity of nuclear delivery systems. Given the enormous demands that the United States' Cold War commitments placed on the military budget, McNamara worried that giving in to never-ending expenditures on ICBMs and bombers would starve other pressing concerns, such as the deepening conflict in Vietnam. To contain the threat of alarmist Strategic Air Command generals and their well-connected political allies, McNamara ordered his staff at the beginning of 1963 to deemphasize counterforce in official Pentagon statements. This step denoted merely a rhetorical shift rather than a dramatic revision in policy. Defense Department studies of nuclear strategy continued to plan for counterforce attacks against Soviet targets as well as a reserve retaliatory force for countervalue attacks.[31]

In a 1963 draft presidential memorandum delivered to President Lyndon B. Johnson, McNamara elucidated his two strategic goals for America's nuclear arsenal: "damage limiting" and "assured destruction." The former included counterforce attacks against Soviet strategic nuclear forces as well as active defenses and civil defense to limit population losses and economic damage to the United States in a nuclear war. "Assured destruction" consisted of the ability of U.S. strategic nuclear forces to inflict "unacceptable losses" on the USSR's population and industry even after a Soviet counterforce attack against the United States. Defense Department researchers developed mathematical models to estimate how proposed changes to U.S. defense capabilities would impact the Pentagon's ability to realize these goals. Unfortunately, these studies found that counterforce attacks on the Soviet Union would still result in enormous civilian casualties, undermining much of the logic of the "no cities" strategy. Moreover, the studies determined that "damage limiting" would be extremely difficult. The additional Minuteman ICBMs proposed by the air force would make little reduction in the damage to the United States from a Soviet retaliatory strike. Meanwhile, the massive Nike-X ABM system sought by the army would provide little additional benefit relative to its immense cost—even while making extremely optimistic assumptions for its effectiveness. Only one element of "damage limiting" emerged from the analyses as both effective and affordable—the OCD's fallout shelter program. McNamara recommended to the president that this program be funded, even as he lost his enthusiasm for additional offensive forces and the ABM.[32]

Initially, "assured destruction" appeared only in classified government reports, but starting in early 1965 McNamara began making public use of the phrase, which in conjunction with the public silence on counterforce led many observers to conclude that the United States had embraced minimal deterrence as official policy.[33] McNamara's reduction of the planned Minuteman ICBM force from 1,400 to 1,000 silos reinforced this impression. Behind the scenes, however, counterforce remained at the heart of American targeting plans for nuclear war, and the extent to which McNamara's public retreat signaled a change in his strategic outlook, rather than merely a rhetorical maneuver to counter domestic political concerns, remains unclear. McNamara continued to support aspects of the "damage limiting" strategy, including his endorsement of the fallout shelter program, even after the departure of Steuart L. Pittman from the OCD in 1964, and he approved the pursuit of a limited ABM system in 1967.[34] Evidence suggests that McNamara always held a nuanced view on nuclear strategy incorporating both counterforce and countervalue elements, and that whatever shift occurred between 1961 and 1968 was likely one more of emphasis than of essence.

By the late 1960s the evolution of U.S. nuclear strategic concepts had slowed down, maturing to a relative equilibrium they would retain until the 1980s. Donald Brennan, the cofounder along with Herman Kahn of the Hudson Institute, merged "mutual deterrence" and McNamara's "assured destruction" to coin the ironic acronym MAD, to poke fun at pro-countervalue arms control advocates like Wiesner.[35] Critics of counterforce targeting concepts retorted with an ironic acronym of their own—NUTS (nuclear utilization target selection). The debate between advocates of MAD countervalue targeting and NUTS counterforce targeting continued until the end of the Cold War, helping to perpetuate the notion, often implicit, that these two terms encompassed the only two possible nuclear strategies and were mutually exclusive. In the West, the common association of civil defense advocacy with counterforce enthusiasts such as Herman Kahn convinced many observers, including both advocates and critics of counterforce, that an inextricable link existed between civil defense and NUTS.

Contrary to the assertions made by Western civil defense critics such as Jerome Wiesner, civil defense bore merely a symbolic, rather than an intrinsic, relationship to any of the positions in the nuclear strategic debate. In the United States, both advocates and critics of counterforce, "warfighting" strategic postures agreed that civil defense would be a desirable component of a counterforce strategy, but they disagreed as to what threshold a civil defense program could reach without becoming destabilizing. In the United States, opponents argued that any civil defense measures would accelerate the arms race and increase the likelihood of nuclear war because of the probable Soviet response. An early version of this contention appeared in a September 1961 article by J. David Singer, a political scientist at the University of Michigan. Singer asserted that "our embrace of civil defense could have a markedly deleterious effect on our entire approach to the war-peace problem," as it would not offer a meaningful deterrent against either direct attack or nuclear blackmail, and "shelters and evacuation plans are likely to generate precisely those expectations in the USSR that will markedly increase their propensity to strike first."[36] Singer premised his argument that the USSR would interpret any civil defense efforts in the United States as threatening on the inaccurate assumption that the Soviet Union lacked a serious civil defense program. In 1961 Singer's strategic objection to civil defense remained exotic—he lamented "the particular irony" that "civil defense is being opposed by those who understand the problem least: the tight-fisted economizers and the Red-hating jingoists"—but it soon became a common refrain in debates over the desirability of fallout shelters.[37]

Physicist Freeman Dyson articulated an extreme version of this argument against civil defense in a 1962 article in the *Bulletin of the Atomic Scientists*, reaching the extraordinary conclusion that "only if we plunge into the vicious circle of building more and more massive bomb shelters do we risk the future of humanity itself."[38] Criticizing the civil defense program of the Kennedy administration, Dyson stated that, while he considered it "quite probable that shelters are ineffective," the possibility existed that "shelters may, against all odds, be effective. And this is why I am so bitterly opposed to them."[39] Referring to rudimentary calculations of the amount of fallout that would result in the demise of half the human population, Dyson asserted that the existence of an effective shelter system would allow the superpowers to fight a lengthy nuclear war that might endanger the survival of humanity itself. The physicist therefore made "a most urgent plea to the populations of the nuclear powers not to commit the supreme folly of building bomb shelters on a large scale." Dyson instead advocated embracing vulnerability as a nation to reduce the threat nuclear war posed to humanity as a whole: "Our present policy of peace through deterrence, so long as we have no bomb shelters, is a policy of finite risk," because "if deterrence fails, the populations of the nuclear powers may die but the rest of the world will survive to carry on the aspirations of the human race."[40]

Both American and Soviet civil defense advocates dismissed Singer's and Dyson's arguments about the strategic implications of shelters. Herman Kahn responded to these concerns in his 1962 book *Thinking About the Unthinkable*, concurring that "some of these and similar problems might be raised by a large crash civil-defense program—say, one that was initiated at substantially more than $5 billion annually." Kahn disagreed, however, that any civil defense would inevitably lead to a shelter race with the USSR, commenting that "I do not believe that the kind of program recommended by the present administration," or the substantial blast shelter program he advocated, "would greatly affect the arms race."[41] Furthermore, Kahn considered a civil defense program at least the size of that pursued by the OCD during the early 1960s as a logical investment even if the United States elected to adopt a minimal deterrence policy, as he considered it a necessary insurance policy against deterrence failure.[42]

A 1962 Soviet pamphlet on the role of civil defense in modern war characterized the notion of a "shelter race" as part of a capitalist plot to undermine Soviet security, and signaled that the USSR would not build more shelters than it considered necessary. Its author, head of the Soviet Civil Defense General Staff O. V. Tolstikov, argued that neither the USSR "nor any present government" could afford to construct blast shelters for tens of millions of people, as attempting to do so would "prevent the satisfaction of the material and cultural demands of Soviet people and limit capital investments in industry and agriculture." According to Tolstikov, "Our foes understand this and seek to lure us into a shelter construction race and by this means weaken the Soviet Union's economy." These enemies fabricated articles such as Dyson's to pursue this end: "The ballyhoo surrounding the question of shelter construction in the American press and radio," he declared, "is undoubtedly calculated upon its export to the Soviet Union in order to inculcate a state of atomic psychosis among us. Not much intelligence is required to recognize the Americans' intentions." Too canny to fall for the capitalists' transparent scheme, Tolstikov assured readers that Soviet civil defense would provide "the necessary shelters" to defend the population, while also utilizing evacuation and dispersal to keep costs manageable.[43]

Civil Defense and Soviet Nuclear Strategy

In the 1950s, the Soviet Union lacked a nuclear strategy in the typical sense. In the early part of the decade, the Soviet government understood nuclear weapons primarily as a means of eliciting respect from the United States, rather than as a usable means of coercion. In addition to Stalin's obstinate refusal to allow meaningful discussion of the military implications of nuclear weapons, Soviet strategic culture also limited the appeal of nuclear force. During the interwar period, Soviet military thinkers developed a distinctive school of military thought emphasizing operational art—the intermediate level of military planning between strategy and tactics.[44] Soviet strategic theory emphasized tanks and large infantry movement, with the basic goal of capturing and holding territory. The experience of World War II confirmed this thinking among Soviet military theorists, who proved resistant to reconsider it in light of the American nuclear threat after 1945. The primary mission for nuclear weapons envisioned by the United States Air Force in the 1940s and 1950s—"city busting" of enemy administrative, industrial, and population centers—served little purpose within the Soviet mentality, discouraging the Kremlin from investment in strategic delivery systems to match American intercontinental bombers.

Nikita Khrushchev hoped that the USSR's burgeoning missile capability after 1957 would help make "peaceful coexistence" a reality, but instead the Soviet Union experienced a series of setbacks that took superpower relations to the brink of nuclear war. Rather than interpreting Sputnik as a reason to "live in peace and friendship" with their communist enemies, Americans instead became terrified of the prospect of a "missile gap" and accelerated their arms buildup in reply. The shooting down of Gary Powers's U-2 spyplane in 1960, along with President Eisenhower's refusal to apologize for its presence over Soviet territory, also helped chill the Cold War into a deep freeze. Finally, Khrushchev's attempt to use assertive measures to modify the status of the city of Berlin on favorable terms for the socialist bloc backfired, leading to a nuclear standoff that ended in a humiliating defeat for the Kremlin. These disappointments impelled the formalization of Soviet nuclear strategy as well as the resurgence of the USSR's civil defense program.

To revive its fortunes after the CPSU's cancellation of the Soviet civil defense program in late 1959, the MPVO General Staff appropriated the writings of German civil defense authority Erich Hampe to develop a strategic justification for civil defense going beyond that of merely surviving nuclear war. Hampe might seem like an unlikely source of inspiration for Soviet strategists, given his personal background as a major general in the army of Nazi Germany, but his immense practical experience dealing with the consequences of Allied strategic bombing during the war provided him with a practical perspective they considered invaluable. After the war, Hampe entered the civil service of the Federal Republic of Germany and became head of that country's nascent civil defense program. Following his retirement in 1955, Hampe published a volume titled *Strategie der zivilen Verteidigung* (Strategy of civil defense), which so impressed Soviet observers that they produced a Russian-language version in 1958.[45] This translation incorporated an introduction signaling to Soviet readers that, while the author's background made it "difficult to expect objectivity in the political interpretation of facts and events," they could learn much from Hampe, in particular calling attention to his argument that civil defense needed to be "all-encompassing" so as to "prevent the paralyzation of the rear of the country into another unsecured front" in case of war.[46]

Hampe's concept of an "all-encompassing civil defense" provided a formidable rhetorical weapon for Soviet civil defense officers aiming to revive their service's fortunes after Khrushchev's decision to dismantle the MPVO. According to Hampe, civil defense in contemporary circumstances meant much more than merely a system of passive defenses against air attack, like those of the belligerents in the previous war. "The experience of World War II," argued Hampe, "demonstrated that the establishment of an all-encompassing civil defense is essential." Only such a civil defense would be able to achieve the goal of "defending the civilian population with the aim of preserving the people."[47] Hampe postulated that civil defense would be essential to securing the survival of the state in a nuclear war and "facilitate the comprehensive preparedness of the country for war."[48] These claims dovetailed neatly with the goals of the Soviet government in case of hostilities and also implied that, in light of the nuclear threat, the role of civil defense in the party-garrison state should be grossly expanded rather than eliminated. Following the transfer of the MPVO General Staff to the Ministry of Defense from the dissolved MVD in 1960, its remaining personnel seized on Hampe's work to argue for a revival of Soviet civil defense as an integral part of the defense establishment. By mid-1960, the MPVO General Staff redubbed itself the Glavnyi shtab Grazhdanskoi oborony (General Staff of Civil Defense), and its members convinced the leaders of the Soviet military to incorporate Hampe's definition of civil defense and its role in national defense readiness into *Voennaia strategiia* (Military strategy), the formal statement of the USSR's military strategy published in 1962.⁴⁹

Authored by a collective of Soviet military officers, *Voennaia strategiia* repurposed Hampe's argument about civil defense by providing it with an acceptable Marxist-Leninist ideological veneer. "In peacetime, preparation of the population for war is conducted in three basic areas," explained the tome, including moral-political indoctrination, preparation of the population for defense against weapons of mass destruction (that is, civil defense), and finally, preparation for military service. Echoing Hampe, *Voennaia strategiia* informed Soviet military officers that "all of these forms of preparation are interrelated and mutually reinforce one another."⁵⁰ Furthermore, the work explained that "the strategic importance of civil defense grows considerably in light of the fact that not merely the defense of the rear of the country, but also the mobilization of the armed forces in the initial period of war, depend upon its effective organization and operation." *Voennaia strategiia* made clear that the primary purpose of civil defense was to allow the Soviet state to continue functioning following a nuclear attack, and suggested that protecting Soviet citizens would serve only as a means to this end. "The primary goals of civil defense boil down to maintaining the necessary conditions for the normal functioning of all organs of the country's leadership in the period of war and the effective functioning of industry," it stated, adding that "these will be attained by means of the maximal defense of the population against weapons of mass destruction, broad and comprehensive aid to the injured, and the rapid liquidation of the consequences of enemy nuclear strikes."⁵¹

Eschewing the Byzantine classifications of possible strategic postures created by Western nuclear strategists such as Herman Kahn, *Voennaia strategiia* indicated that the military purpose of nuclear weapons in war would be the total defeat of the enemy, and made a unitary prescription for how the USSR should plan for such a conflict. As envisioned by Soviet military strategists, a future world war would inevitably involve the use of nuclear weapons, and the authors cited statements by Western military leaders to support this claim.⁵² The introduction of nuclear missile weaponry revolutionized warfare and gave the Soviet Union the power to "take entire countries out of the war as a result of massive missile strikes." The 1959 creation of a new service of the Soviet military, the Raketnye voiska strategicheskogo naznacheniia (Strategic Rocket Forces, or RVSN), reflected the importance of this new technology. *Voennaia strategiia* declared that the "primary goals" of the RVSN would be the destruction of enemy nuclear forces, massed enemy military formations, and "vitally important enemy facilities." Achieving these goals would in turn "enable conditions for the successful action of the other branches of the armed forces, for defending the rear of the country against enemy nuclear strikes, the rapid achievement of the military-political and strategic goals of the war, and, ultimately, victory."[53]

Soviet nuclear strategists therefore endorsed the concept of a preemptive strike. *Voennaia strategiia* stated that, at the opening of hostilities, Soviet nuclear forces needed to degrade enemy military forces as well as destroy targets in the enemy rear and effect its "disorganization."[54] The book ominously prognosticated that these would encompass the enemy's "military, political, and economic might," implying that the USSR planned to attack America's administrative and industrial centers in the opening salvo of a nuclear war. The work also warned that such a war "would have an unprecedentedly destructive, exterminatory character," with the effect that "entire states will be swept from the face of the earth."[55]

The strategic posture outlined in *Voennaia strategiia* superficially met the needs of the party-garrison state, but in practice it posed major liabilities to Soviet security. First, the USSR's nuclear strategy placed emphasis on the utilization of preemptive nuclear strikes, both to destroy Western nuclear weapons before launch and to gain the initiative. While both Soviet theorists and their Western counterparts concurred that in a nuclear war the belligerent that launches first will be much better positioned to limit damage to itself, Soviet ideological and political dogma stipulated that the Western powers would start the war. *Voennaia strategiia* attempted to square this circle with the rationale that Soviet forces would respond on a hair trigger to enemy aggression, launching their retaliatory strike "within minutes."[56] Unlike U.S. secretary of defense Robert S. McNamara, Soviet strategists in the early 1960s did not outline the development of a secure "retaliatory force" intended to punish the enemy even after the destruction of the USSR in a preemptive strike. Implementing the official doctrine in practice would place immense pressure on the leadership to escalate in a crisis situation, making it inherently destabilizing—potentially jeopardizing the security of the Soviet government.[57]

The second barrier to the implementation of the USSR's nuclear strategy in the early 1960s was the reality of the country's technological and military weakness, which denied the Soviet military the ability to carry out its conjectural scheme for defeating its enemies in a nuclear war. The authors of *Voennaia strategiia* blustered that "at the present time the Strategic Rocket

Forces possess the requisite number of launch facilities, missiles, and nuclear weapons, including those in the multimegaton range, so that it is prepared to fulfill the goals with which it is charged"; however, in actuality the USSR's missile forces consisted of a handful of ICBMs when the book appeared.[58] On both sides of the Iron Curtain, the theoretical formulation of nuclear strategy far outstripped the technical capability to implement it, forcing militaries to deviate from official doctrine when developing war plans.

Kennedy's Shelter Effort

John F. Kennedy's interest in civil defense dated to the late 1940s. In October 1949, Kennedy beseeched President Truman to "urge those responsible for civil defense planning to speed up this entire program."[59] Kennedy's support for civil defense continued over the next decade, and his victory in the 1960 presidential election gave him the opportunity to pursue the strong civil defense policy he had long advocated. Unfortunately for Kennedy, the Eisenhower administration left him a dark legacy in the civil defense field. The Office of Civil and Defense Mobilization (OCDM) had constructed a handful of shelters, done some preliminary research, and convinced a few Americans to build fallout shelters, but had not really laid the groundwork for the type of civil defense program Kennedy had in mind.[60] Upon his accession to the presidency in 1961, Kennedy sought the advice of numerous figures about what direction his administration should take with regard to civil defense. Frank B. Ellis, Kennedy's choice to replace Leo Hough as head of the OCDM, reported that the basic idea behind the 1958 reorganization had been sound but that real reform was still required. Carl Kaysen, a member of the White House staff, concluded that the OCDM was "functioning under outmoded concepts." He urged that the government either make a serious civil defense effort or abandon it altogether. Director of the budget David Bell and national security policy advisor McGeorge Bundy opposed substantial investment on civil defense, holding that other spending priorities should have precedence. Defense secretary Robert S. McNamara, meanwhile, strongly supported increased civil defense expenditure, particularly for fallout shelters.[61]

On May 25, 1961, even while his advisors continued to debate the issue, President Kennedy announced his intention to reconstitute and expand the nation's civil defense in a special address to Congress titled "Urgent National Needs." Besides breaking up the OCDM and transferring civil defense to the

Department of Defense, Kennedy's plan also endorsed a large federal shelter effort. This, in Kennedy's view, would serve as "insurance." As he put it:

> The history of this planet, and particularly the history of the 20th century, is sufficient to remind us of the possibilities of an irrational attack, a miscalculation, an accidental war, or a war of escalation in which the stakes gradually increase to the point of maximum danger which cannot be either foreseen or deterred. It is on this basis that civil defense can be readily justifiable—as insurance for the civilian population in case of enemy miscalculation. It is insurance we trust will never be needed—but insurance which we could never forgive ourselves for forgoing in the event of catastrophe.
>
> Once the validity of this concept is recognized, there is no point in delaying the initiation of a nationwide long-range program of identifying present fallout shelter capacity and providing shelter in new and existing structures. Such a program would protect millions of people against the hazards of radioactive fallout in the event of a large-scale nuclear attack.[62]

Kennedy indicated that his new shelter effort would "provide Federal funds for identifying fallout shelter capacity in existing structures, and it will include, where appropriate, incorporation of shelter in Federal buildings, new requirements for shelter in buildings constructed with Federal assistance, and matching grants and other incentives for constructing shelter in State and local, and private, buildings."[63] The president predicted that federal appropriations for civil defense would "more than triple," but he justified this expenditure with the assertion that "no insurance is cost-free; and every American citizen and his community must decide for themselves whether this form of survival insurance justifies the expenditure of effort, time, and money. For myself, I am convinced that it does."[64]

Kennedy emphasized that his shelter system would not add anything to the nation's deterrence posture. "[Civil defense] cannot deter a nuclear attack," he declared. According to JFK, only "retaliatory power" could deter enemy attack, and "if we should ever lack it, civil defense would not be an adequate substitute."[65] This statement contradicted the views not only of nuclear strategists such as Herman Kahn but also of Defense Secretary McNamara, who believed that fallout shelters would increase the credibility of the U.S. nuclear deterrent.[66]

On July 20, 1961, Kennedy signed an executive order making civil defense the responsibility of the secretary of defense, and charging that official with the "development and execution of a fallout shelter program."[67] This effort rapidly began to take shape. One important advantage of transferring civil defense to the Department of Defense was that it removed congressional oversight of the program from long-standing opponents of civil defense such as representative Albert Thomas of Texas. Congress approved Kennedy's $207.6 million supplemental budget request for civil defense in the 1962 fiscal year.[68] In September 1961 the newly established OCD within the Department of Defense, under the leadership of assistant secretary of defense for civil defense Steuart L. Pittman, set off on the task of creating a nationwide fallout shelter system.[69] Pittman's program had four objectives: the identification of shelters in existing structures, the development of additional shelter space where needed using tax and fiscal incentives, the marking of these shelters with readily identifiable signs, and the stocking of the shelters with food, potable water, medical supplies, and radiological instruments.

The Kennedy administration hoped to create fallout protection inexpensively by taking advantage of existing structures. The process of developing shelter space in existing buildings had two phases. In phase one, civil defense would survey all public and private buildings exceeding a particular degree of radiation protection and boasting a capacity of fifty or more occupants with follow-up on-site surveys of the buildings that might offer suitable space.[70] To expedite the survey process, the OCD developed a survey form that could be read optically by computer, adapted from technology used to take the 1960 census. In phase two, contractors would make detailed surveys of potential shelters to confirm the space and ventilation they offered, radiation shielding, and overall inhabitability.[71] Because existing buildings provided only a fraction of the shelter space needed for 240 million spaces, the OCD also hoped to use federal funds to institute the Shelter Incentive Program, which would have provided fiscal payments for the creation of fallout shelter space in existing and new structures. But congressional opposition held up appropriations for this purpose, and in the end the failure of Congress to fund the Shelter Incentive Program led to the resignation of Pittman and the eventual disintegration of the OCD's shelter effort.[72]

Modest compared with the expansive shelter systems advocated by the Gaither Report, the Kennedy shelter effort hoped to produce a large return on a limited investment. The Department of Defense and consulting firms such as the Stanford Research Institute conducted studies on the efficacy of fallout shelters in a wide range of potential nuclear war scenarios. These

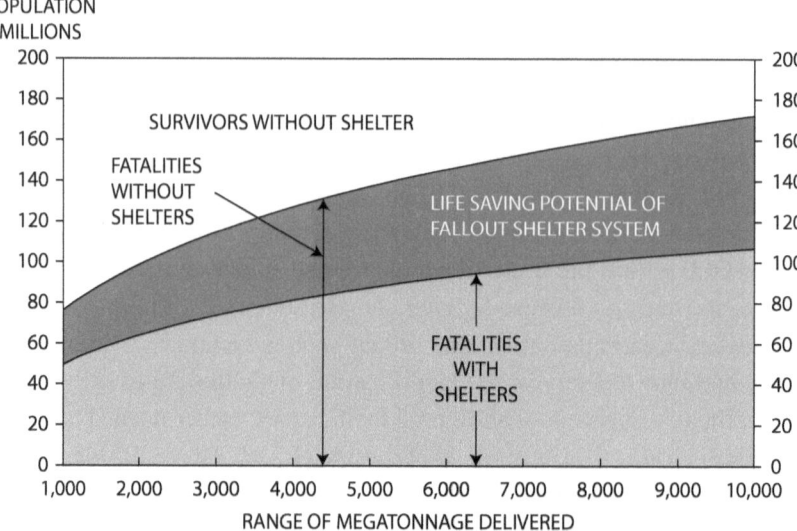

Estimated effectiveness of OCD fallout shelter system. Computer models indicated that the fallout shelter system sought by the Kennedy administration could save tens of millions of Americans who would otherwise die of radiation poisoning, but that a larger fraction of the population in immediate target areas would inevitably perish from the blast and fire. Adapted from Office of Civil Defense, *Personal and Family Survival* (1966).

studies concluded that the availability of effective fallout protection to the entirety of the population would save tens of millions of lives in a nuclear exchange for an investment of a few billion dollars. The complete system projected a total of 240 million shelter spaces, in considerable excess of the 1960 population of the United States—about 180 million. This "overkill" would be necessary to address the difference between daytime and nighttime population distribution. In 1964 the OCD estimated that, of a projected 1970 population of 210 million, 65.7 million would survive without any shelter, while the shelter system would save 48.5 million people who would have otherwise perished, for a total of 114.2 million survivors.[73]

Declassified Department of Defense documents reveal the extent to which McNamara concurred with this optimistic assessment of the community fallout shelter program. In a December 1964 memorandum for president Lyndon B. Johnson, McNamara reiterated his belief that fallout shelters would make a good investment. Proposing an annual expenditure of just over $1 billion for civil defense, he argued that "for a budget level of $5.2 billion, a complete fallout shelter system would be the most effective component of a balanced damage limiting program against large attacks." Furthermore, "at none of the budget levels examined would it pay to spend less for fallout protection." On this basis McNamara urged investment in fallout shelters rather than missile defense, which analysis indicated would save few American lives in comparison with its massive cost. McNamara, however, had no illusions that civil defense could prevent the deaths of a large percentage of the American population in a nuclear war. Even taking into account the possibilities of missile defense and additional offensive forces to destroy Soviet missiles before launch, "there is no defense program which we could expect with confidence to reduce the fatalities to a level much below 30–40 million even if the Soviets delayed their attack on our cities, or much below 60–75 million if they attack our cities on the first strike."[74] According to their Department of Defense backers, fallout shelters could neither preserve "the American way of life" nor prevent the annihilation of America's urban dwellers—but they could indeed serve as the "insurance" called for by President Kennedy.

The fallout shelter program was founded on plausible, albeit counterintuitive, assumptions about what the adversary would do. The Kennedy administration designed it based on intelligence projections of what the USSR's strategic nuclear forces would look like at the end of the decade.[75] At the time, Western analysts believed that the Soviet Union would build a force totaling only several hundred ICBMs, but that those missiles would carry very large thermonuclear warheads with yields of tens of megatons. They furthermore guessed that Soviet war planners would detonate these weapons on the surface to create immense fallout areas. Government officials acknowledged that basically nothing could be done for cities struck by such attacks, yet they confounded contemporary observers by developing fallout shelters even in cities such as Washington that were obviously Soviet targets.

They had a sensible statistical justification for this seemingly obtuse step. Because of the limited number of anticipated Soviet missiles and the unreliability of early ICBMs (which failed in almost half of launch tests), some targeted cities would escape direct attack owing to sheer luck—but those cities would be impossible to identify in advance. With so few missiles, the USSR would be unable to devote much "overkill" even to priority targets without reallocating missiles such that more cities would escape direct attack. As a consequence, even if the enemy targeted its forces optimally so as to kill as many Americans as possible, a fraction of major U.S. cities would survive—but they would need shelters to protect their inhabitants from fallout coming from less fortunate targets upwind. With luck and the support of other forms of "damage limitation" sought by the Kennedy administration, such as missile defense and counterforce targeting, even cities such as New York and Washington might avoid being struck.

Unfortunately, the Soviet Union refused to play along with the assumptions of U.S. civil defense planners. American intelligence agencies seem to have been correct in their assessment of Soviet plans for developing their strategic nuclear forces at the beginning of the 1960s. Soviet weapons designers carried out tests of a missile warhead of around forty megatons in yield and began work on a huge ICBM to carry it, the UR-500.[76] But after considering developing an arsenal like that anticipated by their capitalist adversaries, in the mid-1960s Soviet leaders shifted course. Convinced that numerical parity was essential for their security, they invested in a larger force of over 1,000 smaller ICBMs carrying warheads between one and ten megatons in yield.[77] Western intelligence picked up on this policy shift only after the fallout shelter program had been defeated in Congress. With more warheads, Soviet planners were in a position to target U.S. cities more comprehensively if they so desired—and there is anecdotal evidence suggesting that threatening U.S. urban centers was a major goal of the new policy. A fallout shelter system could still potentially save many lives depending on how the Soviets employed their weapons, but even though the gross megatonnage the USSR could deliver to the continental United States in 1970 was below early 1960s projections, the viability of civil defense was considerably less than hoped.

Unfortunately, the inability of the OCD to overcome congressional opposition resulted in part from serious public relations missteps committed by the Kennedy administration in the fall of 1961 from which it never recovered. Anxious about the ongoing superpower standoff in Berlin and concerned that the community shelter effort would take several years to develop an operational capability, the OCD attempted to bridge the gap with a renewed endorsement of the failed home shelter policy of the previous administration. The September 15, 1961, issue of *Life* magazine enticed readers with "a letter to you from President Kennedy" warning American citizens that "in these dangerous days . . . we must prepare for all eventualities," with the consequence that "the ability to survive coupled with the will to do so are therefore essential to our country." Unfortunately, the associated article about fallout shelters conveyed a glib attitude about the consequences of nuclear war that served to discredit the administration's civil defense efforts. Promising that "prepared, you and your family have 97 out of 100 chances to survive," the piece cajoled Americans to build their own home fallout shelters, illustrating a range of designs costing from $200 to $2,195.[78]

A few months later the OCD published a new civil defense manual titled *Fallout Protection*, which oversold the still-unavailable community shelters while offering relatively little advice about how to survive in the postattack environment. Originally, the administration planned to mail a copy of the booklet to every American home, but it abandoned this plan when the work received withering criticism from both inside and outside the government. Blasting the intrinsically classist nature of home fallout shelters, then-ambassador to India John Kenneth Galbraith complained that "the present pamphlet is a design for saving Republicans and sacrificing Democrats. . . . I am not at all attracted by a pamphlet which seeks to save the better elements of the population, but in the main writes off those who voted for you."[79] Antinuclear activists also found *Fallout Protection* an irresistible target in their efforts to discredit the administration's defense policies. The Pittsburgh Study Group for Nuclear Information concluded that "the government booklet lacks sufficient scope to be used as a basis for sound planning or responsible decisions by local governments, school boards, civic groups, or private citizens."[80] Despite these flaws, the OCD distributed twenty-five million copies of *Fallout Protection* through post offices and defense agencies.[81]

The Kennedy administration's overenthusiastic endorsement of home fallout shelters in 1961 attracted a firestorm of public controversy that severely compromised later efforts to cultivate political and popular support for the community shelter program. Whereas the civil defense programs of the 1950s had rarely found themselves the targets of outright hostility in the mainstream media, in the context of the Berlin Crisis the administration's ill-conceived civil defense publicity campaign struck a raw nerve that elicited attacks from outlets ranging from *Scientific American* to *Consumer Reports*.

The public transferred part of its anxiety about the possibility of nuclear war to fallout shelters and the people who built them, with grotesque results. A woman in California wrote the president stating that when she had told her coworkers about her intention to build a fallout shelter, she had heard "threats and slander." One told her that "a friend told him his neighbor had built a shelter, and it was his intention to wait until his neighbors had gone into their shelter and then he was going to block up the air vents so that they would suffocate and then when he was sure they were dead he and his family would take over the shelter." She noted that "I had a gnawing suspicion that this man was talking about himself and not his friend."[82] Americans' hostility to shelters only intermittently coincided with support for disarmament. An infuriated reader wrote to *Life* after its piece on fallout shelters that "Civil Defense should be replaced by Civil Offense. People who build shelters should be taxed 100 cents on the dollar with all monies to be used for offensive weapons."[83] One letter to Pittman pressed him to "SAVE the money for BOMBS or whatever is needed, but no shelters."[84] Recoiling from this controversy, Kennedy reined in his visible support for the civil defense program, even though he continued to work behind the scenes to convince skeptical congressmen to fund it.

These public relations mistakes placed Pittman in an extraordinarily challenging position as he attempted to overcome opposition in Congress to funding the community shelter program. During the early 1960s, Congress repeatedly denied most of the funds Kennedy's OCD requested. While the OCD received $207 million in supplemental funding for fiscal year 1962, in January 1962 longtime civil defense opponent and chair of the House Appropriations Committee Clarence Cannon reassigned the civil defense budget to a subcommittee headed by Texas Democrat Albert Thomas. Thomas consistently gutted the OCD's budget requests.[85] Shortly thereafter President Kennedy personally requested Thomas's support for the shelter budget—to no avail.[86]

Congressional opponents of civil defense belonged to both parties, but supporters were disproportionately Democrats, and notable Republican politicians calling for strong civil defense policy, such as New York governor Nelson Rockefeller, were members of the GOP's left wing. Generally, prominent congressional foes of civil defense such as Albert Thomas and Clarence Cannon were not known as advocates of reconciliation with the USSR, or of reduced spending on offensive nuclear weapons. Pittman grumbled in a March 1964 letter that Senator Stephen Young of Ohio, a vociferous critic of civil defense, had endorsed provocative moves during the Berlin Crisis that could have sparked a nuclear war.[87] Although their rationales varied, the enemies of civil defense on Capitol Hill generally shared a common concern for fiscal restraint.

After the OCD's initial stumbles in 1961, Pittman conceived a comprehensive strategy to overcome congressional opposition to fallout shelters. Finding that Kennedy and McNamara were no longer inclined to expend much political capital pressuring congressmen to rethink their opposition to civil defense, Pittman in early 1963 persuaded congressman F. Edward Hebert of Louisiana to hold highly publicized hearings on whether to fund or end the shelter program. Initially a civil defense skeptic, Hebert concurred, expecting that his committee would kill the program once and for all. Hebert directed the committee counsel, Phillip W. Kelleher, to draw up a comprehensive list of criticisms of civil defense to see if Pittman and the OCD could refute them. These included arguments that civil defense was technically impossible, that it would be provocative and make nuclear war more likely, and that it would have deleterious cultural and psychological effects on American society. Starting on May 28, 1963, the House Armed Services Committee held six weeks of hearings on the fallout shelter program and heard testimony from 108 witnesses both for and against civil defense.

Pittman and his witnesses effectively countered the arguments of civil defense opponents with their measured case for fallout shelters. One important component of this was an authoritative scientific case for the technical feasibility of civil defense. In 1963, Pittman requested that the National Academy of Sciences produce a summary of the state of scientific knowledge on civil defense. This resulted in a series of conferences over the summer of that year dubbed "Project Harbor." In the early 1960s, even scientists vehemently opposed to civil defense sometimes acknowledged that it could potentially work, but many of Project Harbor's scientist participants were originally skeptical.[88] The ultimate public report, penned by physicist Eugene Wigner, endorsed a public shelter system that was far more extensive than any the United States had ever constructed, even though this went beyond what many of the study's contributors had endorsed.[89] Pittman made extensive use of the Project Harbor reports to coax congressmen to warm up to the wisdom of civil defense.

Much to their surprise, the members of the Hebert Committee found their initial opposition to the OCD's fallout shelter program transforming into strong support. At the end of the summer, the House Armed Services Committee returned a bill authorizing $190 million in fiscal year 1964 for the Shelter Incentive Program. In a climactic debate on the House floor, Hebert's subcommittee described how the hearings had convinced them to abandon their earlier opposition to civil defense, inspiring the full House to vote two to one in favor of the bill. This triumph would not translate into funding for civil defense, however, without equivalent Senate action authorizing the bill.[90] Pittman now turned his attention to jumping this final legislative hurdle. To help lower it, he sought the support of a surprising interest group—arms control proponents.

Civil Defense and Arms Control

Despite the antagonism toward civil defense in American arms control circles in the 1960s, some argued compellingly that these were not merely compatible but complementary. A 1963 contract study conducted for the Arms Control and Disarmament Agency by the Hudson Institute, titled *Arms Control and Civil Defense*, concluded not only that there existed no reason why civil defense would necessarily be destabilizing, but also that "if a [civil defense] program were cast in a suitable framework, it would itself *constitute* an arms control agreement." Civil defense, explained the study, "is intended to achieve one of the objectives of arms control—to reduce the destructiveness of a war if one occurs," with the only difference being that "it is generally oriented to provide unilateral gains . . . rather than joint gains. There is, however, no intrinsic reason why this must be so."[91] The study's authors, including Donald Brennan and Jeremy Stone, maintained that the optimal solution would not be for the superpowers to forgo civil defense but rather for them to pursue it jointly: "Insofar as is possible, programs should emphasize joint gains to both sides and should preferably be pursued cooperatively." As a first step, they recommended that "the President," along with other "relevant high officials of the government," "emphasize that we are glad of Soviet civil defense programs and hope that other powers will continue to provide comparable insurance to their citizens against the possibility of a nuclear war." Such statements of goodwill might be just the beginning of cooperative efforts on civil defense, as "exchanges of U.S., S.U., and other civil defense officials, plans, techniques, unclassified weapons effects, and so on, should be encouraged."[92]

Arms Control and Civil Defense admitted that under certain circumstances some civil defense measures might be strategically destabilizing, but it offered rationales for why they could be the opposite. Its authors emphasized that the dire arguments of Western civil defense opponents that any civil defense would lead to a war hysteria or a deepening of the arms race failed to materialize in response to existing civil defense programs: "Government officials should point out that procurement of U.S. strategic forces has not been increased in response to the (reportedly substantial) Soviet CD program," they recommended. Certain civil defense programs might produce undesirable adverse effects if Soviet leaders believed that "they had been adopted for the purpose of acquiring or enhancing a strategic advantage," and therefore "any civil defense program should be adopted for prudential reasons only."[93] Report contributor Jeremy Stone singled out crisis evacuation as a civil defense tactic that "should be avoided," as it "might appear to provide a differential military advantage that would invite increases in both Soviet hostility and Soviet strategic forces."[94] On the whole, however, the authors held that civil defense "has only a marginal direct strategic impact" and that it "could lose many or most of its negative attributes if the major powers could pursue their civil defense programs in a cooperative framework."[95] This step would signal the benign intentions of America's civil defense efforts to the enemy, as well as help neutralize domestic criticism of the program. This tantalizing prospect appealed to Steuart L. Pittman, who attempted to exploit the arguments made in *Arms Control and Civil Defense* for the advantage of the OCD.

On September 2, 1963, Princeton political economy professor Oskar Morgenstern, a prominent advocate of minimal deterrence, wrote Pittman that "several months ago I developed the idea that civil defense might be an area which could be considered in further arms control discussions with the Soviet Union," and enclosed a memorandum elucidating his thinking on the subject that he had forwarded to Arms Control and Disarmament Agency (ACDA) director William C. Foster and McGeorge Bundy some time before.[96] In this document Morgenstern suggested that "a possibility is for the US to propose an agreement that neither the US nor the USSR engage in civil defense and specifically in shelter building (nor identify any existing shelters)." Morgenstern posited, however, that "such a proposal would make sense only if the SU does not now possess a *significantly* larger Civil Defense system (with shelters) than the US." To determine whether this was the case, he proposed that the CIA "make a thorough survey of the Russian system at present." If it determined that the USSR possessed shelters, then Washington could forgo overtures to ban civil defense and "the existence of a large Soviet effort should then be widely publicized." Either this outcome or a Soviet refusal to cooperate with a U.S. proposal to ban shelters, Morgenstern concluded, would have the result that "civil defense would receive the biggest conceivable push and there can be little doubt that this country would adopt a system going well beyond what is now being proposed by the government."[97]

The manner in which Pittman and his staff responded to Morgenstern's memorandum illustrates both their hesitancy to exploit Soviet civil defense efforts for rhetorical advantage and their enthusiasm for a constructive relationship between civil defense and arms control. Given Morgenstern's considerable influence with the Kennedy administration, Pittman determined that his memorandum deserved an extensive reply. On September 17, OCD staff members prepared a draft letter for Pittman that quoted the Hebert subcommittee report to the effect that "the Soviet civil defense effort far exceeds that of the United States, both in training and in shelter construction," but went on to dispute Morgenstern's argument that Washington should premise its policy on the existence of a Soviet shelter effort. "The presence or absence of a Soviet shelter program constitutes no direct threat to the U.S., so people can't get excited about Soviet shelter efforts," stated the draft, continuing that "a U.S. shelter program can only be sold on the basis of what it would do for the people of the United States."[98] Two days later, OCD staff member J. F. Devaney composed a shorter, less combative draft reply to Morgenstern, which also discounted the notion that "a decision on US civil defense would depend critically on a comparison with that of the USSR" and instead focused on the positive aspects of civil defense. "We see civil defense as being quite similar to arms control in the sense that both are directed to limiting damage," it explained, and therefore "a proposal to limit or reduce the ability to protect people against the hazards of nuclear war would seem inconsistent with the spirit of arms control and I could not support it." This draft offered helpful suggestions for more promising arms control measures that might be pursued instead, such as "the elimination of megaton-yield weapons."[99]

The brief reply Steuart L. Pittman ultimately sent to Morgenstern on September 30 refrained from specific proposals but incorporated an endorsement of the suggestion made in *Arms Control and Civil Defense* that superpower cooperation on civil defense could improve security for both nations. Pittman saw little merit in Morgenstern's proposal: "I do not see shelters as an area for a separate agreement as a phase of disarmament for reasons which I would be glad to offer if and when we might have an occasion to get together." Instead, Pittman wrote that "I believe that a useful development in the United States and other countries, including Russia, would be an appreciation of the ways in which certain types of civil defense can contribute to peace and stability and can, in fact, improve the conditions under which negotiations for arms control might proceed." Under such conditions, "I personally believe that at the right time it might be useful to establish contact with the Soviets on the subject of civilian measures to deal with nuclear catastrophes."[100]

Pittman's attempts to form a political alliance with arms control advocates exemplified his agency's willingness to modify its strategic justification for civil defense in search of political advantage. Pittman attempted to enlist the cooperation of the ACDA to help defend the OCD's shelter programs in the Senate, requesting that the Kennedy administration publicly endorse several concepts from *Arms Control and Civil Defense* and officially repudiate the idea that its civil defense program aimed to complement a counterforce strategic doctrine. On November 4, 1963, Pittman sent a letter to ACDA director William C. Foster reminding him that "as you will recall from our conversation at the time of the House civil defense hearings, I am anxious to see an expression from your agency on the relationship between civil defense and arms control and disarmament." Enclosing a memorandum, "Civil Defense during a Period of Detente," Pittman clarified that this document contained "some of my own thoughts which I would like to see expressed by the Administration in one way or another," and requested that Foster "submit a statement to the Senate Armed Services Committee using some or all of these points."[101]

Pittman's memorandum appropriated the arguments made in *Arms Control and Civil Defense* to neutralize criticisms that his agency's programs were strategically destabilizing and perpetuated the arms race. Both civil defense and arms control, he asserted, were two sides of the same pragmatic coin. "A moderate civil defense program," he explained, "has an objective in common with arms control in that both include the purpose of limiting damage from nuclear weapons, recognizing that the elimination of the possibility of war is unlikely." Fallout shelters would also build trust between the superpowers, as "measures which cut down nuclear damage in any appreciable way contribute to the confidence necessary on both sides for arms control and disarmament negotiations." Taking this logic to heart, Pittman concluded with a provocative proposal: "A more controversial point, but one which I would like to see expressed, is that the nuclear powers have a mutual interest in moderate civil defense activities. Specifically, we welcome the extensive Soviet civil defense effort because we believe that the loss of life in war should be limited as far as possible to a necessary and undesirable by-product of accomplishing military objectives."[102]

Unfortunately for the OCD, Foster and the ACDA refrained from endorsing the idea that civil defense could facilitate arms control. Had the ACDA acceded to Pittman's request, the fate of civil defense in the United States might have proceeded very differently. A declaration that the United States considered civil defense an arms control measure and would work with the Soviet Union to make it more effective might have exploded the notion that civil defense signaled an "aggressive" strategic posture, alleviating the political and cultural barriers to its adoption. In actuality, the dynamics of the ongoing congressional debate over the OCD's fallout shelter program increasingly forced Pittman to curry favor himself with hawkish congressmen who favored greater strategic arms investments. The prospect of cooperating with the Soviet Union on civil defense would likely alienate these figures, on whom the fate of the fallout shelter effort depended.

Pittman faulted the White House for the ultimate collapse of the OCD's shelter efforts in 1964, but blame for this would be more fairly directed at an eternal bottleneck in the weak contract state—congressional budgetary politics. Following Pittman's success in persuading the initially hostile Hebert Committee and the House of Representatives to pass H.R. 8200, he hoped to repeat this achievement with the Senate Appropriations subcommittee appointed to consider the bill, headed by Senator Henry M. Jackson of Washington. In December 1963 Pittman wrote that he believed that the subcommittee members were inclined to issue a favorable report, with the exception of Ohio senator and inveterate civil defense critic Stephen M. Young, but at the end of the hearings Jackson wavered.[103] Unfortunately for the OCD, Kennedy's assassination in November 1963 deprived civil defense of its single most influential proponent. In a January 30, 1964, memorandum to Robert S. McNamara, Pittman stated that "although Senator Jackson told me that he is not going to drag out the decision, I have it from many sources that he is reluctant to go ahead and is giving 'the economy drive' as a reason." The "economy drive" mentioned by Pittman was a promise president Lyndon B. Johnson made shortly after his accession to the presidency to restrain growth in federal spending. Pittman expressed confusion as to Jackson's reasoning but felt that President Johnson could assuage his concerns: "Although I am not familiar with all the crosscurrents of emotion involving this man, I am quite sure that he needs to be wooed and I suspect that this could only be done at this stage by a call or letter from the President."[104]

Pittman's request that President Johnson intercede on behalf of civil defense went unheeded. Throughout the early months of 1964 the White House gave no reply to Pittman's requests for the president to intervene with Senator Jackson. Just before the critical March 2, 1964, meeting of Jackson's subcommittee, Pittman called McGeorge Bundy and asked him to confirm from Secretary McNamara that President Johnson would support the Shelter Incentive Program. Bundy promised to call back with the response, but there was no call. Pittman recalled later that "I appeared empty-handed and Senator Jackson deferred action as he said he would. On returning to my office, I was given the explanation that the President appreciated the effort but that there was not enough time to resolve the matter."[105]

In retrospect, Pittman bitterly concluded that McNamara had not really supported the Shelter Incentive Program, and that the failure of the bill had resulted from the defense secretary's interference. Pittman promptly decided to resign. Before he did so, on March 3 he requested that Senator Jackson issue a statement that his committee's decision had not been based on a rejection of civil defense on technical grounds and to allow the OCD to make some of the changes in the rejected bill on an executive basis, as a "damage control" measure intended to prevent Jackson's move from completely crippling the civil defense program. Pittman enclosed a proposed draft of this statement, which specifically stated that the committee had deferred action because McNamara had related the shelter program to the Nike-X ABM, and that they should be considered together during hearings then scheduled for fall 1964.[106] Pittman's proposed statement contained no mention of President Johnson's economy program. On March 4, Senator Jackson complied with Pittman's request by circulating a letter that was in large part a truncated version of Pittman's proposal. It stated that the decision to defer action "was based on several factors not necessarily related to the substance of the bill. Principally [sic] among them is the fact that ballistic missile defense and the shelter program have been closely related and it is believed that a decision as to both should be similarly related." But Jackson added a sentence notably absent from Pittman's original: "Likewise, all programs involving Federal funds must be reviewed in light of the current program of economy."[107] Jackson's fiscal concerns, rather than the ABM, are the key to understanding his decision.[108] The senator mentioned these in his statement without Pittman's prompting, and documents from earlier in 1964 state that Jackson was concerned about government expenditures, while remaining silent about the ABM issue.

President Johnson's refusal to intervene on behalf of civil defense was a quintessential example of the mechanisms that perpetuated the weakness of the weak contract state. In all likelihood, fiscal politics resulted in the failure of the White House to intervene on Pittman's behalf. When Pittman's request reached President Johnson, he probably determined that civil defense was not worth the potential political consequences of compromising his promise to restrain growth in federal spending, especially in light of his ambitious legislative agenda. Unlike President Kennedy, Johnson had not staked any of his political legitimacy on civil defense and had little incentive to risk any political capital supporting it. Robert S. McNamara, meanwhile, was growing disaffected with incessant demands for greater military spending.[109] During 1963, Pittman had increasingly allied himself with voices in the military and Congress that desired expensive new weapons investments, which McNamara hoped to forestall. As H.R. 8200 portrayed itself as just the first part of a five-year program with sharply raised civil defense spending in fiscal year 1965 and beyond, McNamara likely feared that an open presidential endorsement of it would undermine the credibility of his efforts to restrain calls for higher arms spending. Although later documents show that McNamara continued to support fallout shelters, he had his own reasons at this juncture for not wanting to compromise the economy drive for the sake of civil defense, and in all probability he advised President Johnson not to fulfill Pittman's request. McNamara believed in the value of shelters but rightly doubted the willingness of Congress and the public to make them a reality: as the secretary of defense had told President Kennedy in December 1962, "I don't believe Congress is going to pass the fallout shelter program, and if they did, I don't believe the local community is going to support it effectively."[110] Congress posed the intractable obstacle to the fallout shelter program, not the White House. If Pittman had convinced the Jackson subcommittee to pass H.R. 8200 without any intervention from the president, McNamara would likely have been delighted.

The defeat of the Shelter Incentive Program in 1964 caused the collapse of the U.S. civil defense effort, which in turn enabled an increasing divergence between American and Soviet civil defense capabilities. Upon Pittman's departure McNamara demoted the OCD to a mere subdivision of the Office of the Secretary of the Army. While the Department of Defense insisted that this step was taken in recognition of the OCD's "operational maturity," in reality it signified that civil defense was no longer a serious priority for the administration. Pittman's de facto successor William P. Durkee now bore the title "director of civil defense."

The OCD faced declining budgets throughout the rest of the 1960s, forcing it to curtail even its more modest ambitions. By fiscal year 1969, the OCD had been reduced to a budget of merely $60.4 million, and then-director John E. Davis noted that while the shelter survey and marking efforts continued, they had fallen far behind schedule. Furthermore, the stockpiled shelter supplies that had been purchased under Kennedy would be exhausted within a year, and "while improved supplies have been developed, none have been procured."[111] These supplies included shelter ventilation kits—human-powered fans that OCD researchers had realized during the mid-1960s would be essential to preventing shelters from overheating during the two-week occupancy period they envisioned.[112] Although U.S.

civil defense had identified 160 million shelter spaces, these were not distributed to offer protection to vulnerable populations where they needed it, and congressional refusal to fund the Shelter Incentive Program forestalled the development of new shelter space.[113] In short, while the OCD had developed the rudiments of a cost-effective civil defense system, its real capability was limited and continued to deteriorate. Its institutional status declined as well, as the Nixon administration sought to conserve resources by increasing the involvement of civil defense in "dual-use" programs planning for both nuclear war and peacetime disasters. Defense secretary Melvyn Laird formalized this shift in 1972 by abolishing the OCD and establishing the Defense Civil Preparedness Agency (DCPA) to replace it.[114]

The DCPA proved even more luckless than the beleaguered OCD had been, to the extent that by the end of the Ford administration its capabilities had depreciated to almost nothing. Although appropriations for civil defense remained constant in absolute terms, thanks to inflation the DCPA's real budget continually shrank, and shelter supplies purchased in the early 1960s had become "unfit for use."[115] A 1976 report found that "if a large-scale attack occurred following an intense crisis of about one week, the current program could only add a few million survivors to the estimated 80 million who, because they would be outside the likely areas of attack, probably would survive a large-scale attack with no civil defense." Only after "at least one year of intensive effort" could the program "achieve its full potential of saving about 30 million additional people (about 110 million total survivors)."[116]

The December 15, 1976, meeting of the National Security Council called to determine the defense policy the outgoing administration would leave to president-elect Jimmy Carter illustrated the unenviable place civil defense occupied in the U.S. political establishment by the mid-1970s. Presented with a spectrum of strategic options including a revived civil defense program, the president replied, "I don't like the idea of bomb shelters in backyards. It reminds me of the time I was in Michigan and some shyster salesman tried to sell me one. It was a bunch of crap." Nelson Rockefeller, now the vice president, remarked that "the salesman must have been from New York," eliciting laughter from the attendees.[117] Secretary of defense Donald Rumsfeld called for going "from something that is practically nonexistent to some better planning," but clarified that "I am not talking about going back to bomb shelters."[118] Ford reemphasized that "I am down on civil defense—not one penny for it. Forget it!" In response to Rumsfeld's request for clarification as to whether he wanted to go ahead with the other elements of "a moderately increased strategic emphasis," the president concluded "Amen. Cross civil defense out. We are going ahead strongly with F-15s, F-16s, and A-10s. We are improving our capabilities."[119] Tellingly, the president did not argue against a revived program on the basis that it would be either technically unfeasible or strategically destabilizing. Like Eisenhower twenty years before, Ford rejected civil defense to ensure a continuing emphasis on America's offensive power. Thanks to the president's dismissive attitude, civil defense had literally been reduced to a laughingstock by the end of the meeting.[120] The attitude of his counterpart in the Kremlin, however, could not have been more different. To Comrade Brezhnev and his colleagues, civil defense was anything but a joke.

Opening the "Mineshaft Gap"

The Cuban Missile Crisis caught Soviet civil defense in the process of reconstructing itself. The CPSU Presidium had relaunched the civil defense program in July 1961 as Grazhdanskaia Oborona (literally "civil defense," abbreviated GO), but since the Council of Ministers had fired nearly all civil defense employees and disbanded local civil defense organizations in 1960, all of these needed to be rebuilt from scratch.[121] At the time of the crisis, guidelines for training many important categories of civil defense workers were not yet available.[122] GO had published critical regulations only months or weeks previously, which did not allow enough time to train significant numbers of personnel in them.[123] While public education campaigns were slowly improving, reports to Communist Party officials lamented that these continued to suffer from "many inadequacies."[124]

Despite these obstacles, the Soviet civil defense organization made some effort during the Cuban Missile Crisis to prepare shelters for occupancy. Historian Iurii Aksiutin reports that some Russians he surveyed recalled stepped-up civil defense activities, including educational efforts involving lectures and training exercises, as well as readying some shelters.[125] L. I. Oleinik, a construction engineer from Lytkarino, reminisced that "we dried rusks and prepared a bomb shelter."[126] It is unclear, however, whether local authorities took these steps on their own initiative in light of widespread rumors that nuclear war might be imminent, or whether Moscow ordered them in fear that the events in Cuba might soon degenerate into world war. Some of Aksiutin's interviewees reported that they remained ignorant of the ongoing nuclear standoff until after the fact.[127] In any case, civil defense never issued the "threatening situation" alert that manuals stated would initiate efforts to ready shelters and begin civilian evacuations from urban centers.[128]

Much like Val Peterson a decade before, the inaugural head of GO, marshall Vasilii Chuikov, entered his new position with the expectation that he would keep the costs of the civil defense program manageable. One of the USSR's most important generals during the Second World War, Chuikov became the inaugural chief of the new Grazhdanskaia oborona SSSR (Civil Defense of the USSR) after the Communist Party leadership established it on July 13, 1961.[129] Chuikov not merely gave GO the kind of recognizable figurehead the MPVO had conspicuously lacked in the 1950s; his impeccable military pedigree provided access to the Red Army's enviable reserves of political capital.[130] The revival of civil defense belied the fact that economy-minded Cold War optimists such as Anastas Mikoian retained their influence within the country's leadership, and the Presidium expected that Chuikov would somehow establish an "all-encompassing" civil defense while avoiding the kind of expenditures the shelter construction program of the 1950s entailed.

Chuikov declared that the solution to this riddle lay in an increased reliance on a more rationalized form of evacuation, dubbed *rassredotochnenie* (dispersal), that would allow the USSR to continue critical production even after relocating its population from presumed target areas.[131] Rather than attempt to build costly blast shelters for a substantial fraction of the Soviet Union's city dwellers, all inhabitants of target areas would ideally be either evacuated or, if they worked at a critical production facility, "dispersed." The difference lay in that "dispersed" workers would remain closer to target areas and commute daily to work their shifts. Therefore, blast shelters would be necessary only for members of the largest shifts at factories classified as essential—all other citizens would suffice with comparatively flimsy fallout shelters located in rural areas.

Even this relatively modest goal outstripped the resources available to Soviet Civil Defense in the early 1960s. Shelter construction had ceased at the end of 1959 and remained halted for several years. A few months after the Cuban Missile Crisis, the Ukrainian GO staff fretted to the Ukrainian Communist Party Central Committee that while the condition of civil defense in Soviet Ukraine had "somewhat improved" over that of the previous year, among the continuing obstacles holding up further progress was a lack of cooperation in returning shelters to usable condition. While the Ukrainian government had issued an order in March 1962 stipulating that Civil Defense regain control of the shelters built in the 1950s and ensure that these be maintained in such a state that they could be made ready for use on short notice, some city and regional governments enforced it only when convenient.[132] Just as in the 1950s, shelters served myriad purposes in peacetime, from storage space to repair shops, and local authorities proved loath to enforce an order that posed immediate costs to themselves without any palpable benefit. Perhaps in light of anxieties about the crisis in the Caribbean, Ukrainian civil defense had also developed an expedient plan to build 69,016 "light shelters" (*ukrytii*) in the republic's thirty-nine largest cities, with space for an additional 2,761,000 people.[133] Given that the Ukrainian SSR had some forty-five million inhabitants, even this effort would make only a minor dent in the problem. In conjunction with the USSR's continuing lack of workable plans to provide evacuees and rural populations with fallout shelter, the limited availability of blast shelters posed a daunting obstacle to Soviet civil defense planners.

Soviet efforts to train the population for civil defense also continued to disappoint. While DOSAAF's training campaigns had been one of the few areas of Soviet civil defense activity that continued after the dissolution of the MPVO at the end of 1959, they had suffered considerably during the USSR's civil defense interregnum. As of 1962 the second "Be Prepared for Anti-Air Defense" campaign begun in the waning years of the MPVO remained under way, and according to official statistics 36.2 percent of the Soviet population had passed it.[134] This figure—equivalent to many tens of millions of people—represented less of an accomplishment than it appeared. In May 1962, the presenters at the Fifth All-Union DOSAAF Conference admitted sheepishly that the results of DOSAAF's efforts in this field were generally "unsatisfactory," as "the pace of training is slow and the quality of instruction poor in most cases." An important cause of these shortcomings was a general shortage of civil defense propaganda materials such as posters and films. Official equivocation on the prospect of "peaceful coexistence" with the West had also further confused matters. The director of one collective farm retorted to the local DOSAAF committee's demand that he cooperate with civil defense training: "Don't stoke war psychosis, Comrade! We're fighting for peace, and you're talking about some sort of 'civil defense'!"[135]

Frustrated with the dubious competence of DOSAAF's civil defense training efforts, Chuikov soon began appropriating responsibility for this vital activity for his own organization. In 1964 GO declared that the commanders of volunteer civil defense units would be trained in its own courses, rather than DOSAAF's civil defense schools.[136] This inaugurated a trend that

Evolution of shelter plans of Ukrainian SSR, 1962–66

	1962	1963	1966
Number of blast shelters	10,082	10,287	4,661
Number of blast shelter spaces	1,448,000	1,532,170	670,100
Number of shelter spaces in mines	n/a	n/a	538,400
Sheltered in Kiev Metro	n/a	n/a	12,700
Sheltered in usable basement space	n/a	1,522,000	359,000
Fallout shelter in existing basements and root cellars	n/a	n/a	31,176,500
Rapidly constructed light blast and fallout shelters	n/a	2,761,000	11,355,100

Source: Central State Archive of Social Organizations of Ukraine (TsDAHO).

saw Soviet Civil Defense increasingly consolidate its control over Soviet civil defense training, with the result that by the end of the decade GO carried on its propaganda campaigns directly through state organizations such as the Ministry of Education and the Ministry of Culture, with DOSAAF reduced to merely regurgitating material developed by the GO General Staff.[137]

By the late 1960s Marshall Chuikov came to the realization that even with the reliance on evacuation to protect the vast majority of the Soviet population, the USSR still needed an immense increase in both the quantity and the quality of blast shelters to make its civil defense viable. Soviet Civil Defense built few shelters during the mid-1960s—Ukrainian civil defense declared unequivocally in a May 1966 report that "the construction of new shelters is not envisioned in peacetime"—but since 1963 GO had been developing modernized regulations for shelter construction and design.[138] In the summer of 1967, Chuikov forwarded a missive to the state and party authorities of all the USSR's constituent republics requesting that they "undertake decisive measures to increase the number of shelters" as well as upgrade existing shelters to meet the demanding new norms. The new shelter construction regulations rendered most existing shelters obsolete, making Chuikov's request particularly challenging to fulfill, but he reminded the USSR's communist rulers that "under contemporary circumstances, the possibility of a nuclear-missile war unleashed by the imperialist states cannot be ruled out." Therefore "the further modernization of civil defense and the increase of its readiness" was of "primary significance."[139]

Thanks to the savvy efforts of GO to integrate civil defense more deeply into the party-garrison state, Chuikov's pleas for increased shelter construction did not go unanswered. Initial progress was pitifully slow, however, for many of the same reasons that frustrated the MPVO's shelter-building efforts under Khrushchev. The Ukrainian SSR, for instance, allocated 9.7 million rubles for shelter construction in 1968, but the head of its civil defense found that progress in building the shelters was "absolutely unsatisfactory," and much of the money remained unspent. He blamed this failure in part on "the lack of attention toward these projects from the ministries."[140] By 1970 the tempo of shelter building improved slightly, but Soviet Civil Defense still struggled to convince other institutions to devote scarce resources to shelter construction.[141] The city of Nikolaev, a major shipbuilding center on the Black Sea, possessed a mere seven shelters in 1970 that met the 1966 regulations, with a total of 1,770 spaces. Sufficient shelter for the largest shift at Nikolaev's many factories and shipyards, however, would demand 55,000 spaces, requiring upgrades of fifty-seven existing shelters and the construction of seventy-seven new ones, thirty-seven of which would be incorporated into other buildings. Without a marked acceleration in shelter building, this goal would not be met anytime soon, as the plan for 1970 called for the refurbishment or construction in the city of only nine shelters with 3,600 spaces.[142] At the end of the year, the whole of the Ukrainian Soviet Socialist Republic boasted 2,032 shelters with a total of 338,390 spaces. In theory, plans called for over two million spaces, however, and the number of workers needing shelter was growing faster than the rate of shelter construction.[143]

At this juncture, the ambitions of GO received a boost from an unexpected source—the Kremlin's disillusionment with active missile defenses. In the early 1960s, the USSR had harbored high hopes that effective ABMs would become a reality within the near term. In the 1960s the Soviet military eagerly pursued antimissile technology, and the USSR's leaders initially rebuffed suggestions that forgoing it would bolster Soviet security. On February 9, 1967, Soviet prime minister Aleksei Kosygin told reporters, "I think that a defensive system which prevents attack is not a cause of the arms race . . . perhaps an antimissile system is more expensive than an offensive system, but its purpose is not to kill people, but to save human lives."[144] Enthusiasm faded, however, with increasing recognition of the inadequacies of ABMs. The extreme tolerances required even for an ABM utilizing a nuclear warhead to destroy enemy missiles meant that each ABM would cost more to produce than the ICBM it was to intercept. The imperfect effectiveness of the ABMs would in turn demand multiple ABMs for each enemy missile to make more than a marginal reduction in an enemy attack, so an ABM system directed against the United States would cost considerably more than the USSR's ICBM effort. The ABM technology feasible for the foreseeable future could protect against only a handful of attacking missiles, as it could easily be defeated by overloading it, whether with additional missiles, missiles carrying multiple warheads, or simple decoys.[145] In 1972 the USSR agreed to conclude the ABM Treaty with the United States, which forbade each superpower from fielding comprehensive defenses against strategic ballistic missiles.

Moscow's accession to the ABM Treaty resulted not from a belief that embracing vulnerability would help prevent war, but rather from a growing recognition that the technical obstacles to missile defense made it undesirable in the prevailing strategic context. Soviet leaders, convinced that the United States aimed to mount a first strike against them, feared that in Washington's hands an ABM system would be used to neutralize Soviet retaliation following a preemptive attack, while an extensive Soviet ABM effort would do little to forestall the American threat. In their view, a mutual agreement to forgo ABMs benefited the USSR's strategic interests not because it reinforced the "balance of terror" but because it helped reduce Soviet vulnerability in the prevailing geostrategic circumstances. In addition, the treaty signaled respect by the United States for Soviet military strength, which whetted the political leadership's cravings for affirmation of their nation's great power status. Instead of sinking scarce resources into ABMs, which promised to be ruinously expensive and do little to protect Soviet citizens, the Politburo elected to invest in bomb shelters, which, while still costly, offered a far surer route to reducing the USSR's vulnerability to nuclear attack, if only marginally.

Having soured on the elusive promise of missile defenses, the Soviet Union redoubled its efforts to strengthen its civil defense program. These included a marked increase in the pace of shelter construction, as well as planning efforts envisioning the prospect of surprise attack. In the Ukrainian SSR, for instance, both the budget for shelter construction and the number of shelters completed swelled dramatically compared with a few years earlier. Where Ukraine spent all of 9.7 million rubles on shelters in 1968, in 1973 it budgeted nearly 30 million rubles to build 353 shelters with 138,846 spaces—and this figure did not include an additional 193 shelters with 121,324 spaces incorporated into new buildings, the cost of which was included in its regular construction budgets.[146] These shelters incorporated features that far outstripped those of Soviet shelters built in earlier decades, and those of any shelters ever built in the United States. The 1970 update of the Soviet shelter construction regulations demanded that shelters incorporate not merely substantial resistance to blast and radiation but also elaborate ventilation equipment capable of keeping the shelters habitable even in case of firestorms. Often extremely large to take advantage of economies of scale, many Soviet shelters boasted bottled oxygen, carbon dioxide scrubbers, and multiple diesel generators.[147] Not all citizens could expect to ride out an American nuclear attack in these shelters, however. GO sought to provide shelters only for the largest shift of workers at each plant that would keep operating after most people were evacuated to the countryside, and changes in the classification of such factories actually *reduced* the number of people requiring blast shelters relative to GO's plans a decade before. In Ukraine in 1973, civil defense officials counted these as approximately 1.6 million employees at 3,087 facilities, out of the republic's overall population of over 47 million.[148] Additionally, Soviet Civil Defense planned to construct relatively elaborate prebuilt fallout shelters for workers at these plants who had been "dispersed" while they were not on their shift, along with their families.[149]

Along with the push to build more shelters, during the 1970s GO introduced updated training campaigns expanded to better reach all Soviet citizens, from young schoolchildren to retirees. Along with new classes for primary school students as young as seven, Soviet Civil Defense also launched a new mandatory training course in 1972 that was intended to instruct the USSR's entire adult population, either at work or in their places of residence.[150] The USSR's citizens found themselves bombarded with civil defense propaganda in newspapers, magazines, film, radio, and television, but it did not offer comforting reassurances that Soviet society would weather nuclear war in recognizable form. Instead, civil defense provided them with extensive technical information on the effects of nuclear weapons along with images of death and destruction in a recognizable Soviet environment.[151] Consistent with the institutional goals of GO, which took the possibility of nuclear war very seriously and needed to remain popular only with the tiny circle of men who ran the USSR, the propaganda campaign attempted to provide every citizen with the minimum knowledge needed to survive in a postnuclear world. But unsurprisingly, this effort did not have the effect of making Soviet citizens into enthusiastic supporters of, or believers in, civil defense. They little knew that the civil defense they largely ignored was viewed with intense envy by some of their capitalist enemies.

Gauging the "Mineshaft Gap"

The lull in U.S. civil defense activity in the late 1960s coincided with the emergence of a new group of articulate civil defense advocates—the Civil Defense Study Group at Oak Ridge National Laboratory—that played a preeminent role in American studies of Soviet civil defense during the 1960s and early 1970s. Enthusiastic about the results of the 1963 Project Harbor study, Eugene Wigner utilized his position as research director of the Oak Ridge National Laboratory to establish the Civil Defense Study Group in 1964. This twenty-member interdisciplinary team investigated questions ranging from the possible environmental effects of nuclear war to expedient shelter construction and the civil defense programs of other countries, including the Soviet Union. The Civil Defense Study Group's interest in Soviet civil defense emerged serendipitously from its efforts to develop a computerized keyword index of available documents related to civil defense, among them numerous translated titles of Soviet origin. In late 1965 it hired Joanne Gailar, a local resident with no background in civil defense, to develop the catalog. The lack of abstracts on the translated Soviet documents forced Gailar to read them in their entirety, and their contents made a strong impression on her. One day, Wigner called an impromptu meeting at which he asked all members of the Civil Defense Study Group to say what they would do to prepare if they knew a nuclear attack would occur the next day. Gailar recalled later that "the only thing I could think of that made any sense was what the Russians were doing."[152]

As Gailar discovered, Wigner "was extremely impressed" with Soviet civil defense, and he used his influence as a prominent nuclear scientist to draw Americans' attention to the Soviet civil defense program.[153] Wigner encouraged Gailar to write an article about Soviet civil defense based on the translated documents; titled "Seven Warning Signals: A Review of Soviet Civil Defense," the article appeared in the *Bulletin of the Atomic Scientists* in December 1969.[154] Following the success of this article, Wigner decided to free Gailar of her indexing duties and have her study Soviet civil defense full time. In addition to composing twenty articles on Soviet civil defense, three of them coauthored with Wigner, Gailar also oversaw a project to translate a Soviet civil defense manual in its entirety into English.[155] Lacking a working knowledge of the Russian language, Gailar remained entirely dependent on translated Soviet sources in her research. Civil Defense Research Project member Cresson Kearny undertook studies to determine whether the improvised shelters described in Soviet manuals would be effective and could be constructed by individuals without special equipment or training, reaching affirmative conclusions on both counts.[156]

Within a few years, Gailar and Wigner grew alarmed about the possible strategic consequences of the Soviet civil defense program. In mid-1972 they wrote the article "Will Soviet Civil Defense Undermine SALT?"[157] The duo announced in the May/June 1974 issue of the Defense Civil Preparedness Agency publication *Foresight* that their calculations indicated that Soviet civil defense could reduce the USSR's losses in a nuclear war to "about 4% of their people—very much less than they lost in World War II." They fretted that "what appears to us most surprising is that very few American leaders know at all about these preparations, and fewer yet have formed an estimate of their effectiveness."[158] Wigner made vigorous personal efforts to apprise politicians of the Soviet civil defense menace.[159]

Disappointed by the impotence of prevailing U.S. civil defense policy, Oak Ridge's civil defense enthusiasts took matters into their own hands and developed their own strategic evacuation plan. Firmly confident that the Soviet Union would concentrate a nuclear attack solely on American strategic nuclear forces and therefore not target their city despite its centrality in the United States' nuclear weapons complex, Oak Ridgers planned to develop fallout shelters within the commodious buildings of K-25 and X-10, facilities built during the Manhattan Project to produce the original atomic bombs. Their location some distance away from the residential section of Oak Ridge necessitated the development of an evacuation plan for the city. Oak Ridge itself boasted a mere 7,000 fallout shelter spaces for its 29,000 residents, but K-25 contained shelter for about 30,000 and X-10 an additional 15,000. The Oak Ridge Office of Civil Defense circulated a photocopied "fallout shelter and evacuation map" showing residents of eastern and western Oak Ridge whether they should evacuate to X-10 or K-25, as well as explaining how they would learn of the evacuation. "No lives need to be lost from traffic accidents or radiation sickness," it explains, "if we keep calm, drive slowly, follow directions, and let our actions be guided by the Golden Rule."[160]

Leon Gouré's abandonment of his studies of Soviet civil defense in the mid-1960s to focus on the Vietnam War opened the field for Wigner and Gailar, but starting with a 1969 RAND report, *Soviet Civil Defense Revisited*,

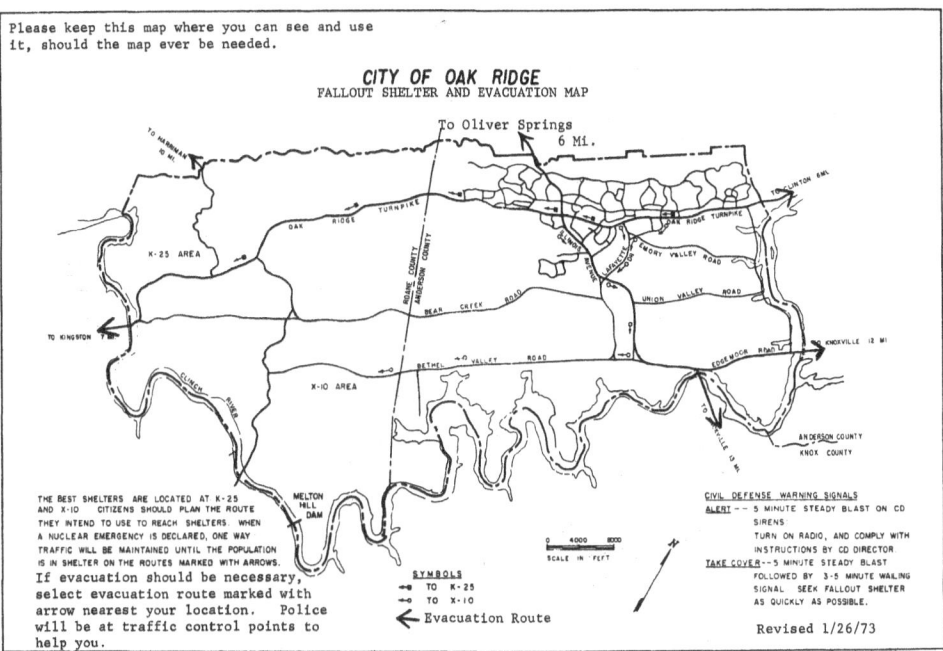

As part of its unique homegrown civil defense program, Oak Ridge, Tennessee, distributed photocopies of this evacuation map to its citizens in the early 1970s. Author's collection.

1966–1969, Gouré again devoted his attention to the topic.[161] Gouré departed RAND shortly thereafter, perhaps as a result of his leading role in an infamous study asserting that aggressive bombing campaigns could win the Vietnam War, which played a key role in convincing President Johnson to deepen U.S. involvement in southeast Asia.[162] Echoing Gailar and Wigner with his increasingly shrill pronouncements about the Soviet program, Gouré followed up with *Soviet Civil Defense, 1969–1970* in 1971, in which he tracked the progress of Soviet civil defense from his new position at the Center for Advanced International Studies. Although Gouré acknowledged the continuing shortcomings of Soviet civil defense, including a noticeable lack of enthusiasm among the Soviet population, he warned of "the increased scope and momentum of Soviet civil defense activities" and the "progressive improvements" being made to it.[163] Ominously, Gouré concluded that Soviet civil defense might possibly be "something more than a very large but otherwise routine defense preparedness effort."[164]

As analysts in the United States scrutinized Soviet civil defense activities, observers in the USSR found multiple propaganda uses for Western civil defense programs. To whet growing demand for information about foreign civil defense among its personnel, in the late 1950s the MPVO General Staff introduced a classified journal devoted to the subject.[165] *MPVO—informatsionnyi sbornik po materialam zarubezhnoi pechati* (Civil defense—information compiled from foreign sources) collected information from Western periodicals on civil defense, particularly its technical aspects, to keep Soviet civil defense professionals abreast of international developments in their field. Largely composed of summaries of open Western literature on civil defense, primarily from West Germany, Switzerland, and the United States, the journal also occasionally featured anonymous summary articles presenting dire accounts of Western civil defense activity, especially after the announcement of President Kennedy's expanded civil defense effort.

Selective choice and treatment of their source material enabled the editors of *Civil Defense—Information Compiled from Foreign Sources* to deemphasize the obstacles facing American civil defense and exaggerate the extent of its efforts. For instance, a January 1962 article on civil defense in the NATO countries states erroneously that U.S. law dictated construction of shelters in all new residential buildings.[166] Translators employed selective language to overstate the scale of the Kennedy administration's fallout shelter program. By calling the basement fallout shelters "*ubezhishche*," used in Russian to denote blast shelters, rather than "*ukrytie*," which Soviet civil defense used for its own fallout shelters, the journal implies that the United States pursued an immense effort to build light blast shelters for tens of millions of people.[167] The editors summarized some of the articles emerging from the raging controversy in the United States over fallout shelters without giving any indication of the growing hostility toward civil defense among many Americans. Characterizing a March 1962 article in the *New Republic* on the shelter controversy, they merely stated that it contained "the comments of various leading figures, politicians, and journalists on questions of civil defense."[168] The summary of *Nation* editor Roger Hagan's scathing August 1962 article on Kennedy's community shelter system simply repeats figures on the scale and cost of the proposed program, along with the effects of various attacks on the United States, omitting any mention of Hagan's antipathy toward civil defense.[169] Occasionally material slipped in about weaknesses of American civil defense, such as in the September 1962 issue, which summarizes Steuart L. Pittman's statements on the shortcomings of the OCD's shelter program.[170] Taken together, the accounts given in the journal formed a powerful argument for the robust civil defense effort sought by Soviet Civil Defense General Staff in the early 1960s.

In the late 1960s, Soviet civil defense repackaged the rhetoric it directed at the Communist Party in the 1950s—justifying its preferred policies for public consumption by attributing them to Western civil defense programs—for a wider audience. A 1969 work by propagandist Lev Korzun, *Grazhdanskaia oborona v stranakh NATO* (Civil defense in the NATO countries), explained that the primary reason nations such as the United States and West Germany pursued civil defense programs was their understanding "that aggression would not go unpunished" but that it had other purposes as well, such as preparations for aggressive war, the militarization of all areas of life in those states, and finally inciting hatred toward the Soviet Union and its socialist allies.[171] Korzun made the rather anachronistic argument that "civil defense preparations in the NATO countries are proceeding intensively and constantly increasing," while contradicting himself with admissions of the shortcomings of the United States' fallout shelter system.[172] Korzun explained that given its weaknesses and the statements of American military figures that fallout shelters would enhance the United States' deterrence capabilities, the fallout shelter campaign was really a "bluff" intended to bolster American claims to overwhelming military superiority over the USSR. The author drew a direct analogy between the disrespect for Soviet power embodied by Kennedy's impotent fallout shelters and Nazi propaganda characterizing the USSR as "a giant with feet of clay," reminding readers of the unenviable fate that Hitler's Germany received for its arrogance.[173] Korzun's logic inverted that of American critics of civil defense who argued that a strong shelter policy would be provocative, and implied that the Kremlin might prefer a stronger American civil defense program acknowledging Soviet strategic might.

Eager to further discredit the capitalists' civil defense efforts, Korzun expanded his study in 1970 to include Switzerland and published it as *Grazhdanskaia oborona v kapitalisticheskikh stranakh* (Civil defense in the capitalist countries). Perhaps recognizing that his statements that the weakness of American civil defense reflected Washington's contempt for Soviet power undermined his thesis that capitalist countries were expanding their civil defense programs, Korzun eliminated them in the new edition, but he took the opportunity to denounce Herman Kahn's theories about the possible strategic applications of civil defense evacuation. Citing Kahn's 1965 work *On Escalation,* Korzun charged that "it is apparent that apologists for imperialism seek to use the evacuation of the population as a means of nuclear blackmail and political coercion. It can be said confidently, however, that attempts at blackmail of this sort, as well as any other sort, are doomed to complete and utter failure."[174] In addition to elaborate evacuation plans, Korzun asserted that President Nixon was considering a new program of public blast shelter construction, despite the failings of the existing shelter program.[175] Korzun called attention to the opinions of "bourgeois specialists" who recognized the USSR's advantageous position to apply both shelter and evacuation measures in its own civil defense.[176]

Like earlier Soviet accounts of American civil defense, *Civil Defense in the Capitalist Countries* selectively presents evidence to bolster the case for the ongoing Soviet civil defense program, offering highly exaggerated Western examples to justify costly shelter construction and evacuation planning. According to Korzun, the imperialists invested in civil defense to enable their plans to launch an aggressive nuclear war against the Soviet Union as well as to blackmail and instill hatred toward the Soviet Union among their populations. Although at that moment these programs did not meet the demands of nuclear war, a fact he attributed to "the unpopularity of civil defense among the broad mass of the population," the capitalist states continued to devote larger and larger resources to overcome these weaknesses. Meanwhile, people of goodwill everywhere recognized the peace-loving policies of the Soviet Union, so much so that "even avowed anticommunists must acknowledge that it is unbelievable that the Soviet Union would start a war or mount a nuclear attack on other countries."[177] Korzun cited none other than Herman Kahn, "one of the most prominent military ideologues of American imperialism," to support this point, quoting a comment Kahn made in a 1967 *Der Spiegel* interview that "the Soviets are entirely uninterested in killing as many Europeans as possible." American aggression compelled the USSR to take reasonable precautions to protect itself, despite its desire for peace, wrote Korzun, who concluded that "under these circumstances the Soviet Union and other socialist states are compelled to take measures to strengthen their defense capabilities, including civil defense."[178] Like his counterparts in the United States, Korzun cherry-picked available data to make the case for Soviet Civil Defense's preferred policies while assessing enemy civil defense.

Conclusion

By the mid-1970s, U.S. civil defense had fallen into a nadir even as its Soviet counterpart had reached the pinnacle of its institutional success. At the beginning of the 1960s, both programs experienced renaissances after being defunded by their respective governments in the late 1950s, but the Kennedy administration's civil defense program failed to navigate the political minefield of the American weak contract state. Kennedy's scheme for a national fallout shelter system was the most realistic U.S. civil defense proposal of the Cold War, and came the closest to being implemented, but it still foundered in the face of congressional skepticism and limited popular support. Congress refused to fund the fallout shelter program not because of a strong conviction that civil defense was impossible or that it would be strategically destabilizing, but rather because of the intractable opposition of a few key congressmen motivated largely by the same kind of vague fiscal logic directed against the FCDA's shelter proposals in the 1950s. Civil defense advocates attempted to appropriate nuclear strategy for their own ends, whether by forging a linkage between civil defense and the credibility of deterrence, or by characterizing civil defense as a form of arms control, but both of these gambits failed. However strong the merits of the technical and strategic arguments against civil defense, they did not determine the fate of U.S. civil defense policy in the 1960s.

Thanks to its fortuitous institutional alliance with the military, Soviet Civil Defense rebranded itself as an indispensable component of the party-garrison state and managed to embark on the kind of civil defense effort only dreamed of in America. Where Kennedy's fallout shelters were merely ordinary basements with signs on them, occasionally garnished with cardboard boxes of shelter supplies, the USSR spent hundreds of millions of rubles a year constructing elaborate blast shelters. The leaders of the Soviet Union tolerated this expense not because of their belief that civil defense would enable them to coerce or blackmail Washington, but rather because of their genuine anxiety about the possibility of a nuclear war with the United States. Its considerable size, however, belied the fact that the USSR's civil defense was as much of an economically motivated compromise as its stillborn U.S. counterpart, particularly in its reliance on strategic evacuation to protect all but a small fraction of the population. This fraction actually shrank over the course of the 1960s as GO reduced the number of cities and factories categorized as probable targets, even though it expended increasing sums constructing more, and more elaborate, blast shelters. Soviet civil defense officials fretted constantly about how in the absence of strategic warning all of their preparations would be useless, and advocated for even more costly and elaborate programs that could plausibly operate during a surprise attack. Despite the contrast between the U.S. and Soviet civil defense programs, the largest "mineshaft gap" of all remained that between the institutional ambitions of civil defense and its accomplishments.

5   Strategy for Survival

We came closer than we realized. In the early 1980s, the U.S. intelligence community wrote off Soviet fears of an American preemptive strike as sheer paranoia. Neither the public statements of Soviet leaders such as Iurii Andropov nor increases in military readiness resulting in costly disruptions to the USSR's economy could convince either intelligence analysts or the Reagan administration that the Kremlin genuinely believed Washington might try to fight and win a nuclear war. Instead, U.S. leaders interpreted these as just a Soviet scheme to undermine support for Reagan's assertive defense policies. Soviet talk of a "war scare" was sheer hokum, they insisted, and they doubled down on steps meant to demonstrate U.S. resolve. Not least of these was a fall 1983 U.S.-NATO military exercise dubbed "Able Archer," which envisioned a nuclear conflict with the USSR and Warsaw Pact.[1]

The United States realized only years later that the Kremlin feared that Washington might be using this exercise as cover to start a nuclear war. In 1990, the President's Foreign Intelligence Advisory Board concluded in a highly classified report that "the Soviets perceived that the correlation of forces had turned against the USSR, that the US was seeking military superiority, and that the chances of the US launching a nuclear first strike—perhaps under cover of a routine training exercise—were growing." This body sheepishly admitted that "the US intelligence community did not at the time, and for several years afterwards, attach sufficient weight to the possibility that the war scare was real."[2] Given the razor-sharp tension between the superpowers at the time, this oversight could easily have triggered a nuclear apocalypse. An accident or technical mishap, such as the notorious September 1983 malfunction of the USSR's early warning satellites, was very liable to be misinterpreted by the country's terrified leadership as a U.S. attack, precipitating an accidental nuclear war.[3]

Nor was the 1983 "war scare" an isolated incident in the history of the nuclear arms race. While scholars disagree about the exact number of nuclear "close calls," the increasing availability of U.S. and Soviet documents has exploded sanguine interpretations holding that events such as the 1961 Berlin Crisis, the 1962 Cuban Missile Crisis, or the Andropov-era paranoia about a U.S. preemptive strike had little chance of escalating to nuclear war.[4] Given the reality of the nuclear threat, the willingness of U.S. and Soviet leaders to risk nuclear war is extraordinarily difficult to rationalize, particularly in light of the weakness of their civil defense programs. Even if a well-funded civil defense could theoretically save some viable kernel of civilization from perishing in a nuclear holocaust, neither American nor Soviet leaders believed they possessed such a program, much less actually had one.

The 1980s war scare demonstrates that civil defense lacked the straightforward relationship to nuclear strategy often attributed to it. During the 1970s, critics of détente pointed to the USSR's civil defense program as proof that the Kremlin aimed to win, rather than deter, a nuclear war. In the early 1980s, critics of the Reagan administration's civil defense proposals argued that any attempt to protect Americans from nuclear attack would be interpreted by Soviet leaders as a sign that the United States was planning a first strike. The elegant theories of nuclear strategists, however, made relatively little impact on the fate of Cold War civil defense. Both Soviet and some Western strategists rejected the premise that civil defense was intrinsically linked to "aggressive" nuclear strategies. The Soviet Union did not invest in an extensive civil defense program in hopes that it might emerge victorious in a nuclear war, nor did the United States reject civil defense because it might be taken by Soviet leaders as a signal of aggression and upset the "delicate balance of terror." The U.S. weak contract state prevented Washington from following a coherent nuclear strategy, and it instead promulgated hodgepodges of contradictory policies advocated by various interest groups. More surprisingly, the USSR also lacked a self-consistent nuclear strategy, despite centralized control of the party-garrison state and its defense obsession.

This chapter outlines the troubled fate of both superpowers' civil defense programs during the final fifteen years of the Cold War. A belief that the Soviet civil defense program might give the USSR an edge in the arms race inspired an ill-fated attempt by the United States to match it by pursuing an inexpensive policy of strategic evacuation. Overenthusiastic promotion of the Crisis Relocation Planning (CRP) program helped destroy what little legitimacy civil defense still enjoyed with the American public during the early 1980s. Furthermore, poor leadership of the Federal Emergency Management Agency (FEMA) during the Reagan administration helped undermine the quality of U.S. emergency management in peacetime disasters in years to come. In the USSR, criticism of civil defense became ubiquitous in

Soviet media even in the final months of Brezhnev's life, and the reformist government of Mikhail Gorbachev formally repudiated the civil defense policies of his predecessors. Additionally, the catastrophic consequences of the 1986 Chernobyl disaster demonstrated considerable inadequacies in the USSR's civil defense program, but it also helped spur its surprising transformation into one of the world's most effective emergency management agencies for peacetime disasters.

The ouster of Nikita Khrushchev in 1964 seemingly rescued the Soviet party-garrison state from a man determined to dismantle it. His successor, Leonid Brezhnev, rewarded his military allies for their political support by financing their ambitions to pursue parity with the United States. Khrushchev had hoped that a finite arsenal of powerful nuclear missiles would secure the USSR's defense, but the Soviet military leadership contended that unless their country matched America's armed might as closely as possible, humiliating setbacks such as the withdrawal from Cuba might be the least of Moscow's problems. Yet while Nikita Sergeevich failed to undermine economic support to the party-garrison state, his reforms mortally wounded the social foundations Stalin had laid for it. Khrushchev promised the population that the privations of the Stalin years were a thing of the past, and the 1962 Novocherkassk riots revealed that the party could not renege on those promises without risking massive internal disorder. Brezhnev's USSR could not demand the kind of sacrifices from the population for defense needs that Stalin regularly extracted with ferocious brutality. Moreover, external military threats had lost most of their power to impel Soviet citizens to sacrifice for the motherland—in part because Khrushchev had promised that the USSR's missiles had rendered such sacrifices obsolete.

Brezhnev's Soviet Union initially proved surprisingly successful at splitting the difference between the expectations of its citizens for improved living standards and its military's insatiable demands for additional weaponry. Buoyed in part by exports of oil and other raw materials, the party could both match U.S. strategic forces and provide every Soviet family with a television set. But the USSR's planned economy was maladapted for the seemingly endless strategic competition with the United States, helping drag it into the "stagnation" of the late 1970s and early 1980s. The institutional basis of the party-garrison state inherited from Stalin continued to exist as it had before, perpetuated by the Brezhnev Politburo's aversion to political or economic reform, but it failed to reproduce the defense-oriented mentality of the 1930s. The rising generation of communist politicians, such as Mikhail Gorbachev and Boris Yeltsin, saw the decaying remnants of the party-garrison state as an obstacle to desperately needed reforms. Once they gained dominance over the country in the mid-1980s, they went to work dismantling it once and for all.

The abysmal fate of U.S. civil defense in the late Cold War, meanwhile, showed how the weak contract state could no longer generate popular acquiescence as it had in the 1950s. Almost no stakeholder groups were strongly supportive of civil defense in any form, while more than a few were vociferously opposed to it. The myriad shortcomings of the crisis relocation policy endorsed by the Carter and Reagan administrations made these pitfalls even deeper. The CRP program proved uniquely ill suited to incentivize either interest groups or individual citizens to participate. CRP was essentially a strategic gambit intended to send signals to the USSR, and as the program stood to be inexpensive even if fully funded, there were few profits to be gleaned, and little to lose if it was crushed.

Civil Defense and Nuclear Strategy in the Late Cold War

Opponents of civil defense in the United States during the 1970s and 1980s placed nuclear strategy at the center of their critique. These critics argued that civil defense made nuclear war more likely because it sought to limit the human damage caused by nuclear attack, undermining "Mutual Assured Destruction" (MAD). The USSR's ratification of the 1972 Antiballistic Missile (ABM) Treaty and Strategic Arms Limitations Talks (SALT), they asserted, demonstrated that the Soviet leadership agreed that nuclear war could not be won. Proponents of revived U.S. civil defense efforts, such as Edward Teller and Eugene Wigner, meanwhile, countered that Soviet civil defense lay at the core of a "war survival" strategy intended to make the United States vulnerable to Soviet nuclear blackmail. The mere existence of the Soviet civil defense program, in their view, proved that the Kremlin rejected MAD. To contain the growing Soviet threat, they held that America needed both a bolstered civil defense and a more aggressive strategic posture.

By the mid-1970s some American arms control advocates became so invested in MAD that they opposed all forms of population protection. Some, such as Paul Warnke, the Carter administration's choice to head the Arms Control and Disarmament Agency (ACDA), arrogantly imagined they could press this thinking on Soviet leaders. Asked by a reporter for the *New Republic* in early 1977 about Soviet preparations to survive a nuclear war, he replied that "in my view this kind of thinking is on a level of abstraction which is unrealistic." Rather than "indulge what I regard as the primitive aspects of Soviet nuclear doctrine," Warnke thought that "we ought to be trying to educate them into the real world of strategic nuclear weapons, which is that nobody could possibly win."[5]

Soviet commentators dismissed this critique of their strategic culture because they thought that the Americans' missiles spoke louder than their words. For political and operational reasons, Washington continued to develop and deploy new weapons that contradicted the prescriptions of minimum deterrence theory throughout the 1960s and 1970s. To the alarm of Soviet military analysts, U.S. policy pronouncements wavered dramatically between the Nixon, Ford, and Carter administrations as the military deployed more-accurate missiles with multiple warheads. Without any clear definition of "official" policy, military planning leaned toward counterforce attacks against Soviet strategic nuclear forces. The Department of Defense evolved away from McNamara's "Assured Destruction" toward "Assured Retaliation," which sought more flexible nuclear employment options to deter a broader array of possible Soviet provocations. Secretary of defense James Schlesinger (1973–75) publicly flirted with the idea of planning for limited nuclear war, while arms control officials such as Warnke insisted that the United States eschewed such "war-fighting" doctrines. Perceptive Western commentators recognized this contradiction, leading Aaron Friedberg to conclude waggishly in 1980 that the "United States has had a strategic doctrine the same way a schizophrenic has a personality. Instead of a single integrated and integrating set of ideas, values, and beliefs, we have had a complex and sometimes contradictory mélange of notions, principles, and policies."[6]

Bewildered by the inconsistencies in American declarations and behavior, Soviet observers scoffed at claims that the U.S. government followed the "nonthreatening" policy of MAD. As Scottish political scientist John Erickson noted in 1980, "Soviet opinion from the outset was not inclined to accept what might be called the metaphysics of deterrence, or any arcane system of scholasticism that merely screened the American policy of containment." The Soviet government believed that the "real world of military procurement"—in which the United States was deploying new, multiple-warhead Minuteman III and Poseidon missiles—revealed what its capitalist rival was really up to. As Erickson concluded, "It was impossible for the Soviet Union to subscribe to the mutuality of 'assured destruction' (or MAD) when military reality appeared to suggest further expansion of US counterforce capability."[7]

Even though they lacked confidence in the effectiveness of civil defense, Soviet leaders embraced it as part of a general strategy aiming to maximize the chances that their government would survive a nuclear war. Arguments against civil defense efforts, such as those made by Anastas Mikoian in the late 1950s, could be expected to appear unconvincing in light of what appeared to the Kremlin and Soviet General Staff as a concerted design against their nation—even if they did not believe civil defense to be anything more than a desperation measure. Soviet defense analyst Vitalii Tsygichko commented in a 1991 interview that "it was well understood among the General Staff that the Soviet Union would not come out of such a war in anything like the same state in which it began the war. The general hope was that some pocket of undestroyed civilization would survive, perhaps in Siberia, that might serve as a nucleus for rebuilding the state."[8] Therefore, the goal of Soviet civil defense was quite earnest: to attempt to create preparations that might allow the Soviet state and some fraction of the populace to survive in a postnuclear world. The role of civil defense in Soviet nuclear strategy, so much as it had one, consisted of providing an ultimate form of insurance for the Soviet party-garrison state against the possibility of nuclear annihilation, rather than to bolster deterrence or facilitate strategic coercion.

Soviet writers rejected not only American strategic theories but also the analytical categories used to express them. The Russian language lacks words that accurately convey the meaning of many English-language strategic terms, encouraging the use of loaded translations chosen to discredit Western strategic ideas. Soviet discussions of enemy strategic thought rendered "deterrence" as *ustrashnenie*, a word with undertones of terror and coercion, while "containment" became *sderzhivanie*, which also implied that the United States aimed to force the USSR to obey its will. A 1988 primer on American nuclear strategy for Soviet readers explained that Washington's policy consisted of *sderzhivanie putem ustrashneniia* (containment by means of deterrence), dismissing and delegitimizing enemy strategy via selective translation.[9] Soviet writers refrained from using these terms to describe the policies of their own government for obvious reasons. The concept broadly referred to in English as "nuclear deterrence" or "MAD"—the idea that nuclear weapons would deter enemy attack—generally became *paritet* (parity) in Soviet publications, which meant something considerably different. This term reflected the Soviet military and political establishment's lack of faith in minimal or finite deterrence, as the experience of the 1950s and 1960s convinced them that only rough numerical equality in forces with the United States would elicit respect for Soviet national interests.

In addition to discounting the frameworks employed by Western nuclear strategists, Soviet commentators dismissed the strategists themselves as intellectually dishonest sellouts to imperialism. Herman Kahn received particular abuse in this regard. Not only did the introduction to the Soviet translation of his 1965 book *On Escalation* warn that "it must be underscored that military cadres should regard the theories outlined within in the most critical possible light," but it also suggested that Kahn wrote the work at the behest of the Mellon and Rockefeller business interests.[10] Soviet translations of Henry Kissinger and Bernard Brodie proved only slightly more flattering to those theorists.[11] A 1973 Soviet monograph about American "think tanks" characterized Kahn as "an odious figure" whose works were not merely intellectually worthless but dishonest as well, as he must have recognized that any attack on the Soviet Union would prove suicidal for Washington.[12] According to its author, Kahn's flaws exemplified a basic truth about all of his ilk: "The slightest examination reveals the total bankruptcy of the pretensions of the 'academic strategists,'" she concluded.[13] Such official pronouncements signaled to Soviet military officers and analysts that American strategic theories were ideologically unacceptable and suitable primarily as a means of better understanding the inhuman designs of their capitalist enemies.

Impressed by an extreme sense of its own vulnerability, the Soviet political and military leadership in the 1970s diversified its strategy for nuclear war to accommodate a wider range of scenarios. Although very influential figures in the USSR's defense establishment, particularly defense minister Andrei Grechko, vehemently opposed the notion that the USSR might not be able to regain the initiative and turn the tables on the Americans if they were foolish enough to attack the Soviet Union, technical analyses carried out by Soviet defense researchers convinced Leonid Brezhnev that the emphasis made by earlier Soviet nuclear doctrine on somehow detecting and preempting a U.S. nuclear strike could not form the basis of a sound defense policy.[14]

As a consequence, Soviet strategic nuclear forces expanded their plans to encompass three possible scenarios. The first of these was a refined version of the preemptive attack against U.S. counterforce targets outlined in *Voennaia strategiia* a decade before. While this option offered the best hope of limiting damage to the USSR in a nuclear exchange, the Soviet military doubted that the nation's political leadership would ever authorize its use, or that circumstances would allow enough advance warning to enable it. As an alternative, military strategists developed a second plan—to launch a Soviet retaliation while under attack from the United States. This launch-under-attack option (called the *otvetno-vstrechnyi udar* in Russian) would include strikes on U.S. strategic forces, as well as critical economic and administrative centers, with the goal of both limiting damage to the Soviet Union and punishing the enemy for its aggression. Finally, they introduced a third option—a purely retaliatory strike launched with whatever forces survived an enemy first strike, directed predominantly against "countervalue" (i.e., urban) targets.[15] Taken together, these war plans defied easy characterization within the Western schema of "counterforce" and "countervalue," although they included "war-fighting" elements. While starting in the late 1960s Soviet strategic thinkers increasingly emphasized the importance of a secure retaliatory force to deter a U.S. attack, Soviet nuclear strategy always sought to maximize the chances that the Soviet state would survive in a wide range of possible wars.[16]

Buoyed by this strategic outlook, the Soviet civil defense program reached its peak during the 1970s. Leonid Brezhnev's government granted vast funding to civil defense, which it used to launch an ambitious program of shelter construction. During the mid-1970s, the Soviet Union invested considerable resources in these shelters, completing blast shelters for about one million occupants and fallout shelters for three to four million occupants every year.[17] The increase in funding coincided with the formal transfer of *Grazhdanskaia Oborona* (GO) to the Ministry of Defense and the promotion of colonel-general Aleksandr T. Altunin to the command of the organization in 1972. A highly decorated veteran of World War II, the ambitious Altunin brought a new dynamism to Soviet civil defense.

General Altunin lacked confidence that Soviet civil defense could depend on the strategic warning essential for its evacuation plans. In an article in the February 1974 issue of the Soviet military journal *Voennaia mysl'* (Military Thought), he asserted that shelters would necessarily play the "leading role" among civil defense preparations, particularly as under threat of surprise attack "all others may prove insufficiently effective."[18] The colonel-general declared that one of the primary goals of civil defense was "the search for more effective means of providing the entire population with defensive structures" and conducting research to determine how to find the optimal balance of cost and protection.[19] Although Altunin hinted that GO would prefer even more investment to create a blast shelter program capable of protecting urban populations from a surprise attack, behind the scenes the Soviet government elected to invest in a smaller number of high-quality shelters, relying on evacuation and therefore significant warning time for most of the population.[20]

In private, Soviet officials fretted extensively about the weakness of their civil defense program in the face of a surprise attack. In a secret 1972 report on the readiness of civil defense in the Ukrainian SSR, marshall Kirill Moskalenko lamented that "all measures for the protection of the population are premised on the availability of the warning period" and that civil defense had not planned what it would do "in the extremely difficult circumstances of the surprise outbreak of nuclear war." Moskalenko concluded that, "obviously, this colossal vulnerability must be corrected."[21] Shortly thereafter the Ministry of Defense directed that both the armed forces and civil defense prepare for surprise nuclear attack, and regional civil defense organizations began drawing up plans accordingly.[22] In 1974, the commander of the Carpathian Military District reported that "under these challenging conditions the possibilities of action by civil defense are extremely limited" and that these obstacles could be overcome only with "thorough preparations," especially increasing the number of blast and fallout shelters.[23]

In addition to fears that nuclear attack might occur without a preceding period of strategic warning, research and testing during the 1960s and early 1970s revealed that even under ideal circumstances GO's evacuation plans would be difficult to actualize. In 1966 General Chuikov criticized the poor state of existing evacuation efforts, including inadequate accounting of populations to be evacuated, inefficient allocation of available transportation, and troubling mismatches between the plans of cities evacuating their citizens and the districts receiving them.[24] For instance, Chuikov noted that Moscow's plans to evacuate its residents through waypoints would result in massive backlogs, leaving hundreds of thousands waiting in those cities for days or even weeks before departing for their final destinations. Acknowledging that during a period of strategic warning the use of automobiles and trucks would be difficult owing to shortages of drivers and fuel, he ordered that evacuation plans emphasize trains instead.[25] Furthermore, tests in Ukraine to determine how quickly civilians could construct the improvised shelters envisioned in civil defense plans found that these would take several days to complete—far longer than hoped.[26] Over the next several years Soviet civil defense worked to overcome these challenges, shortening the predicted time to complete evacuations and developing better methods for use of the basements of rural buildings and root cellars as improvised fallout shelters, but overwhelming problems remained.[27] In 1972 Marshall Moskalenko disapprovingly concluded that plans for the evacuation of Ukrainian cities remained "poorly developed" and would take too long to implement. Evacuation of Kiev would require forty hours, and Kharkov fifty. More worryingly, he felt that ordering the evacuation would result in chaos, commenting that "it is unlikely that even the most stringent measures of maintaining public order can keep people in cities for long after an evacuation is ordered."[28]

Soviet civil defense propaganda put a positive spin on the numerous challenges of the evacuation policy, but GO's goal of making its plans realizable necessitated admitting some of its shortcomings. Civil defense publications asserted that the combination of urban evacuation and blast shelters would be highly effective. One 1969 manual stated that it "could reduce the losses among the population of major cities in a nuclear missile attack by 90–95 percent."[29] In January 1975 DOSAAF's magazine published an article about a civil defense exercise at a collective farm in which General Altunin and two members of the Moscow oblast government approvingly observed preparations to provide fallout shelter to urban evacuees. In addition to the commodious basement of one of the many multistory apartment buildings on the collective farm, which boasted a fully equipped built-in fallout shelter, residents of more traditional homes modeled how good Soviet citizens would help one another during a nuclear war. Altunin and the officials visited one ordinary rural house with a basement and a root cellar, both of them outfitted as improvised fallout shelters. They asked the housewife:

"How many people are there in your family?"

"Three."

"One fallout shelter would've been enough."

"But won't evacuees be arriving from the city? What would I do with them, if there's radiation?"

"Now that's thinking ahead!," concluded the article.[30]

The neighborly Soviet housewife might be waiting a long time for her urban guests, however, as they probably would be making their way to her on foot. In redeveloping its evacuation plans, Soviet civil defense discovered that the USSR's available transportation resources could accommodate merely a fraction of the urban population, meaning that many unlucky citizens would have to walk. The 1977 manual for the mandatory adult civil defense training course detailed how citizens would arrive at an evacuation point carrying a minimum of their belongings, after which authorities would register them and determine where they should go and by what means. Those not lucky enough to travel by vehicle would join "columns" and make an organized march to their destinations, even in unforgiving weather conditions and at night. The manual refrained from informing them that some would be traveling tens of kilometers in this arduous fashion.[31] Recognizing how little this portrayal of evacuation would appeal to most Soviet citizens, civil defense informed them that "it is critical that everyone understands that these difficulties and deprivations are unavoidable, that they must be tolerated to save life, and that therefore it is the duty of every citizen of the USSR to obey the orders of responsible authorities."[32] The earnest portrayal of the hardships of evacuation in Soviet propaganda offered scant comfort to the USSR's citizens.

The American notion that evacuation might prove a useful means of coercion in an international crisis left Soviet officials flabbergasted. Incredulous of Western strategic theories that conflated any preparation to survive a nuclear war with a determination to start or threaten one, they considered evacuation an essential, if utterly desperate, expedient that might be the only way to save most of their citizens from annihilation in a nuclear war. Chastening experiences taught Soviet civil defense that strategic evacuation would not provide a simple solution to the challenge of protecting civilians from nuclear attack. Soon the government of the United States would learn the same hard lesson.

The Wizards of Armageddon and Strategic Evacuation

Unlike the Soviet Union, the United States possessed a small but influential body of civilian nuclear strategists who played an important role in shaping debates on both nuclear strategy and civil defense policy. In the 1950s, thinkers such as Herman Kahn generally favored costly public blast shelter programs, but in the mid-1960s some of them became enamored with strategic evacuation as their thinking evolved about the probable form a nuclear war would take. At first their opinions made little impact on U.S. civil defense policy, but Soviet civil defense plans for strategic evacuation ultimately clinched the argument in their favor, resulting in the adoption of an analogous scheme by American civil defense in the late 1970s.

In the 1970s, the USSR's civil defense evacuation plans drove a growing belief in the American defense community that the Kremlin might evacuate Soviet cities in a nuclear crisis to put pressure on the United States, inspiring arguments that the United States might need similar capabilities to retain parity. In 1971 Leon Gouré expressed his alarm about "the increased scope and momentum of Soviet civil defense activities," claiming that "Soviet capabilities to accomplish a large-scale evacuation of its major cities is [*sic*] undoubtedly improving." He warned that "this could provide Moscow with a major advantage in a negotiating situation with the West. One cannot overlook also the possibility that once the evacuation has been successfully accomplished the Soviet leaders may be greatly tempted to exploit this favorable and possibly unique situation to launch a first strike."[33] In the view of some analysts, such as Kahn and Gouré, the improved Soviet strategic capability resulting from its MIRVed SS-18 and SS-19 intercontinental ballistic missiles (ICBMs), in conjunction with its civil defense program, could allow the USSR to successfully mount, or at least plausibly threaten, limited nuclear attacks such as "demonstration strikes," "city exchanges," or even a comprehensive counterforce attack designed to destroy American strategic nuclear forces while causing the minimum possible number of civilian casualties. By this logic, the USSR's civil defense could conceivably help make Soviet nuclear threats credible even if the program could not protect citizens from a nuclear attack.

Many in the American defense community concurred with Gouré's worries, even if they did not necessarily agree about their magnitude. In February 1972, defense secretary Melvin Laird (1969–73) announced that the nation's civil defense program would reorient itself to emphasize crisis activities, including maintaining the current shelter system with an eye toward crisis use in addition to "evacuation planning guidance for high-risk areas."[34] Thus began the efforts of the Defense Civil Preparedness Agency (DCPA) in pursuit of what it dubbed crisis relocation planning.

The DCPA could not implement CRP immediately, as neither it nor its predecessor agencies possessed practical experience planning for strategic evacuation. To overcome these obstacles, the agency initiated a pilot project in San Antonio, Texas, in 1973. This experience allowed the DCPA to develop a preliminary manual for CRP. With their new manual in hand, DCPA officials trained federal-state teams in CRP and launched nine additional pilot projects. At the direction of the Pentagon, in 1976 the agency began working with the states on the general implementation of crisis relocation plans, and by the spring of 1979 such efforts were under way in all fifty states. The DCPA incorporated a chapter on crisis relocation in its February 1977 manual for citizens, *Protection in the Nuclear Age*.[35] The DCPA understood, however, that the United States remained far from an operational strategic evacuation capability, instead characterizing its accomplishments as "a modest start."[36] Its officials believed that even with full funding, the CRP program would require at least until the mid-1980s to become operational.[37]

The DCPA's increasing involvement in emergency management planning for peacetime as well as nuclear hazards during the mid-1970s proved a troublesome burden, as the agency gained new responsibilities while retaining the anemic budget of its already-underfunded predecessor. Between 1972 and 1976 the DCPA developed plans for "on-site assistance" in nonmilitary emergencies, and it continued the practice of its predecessors of providing matching funds and practical assistance to state emergency management agencies.[38] To make matters worse, the Nixon administration's 1973 abolition of the Office of Emergency Planning and the reallocation of its emergency management functions to the Department of Housing and Urban Development left the United States' federal emergency management planning fragmented and disorganized.[39] In light of the DCPA's limited funding, some officials, including defense secretary James R. Schlesinger and his successor Donald Rumsfeld (1975–77), argued that the agency should divest itself entirely of its peacetime emergency management functions and concentrate exclusively on its plans for nuclear war. This move elicited howls of protest both from the states and from the DCPA itself, which recognized that state and local cooperation with civil defense planning could be jeopardized without the carrot offered by the dual-use programs.[40] Congressional action rescued the DCPA from this impasse by boosting the DCPA's budget and enacting legal changes to authorize the use of these funds for dual-use programs.[41] Partially in response to this episode, in early 1977 the Joint Committee on Defense Production, chaired by Senator William Proxmire of Wisconsin, recommended that all federal emergency management functions, including those of the DCPA, be merged into a single independent agency, the Federal Preparedness Administration.[42]

More than ever, civil defense in the United States suffered from "guilt by association" owing to the increasing overlap between enthusiasm for civil defense and skepticism of arms control and détente. An example of this mentality appeared in Paul Nitze's January 1976 *Foreign Affairs* article "Ensuring Security in the Era of Détente," which charged that, in light of the Soviet civil defense program, the Kremlin obviously aimed to "produce a theoretical war-winning capability."[43] Unlike during the fallout shelter campaign of the early 1960s, when civil defense advocates could be found on both sides of the political aisle, during the 1970s those favoring a bolstered civil defense effort increasingly hailed from the ranks of conservative Republican hawks. The association between fears of Soviet civil defense and advocacy of continued investment in offensive nuclear weapons as well as "limited nuclear use options" alienated proponents of arms control and détente both inside and outside the government against further U.S. investments in civil defense.

Soon proponents of détente and disarmament decided to counter shrill warnings about the menace of Soviet civil defense by arguing it was really just a figment of their opponents' imaginations. Physicist and arms control advocate Sidney Drell pioneered this rhetorical strategy in a debate with Arthur Broyles and Eugene Wigner appearing in the pages of *Physics Today* in April 1976. When Broyles and Wigner contradicted Drell's assertion that the development of civil defense evacuation plans "could be viewed with alarm by an opponent as preparation for a first strike" (a sentiment with which they expressed agreement) by chiding him for failing to take the existence of Soviet evacuation plans into account, Drell swung back with a charge that Soviet civil defense was too feeble and incompetent to be worthy of American concern. "To the best of my information no evidence exists that [the Soviets] have in fact exercised a civil defense system capable of massive population relocation or evacuation," he wrote. Acknowledging that the Soviet program was both more extensive and better funded than its American counterpart, Drell shifted the goalposts by declaring that "I believe that in view of the unprecedentedly large scale of the nationwide disaster we are considering, an effective civil defense program must also include, as one of its components, full-scale rehearsals and survival living exercises involving the population."[44] He then cited the preface of one of the Soviet civil defense manuals translated by the Oak Ridge National Laboratory (ORNL) Civil Defense Research Project, which concluded that, in light of the inadequate air-supply requirement named for shelters, "the Soviet Union has not conducted mass shelter living experiments or even simulated ones as is the case in the US."[45] Drell asserted that "in my judgment, plans and manuals, on the one hand, and an effective operating system, on the other, are very different things!," implying that Soviet civil defense posed no threat and Washington could safely ignore it.

In 1976 Leon Gouré published his magnum opus, *War Survival in Soviet Strategy: USSR Civil Defense*, which asserts that "the Soviet Union has the largest and most comprehensive war-survival program in the world today."[46] Warning that "Moscow categorically rejects any concept of security based on a balance of 'mutual assured destruction'" and that "the advent of 'detente' in U.S.-Soviet relations has not led to any decline in Moscow's efforts to continue to improve Soviet war-survival capability," Gouré found that the investment of an estimated $20 billion in civil defense during the previous several decades had "already provided the Soviet Union with a considerable capability" to survive a nuclear war and recover from it.[47] Moreover, Gouré cited Soviet publications to support the claim that "Soviet military analysts are well aware of the asymmetries in Soviet and U.S. war-survival capabilities," which he characterized as "one of the factors which influence the Soviet belief that the 'correlation of world forces' is shifting in favor of the USSR." Although Gouré remained nominally agnostic as to whether the USSR could actually win a nuclear war, he remarked that the Soviet advantage in civil defense "bears importantly on Moscow's strategic and risk calculations and on assessments of the probable outcome of a nuclear war between the USSR and the United States."[48]

Critics of rapprochement with the Soviet Union found Gouré's arguments irresistible, and soon repackaged them for a popular audience. In 1977, Richard Pipes, Harvard historian and member of "Team B" (a group of outside experts engaged to critique CIA analyses of the USSR noted for their hawkish appraisal of Soviet intentions), published an article in *Commentary* reiterating Gouré's argument titled "Why the Soviet Union Thinks It Could Fight and Win a Nuclear War."[49] For his part, coarchitect of détente Henry Kissinger pooh-poohed these alarmist views. "[The Soviet] civil defense program poses no major problems," he insisted in a January 1977 meeting with the General Advisory Committee on Arms Control and Disarmament, as "assuming they could evacuate their cities, the US could move to launch on warning." In Kissinger's view, the Soviet shelter program had a "strategic" aspect and a "moral" one consisting of "responsibility to a portion of the population." Since the USSR's civil defense did not give the Kremlin a strategic "decisive edge," Kissinger concluded perceptively that its main purpose had to be saving lives rather than bolstering Soviet power.[50]

CRP and the Creation of FEMA

The breakdown in détente during the administration of president Jimmy Carter (1977–81) helped restore the flagging fortunes of civil defense in the United States. Carter initially lacked enthusiasm for either the nuclear arms race or civil defense, yet by the time he left office he threw his support behind both greater arms spending and CRP. Concerns about Soviet civil defense tipped the scales in the favor of advocates of a stronger American civil defense policy. In September 1978 Carter signed Presidential Directive-41 (PD-41), which both declared civil defense an integral component of the United States' strategic posture and specifically endorsed the CRP concept.

The invocation of Soviet civil defense by critics of détente such as Paul Nitze and Richard Pipes led to the outbreak of open conflict between different agencies within the Carter administration over the Soviet civil defense threat and the possible revival of the United States' civil defense program. While the Department of Defense and the DCPA pushed the White House to endorse CRP to match Soviet civil defense, the ACDA and the State Department, worried about the erosion of their efforts to improve relations with Moscow, sought evidence that the Soviet program was overrated and that civil defense was generally impracticable in nuclear war. Secretary of state Cyrus Vance and the leadership of the ACDA hoped that a future SALT treaty would include civil defense, possibly resulting in the curtailment of both the Soviet and American civil defense programs.[51] Strenuously dissenting from motions by the Department of Defense and the DCPA to declare a strategic rationale for a reinvigorated civil defense effort, the ACDA regarded CRP as dangerous because it perceived civil defense as a threat to its political agenda.

A series of studies conducted by the Department of Defense analyzing the prospective cost and effectiveness of various possible civil defense programs convinced defense secretary Harold K. Brown to endorse a revived civil defense. Utilizing several different computer models and possible war scenarios, these studies estimated the proportion of the United States population that would survive a hypothetical Soviet attack in the mid-1980s in the presence of six different civil defense programs. These options ranged from "A," the essential abandonment of civil defense, to "F," the construction of a system of 100 psi blast shelters for urban Americans at a cost of $58 billion over a period of five years. This research found that, without any civil defense, a mixed Soviet attack against both military and civilian targets would kill between 80 and 85 percent of the U.S. population. Successful relocation, however, appeared capable of reducing these losses enormously, to a mere 15–25 percent. The computer models also found that even a Soviet attempt to thwart the relocation by retargeting the evacuated population would leave most Americans alive, thanks to their lower population density after evacuation. If the USSR limited its attack to military targets, relocation appeared nearly as effective as the ruinously expensive blast shelter system, at a miniscule fraction of the cost.[52] Defense Secretary Brown selected program "D'," the least expensive of the evaluated relocation programs, as the basis of the DCPA's future civil defense efforts.[53]

Estimated effectiveness of alternative civil defense programs considered by the U.S. Department of Defense, 1977

Percentage of total U.S. population surviving a mid-1980s threat

	Program description	Approx. costs ($M) FY79/FY79–83	Counterforce only	Counterforce and countervalue attacks		
				Population in place	Population relocated	Population relocated and targeted
A	No U.S. civil defense (i.e., warning only)	10/50	92–98	15–20	—	—
B	Best effort (at current funding level) for protection-in-place, one year needed to surge	100/500	95–98	25–30	—	—
C	Fallout protection for population-in-place under counterforce attack (1–2 weeks to surge)	120/700	97–99	30–40	—	—
D	Relocation of risk-area population to farms and hamlets (<2,000 population), with protection factor (PF) of 50 for fallout, plus plan C for in-place protection	140/1,600	98–99	30–40	75–85	55–70
D'	Same as D, with more deliberate pace (mid-1980s operational capability)	140/1,100	98–99	30–40	75–85	55–70
E	Relocation of risk-area population to small and medium-sized towns (~5,000–10,000 population) after 1–2 weeks surge with 15 psi blast/PF 200 fallout protection plus plan C for in-place protection	145/11,600	98–99	30–40	80–90	60–75
F	100 psi blast/PF 500 fallout protection for in-place risk-area population and PF 100 fallout protection for population outside risk areas (implementable on tactical warning)	175/58,000	99+	85–90	—	—

Source: National Security Archive, Civil Defense/Emergency Management Collection (Rumbarger Donation), Box 10, Folder "DoD (PA&E) review of CD program "77–78.""

Projected to cost a mere $1.1 billion between 1979 and 1983, program D' combined strategic evacuation with a less ambitious version of the Kennedy-era fallout shelter program. The Department of Defense studies estimated that it would double the percentage of Americans who would survive a nuclear attack, relative to no civil defense, to 30–40 percent even if the attack came before evacuation, and save 75–85 percent of the population after relocation.

As the hawks determined to undermine arms control negotiations with the USSR cited Soviet civil defense as proof of the Kremlin's nuclear malevolence, the ACDA and State Department needed to either coax Moscow to curtail the program or, alternatively, convince the American government and population it did not pose the strategic threat Gouré and others claimed. Tasked with producing a definitive account of available information on the subject, the CIA issued a report in July 1978 titled *Soviet Civil Defense*. To the consternation of both advocates and opponents of reinvigorated U.S. civil defense efforts, the CIA's assessment remained agnostic about the ongoing debate. According to the report, "by developing an extensive and active civil defense," Soviet leaders "hope to convince potential enemies that they cannot win a war with the USSR."[54] Furthermore, CIA analysts concurred with Gouré that Soviet leaders placed considerable faith in their civil defense efforts. "The Soviets almost certainly believe that their present civil defenses would improve their ability to conduct military operations and would enhance the USSR's chances for survival following a nuclear exchange." They parted from Gouré, however, regarding the impact of civil defense on Soviet strategy. Soviet leaders, in the view of the CIA, "cannot have confidence, however, in the degree of protection their civil defenses would afford them, given the many uncertainties attendant to a nuclear exchange. We do not believe that the Soviets' present civil defenses would embolden them to deliberately expose the USSR to a higher risk of nuclear attack."[55] Post-1991 revelations by the successor agencies of Soviet civil defense show that the CIA's evenhanded account accurately ascertained the approximate cost and objectives of the Soviet civil defense program in the 1970s.[56] Both the ACDA and the DCPA selectively quoted the report to assert that the CIA concurred with their position.

Tensions between advocates and opponents of civil defense in the Carter administration came to a head at a series of White House meetings on the subject in August 1978. Secretary of defense Harold Brown, acting as chair, declared at a meeting on August 3 that U.S. civil defense "would necessarily be driven in part" by Soviet efforts in the field. Representatives of various agencies present, particularly the ACDA, argued that civil defense expansion should be kept within "SALT established limits." Following a CIA briefing on the Soviet civil defense program, most of the attendees endorsed the conclusion that "we do not want the president, if the Soviets evacuate in a crisis, to have no options other than yielding or preemption. Civil defense is, for that reason, part of the strategic equation."[57]

The ACDA dissented from this position.[58] At a follow-up meeting on August 18, the ACDA continued to protest the drift toward the official endorsement of a strategic role for civil defense even after the State Department demonstrated a willingness to cooperate with the Department of Defense on the issue. Owing to the lack of prior precedent, the ACDA worried that tying civil defense to the strategic balance "constituted a significant change that can be construed to require a much larger civil defense buildup than is intended." Others at the meeting disagreed, contending that President Carter had already accepted that civil defense possessed strategic relevance by suggesting its inclusion in SALT. As an alternative to the Defense Department's preferred policy of acknowledging a strategic role for civil defense, the ACDA proposed language emphasizing a "very limited" role for civil defense as "insurance" against enemy attack. The meeting adjourned with the dispatch of drafts of both versions to President Carter.[59]

The final impetus overcoming the Carter administration's initial skepticism on civil defense came from Moscow's unwillingness to include civil defense on the agenda for the projected follow-on treaty to SALT II. Carter hoped that this treaty might convince the USSR to abandon civil defense the same way it had abandoned ABM defenses following the implementation of the 1972 ABM Treaty, but he found the Kremlin unwilling to even discuss the idea. The *Washington Star* reported in November 1978 that, while preliminary talks on all other topics for SALT III had begun, "the two sides could not agree to begin negotiating on civil defense."[60] In September 1978 Carter signed PD-41, giving program D' his implicit presidential endorsement.[61]

Aiming to salvage their position, the ACDA and State Department took measures to contradict alarmist claims made about Soviet civil defense.[62] The State Department struck first by circulating the July 1978 CIA report on Soviet civil defense as a "special report" via its Office of Public Communication.[63] Considerably more threatened than the State Department by its defeat on the civil defense issue, the ACDA decided to delegitimize the dire interpretations of Soviet civil defense that carried the day for its opponents. In 1977 the agency developed a classified study of how effective Soviet civil defense would be at limiting losses to the USSR's population and industry after a nuclear exchange. In December 1978, the ACDA published a sanitized version of this report as *An Analysis of Civil Defense in Nuclear War.* Assailing the claims made by Wigner and Gailar that Soviet civil defense could reduce the USSR's casualties in a nuclear war to a small percentage of its population, the ACDA opined that even urban evacuation, "if it can be implemented," would reduce short-term Soviet fatalities only to 25–35 million. The ACDA noted that Washington, if it so desired, could thwart Soviet evacuation by retargeting available warheads "against the evacuated population in groundbursts, causing as much as 70 to 85 million fatalities in the Soviet Union even if the Soviet evacuation and sheltering plan is fully implemented." Listing other findings of its analysis, including "the destruction of 80% of all Soviet cities with populations over 25,000" and "large casualty rates for people located in even very hard blast shelters," the ACDA concluded dismissively that "while some civil defense activities, such as evacuation, have some effect on the immediate post attack environment, their benefits in the long run have not yet been established."[64]

Curiously, the findings of the ACDA study roughly agreed with those of the 1977 Department of Defense study, but the tone differed enormously. The ACDA estimated fatalities for a Soviet "direct population attack" on the United States with in-place shelter and urban evacuation at 87–109 million, about 40–45 percent of the U.S. population.[65] The ACDA released this and another study, *US and Soviet Strategic Capability through the Mid-80's: A Comparative Analysis,* without clearing them through proper channels, inciting the anger of Defense Secretary Brown. Brown wrote a letter of protest to the ACDA complaining that it had distributed copies of the two studies to members of Congress where they "were subsequently used in open hearings on the Hill to provide the basis for questioning Administration witnesses." According to Brown, "To assure that data and analyses on especially sensitive strategic policy issues—among which civil defense is one—are not inconsistent," the studies ought to have been "cleared through the SALT working group." Frustrated by the ACDA's bold attempt to overcome its defeat on civil defense within the Carter administration, Brown asserted, "I think that our interests might be better served if the prescribed clearance procedures were strictly adhered to in connection with the release of information on sensitive strategic policy issues. It would be useful to remind our staffs of the agreed procedures."[66]

At the same time that Carter pondered the redevelopment of American civil defense policy, he also streamlined federal responsibility for emergency management. Not everyone in the government agreed with the wisdom of merging the DCPA's civil defense functions with peacetime emergency response. Defense Secretary Brown worried that moving civil defense out of the Department of Defense would compromise America's strategic posture and that the combined agency might neglect civil defense in favor of nonmilitary disaster management. The lackluster record of the DCPA, however, made defending the existing arrangement impossible, and Brown had to make do with assurances that the new agency would maintain links with the Defense Department. In June 1978, President Carter declared his plans to implement executive orders creating FEMA, eliciting protest from some members of Congress. Implementation of the reorganization proved more difficult than anticipated, as finding leadership, transferring functions, and merging various regional organizations all presented complex obstacles. President Carter activated FEMA with Executive Order 12127, issued March 31, 1979, and effective on April 1—inauspiciously, in the midst of the crisis at the Three Mile Island nuclear power plant in Pennsylvania, whose second unit experienced a meltdown on March 28.

Although the outlines of the new civil defense program remained murky, the Carter administration's endorsement of crisis relocation swiftly attracted vociferous criticism both inside and outside the government. Members of Congress soon began echoing the ACDA's critiques of Carter's civil defense policy. Representative Thomas Downey of New York asserted that the new effort would threaten to escalate a nuclear confrontation and would fail to protect the population, advocating instead that the goal of civil defense should be "planning to maintain calm and rational order in American cities during a crisis," much as Phillip Wylie argued three decades before.[67] Private citizens also criticized the idea of reviving civil defense. David F. Cavers, who had been a bugbear of Steuart L. Pittman's during congressional hearings about civil defense in the 1960s, blasted the proposal in the *Bulletin of the Atomic Scientists*.[68] Even the few positive responses offered only lukewarm praise. William H. Kincade of the Carnegie Endowment for International Peace expressed his concerns about the "problematic assumptions" behind crisis relocation but concluded it was "prudent" because "the government has the most fundamental obligation to try to save lives, even if it can only alter the casualties from a large-scale nuclear exchange by a few percentage points or tenths of a percentage point."[69]

Chastened by this torrent of criticism, President Carter hesitated to request the funding necessary to begin implementing the policies in PD-41.

Some commentators, including the *New York Times* editorial page, assumed that the president endorsed reviving civil defense only as a gambit to coax congressional hawks to support ratification of the SALT II treaty. President Carter denied these claims, but also distanced himself from the civil defense controversy.[70] In congressional testimony, DCPA head Brandyl Tirana, requested a mere $108 million instead of the expected $140 million stipulated for D'. Tirana admitted that this amount could not allow more than token steps to develop a crisis relocation capability, but Congress elected to act as it had in the past and reduced the civil defense budget to only $100 million. Adjusted for inflation, this was the lowest amount budgeted for United States civil defense since 1951.[71]

Observers in the USSR responded to the American controversy over Soviet civil defense efforts with a mixture of bewilderment, incredulity, and horror, in part because few of them understood their own country's civil defense policy. For instance, in a 1977 article published in the *Bulletin of the Atomic Scientists*, Georgi Arbatov of the Soviet Academy of Sciences Institute of USA and Canada Studies dismissed Gouré's book as "part of a propaganda campaign" portraying Soviet civil defense as "evidence of Soviet preparation to make a preemptive strike on the United States." Arbatov himself, however, did not discount the existence of the program. Instead, he maintained that the Soviet government pursued civil defense against smaller, more manageable threats—implicitly, that of China—an interpretation that is not borne out by the archival record.[72] In 1978, the Soviet military commissioned a Russian-language translation of Gouré's *War Survival in Soviet Strategy*. Considered a classified document and circulated only to a select readership, the Soviet edition includes an introduction characterizing the work as an example of how "aggressive American political circles" sought to construe civil defense as another basis for fear of the illusory "Soviet military threat" and sabotage good relations between the superpowers.[73]

In February 1978, the man best positioned to know the true capabilities and intentions of the Soviet civil defense system, General Altunin, publicly declared that both sides of the American debate were erroneous. Writing in the military newspaper *Krasnaia zvezda* (Red Star), Altunin remarked that "it would be strange to deny that certain measures to improve [Soviet civil defense] are being carried out." Dissenting from contentions that he presided over a moribund and unworkable "paper program," Altunin explained that "the main purpose of our civil defense is, along with the armed forces, to ensure the population's defense against mass destruction weapons and other means of attack from a likely opponent." At the same time, however, Altunin repudiated the strategic role for civil defense emphasized by Gouré. "We state unequivocally," wrote the general, that "the USSR's civil defense has never threatened anybody and threatens nobody, poses no danger for Western countries and moreover does not and cannot upset the Soviet-American balance of forces."[74]

Meanwhile, American opponents of nuclear weapons seized on alarmist claims regarding Soviet civil defense as a potential weak spot in their enemies' rhetorical fortifications. In 1980, members of the antinuclear organization Physicians for Social Responsibility (PSR) visited the Soviet embassy in Washington, where they questioned assistant ambassador Aleksandr Bessmertnykh about the Soviet civil defense program. In reply, Bessmertnykh reassured them that "the system has been highly exaggerated in the US press," that "civil defense in the USSR is largely for conventional weapons," and finally that "civil defense provides no security against nuclear [attack]."[75] These answers reinforced Soviet diplomats' pursuit of further arms control objectives, but would have come as a surprise to the employees of Soviet civil defense. In all likelihood Bessmertnykh was not being deceptive, but he lacked a clear idea of what his country's civil defense policy was.

Following the precedent of previous decades, Soviet writers seized on the Carter administration's decision to reinvigorate American civil defense efforts to justify their own civil defense program. In a 1980 article published in the Soviet journal *USA: Economics, Politics, Ideology*, V. S. Frolov denounced the new program not only as a means of deceiving Americans into believing in a nonexistent "Soviet military threat" but also as potentially disastrous as it might convince Washington that it could risk waging a nuclear war. Frolov basically inverted Gouré's argument while echoing earlier Soviet assertions that American war planners invested in civil defense to enable their offensive war plans against the Soviet Union. Even more remarkable, however, were Frolov's claims that most of the assets and expenditures of American civil defense were hidden from the public and that civil defense remained under the control of the Department of Defense. To maintain the plausibility of his position, the author disregarded the ample evidence that American civil defense had been moribund for years and that Congress had not funded implementation of the Carter administration's CRP proposal. Frolov's article intimated that American civil defense was a mirror image of its secretive, military-controlled USSR counterpart, therefore legitimizing contemporary Soviet policy.[76]

"It's the Dirt That Does It": Ronald Reagan's CRP Debacle

The election of Ronald Reagan to the White House in 1980 seemed to portend a renaissance in the fortunes of American civil defense. Reagan was the first president since JFK with apparent enthusiasm for civil defense, but unlike Kennedy, who knew that admitting his belief that civil defense would strengthen America's strategic posture might alienate the public, Reagan associated himself politically with strategic thinkers who considered civil defense a vital tool of coercion, such as Paul Nitze. Furthermore, although the Reagan administration claimed greater effectiveness for its civil defense program than Kennedy had, in most respects it was less ambitious than that of the OCD in the 1960s. While Reagan essentially continued the CRP policy approved by his predecessor, a poor choice of FEMA director, multiple embarrassing public relations gaffes, an obstinate refusal to acknowledge the weaknesses of the CRP policy, and growing hostility from both state and local emergency management agencies as well as the public all contributed to make the Reagan years the nadir of American civil defense history.

President Reagan tapped Californian Louis O. Giuffrida as his choice for director of FEMA. A career army officer born in 1920, Giuffrida rose to the rank of colonel before becoming a general in the California National Guard. During his military service Giuffrida took a special interest in policing and managing popular disturbances; while studying at the U.S. Army War College he authored a 1970 thesis titled *National Survival—Racial Imperative*, in which he contemplated the use of martial law and internment camps to contain a Black Nationalist uprising.[77] Giuffrida's dubious record on race issues attracted little media attention at the time of his nomination, rising to notoriety only when an investigative reporter published an article asserting that *National Survival—Racial Imperative* formed the basis of a classified 1984 FEMA continuity-of-government exercise developed by National Security Council (NSC) liaison to FEMA lieutenant colonel Oliver North.[78] Giuffrida owed his position to his association with Reagan during his tenure as governor of California, when he served as an advisor on terrorism and emergency management. At the governor's request, Giuffrida also organized and directed the California Specialized Training Institute, which trained police, firefighters, and emergency managers.[79] In addition, Giuffrida shared a close friendship with Reagan associate Edwin Meese.

Powerful patrons, however, ultimately proved inadequate to save Louis Giuffrida from himself: he demonstrated incorrigible corruption and cronyism that led to his departure from FEMA in September 1985. His appointment of a friend, Fred J. Villella, as FEMA's executive deputy director played an important role in his undoing, as Villella created a public scandal for the agency by embezzling FEMA money to convert an agency building in Emmitsburg, Maryland, into a personal residence. Villella resigned in August 1984 amid hostile congressional scrutiny of not merely his misuse of government funds but also allegations of sexual harassment.[80] A few months after Villella's departure, FEMA fell under additional criticism for alleged favoritism in the dispensation of no-bid contracts. The refusal of Giuffrida and several of his subordinates to respond to congressional subpoenas on this subject in late 1984 and inconsistent testimony led the Justice Department to investigate the case for possible perjury. In addition to "fraud" and "favoritism," witnesses alleged that Giuffrida evinced simple "mismanagement" of FEMA.[81] Under increasing assault from all sides, Giuffrida announced his imminent resignation in July 1985, denying any connection between this step and the ongoing investigations into his questionable conduct.[82]

Starting in June 1981, President Reagan took steps to deepen the connection between civil defense and the United States' strategic nuclear posture established by his predecessor in PD-41. During the second half of 1981, the NSC developed a National Security Decision Directive outlining the administration's civil defense policy.[83] In March 1982, the president approved an unclassified version of the final document, dubbed NSDD-26, which declared that "civil defense is an essential ingredient of our nuclear deterrent forces" and that "it is a matter of national priority that the US have a civil defense program which provides for the survival of the US population." According to NSDD-26, this program would "enhance deterrence and stability" as well as "reduce the possibility that the US can be coerced in a crisis." Like the CRP program endorsed by the Carter administration, NSDD-26 emphasized strategic evacuation, but it also added research programs into industrial hardening and the provision of blast shelters for critical workers, with the assumption that a "funding decision" on these would be made subsequently. Additionally, NSDD-26 dictated that the CRP capability would become operational by the end of fiscal year 1989. NSDD-26, however, lacked any mention of one vital component of the Carter administration's program—the provision of an in-place fallout shelter system such as that championed by President Kennedy to protect American citizens in the absence of strategic warning.[84] The resulting dependence of Reagan's civil defense proposals on strategic warning became a lightning rod for critics.

Even before the promulgation of NSDD-26, pundits and antinuclear activists realized that civil defense offered an easy means of attacking Reagan's nuclear arms policies. Declarations that civil defense contributed to America's "deterrence posture" combined with sanguine statements about the survivability and winnability of nuclear war made FEMA and its CRP efforts irresistible for comedians and protesters alike. In an interview with Robert Scheer, a reporter for the *Los Angeles Times*, deputy undersecretary of defense for strategic nuclear forces and CRP advocate T. K. Jones inadvertently gave FEMA's critics the ultimate punchline. Claiming that, with a civil defense program comparable to that in the USSR, the United States could recover from a nuclear attack within two to four years, Jones asserted that "everybody's going to make it, if there are enough shovels to go around." He clarified that all one needed to do was "dig a hole, cover it with a couple of doors and then throw three feet of dirt on top. It's the dirt that does it."[85]

Contrary to Jones's glib assertion, preparing America to survive nuclear war proved much more complex than simply distributing shovels. FEMA's strategic evacuation plans posed numerous organizational and logistical challenges, often exasperating the state and local officials charged with carrying them out. Planning for evacuation necessitated not only developing schemes to conduct simultaneous traffic movement of an unprecedented number of people, but also housing, feeding, and clothing them at their destinations. Few emergency management officials were enthusiastic about CRP, but as the federal budget provided funding for it that could be applied to other hazards under the dual-use policy, only a handful publicly rebelled. The most prominent of these emerged in Greensboro, North Carolina, where Marilyn J. Braun, the director of the Greensboro-Guilford County Emergency Management Assistance Agency, publicly declared her refusal to participate in CRP. Disenchanted with the concept during the Carter years, Braun had already attracted the ire of federal and state civil defense officials in December 1981 when she removed all buildings in Greensboro from the national fallout shelter registry and began taking down shelter signs in the city. Braun testified before the House Sub-Committee on Environment, Energy, and Natural Resources on April 22, 1982, stating that her office had concluded that "the planning concept was placed on very broad and wishful assumptions" that "were not realistic to us." Noting that government authorities claimed that "any plan was better than no plan at all," she retorted that "our analysis showed that the crisis relocation plan *was no plan at all*." Emergency managers, in her view, had a responsibility to promote measures to the public providing "minimal, predictable protection," but no conceiv-

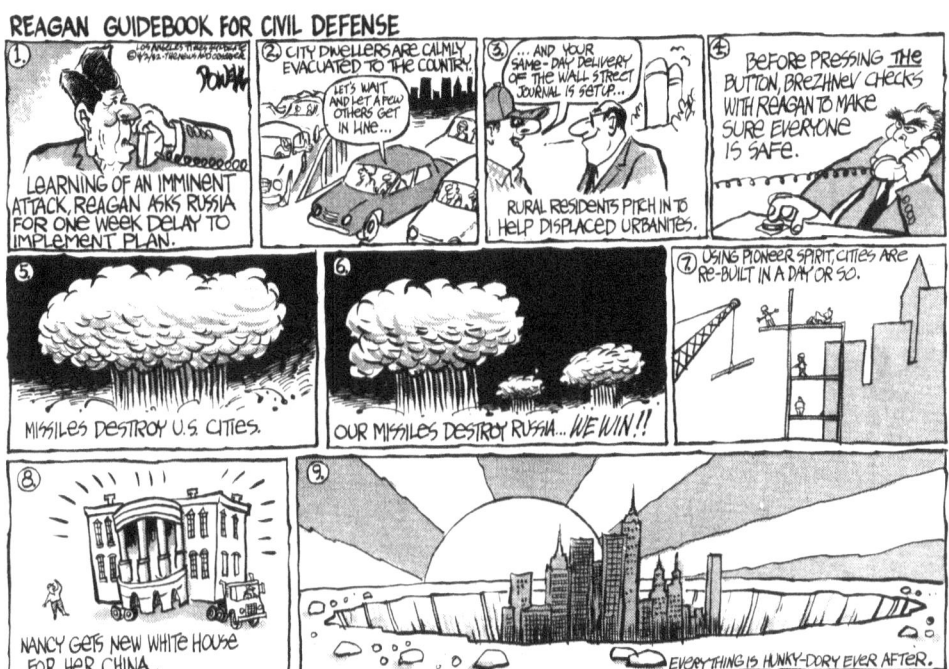

This April 1982 political cartoon illustrated the absurdities of Reagan's CRP plan. Reprinted with permission from *The News & Observer*, Raleigh, NC.

able civil defense program could do this for nuclear attack.[86] While few emergency managers followed Braun's example, some readily admitted the shortcomings in their crisis relocation plans. The architect of the plan for Montgomery County, Maryland, confessed that his effort remained "incomplete" and that it would "require a lot more regional planning" to become effective.[87]

With the encouragement of antinuclear activists, some local governments voted to reject CRP as a means of protesting the nuclear arms race. The first community to take this step was Cambridge, Massachusetts, home of Harvard University and the nexus of the revived PSR, an antinuclear organization that took special glee in attacking FEMA's CRP policy. Goaded by PSR members from the Harvard faculty, the Cambridge city government voted in 1981 against participating in crisis relocation efforts, instead electing to use city funds to circulate a pamphlet about the effects of a nuclear attack on the city.[88] Antinuclear activists and opponents of Reagan's defense policies nationwide sought to replicate this success. They did so with spectacular results in March 1982, when the *MacNeil-Lehrer Report* aired the Boulder, Colorado, city council meeting on the topic of CRP. Civil defense critics humiliated proponents of FEMA's program on national television, and the city council voted to establish a Nuclear War Education Committee to produce a booklet similar to Cambridge's.[89] Other communities simply voted either to reject CRP or not to accept their particular CRP plan. Despite some high-profile cases such as New York City and San Francisco, this trend spread to only a limited number of communities. By mid-June 1982 FEMA counted just twenty-four jurisdictions opposed to CRP as a concept, all but one of them in New England or California, and four that rejected their specific evacuation plan.[90]

With the battle over FEMA's budget request for crisis relocation raging in Congress, the conflict between civil defense proponents and critics became one of competing scenarios. Out of necessity, FEMA asserted that a nuclear war would probably occur with sufficient strategic warning to allow for evacuation, and that the war itself would cause only a manageable amount of damage to evacuation zones. Ironically, this constituted a claim that the Soviet Union would cooperate with American civil defense. However popular these assumptions were with certain strategic theorists, they struck many Americans as self-evidently absurd. Critics of crisis relocation painted a very different picture, in which war began suddenly and the USSR attacked American population centers with its largest weapons. For example, *The Nuclear Threat to Marin County: A Prevention and Source Document*, a booklet circulated by the Marin County, California, Board of Supervisors in opposition to civil defense, described the horrific consequences of the detonation of a twenty-megaton warhead over San Francisco at 3 P.M. on "a clear, sunny weekday in autumn." The authors characterized this as an optimistic scenario, as there was no reason to assume there would not be more bombs, or that the attack would not utilize weapons designed to create additional fallout ("salted" bombs). Furthermore, evacuating would simply incite a nuclear war, as "it could mean that the U.S. was preparing to deploy its first-strike weapons, thereby provoking a first strike by the adversary." They concluded that "such considerations are logical, lethal, and apparently disregarded by civil defense planners."[91] This scenario bore little resemblance to either actual Soviet war planning or American analysts' expectations of what form nuclear war would take, but it resonated with citizens inclined to regard nuclear war as an irredeemable catastrophe.

FEMA received an invaluable opportunity to tell its side of the story during the production of the ABC television film *The Day After*, which portrayed life after a nuclear attack. Thanks to the desire of ABC films for government cooperation to access military facilities and equipment, the Department of Defense successfully pressed for modifications to the filming script, among them several changes requested by FEMA. *The Day After*, disappointingly, did not show FEMA's crisis relocation plans in action, but Giuffrida gleefully reported to Edwin Meese that "the film's scenario makes two points which are key premises in the Civil Defense Program: 1. That there likely would be strategic warning in advance of an actual attack; 2. That most people, after leaving the cities, would survive."[92] In August 1982, FEMA Public Affairs director Jim Holton reported that ABC had made "nearly all" of the requested script changes, such as a discussion between two restaurant patrons in the background of one scene about the possibility and desirability of evacuation.[93] Unfortunately, *The Day After* proved less useful for FEMA than hoped, as ABC elected to edit the original four-hour filmed version to two hours and air it in November 1983 instead of in February as originally planned. The aired version still upheld important components of FEMA's argument for civil defense, including a news report announcing the evacuation of Soviet cities.[94]

In contrast to the civil defense programs of the 1950s and 1960s, which enjoyed either polite support or at least neutrality from most of the mainstream press, in the 1980s influential news outlets joined antinuclear activists in condemning the civil defense program. Multiple editorials in the *New York Times* and *Washington Post* assailed FEMA and its CRP effort.[95] Broadcast media also proved hostile. An internal FEMA report found that "with a few exceptions, print and broadcast news accounts of civil defense have been negative," and described plans to "be aggressively responsive to flagrantly erroneous and misleading news items, columns, and editorials," a task for which the FEMA Office of Public Affairs had "contracted for the services of a skilled ghost writer."[96] The publication of Jonathan Schell's *The Fate of the Earth* in early 1982 provided a touchstone for critics of civil defense, even though its thesis that nuclear war might result in the extinction of mankind elicited howls of protest from the technical experts Schell consulted, who pointed out that they had concluded the opposite.[97]

FEMA's plans for strategic evacuation attracted withering scrutiny from antinuclear organizations, which often made up in enthusiasm what they lacked in technical expertise. The PSR led this charge, organizing debates with well-meaning representatives of local emergency management organizations and utilizing the opportunity to humiliate them when they attempted to justify their CRP efforts. Although this tactic often generated effective publicity, the PSR officially repudiated it in late 1982 after recognizing that it was not merely mean-spirited and unfair, but that many emergency management professionals disliked how nuclear war planning distracted them from their efforts to prepare for peacetime disasters. Jennifer Leaning, the organization's medical director, issued a memo beseeching that PSR spokespeople "distinguish between the role of FEMA and the role of local emergency management officials."[98] Leaning subsequently co-edited *The Counterfeit Ark: Crisis Relocation for Nuclear War*, a book-length attack on the Reagan administration's civil defense policies.[99]

In addition to broadly antinuclear organizations such as the PSR, a small group of activists devoted their primary attention to critiques of civil defense and crisis relocation. Peter Dyke, a retired CIA employee living in Santa Fe, New Mexico, published a newsletter titled *The Front Line*, which circulated information about civil defense among the antinuclear community.[100] In February 1985, Dyke and like-minded activists including Matthew Leighton of the Traprock Peace Center organized a conference specifically devoted to the topic.[101] Dyke focused his efforts on civil defense because he considered it "an easy vehicle for educating the public at the grass roots in the effects of nuclear weapons and the orientation of the Administration's overall nuclear war strategy." Ironically, by February 1985 the failure of FEMA to persuade Congress to fund the CRP meant that conference participants had relatively little to discuss. In a subsequent memo, Dyke lamented that "Crisis Relocation as a national strategy is dead."[102]

Perversely, neither FEMA nor the White House utilized some obvious rhetorical strategies available to them to support the CRP program. When FEMA submitted its $252 million budget request for fiscal year 1983 as the beginning of a projected $4.2 billion program lasting seven years, it failed to anticipate the arguments opponents would adopt and take steps to preempt them. For instance, FEMA publicity materials ignored the fact that the Carter administration tried, and failed, to convince the USSR to include its civil defense program in disarmament talks in 1978 and that negotiators might need CRP as a bargaining chip. This argument might appeal to the numerous Americans skeptical of civil defense but fearful of the Soviet Union. FEMA also neglected to exploit fully the idea that the mere existence of an American strategic evacuation capability, however impotent, might dissuade the Kremlin from attempting to evacuate its cities in a crisis and therefore help prevent escalation. The agency instead emphasized scenarios in which the government successfully utilized strategic evacuation, either to convince the USSR to back down in a nuclear standoff or to actually survive a nuclear war. FEMA claimed that Soviet civil defense could save over 90 percent of the Soviet population and that the CRP program could save 80 percent of the U.S. population, without circulating the supporting analysis.[103] This posed a marked contrast to the statements of Val Peterson, Steuart L. Pittman, and Brandyl Tirana, who readily admitted the weaknesses of existing civil defense programs and that even their perfect implementation would leave tens of millions of Americans vulnerable. FEMA's presentation of the CRP policy alienated even the framers of PD-41. Harold Brown told the *National Journal* that, while he supported a modest civil defense program for its publicity value, he doubted that it could save that many people.[104]

Still No Technical Consensus

Even in the 1980s, scientific consensus on the feasibility of civil defense remained elusive. *The Medical Implications of Nuclear War*, published by the National Academies Press in 1986, summarized findings presented by prominent researchers into the effects of nuclear weapons at a symposium held in September 1985. The resulting book expounds on various then-prominent hypotheses about the consequences of nuclear war, including nuclear winter (the theory that nuclear war would result in drastic global cooling), and the idea that radiation exposure might cause the equivalent of AIDS. Reading it, one might get the impression that scientific opinion concurred about all of these "discoveries," as participant Carl Sagan termed them.[105] Behind the scenes, however, the symposium participants disagreed, sometimes vehemently.[106] The apparent consensus was illusory.

In the mid-1980s a group of American physicists attempted to produce a definitive statement on the science of civil defense, only to learn firsthand the formidable obstacles to such a project. Eleven physicists working under the auspices of the American Physical Society's Forum on Physics and Society, including both advocates and detractors of civil defense, attempted "to create as impartial a report as possible" on the topic, but even though "most members have tempered their views during the course of this study," they could reach no agreement. The preface to the final product, published in 1987 as *Civil Defense: A Choice of Disasters*, expressed the editors' thanks that "constructive criticism and considerable good will on the part of the group members produced a preface which has attained, if not consensus, at least the consent of all." They confessed, however, that "the same cannot be said for the whole report," as the different authors penned the eleven chapters and these advocated positions ranging from support for massively expanded civil defense programs to dismissals of civil defense in any form.[107]

In the charged political atmosphere surrounding nuclear weapons in the early 1980s, civil defense found few defenders, yet popular opinion on the subject remained equivocal. The weak contract state was weak in this case, as in many others, less because of widespread opposition than because of the objections of various spoilers. A small but enthusiastic cohort of civil defense enthusiasts existed, but they remained outside the political and media mainstream.[108] Major publications published few pieces supporting civil defense, with one of the few exceptions being a 1984 *New York Times* editorial by physicist Edward Teller.[109] Yet the deficit of positive publicity failed to prevent many Americans from agreeing with FEMA about the possible merits of the CRP program. A May 1982 poll found that 55 percent of Americans believed that strategic evacuation plans should be made for cities considered likely targets of nuclear attack versus 39 percent who did not.[110] This result echoed the findings of several other polls in early 1982, which found that a majority of Americans preferred continuing the civil defense program. In late May and early June of that year, FEMA conducted its own Gallup poll, which found that only 18 percent of respondents would approve of ending the civil defense program entirely, while 59 percent disapproved. Fifty percent also backed President Reagan's decision to increase civil defense funding, while 39 percent disapproved, and 67 percent agreed that the United States should have a relocation plan.[111] The findings suggested that a sizable proportion of Americans might be sympathetic to FEMA's civil defense plans if the agency found the right means of appealing to them.

But the ultimate fate of Reagan's crisis relocation plan lay not in the court of public opinion but in the halls of Congress, where the civil defense efforts of Truman and Kennedy both met their demise. FEMA's 1983 budget request for civil defense fared well in the House Armed Services Committee, which voted to approve the entire $252 million budget request; and the House also voted down an amendment sponsored by vociferous civil defense critic Massachusetts representative Edward Markey, which sought to reduce the appropriation to $144 million. In accordance with past precedent, however, the House Appropriations Committee approved a stingy $133 million, the Senate authorized a mere $144 million, and the budget that emerged from reconciliation allotted only $147.8 million, preventing implementation of the crisis relocation plan.[112] To salvage the strategic evacuation program, FEMA authorities considered cannibalizing the agency's funding for peacetime disaster planning to underwrite its civil defense efforts and leaning more on state and local authorities.[113]

To discourage state and local governments from opting out of strategic evacuation planning as Cambridge and San Francisco had, FEMA threatened to deny them dual-use funds from the civil defense budget if they refused to participate. In May 1982, the agency announced its intentions to establish formal regulations to this effect. To evade negative publicity, FEMA wrote the regulation so that, instead of automatically denying the funds under particular circumstances, eligibility would be "based on several factors, including overall program acceptance." Therefore, FEMA could intimidate state and local authorities into cooperation with CRP by maintaining an omnipresent threat of withdrawing matching funds used, among other things, to help pay for the salaries of emergency managers, and plausibly deny that it used the money as a tool of coercion.[114] This strategy successfully stemmed the tide of local governments turning against FEMA's civil defense proposals, although the roster of jurisdictions that did so continued to expand.[115]

To rescue the crisis relocation effort, FEMA elected to make its plans for nuclear war survival more acceptable by emphasizing their possible dual-use functions in peacetime disasters. To improve the program's image, FEMA repudiated the term "crisis relocation planning" and introduced "Integrated Emergency Management Systems" (IEMS) in its stead. According to FEMA, this arrangement would provide "multiple-hazard preparedness" for extreme weather events, nuclear power plant accidents, and hazardous materials events in addition to nuclear war.[116] Civil defense critics dismissed IEMS as a cynical rebranding of the same CRP program. Marilyn J. Braun scoffed that "deception by any other name is still deception," denouncing the new scheme as "merely a terrible gimmick to sell war planning to the public."[117] As a defense of the concept, FEMA offered the example of a 1982 incident in Waterford, Louisiana, when emergency managers relocated 17,000 people threatened by the possible release of toxic chemicals in over just two hours by utilizing the evacuation plan for a nearby nuclear power plant.[118] For fiscal year 1984 FEMA again requested $253 million, but the House Appropriations Committee concurred with Braun that the new program represented little substantive change. The final approved civil defense budget for that year came to $169 million, allowing 9 percent real growth accounting for inflation.[119]

The dismal fate of FEMA's crisis evacuation efforts resulted both from the agency's incompetence and the intrinsic shortcomings of the CRP concept. Louis Giuffrida's record of corruption, cronyism, and mismanagement, in addition to the dysfunction resulting from FEMA's institutional structure, would have made practical implementation of even a theoretically sound emergency management program extremely difficult. FEMA's deep involvement in shadowy and sometimes bizarre plans for continuity of government and war mobilization also distracted attention and resources away from both civil defense protection for the general population and peacetime emergency management. Furthermore, the Reagan administration and some within FEMA expected far too much of CRP, promising that it would save most of the population in a nuclear attack at minimal expense. FEMA also failed to promote the program effectively, allowing civil defense critics to dominate public discourse. One exasperated local civil defense official sent a copy of an anti-CRP tract published by the Center for Defense Information to FEMA, stating that it contained the best exposition he had seen and suggesting that "we need something similar supporting the program."[120]

FEMA's civil defense woes also stemmed from the desire of the American weak contract state to impose political solutions on technical problems. A scientifically defensible civil defense would require extensive investment in bomb shelters, even if it relied heavily on strategic evacuation like the Soviet program. Unfortunately, over the course of the Cold War both voters and Congress repeatedly demonstrated their unwillingness to support substantial public expenditures on shelters, so the American defense community turned to strategic evacuation in the hope it would prove politically acceptable. As envisioned under Carter, the civil defense program would include a fallout shelter system like that of the Kennedy years in addition to crisis relocation, but the Reagan administration neglected this component. Without these shelters, the effectiveness of the system if attack came without strategic warning would fall sharply. "The in-place shelter capability has been unduly deemphasized and too much emphasis has been placed on relocation plans, the credibility of which depend on speculations on how the crisis develops," complained Steuart L. Pittman in a July 1982 letter.[121] As few Americans felt confident of FEMA's assumptions, CRP proved no more politically acceptable than the rejected shelter programs of previous decades. As time passed, the extreme technical and logistical challenges posed by strategic evacuation grew increasingly apparent, undermining the already-limited faith of both the populace and local emergency management workers in its feasibility.

FEMA's civil defense efforts exhibited several of the flaws critics levy at civil defense in general. FEMA claimed that simple, inexpensive measures could save most Americans even in the face of a full-scale nuclear attack from the Soviet Union. The agency's plans favored government leaders over the general population, envisioning the construction of costly blast shelters for a subset of officials while leaving individual citizens largely responsible for their own survival. FEMA also claimed that its program would enhance America's strategic posture. In these respects, Reagan's civil defense program differed from those of his predecessors, which promised much less while costing considerably more. Yet despite its unsavory history, the archival record fails to support accusations that the Reagan administration supported civil defense because of cynical motives. FEMA analysts and officials earnestly believed in the potential effectiveness of crisis evacuation to protect civilians from nuclear attack.[122] They also lacked an intention to lull the citizenry into complacency about the threat of nuclear war, as critics charged. On July 26, 1982, FEMA issued a miffed rebuttal to the Center of Defense Information's attack on CRP declaring that "every sane person is horrified of nuclear war and the horrifying suffering and destruction it would cause, even if the most elaborate civil defenses imaginable had been developed—for example, blast shelters for 145 million urban residents, rather than the moderate program proposed by the administration." Citing a 1978 opinion survey that found that "while people believe enhanced civil defense will improve their chances of survival, they attribute lower performance to such systems than Defense Department and other studies," FEMA observed that "the American people entertain no exaggerated ideas about the effectiveness of civil defense, and will not become 'fearless' about nuclear war."[123]

President Ronald Reagan's March 23, 1983, announcement of the Strategic Defense Initiative (SDI) distracted attention away from civil defense and transformed the political debate on nuclear weapons in the United States. In a televised speech, Reagan called on "the scientific community" to "give us the means of rendering these nuclear weapons impotent and obsolete," by developing a space-based missile defense system capable of defeating a full-scale nuclear attack. Skeptical members of the media soon dubbed Reagan's proposal "Star Wars," after George Lucas's wildly popular 1977 science fiction film. Although historian Dee Garrison characterizes SDI as "the greatest civil defense fantasy of all," as an active defense system it cannot be categorized as a form of civil defense.[124] As envisioned by Reagan and his backers, conjectural technologies such as space-based nuclear-pumped

X-ray lasers would destroy attacking missiles before they reached their targets. Technical experts largely dismissed the feasibility of such a system, because even if it worked as envisioned, a determined enemy could always overload it with decoys or deploy nonmissile delivery systems. But as an instrument of domestic politics, "Star Wars" really was a superweapon. SDI allowed Americans to have their cake and eat it too by offering an imaginary escape from nuclear war without having to come to an accommodation with the "Evil Empire," and soon Reagan's "Star Wars" won favor with much of the public. Starting in 1983, SDI supplanted civil defense in the rhetoric of the Reagan administration, effectively neutralizing much of the political momentum behind the antinuclear movement and other attacks on Reagan's defense policies.[125]

The prospect of "Star Wars" not only distracted the attention of the American electorate and the antinuclear movement away from CRP, it also sapped the Reagan administration's enthusiasm for civil defense. The civil defense budget for fiscal year 1985 allowed a modest increase beyond inflation to $181 million but still prevented FEMA from pursuing the goals set out in NSDD-26, particularly after two years of lackluster funding. As of late 1984 the agency still hoped to implement the crisis relocation plan by the end of 1989 and stated its intention to request $345 million for the next fiscal year. Instead, FEMA asked for a mere $119 million for civil defense, seemingly signaling the Reagan administration's abandonment of its strategic evacuation scheme.[126] Shortly thereafter the scandal-ridden Giuffrida resigned from his post.

President Reagan's choice to succeed Giuffrida, Julius W. Becton, contrasted remarkably with his predecessor. The highest-ranking African American general in the history of the U.S. Army, Becton took over the troubled agency in November 1985. Before becoming head of FEMA, Becton served as director of the United States Agency for International Development's Office of Foreign Disaster Assistance, giving him some administrative experience in the emergency management field. Becton later recounted in his memoirs that he "was flattered to be asked" if he would be interested in managing FEMA, as "it meant higher pay and a new challenge." Thanks in part to the support of vice president George H. W. Bush and major general Colin Powell, Becton won out over other candidates for the top post at FEMA.[127] At his October 23, 1985, nomination hearing, he provided equivocal answers to questions about how he would approach FEMA's plans to protect civilians against nuclear attack. Becton stated that "I would want to look at the issues carefully before reaching any final conclusion," but that "perhaps the best solution would be evacuation plans for some areas and best-available existing protection in other areas—at state and local option."[128]

Under Becton, FEMA continued its nuclear war planning, albeit at a less ambitious level than during the early 1980s. FEMA efforts in this area increasingly focused on ensuring continuity of government in case of a nuclear attack on the United States. In early 1986 the agency announced a $1.5 billion plan to construct 600 shelters between 1988 and 1992 to protect local government officials, in addition to vital records. Citizens, however, would be forced to rely on "self-help." On May 8, 1986, Senator William Proxmire wrote a scathing letter to Becton complaining that the new plan "appears similar to the Soviet civil defense system that protects its government and Party elite."[129] A few months later, FEMA submitted a report to Congress admitting that "U.S. civil defense capabilities are low and declining" and that in case of nuclear war "national survival would be in jeopardy." FEMA stated that civil defense readiness would continue to deteriorate without additional funding, noting that a public blast shelter program like that in Switzerland would require sustained expenditures of $9 billion a year. For the coming fiscal year, however, FEMA planned to request only $130.8 million for civil defense.[130]

Under Becton's leadership, FEMA maintained pressure on state and local governments to cooperate in response plans for nuclear attack. In contrast to the equivocal regulation promulgated in 1982 regarding matching funds appropriated under the Civil Defense Act, in the summer of 1986 FEMA announced that state governments refusing to participate in civil defense and continuity-of-government preparations would be ineligible, evoking angry protests from some governors and emergency managers.[131] FEMA's threats failed to coerce some states, and in March 1987 the governors of Washington and Oregon defiantly refused to participate in a "war game" designed to evaluate state civil defense response to a nuclear attack. Washington governor Booth Gardner dismissed the exercise scenario, based in part on Tom Clancy's best-selling novel *Red Storm Rising*, as "unrealistic," while Governor Neil Goldschmidt of Oregon refused to participate but offered to cooperate in a test envisioning natural disasters, terrorist attacks, or a nuclear power plant accident. In retaliation, FEMA threatened to withhold $1.4 million from Washington and $1.1 million from Oregon, but Oregon senator Mark Hatfield retorted that he would cut FEMA's budget if it did do.[132]

Soviet Civil Defense and Antinuclear Protest in the 1980s

Opponents of the Reagan administration's defense policies quickly seized on alarmist claims about Soviet civil defense as an attractive means of belittling the president's position on nuclear war. In an issue of its publication *The Defense Monitor*, the Center for Defense Information dismissed the notion that the United States needed CRP to match a possible Soviet evacuation, maintaining that "it is unlikely that the Soviets would ever risk such an adventure" because it would provide Washington with strategic warning, and "missiles could be quickly retargeted." Soviet civil defense, argued the Center for Defense Information, "performs other functions besides trying to limit the effects of nuclear war," namely, "to instill and maintain a garrison-state mentality and the belief that the leaders are protecting their people."[133]

In testimony before the Senate Foreign Relations Committee on March 16, 1982, retired admiral Noel Gayler, a favorite spokesman of antinuclear campaigners owing to his prestigious military background, declared that "there is no need to match the Russians" in civil defense, because "they make mistakes, too."[134] Gayler stated that "qualified Russian observers concede that civil defense is a phony, a Potemkin village."[135] The admiral held that "their civil defense program is a turkey" and that "many of them are beginning to realize that."[136] If the USSR evacuated its cities, Gayler opined that the president would simply retarget available nuclear forces to attack the evacuated Soviet population and then publicly declare he had done so—a position that elicited howls of protest from Eugene Wigner, who also testified at the hearing.[137] In 1984, Gayler repackaged his comments on Soviet civil defense as a chapter of *The Counterfeit Ark*, in which he claimed that Soviet citizens considered civil defense "in the same way we regard TV advertisements." Concluding, without any supporting evidence, that "Soviet civil defense cannot have strategic value in the eyes of Soviet planners because they know its emptiness even better than we," Gayler asserted that "there is no strategic usefulness either in active or passive defense when applied to relations between the superpowers."[138]

Some of the men in the Kremlin apparently disagreed, as civil defense figured prominently in "Operation RYAN," the KGB's effort to monitor Western defense activity to detect signs of an impending preemptive nuclear attack against the Soviet Union. Iurii Andropov, head of the KGB and Brezhnev's successor as general secretary, initiated RYAN (an acronym for the Russian phrase for "nuclear-missile attack," *raketno-iadernoe napade-*

nie) in 1981 out of concerns about increasing U.S. hostility toward the USSR. Operation RYAN directed the intelligence agencies of the Soviet Union and its allies to gather information in search of signs that the United States was preparing to launch a nuclear strike against the socialist bloc. According to KGB defector Oleg Gordievskii, RYAN specifically targeted information about Western civil defense activities. In early 1983, the KGB ordered Soviet spies in the West to determine "the location of specially equipped Civil Defence shelters or premises which could if necessary be used as shelters (underground garages and depots, basements, tunnels) and arrange for a periodical check on their state of preparedness to accommodate the population at a particular time." Should they discover that "shelters are being taken out of storage or a start is being made on preparing certain premises for accommodation of the population," they were to report this immediately.[139] The KGB apparently believed, as intimated by V. S. Frolov's 1980 article, that the United States possessed a clandestine civil defense program similar to that of the USSR.

Meanwhile, the mainstream American media took the side of the skeptics in the debate over Soviet civil defense. On June 11, 1982, the *New York Times* published an article, "Russians, Too, Joke Sadly on Atom-War Survival," describing the widespread apathy among Soviet citizens regarding their country's civil defense program. Admitting that Soviet civil defense "dwarfs similar undertakings elsewhere," America's "paper of record" asserted that it was nonetheless on the wane: "The momentum of the program continues to carry it forward. But some Western analysts believe it has begun to slow down under the impact of public and professional skepticism, budgetary constraints and a growing sense in the Kremlin that war is, after all, an unthinkable prospect." Illustrated with a photo of twelve-year-old Muscovites trying on gas masks in a civil defense class, the article closed with quotations from Leonid Brezhnev and oncologist Nikolai Blokhin characterizing nuclear war as an unprecedented catastrophe.[140]

The *New York Times* accurately detected a new trend in the Soviet leadership, for amid the atmosphere of mounting superpower tensions, influential figures within the Soviet government enabled greater public criticism of civil defense. In the summer of 1982 the growing clout of civil defense skeptics in the Soviet regime resulted in the broadcast of an uncensored discussion of the consequences of nuclear war and civil defense on Soviet television by members of the International Physicians for the Prevention of Nuclear War (IPPNW), an antinuclear organization including both American and Soviet medical professionals. The far-reaching influence of eminent

Soviet cardiologist Evgenii Chazov—CPSU Central Committee member, IPPNW cofounder, and personal physician to Leonid Brezhnev—enabled the IPPNW to arrange a one-hour timeslot on the evening of Saturday, June 26, 1982, for the broadcast. The roundtable consisted of three American participants (physicians Bernard Lown, Jim Muller, and John Pastore) and three Soviet participants (medical experts Mikhail Kuzin and Chazov, and biophysicist Leonid Il'in). Expecting that the final broadcast would be subject to extensive Soviet editing, the three Americans waited for Chazov to brief them on what they could and could not say, but owing to the demands of chairing the ongoing World Congress of Cardiology Meeting, Chazov had time only to suggest that they avoid the topic of civil defense. Caught up in the heat of the moment and afraid of criticism from the Western press, Lown decided to raise the issue anyway during the taping on June 24.[141] "There has been much controversy about civil defense," he commented, then made clear what side of the debate he took. "Shelters in targeted areas," he claimed, "will become crematoria with the exhaustion of oxygen from firestorms, the buildup of noxious gases."[142] Furthermore, Lown declared that "evacuating is insane," as in his view it would be ineffective and foster a false sense of security while simultaneously making nuclear war more likely. "If any nation begins to evacuate its people, it means it's preparing to strike, so it invites preemption." Lown summed up that "we physicians have concluded that the only remedy is prevention—not civil defense measures."[143]

Lown feared that his impulsiveness might inspire the Soviet authorities to edit his remarks or cancel the broadcast altogether, but to his delight they aired it as recorded. Apparently Lown's message met with approval from people in high places, for Soviet television rebroadcast the program in its entirety the following week. The *New York Daily News* editorialized that the broadcast was "an astonishing blow against the Soviet military establishment" and that "Lown knocked the stuffing out of the Soviet civil defense system." Lown commented in his memoirs that "after the telecast, the subject of the civil defense gap ceased to be a favorite target of cold warriors," implying that he deserved credit for this development.[144] Lown's outburst exposed large numbers of Soviet citizens to the previously unfamiliar fact that many Americans viewed the USSR's civil defense system as destabilizing, and whatever the impact of the IPPNW's broadcast on Soviet public opinion, it signaled the growing strength of civil defense opponents in the Soviet elite.

The following year brought further signs of mounting skepticism toward civil defense within the Soviet government. In March 1983 the Knowledge

Society printed an outline for a lecture by medical professor Vasilii Legchaev, *Iadernoe oruzhie—ugroza biosfere i zhizni na zemle* (Nuclear weapons: A threat to the biosphere and life on earth), in which the author blamed the United States for the arms race and for perpetuating nuclear recklessness, but offered little hope that nuclear war might be survivable or winnable. Citing Chazov as an authority, the brochure states that nuclear war would cause "the total destruction of nature and depletion of the Earth's protective ozone layer" along with "especially virulent forms of microorganisms and dangerous vermin" resulting from radiation exposure to the environment. Answering Khrushchev's riddle on the aftermath of the nuclear war, the author wrote that "the living would envy the dead" as a result of the "horror of extended death agony" as well as the possibility of heritable diseases.[145] The publication at the beginning of 1984 of the earliest Soviet nuclear winter studies, even more pessimistic than those of their American counterparts, reinforced the swelling chorus of Soviet voices asserting that civil defense would be essentially futile in a nuclear war, as well as provided ammunition for the growing number of reformers hoping to break the Soviet military's stranglehold on the USSR's economy.[146]

The mounting controversy in the USSR about the consequences of nuclear war and feasibility of civil defense likely resulted from increasing dissension within the party-garrison state as the country's domestic situation continued to deteriorate. The Ministry of Foreign Affairs, the USSR Academy of Sciences (which supported the nuclear winter studies), and the Soviet Peace Council contested the Ministry of Defense with the argument that only by reining in defense expenditures would the Soviet Union be able to escape what Mikhail Gorbachev later dubbed "stagnation." The prestige enjoyed by the civil defense program among the Soviet population, never high, dropped considerably in the late 1970s and 1980s. Interviews made of expatriates from the USSR in the United States showed that, despite civil defense propaganda and mandatory civil defense classes in Soviet schools, Soviet youth did not believe that the USSR could survive a nuclear war with the United States.[147]

The ascent of the reformist Mikhail Gorbachev to power in 1985 further bolstered the fortunes of Soviet civil defense opponents. The new general secretary came to believe that the only way to save socialism was to dismantle the "garrison" aspect of the party-garrison state. As a step in this direction, Gorbachev established a policy of allowing more open discussion of previously sensitive political issues, making it possible for well-connected civil defense skeptics to popularize their views. The patronage of Anatolii

Gromyko—historian, member of the USSR Academy of Sciences, and son of Soviet foreign minister Andrei Gromyko—enabled the production by Lenfilm in 1986 of the first portrayal of the aftermath of nuclear war in Soviet cinema, *Dead Man's Letters*. Political taboos necessitated setting the film in the West. Directed by Konstantin Lopushanskii and cowritten by the noted Soviet science fiction authors Viacheslav Rybakov and Boris Strugatskii, the film portrays the desperate existence led by a dwindling number of survivors of a nuclear holocaust huddling beneath a city in bomb shelters. As lingering death by radiation poisoning thins their numbers, the government selects the fittest of those remaining to take to the "primary bunker," where they will wait decades for the surface world to become habitable again. According to the film, the government had taken steps of limited, but still meaningful, effectiveness to protect the population, such as building bomb shelters for urban residents and stockpiling gas masks. The use of Soviet civil defense equipment in the film, including gas masks and shelter equipment, makes its portrayal of Western civil defense an eerie mirror image of the Soviet program. *Dead Man's Letters* gave the Soviet Union a counterpart to Western films about life after nuclear war such as the American *The Day After*, which appeared on Soviet television in 1987.[148] That same year Ted Turner's "cable superstation" WTBS purchased the rights to show *Dead Man's Letters*, making a political statement by airing it against *Amerika*, a dystopian twelve-hour CBS miniseries about what the United States would be like as a Soviet satellite state.[149]

In the United States, worries about Soviet civil defense increasingly became the province of extreme anticommunist hawks and fringe survivalist groups. Organizations such as the Oregon Institute of Science and Medicine (OISM), which promulgated Leon Gouré's alarmist warnings about Soviet civil defense from its corrugated-metal shed in the American northwest, produced publications appealing to a small, but enthusiastic, audience.[150] Arthur Robinson of the OISM circulated a newsletter on nuclear war survival, *Fighting Chance*, which found favor with survival enthusiasts, and published numerous articles on Soviet civil defense. The OISM also produced videotapes about civil defense, among them a series of six cassettes devoted specifically to Soviet civil defense and starring a pipe-smoking Leon Gouré.[151] Other popular survivalist periodicals included *Survival Tomorrow*, whose female editor expressed dismay at how survivalism attracted "mentally unbalanced" people who "paid scant attention to the common-sense underpinnings of survival and used the notion of impending doom to escape from personal problems and buy quantities of expensive gear—'big boy toys.'"[152]

Despite continuing belief in some corners of U.S. political opinion about the menace of Soviet civil defense, by the mid-1980s even paranoid American fantasies of Soviet nuclear attack dismissed the Kremlin's survival programs as a paper tiger. The 1985 thriller novel *The Guardians*, about a postapocalyptic commando team charged with extracting the president from his bunker beneath the smoldering radioactive ruins of the nation's capital and transporting him to the Midwest so he can carry out the top-secret "Blueprint for Renewal," exemplifies this trend. In the novel, set in the near future, the leaders of the Soviet Union decide to launch a nuclear attack on the United States following military reversals in Central Europe, leading to the "One-Day War." As envisioned by the author, civil defense proves totally impotent in the face of the onslaught: "The United States's shiny new civil defense came apart at the seams. The Soviets' vaunted system had never existed except on paper. A nation that could not feed or shelter its population *before* the holocaust could hardly be prepared to cope with the greatest catastrophe in the history of the human race. Not that anyone could."[153]

Nuclear Strategy beyond MAD and NUTS

In the United States, civil defense critics selectively employed the rhetoric of counterforce and countervalue to undermine their opponents' arguments, but often rejected both these paradigms and advocated disarmament as an alternative. Civil defense opponents asserted that a U.S. CRP program would stoke Soviet paranoia and make war more likely. As Jennifer Leaning and Langley Keyes put it in *The Counterfeit Ark*, civil defense "could reinforce a tendency in Soviet thinking" that they might gain maximal advantage with "a surprise Soviet attack, prior to the initiation of U.S. evacuation measures."[154] Largely premised on emotional appeals rather than public pronouncements of Soviet strategic doctrine, the arguments made by civil defense opponents such as Leaning and Gayler incorporated a major contradiction in that they tended to reinforce MAD rather than to support the disarmament measures groups like the PSR endorsed. Scrambling to discredit counterforce, opponents of civil defense inadvertently perpetuated the logic of stalemate and mutual annihilation.

The ongoing debate over nuclear weapons in the first half of the 1980s led to a flowering of contending strategic postures to supplant MAD and nuclear utilization target selection (NUTS). Ronald Reagan's proposal for space-based missile defenses, the SDI, stood foremost and most debated among these. Reagan denounced mutual annihilation as immoral and unacceptable, and promised that SDI would abolish MAD by "making nuclear weapons impotent and obsolete." While the arms race continued, by the second half of the 1980s nearly everyone debating nuclear strategy in the United States wanted some change from old paradigms: either a unilateral or bilateral nuclear freeze, a restructuring of the nation's nuclear deterrent to emphasize "survivable" retaliatory forces to better implement MAD, SDI (which, according to Reagan, would be shared with the USSR), or some combination thereof. Not least among these were a surprising assortment of thinkers who argued that the active missile defenses and civil defense should be combined with bilateral reductions in strategic arsenals.

During the 1980s, a limited number of strategic theorists and civil defense advocates returned to the logic pioneered by researchers at the Hudson Institute in the mid-1960s that civil defense was not only a moral obligation in light of the possibility of deterrence failure but could be a valuable component of a stable deterrent posture also. Prominent advocates of this position included nuclear physicist Alvin Weinberg and political scientist Jack N. Barkenbus of the ORNL, who produced a series of articles in the mid-1980s advocating what they termed a "defense-protected builddown," or DPB. Noting that "Soviet objections to the SDI appear to be related to the concurrent and vigorous build-up of United States strategic offensive forces," Weinberg and Barkenbus explained that "DPB is predicated upon maintaining rough superpower parity while winding down offenses," which "should not be measured by the number of weapons ready to be launched on each side but rather by approximate estimates of the number that get through."[155] Weinberg contended that "a disarmed, stable peace is hard to contemplate except from a position of defensive strength," and therefore defenses would be essential to achieve disarmament.[156] Although this definition and most discussion of the DPB concept focused on active missile defenses as opposed to civil defense, ORNL scientist Conrad Chester contributed a plea to Weinberg and Barkenbus' 1988 edited volume on DPB arguing that "civil (passive) defense would appear to be indispensable as the foundation on which all programs leading to a defensive strategy must be built," particularly as "it would appear to be a very valuable form of insurance against less-than-desired performance of active defense systems."[157]

Advocates of using civil defense to facilitate an end to the nuclear arms race hoped that their new paradigm would prove more politically acceptable than other disarmament proposals for both Washington and Moscow.

Abandoning his earlier objection to civil defense, Freeman Dyson articulated his own vision of a transition to a defense-dominated world in his 1984 book *Weapons and Hope*. More idealistic than Weinberg's DPB concept, Dyson proposed what he termed "Live and Let Live," in which the superpowers would eliminate their nuclear arsenals entirely. As a hedge against cheating or attacks by minor nuclear powers, both the United States and the Soviet Union would field nonnuclear defensive weapons and civil defense adequate to contend with such threats.[158] Jonathan Schell, author of the popular 1982 antinuclear treatise *The Fate of the Earth*, emerged as another surprising advocate of civil defense as a means of facilitating disarmament. In his 1984 book *The Abolition*, Schell proposed an international agreement to ban nuclear weapons, suggesting that "with an abolition agreement in force," civil defense "would be helpful, because it would reduce the effectiveness of blackmail."[159] Dyson, Weinberg, and others favoring a combination of defenses and arms control were frustrated by the stagnation in superpower disarmament negotiations during the early 1980s, which remained acrimonious and fruitless prior to Mikhail Gorbachev's succeeding Konstantin Chernenko as general secretary of the CPSU in 1985, and hoped their approach could break this impasse.

Gorbachev's "New Thinking" enabled a breakthrough in arms control talks in the late 1980s, as he and his allies hoped that curbing weapons spending would facilitate desperately needed economic and political reforms in the USSR. The roots of the "New Thinking" predated Gorbachev's rise to power, as the term appeared prominently in the title of a 1984 book about the arms race by Anatolii Gromyko, *Novoe myshlenie v iadernyi vek* (The new thinking in the nuclear age).[160] Glasnost finally allowed public discussion of nuclear strategy in the USSR, but few Soviet citizens learned what their country's strategy was. Genuinely alarmed about the possibility of nuclear war and eager to rein in the arms race to free up resources for his domestic reforms, Gorbachev proved far more willing than his predecessors to make concessions in arms control talks. The Intermediate Nuclear Forces Treaty in 1987, and the Strategic Arms Reduction Treaty four years later, led to sizable numerical reductions in American and Soviet strategic arsenals.

Under Gorbachev, the USSR moved toward adopting a nuclear strategy much more akin to MAD than it had in the 1960s and 1970s. To counter the possible threat posed by Reagan's SDI program, as well as the introduction of new delivery systems by the United States (such as the Trident II SLBM), Gorbachev introduced two new concepts to Soviet nuclear strategy to guide arms development decisions. The first of these, "sufficiency," repudiated the tendency during the Brezhnev era to match American military capabilities both quantitatively and qualitatively, which led to expensive programs to develop aircraft carriers, new manned bombers, and the like simply because the United States possessed them. Now the Soviet Union would acquire only those weapons sufficient to secure its defense, which fed into Gorbachev's second concept, "asymmetry." Rather than attempt to match possible space-based missile defenses in kind, the USSR would deploy more inexpensive technologies to defeat it. This program led to the development of the road-mobile Topol ICBM, which incorporated special features to survive the still-hypothetical directed energy weapons emphasized in U.S. SDI research.[161] Although Soviet defense interests succeeded in forestalling the full adoption of the new strategic paradigm, the increasing reliance on deterrence sapped Soviet civil defense's institutional legitimacy.

Civil Defense and the Twilight of the Cold War, 1986–1991

The April 26, 1986, accident at Chernobyl Nuclear Power Plant and its aftermath confirmed the opinion of Western skeptics of Soviet civil defense and seriously impaired the program's prestige within the USSR. Mathematical physicist Evans M. Harrell wrote in 1987 that "even though the circumstances were vastly more favorable than would be expected in a nuclear war, there have evidently been several foul-ups," citing the delay in evacuation and lackluster radiological control procedures both inside and outside the exclusion zone.[162] The reputation of Soviet civil defense suffered further in subsequent years as more information about the aftermath of the Chernobyl accident became available. Political scientists William Potter and Lucy Kerner wrote in a 1991 *Soviet Studies* article that "on the balance, the typical, pre-Chernobyl, Western image of a massive, well-equipped, finely tuned and vigilant Soviet civil defense apparatus corresponds poorly to the actual conduct of civil defense forces prior to and in the immediate aftermath of the Chernobyl accident." They maintained that "instead, one finds a poorly-trained, ill-equipped and, at least with respect to the accident at hand, understaffed body of Civil Defense units."[163]

As it turns out, these assessments denied Soviet civil defense the credit it deserved for attempting to mitigate the effects of the Chernobyl disaster. Civil defense officials were among the few pushing in the critical hours after the explosion for decisive measures to protect the population, particularly evacuation. The plant's civil defense director, Serafim Vorob'ev, recognized the severity of the accident and attempted to report it to authorities in Kiev and Moscow, only to be silenced by the plant's administration. The plant's director, Viktor Briukhanov, convinced Moscow that while the accident had damaged the plant building, the reactor itself remained intact. The Soviet government mobilized a response appropriate for this understanding of the accident. Even after it became apparent that the reactor had exploded and that it was releasing immense amounts of radioactivity into the Ukrainian countryside, party, KGB, and military officials hesitated to inform the public that the accident had occurred, much less order evacuations. Soviet civil defense officials at the scene of the accident rightly protested this outrageous breach of responsibility. They tried to minimize the delays in evacuating the communities closest to the stricken reactor, delays that constituted the largest failure of emergency management at Chernobyl. General Boris Ivanov, General Altunin's second-in-command whom he dispatched to Chernobyl, even circumvented party officials to order one of these evacuations on his own initiative. When the evacuations finally took place, they proceeded relatively quickly and smoothly, even though they resulted in the abandonment of the evacuees' potentially contaminated personal belongings. While Soviet civil defense failed at Chernobyl, this was primarily because the party and KGB were so petrified by the effects that revealing the accident might have on their legitimacy that they prevented civil defense from doing its job.[164]

Even in conjunction with Gorbachev's "New Thinking" and the dramatic revival of arms control negotiations in the late 1980s, the Chernobyl disaster failed to dissuade die-hard Soviet civil defense alarmists of their views. A handful of professional defense analysts in the United States fretted about Soviet civil defense even as the USSR teetered toward its collapse. Leon Gouré continued to write studies of Soviet civil defense under contract for the government, barely tempering his views despite the underwhelming performance of the organization in both the Chernobyl disaster and the 1988 Armenian earthquake. He penned a draft report on the subject in 1989 in which he argued that "it should be cautioned that experiences with peacetime disasters do not provide a comprehensive test of Soviet Civil Defense capabilities and effectiveness in a war situation."[165] An extraordinarily dire appraisal of Soviet civil defense appeared in a 1990 book by Peter Pry, an employee of the CIA's Office of Soviet Analysis. Ignoring Chernobyl's implications for the effectiveness of Soviet civil defense entirely, Pry concluded that "conceivably, the USSR's superior survivability could move Soviet leaders, after largely disarming the United States with counterforce attacks, to make massive countercity attacks, the object being to wage a war of extermination to a 'final solution' to the world historical problem that, in the Marxist-Leninist view, is the United States."[166]

Ironically, Gouré's and Pry's assertions about the continuing menace posed by the USSR's ostensibly superior capability to survive nuclear attack coincided with major reforms to Soviet civil defense deemphasizing nuclear war survival in favor of preparations for technological and natural disasters. Instituted at the behest of the Communist Party leadership in 1988, these reforms led Soviet civil defense to reorient its planning efforts away from nuclear attack to focus on nuclear power plant accidents, earthquakes, forest fires, and other peacetime disasters.[167] By 1991 public education campaigns largely ignored the enemy nuclear threat and instead treated readers to illustrations of the Chernobyl Nuclear Power Plant and statistics about the 1988 Armenian earthquake.[168] Chernobyl both delegitimized Soviet civil defense's previous institutional mission and endowed it with a new raison d'être—one far more compelling for most Soviet citizens than that of surviving nuclear war.

The turbulent developments that wracked the Soviet Union in the late 1980s led to increasing skepticism of the utility of civil defense in a nuclear war, but the organization's shift to emphasize peacetime disasters never entirely supplanted planning for nuclear attack. Some high-ranking officers within GO doubted that their efforts would make much difference in a nuclear war, and heartily endorsed transitioning from what they considered an exercise in futility to the immediate need for better emergency management in more mundane disasters.[169] The change in the USSR's civil defense policy, however, did not indicate any reduction of Soviet skepticism regarding American strategic categories, and Soviet strategists never accepted the notion that defenses were inherently undesirable—just that they were technically unworkable.

Ironically, the humiliation of civil defense following Chernobyl resulted in its rebirth as a larger, more prestigious organization in the post-Soviet era. Russia's post-Soviet civil defense organization, the Ministerstvo po Chrezvychainym Situatsiiam (Ministry of Extreme Situations, or MChS), saw the Chernobyl liquidation and the Armenian earthquake as proof of its relevance and legitimacy.[170] Under the leadership of the charismatic Sergei Shoigu, the MChS gained new responsibilities during the 1990s, most dramatically absorbing Russia's firefighting services in 2002. Unlike the old civil defense, which Soviet citizens often made the butt of jokes, the MChS enjoys unusually high popularity among Russians compared with other government agencies.[171] The contrast with FEMA could not be more marked.

During the twilight years of the Cold War, FEMA still maintained some hope of a revived civil defense program. On February 4, 1987, President Reagan signed National Security Decision Directive 259, which rescinded the policy in NSDD-26 and instead emphasized "state and local crisis management and improvement of population protection capabilities through voluntary self-help capabilities and emergency public information."[172] Later that year, FEMA introduced revised estimates of a Soviet attack on the United States, finding that the evolution of the Soviet arsenal to encompass more accurate delivery vehicles with lower-yield warheads, in addition to changing assumptions about targeting, would markedly reduce the hazard to American citizens anticipated from a nuclear attack. Where a 1975 study found that 155.86 million Americans would be in areas subject to nuclear blast effects in a nuclear attack, FEMA's new figures counted only 111.91 million out of an increased U.S. population of 241.6 million. FEMA civil defense director Joseph Moreland told the *Washington Post* that, in light of these optimistic findings, he hoped for a possible boost in the next year's budget for civil defense to $190 million.[173] Civil defense critics expressed confusion about the new initiative, which seemed to repudiate evacuation and remained highly vague about how the population would be protected. Jennifer Leaning theorized that FEMA assumed a fully functional missile defense, despite the lack of any explicit admission of this from the agency. "Without support from SDI," she commented, "this plan turns on a colossal non sequitur." She worried that the momentum behind SDI might finally give a boost to the demands of civil defense enthusiasts who still hoped for the introduction of a public blast shelter system.[174]

Conclusion

The Cold War rivalry between the United States and the Soviet Union never resulted in a nuclear exchange, because neither superpower aimed to start a new world war and because both superpowers were uncertain about the physical and political consequences of using nuclear weapons. While Western strategic thinkers tended to premise their theoretical paradigms, including those emphasizing countervalue targeting and those emphasizing counterforce targeting, on a high degree of confidence regarding weapons effects and performance, advocates of these contrasting views disagreed dramatically about the political effects of nuclear threats. Soviet military planners, meanwhile, acknowledged a higher degree of uncertainty as to what form a nuclear exchange might take and what physical effects it might have, but the ideological blinders imposed by the party-garrison state led to an insistence that the socialist experiment could somehow survive in any war scenario. This assumption convinced the USSR to invest much more in civil defense than the United States, but it also inspired the adoption of force postures that, in practice, increased the chances of escalation and nuclear war. Because of uncertainty about the possible nature of nuclear war, none of the strategies postulated by the two Cold War superpowers was necessarily superior. Under unfavorable circumstances all threatened to fail spectacularly, and no one could predict which would prove most effective in future circumstances.

The unenviable trajectory of the strategic evacuation efforts of the Carter and Reagan administrations illustrates just how tenuous the connection between civil defense and nuclear strategy really was. Even though CRP was motivated by strategic concerns and justified by strategic rationales, its abject failure made little observable impact on other areas of U.S. nuclear weapons policy. Political and institutional considerations played a far greater role in shaping the superpowers' responses to the arms race than the prescriptions of strategic theorists. Both Washington and Moscow expended immense sums on weapons that made political sense for the weak contract state or the party-garrison state but served no logical strategic purpose—leading to decisions that fed into their adversary's paranoia. Institutional and political, rather than strategic, obstacles sealed the fate of the superpowers' Cold War civil defense programs.

Historical experience fails to support the contention that civil defense was an intrinsically destabilizing component of a nation's defense posture, as Western critics of civil defense often asserted. While this conclusion flows logically from assumptions common in some parts of American strategic culture, both Soviet and American theorists contested these views. In light of the human tendency to assume the worst of one's enemy, the possession of a civil defense program by another power might be seen as a signal of possible aggression, but it can also signal respect for one's own offensive capabilities. Evidence exists that at least a few Soviet observers viewed the mismatch between formidable U.S. offensive nuclear forces and its weak civil defense program as a symptom of an arrogant belief in the power of its first-strike capabilities.[175] The general tendency of Soviet analysts to overestimate the scale of the U.S. civil defense effort, however, probably prevented this interpretation from becoming a common view in the USSR.

The true threat to peace and stability in the Cold War nuclear standoff lay in offensive weapons, rather than civil defense. Missile defenses were destabilizing only in the Cold War context of superpowers armed with massive arsenals of ICBMs that could destroy all but a token retaliatory force. Effective missile defenses could then conceivably make nuclear war a winnable proposition for an aggressor, while offering minimal benefit for a defender. Civil defense, meanwhile, could never prevent colossal property damage against a determined enemy, even if it were so perfect as to prevent all civilian casualties, and when wielded by a nonnuclear state it could never be construed as threatening. Switzerland, the quintessential neutral power, boasted the most comprehensive civil defense program of the Cold War, and no one imagined that Bern pursued an aggressive "war-fighting" nuclear strategy.[176]

The United States did not forgo civil defense for strategic reasons, nor did the Soviet Union invest in civil defense in pursuit of strategic advantage. Furthermore, the superpowers' actual civil defense programs played little role in either the nuclear strategic balance or enemy perceptions of it. Highly selective interpretations of intelligence about enemy defense activities allowed interest groups in both superpowers to confirm their suspicions of enemy malevolence, characterizing any civil defense policy as an element of a threatening strategic posture. Rejecting civil defense while the superpowers possessed huge nuclear arsenals neither necessarily reassured the enemy nor made deterrence more stable.

Conclusion
Insurance Forgone

An unwitting viewer of Russian broadcast television in the fall of 2016 could have been forgiven for concluding that nuclear war was imminent. Following the Russian seizure of Crimea in February 2014, the state-dominated Russian media began employing bombastic nuclear rhetoric unprecedented even in the darkest days of the Cold War. On March 16 of that year, television personality Dmitrii Kiselev warned darkly on his weekly show that Russia was "the sole country that could turn the United States into radioactive ash."[1] Since Kiselev was head of the Russia Today news agency, many assumed him to be an unofficial Kremlin mouthpiece, and both Western and Russian observers took his frightening declaration as a warning that any Western attempt to interfere with the annexation of Crimea would be risking nuclear war. Over the next two years such rhetoric continued, and while the Russian government officially dismissed Kiselev's belligerence it took some steps that reinforced his narrative that nuclear war was again a serious possibility. Not least of these were efforts to reinvigorate Russia's civil defense program.

While civil defense planning for nuclear attack never entirely vanished in Russia, it had receded into the background after the collapse of the USSR. As it happened, Russia's emergency management agency, the Ministry of Extreme Situations (MChS), had the good fortune to be run by one of Russia's most competent and popular political figures, Sergei Shoigu. Shoigu became head of Russian emergency management at the beginning of the 1990s and successfully navigated it through that tumultuous decade, transforming the remnants of the troubled Soviet civil defense organization into a competent, professional emergency management agency.[2] After years of rumors that Vladimir Putin would promote Shoigu by making him prime minister or possibly even his chosen successor, the president named him defense minister in 2012. Shoigu's successor at the MChS, lieutenant-general Vladimir Puchkov, started his career as a Soviet Civil Defense staff officer. In light of Russia's increasingly contentious relations with the West following the seizure of Crimea, Puchkov's agency stepped up its planning for war with a peer power, introducing nationwide civil defense exercises in 2014. Russian civil defense received an important endorsement in October 2015, when deputy prime minister Dmitrii Rogozin, overseer of the country's defense industry as head of the Military-Industrial Commission, declared that civil defense in the country "should be recreated" so that it could provide "individual protection for the population" against radiological and other threats.[3]

In the fall of 2016, Russian media made it seem as if the revival of civil defense was truly at hand. In September and early October news programs featured tours of bomb shelters and warned citizens that they should make sure they knew where the nearest shelter was located.[4] Muscovites, at least, could be confident they could find a place underground with their fellow citizens: the MChS declared that Moscow had shelter space for all twelve million of its residents.[5] As the government reprised Soviet practice by refusing to divulge the location of all the shelters, concerned citizens resorted to crowdsourcing to try to ascertain where they were.[6] In early October, the MChS ran a nationwide drill as part of "Civil Defense Week" involving over forty million civilians, along with 200,000 emergency management personnel and 50,000 pieces of equipment.[7] Simultaneously, the Russian military ran a major exercise envisioning the full mobilization of the country for a war with the West, including the transfer of comprehensive government authority to district military commanders and the imposition of martial law.[8]

Much like its predecessor in 1927, the war hysteria of 2016 petered out without any armed confrontation. Kremlin leaders seem to have decided that the "nuclear hysteria" that had gripped the country had gotten out of hand. In late October, Vladimir Putin condemned Kiselev's cavalier assertions about nuclear war, denouncing the journalist's "dangerous rhetoric" and reassuring listeners that "we are not threatening anyone."[9] The surprise victory of Donald Trump in the United States presidential election on November 8 marked a definitive conclusion to the war hysteria. Russian media had asserted that the election of Hillary Clinton would be a disaster for Russo-American relations that might lead to war; Trump, meanwhile, seemed like he might be willing to accommodate Russian interests. For his part, Kiselev celebrated Trump's election so much that even members of Putin's political party condemned his "Trumpomania."[10]

What are we to make of the 2016 war hysteria and the place of civil defense in it? In many ways it seems more reminiscent of the 1927 War Scare than actual nuclear "close calls" such as the Cuban Missile Crisis or Andropov's worries about a preemptive strike in the early 1980s. In those cases, Soviet leaders had taken disruptive and costly measures to try to mitigate the perceived threat but had been extremely reluctant to share their concerns with the public. As in 1927, the war fears of 2016 played out in a brash publicity blitz taking advantage of all forms of media. In other words, it had all the hallmarks of being primarily an agitation campaign rather than a serious attempt to mobilize the Russian public for an imminent war. Neither Russian nor Western observers reached much agreement as to what the goals of this campaign really were, however. One strain of thought contended that the primary intended targets of the campaign were foreign governments that might interfere with Russia's ongoing military operations in Syria. A second argued that the "war hysteria" was intended to consolidate political support for Putin and his government inside Russia by distracting the public from domestic problems.

This is not to say that President Putin and his associates did not actually worry about a major war with the United States and its allies. His government's massive program of rearmament, which Russia's stagnant economy could hardly afford, included extremely costly investments in systems apparently intended for this scenario. It just seems that Putin, like Stalin in the 1920s, believed that war was an intermediate-term possibility rather than an immediate threat. Yet, as in 1927, the war hysteria also served as a basis for cultivating militarily useful mobilization capabilities. While alarmist commentators such as Kiselev distracted television audiences with talk of nuclear war, the Russian government quietly laid the groundwork for disruptive wartime economic mobilization. Might Putin's Russia be erecting a twenty-first-century counterpart to the Soviet party-garrison state? Only time will tell whether the trends observed in 2016 will conclude in such an outcome, and what role civil defense will play in it.

The United States has also seen calls to revive civil defense in the mid-2010s. The increasing sophistication of North Korean nuclear forces and particularly its sudden development of intercontinental ballistic missiles (ICBMs) in 2017 led some lawmakers to propose renewed civil defense efforts. Brad Sherman, a Democrat representing part of Los Angeles, complained in a House Foreign Affairs Committee meeting that "we ought to have civil defense in this country," but "we have a foreign policy establishment that will not admit to the American people that [deterrence] may fail to prevent us from being hit." He concluded darkly that while "we could prepare to minimize casualties, we won't, because that means we'd have to admit that there's the possibility we will face casualties."[11] Politicians in Hawaii were more proactive: the state's House Public Safety Committee called for the Hawaii Emergency Management Agency (HEMA) to restart the state's fallout shelter system. HEMA's director Toby Clairmont replied that the shelter survey had last been updated in 1985 and that it would take over seven years to provide stocked shelter spaces for the state's 1.42 million residents.[12] On January 13, 2018, HEMA inadvertently terrorized the state's inhabitants when it accidentally circulated an erroneous phone alert stating that a missile had been launched at the islands. Washington state lawmakers introduced a bipartisan bill to rescind the ban on civil defense preparations for nuclear war passed in the 1980s. Republican state senator Mark Miloscia, who cosponsored the bill, scoffed that "to throw your hands up and say, 'Everyone's going to be destroyed,' I think that's silly." His Democratic colleague state senator Guy Palumbo, who also cosponsored the legislation, concurred: "Are you kidding me? We have a law that prevents emergency planning?" and noted "we (legislators) were dumbfounded we wouldn't have contingency plans for any kind of harmful nightmare like that."[13]

It therefore seems that civil defense might return in both Russia and the United States. What kind of lessons should a revived civil defense derive from the experiences of the twentieth century? The history of civil defense in America and the Soviet Union during the Cold War suggests that whether or not civil defense *should* be revived, cultivating a program with a meaningful capacity to protect people from nuclear attack is an extremely challenging task. There is little other reason to pursue such a program, however. Cold War experience showed that civil defense has scant utility for propaganda and agitation, particularly in the long term. Moreover, civil defense proved worse than useless as a means of signaling one's intentions to potential adversaries.

The five chapters of this book traced the troubled evolution of both U.S. and Soviet civil defense during the Cold War. The first chapter examined why both Washington and Moscow hesitated to begin serious civil defense planning for nuclear war. Both Truman and Stalin dallied about civil defense because of political and ideological concerns, as well as skepticism about the imminence of a new world war. The second chapter investigated why neither superpower took decisive steps to develop a robust civil defense during the early 1950s, when nuclear war appeared winnable and superpower relations were often explosive. The third chapter explored the impact of the sudden introduction of thermonuclear weapons and missiles to deliver them on civil defense in the mid to late 1950s. Both U.S. and Soviet civil defense officials attempted to turn the new threat into an argument for massively costly shelter efforts, only to have political leaders curtail or eliminate civil defense instead. The fourth chapter elucidated reasons for the marked divergence of the U.S. and Soviet civil defense programs after superpower leaders revived them during the 1961 Berlin Crisis. Soviet civil defense successfully influenced the formulation of the USSR's nuclear strategy to win the patronage of the Soviet military, but the often-creative efforts of U.S. civil defense officials to cultivate institutional allies failed. The final chapter characterized the ultimate fate of American and Soviet civil defense in the final years of the Cold War. An attempt by the U.S. government to couple civil defense to nuclear strategy utilizing a dubious policy of strategic evacuation became a laughingstock while drawing resources away from peacetime emergency management. In contrast, growing skepticism of civil defense among Soviet leaders, as well as the Chernobyl disaster, ultimately led to its reinvention as a surprisingly effective emergency management agency in the post-Soviet period.

Both U.S. and Soviet civil defense failed abjectly to achieve the goal of fortifying their societies to survive nuclear war. In the 1950s, the Federal Civil Defense Administration (FCDA) and Office of Civil Defense Mobilization admitted frankly that without vastly increased funding, their ability to protect Americans from a Soviet nuclear attack would remain nonexistent. Even at the height of the fallout shelter effort in the mid-1960s, the leaders of U.S. civil defense recognized that their program would require several years of work and billions of dollars before it would achieve operational readiness. Starved of investment, the U.S. civil defense program entered a decline after this point from which it never escaped. Soviet civil defense appears successful only relative to its U.S. counterpart. The MPVO's costly shelter construction effort of the 1950s squandered immense resources building shelters that American hydrogen bombs had already rendered obsolete. Although by the 1970s Soviet civil defense had developed shelter designs that might plausibly withstand thermonuclear attack, these proved so expensive that the program found itself forced to rely on a questionable policy of strategic evacuation to protect all but a small fraction of the country's population. Contrary to Leon Gouré's 1976 assertion that the USSR "already" possessed "a considerable capability" to survive a nuclear war and recover from it, in private, Soviet civil defense officials lamented the myriad weaknesses of their program.[14] Far from sanguine about the consequences of nuclear war, the leaders of U.S. and Soviet civil defense were perhaps more aware than anyone else of just how vulnerable their countries really were.

The sensible choice was to reduce the probability of nuclear war as much as possible, or at least invest in civil defenses adequate to protect their populations from total annihilation if war occurred. Instead, Washington and Moscow doubled down on investments in strategic nuclear weapons while starving their civil defense programs. By forgoing "Armageddon insurance" while stoking the possibility of nuclear war, U.S. and Soviet leaders risked the demise of their respective civilizations.

What accounts for the irrationality of the superpowers' civil defense policies? A comparison of the U.S. and Soviet civil defense programs suggests that it resulted from far more than collective skepticism about the feasibility of civil defense. The two superpowers did not embrace or reject civil defense on the basis of its feasibility, cost, or potential strategic implications. First, in the United States as well as the USSR, scientific opinion remained divided about the extent to which civil defense could protect citizens from the effects of nuclear war, with a sizable contingent of technical experts continuing to endorse it even in the late 1980s. Second, the costs of civil defense did not pose an insurmountable obstacle. Ambitious civil defense programs proposed in both the United States and the Soviet Union, though costly, still represented a mere fraction of the countries' massive defense budgets. For instance, Millard Caldwell's half-billion-dollar budget requests for the FCDA in the early 1950s amounted to about 1 percent of federal defense spending at the time, and even Val Peterson's 1956 proposal for a $30 billion public shelter system likely would have translated into annual expenditures of about 10 percent of the U.S. defense budget in the late 1950s. The Department of Defense's 1977 "plan F" proposal to construct blast shelters for all inhabitants of America's cities also foresaw an annual cost of about 10 percent of defense spending. The Department of Defense projected a total expenditure by the mid-1980s of $58 billion for "plan F," in comparison with the 1977 U.S. defense budget of $131 billion.[15] Archival evidence on Soviet shelter construction costs suggests that even the much-poorer USSR could afford a similarly ambitious program if it reallocated resources from the military. Increasing Soviet civil defense expenditures from its likely value of 1 percent of the annual Soviet defense budget in the mid-1970s to 5 or 10 percent would have been sufficient to construct shelters adequate for the entire urban population of the USSR within a few years.[16] The case of Switzerland, which actually enacted a comprehensive blast shelter system, offers further evidence that such efforts could come to fruition. Third, American and Soviet analysts disagreed about the strategic effects of civil defense, as under different circumstances it might be either stabilizing or provocative. Rather than the factors traditionally cited as dooming civil defense, a study of both superpowers demonstrates that institutional politics and, ultimately, the nature of their respective political systems played the critical role in determining civil defense's development during the Cold War. Civil defense was hard, and neither the American weak contract state nor the Soviet party-garrison state proved equal to the task.

In the decades after 1945, advances in weapons technology transformed the nature of nuclear war, and civil defense evolved accordingly for its institutional advantage. In the early years of the arms race, the U.S. and Soviet militaries envisioned a war fought with a handful of weapons similar to those dropped on Japan. This nuclear conflict would be not only survivable but winnable, and civil defense aimed to help win it. A mere decade later, the introduction of multimegaton warheads and ICBMs, along with enormous growth in the size of nuclear arsenals, utterly transformed the nature of the nuclear threat. Now nuclear war could exterminate entire peoples and might precipitate an ecological apocalypse. Strategists and philosophers argued about whether "victory" had any meaning in such a conflict. Thus, by the early 1960s civil defense focused on survival.

Civil defense officials quickly turned the seemingly insurmountable technical challenge of surviving thermonuclear war to their institutional advantage by using it to advocate for larger and more expensive programs. From fallout in the 1950s to nuclear winter in the 1980s, civil defense proponents made every new threat into a sales pitch. Both American and Soviet civil defense officials made earnest efforts to develop credible measures to protect their populations, but they did so in part because the scale of these would maximize the power and prestige of civil defense.

In the United States and the Soviet Union, the interplay of different institutions acting in their own self-interest yielded divergent results in civil defense efforts. U.S. civil defense struggled, and repeatedly failed, to attract reliable political support, and well-placed congressional opponents hamstrung the nascent planning efforts of the Truman, Kennedy, and Reagan administrations. In the USSR, the alliance of civil defense with powerful military interests rescued the program from oblivion in 1961 and allowed it to enjoy two decades of relative prosperity. American and Soviet civil defense officials proclaimed varying—and occasionally contradictory—rationales for their preferred programs to appeal to a range of constituencies.

For both countries, however, the meager influence of civil defense relative to other interest groups limited their prospects over the course of the Cold War. The lack of a comfortable institutional home for U.S. civil defense efforts during the late 1940s delayed the founding of the FCDA until late

1950 and hobbled that organization with provisions intended to maintain state and local political control. In the Soviet Union, the pervasive influence of Joseph Stalin forestalled attempts to adapt Soviet civil defense and military planning to the realities of the nuclear age. Freed from this obstacle by the dictator's death in 1953, his successors rapidly introduced policies to address the Western nuclear threat, including changes to civil defense. The USSR built bomb shelters on a significant scale, but these were far fewer than needed to protect the country's swelling urban population. To overcome the inadequate shelter availability, American and Soviet planners turned to evacuation as a more affordable substitute, but this expedient failed to solve the political and operational obstacles facing civil defense.

Like their American counterparts, the leaders of the USSR developed a conflicted attitude toward nuclear war and found themselves hemmed in by politics and ideology in a manner that encouraged irrational policy choices. In contrast to the United States, where the possibility of a nuclear war struck many as "unthinkable," in the Soviet Union the political leadership saw the destruction of the Soviet state as equally inconceivable. This proscription made civil defense an ideological necessity, but Soviet statesmen such as Nikita Khrushchev and Leonid Brezhnev also sought to assuage their acute sense of vulnerability by devoting the cream of their nation's technical and economic resources to offensive nuclear weapons. Rather than developing a comprehensive program intended to minimize civilian casualties in case of an unprovoked nuclear attack, they elected to create a relatively inexpensive program intended to preserve the Soviet state in some form, which could work only in a narrow range of circumstances.

Civil defense was one facet of the party-garrison state's increasing dysfunction over the course of the Cold War. The same relentless pursuit of security that motivated Soviet leaders to develop a civil defense system also encouraged them to adopt strategic postures that, under less favorable circumstances, might have inadvertently resulted in the outbreak of a general nuclear war. The Soviet military's emphasis during the 1960s and early 1970s on preempting an enemy nuclear attack, in conjunction with the availability of adequate strategic resources and an atmosphere of international tension, would have significantly increased the chances that a crisis situation would escalate into a full-blown nuclear exchange. Fortunately, the Soviet military implemented a more flexible nuclear strategic doctrine before another superpower standoff like the Cuban Missile Crisis occurred. The USSR's attempts to create a nuclear arsenal capable of retaliating to, rather than preempting, a U.S. nuclear attack ironically convinced American observers such as Leon Gouré and Richard Pipes that the Soviet Union sought a first-strike capability, producing a vicious cycle that brought the Cold War to a new nadir in the early 1980s.

U.S. and Soviet civil defense officials used enemy civil defense activity as ammunition in their battles for influence and resources, but abandoned their inclination for mistrust when it appeared advantageous. In their attempts to monitor enemy civil defense, Soviet and American analysts alike demonstrated a powerful propensity for motivated reasoning, selectively interpreting available evidence to support their institutional interests. Mutual suspicions encouraged both superpowers to characterize almost any civil defense policy as a threat. The USSR's civil defense investments bolstered alarmist U.S. analyses of Soviet intentions during the 1970s and undermined détente. The relatively weak civil defense policies of the United States, in conjunction with its bountiful arsenal of offensive nuclear weapons, persuaded some Soviet observers that Washington believed it could neutralize the USSR's retaliatory capability and win a nuclear war.

Within the limitations of their political and cultural contexts, Soviet and American civil defense officials fashioned narratives of a possible war to suit their institutional needs. Convinced of the feasibility and necessity of their institutional mission, they sought to harness nuclear anxiety for their own ends, and adjusted their portrayals of nuclear war to better exploit new circumstances. As the Cold War waned in the 1980s, American and Soviet civil defense increasingly turned away from planning for nuclear war and toward creating new narratives of concern about natural and technological disasters to appeal for government resources and win popular support.

The Cold War civil defense efforts of the United States and the Soviet Union left a mixed legacy for the countries' subsequent emergency management programs. Both the Federal Emergency Management Agency and the Russian Ministry of Extreme Situations inherited institutional resources originally created to survive nuclear war. As no such conflict ever broke out, these investments never served their intended purpose, but on occasion they proved invaluable. Following the nuclear accidents at Three Mile Island and Chernobyl, civil defense authorities drew on supplies and expertise developed for nuclear attack to assist in the emergency responses. Unfortunately, in both superpowers nuclear war planning served as a constant distraction from preparations for more mundane disasters. Lackluster emergency management performance after the 1988 Armenian earthquake and Hurricane Andrew in 1992 evidenced this lamentable neglect.

Finally, beyond institutional considerations, civil defense officials in both nations struggled to motivate their citizens to participate in civil defense seriously. The largely voluntary nature of civil defense in the United States exacerbated this problem, with a limited number of civil defense enthusiasts providing the bulk of personnel without attracting much interest among the general population. Given the choice between building a fallout shelter and watching a *Twilight Zone* broadcast about a fallout shelter, most Americans clearly preferred the latter. American popular culture also proved unfriendly ground for civil defense propagandists, as even in the late 1940s popular narratives about nuclear war strongly contradicted the needs of civil defense and grew increasingly hostile with time. Despite their experiences during World War II, most Soviet citizens seem to have evinced no more enthusiasm for civil defense than their American counterparts. While Soviet civil defense possessed the ability to make participation in its efforts "compulsory," Soviet citizens benefited from ample practice shirking state-mandated activities, and local authorities often demonstrated little inclination to enforce civil defense edicts. At the same time, civil defense in the USSR enjoyed a relatively friendly media environment that limited the circulation of narratives about nuclear war contradicting those endorsed by the government, and to the extent that Soviet popular culture addressed nuclear war it proved more amenable to civil defense than its American counterpart. The few Soviet novels and films portraying a nuclear war show civil defense measures such as shelters successfully preserving at least some survivors. Instead of signaling popular acceptance of civil defense, however, these isolated examples probably reflect the rarity of tales about nuclear war in Soviet popular culture.

While both Russia and the United States exploited civil defense for the purpose of agitation prior to the Cold War, civil defense propaganda during the Cold War generally aimed to further the institutional goals of civil defense. In the 1920s and 1930s, the civil defense propaganda activities of OSOAVIAKhIM helped socialize Soviet citizens in the emerging Stalinist culture and consolidate Stalin's grip on power. During World War II, the U.S. Office of Civilian Defense crafted propaganda campaigns that helped people on the home front feel like an integral part of the war effort. Neither superpower regularly employed such gambits in its Cold War civil defense propaganda, however. Civil defense was too unpopular in both countries to serve as a promising foundation on which to agitate for other, unrelated goals. U.S. civil defense propaganda typically sought to cultivate political support for the agency's ambitious programs. On the occasions that it did not, such as during the early and late years of the Eisenhower administration, it aimed to placate the few influential U.S. politicians who pressed for more aggressive civil defense efforts, such as Chet Holifield. To the extent that Soviet civil defense propaganda between the 1950s and 1980s had functions outside of teaching citizens how to survive enemy attack, such as inculcating fear of the USSR's capitalist enemies, it was merely one small piece of the regime's comprehensive system of agitation.

Civil defense failed in the United States because, despite the unprecedented Cold War peacetime mobilization, America truly remained a "weak contract state." In order to realize anything beyond an insipid program consisting largely of publicity campaigns, civil defense officials needed to win the support of myriad constituencies on both the national and local levels. All of these groups wielded their respective vetoes early and often. Unlike its Soviet counterpart, civil defense could not force congressmen, state and local governments, or individual citizens to support its programs. Nor could civil defense officials offer many positive inducements to any of these constituencies. Had civil defense received the generous funding it tried so persistently to wrest from Congress, the possibility of disbursing these resources would have given its leaders vast leverage to bolster its agenda. In the absence of funding, civil defense faced an insurmountable chicken-and-egg problem, as it could not lobby very effectively for an expanded budget without more resources to employ as incentives. This vicious cycle ensured that U.S. civil defense never attained most of its ambitions. The inability of U.S. presidents to secure more resources for civil defense offers further evidence of the weakness of the U.S. contract state. Even the direct intervention of President Kennedy, the only enthusiastic civil defense advocate to occupy the White House, managed to secure only a brief surge of funding far smaller than what he sought.

Furthermore, the failings of Soviet civil defense illustrate the limitations of the USSR's party-garrison state. The peculiar unwillingness of the communist leadership to devote more resources to civil defense is especially perplexing given that they genuinely feared nuclear attack and that the purpose of the program was to preserve some sort of nation for them to rule over in the aftermath of one. The Soviet state could, and did, devote an immense share of its national resources to defense, so cost was not the immediate obstacle. There was no need to cultivate a broad political consensus for civil defense among legislators, as the Congress of People's Deputies served as a formal rubber stamp for policies developed by the CPSU Central Committee. Nor were communist leaders particularly dissuaded by the fact that the general population of the country hated many of their policies. Even though individual citizens would have grumbled about the impositions of a more ambitious civil defense program, they were spared from these because their rulers had conflicting views about the desirability and feasibility of civil defense. The Soviet Union's contradictory civil defense policies can be traced to disagreements within the uppermost level of the Communist Party leadership. The party, as it turned out, was the weak link in the party-garrison state.

The stereotypical view in the West during the late Cold War was that the Soviet leadership was obsessed with preserving and perpetuating its power. That a substantial subset of this group self-consciously dismantled the party-state at the twilight of the USSR shows that the reality of Soviet governance was much more nuanced than Western observers acknowledged at the time.[17] The USSR's civil defense program offers further insight into the peculiar, ultimately self-defeating preoccupations and blind spots that eventually doomed the Soviet experiment. The party-garrison state was designed to protect the USSR from a particular kind of threat to its existence—the mass, industrialized warfare envisioned by Western and Soviet military theorists in the aftermath of the First World War. Such wars would involve millions of men under arms as well as immense numbers of machines: tanks, airplanes, and submarines. Despite its disastrous defeats in the early part of the Nazi invasion, the party-garrison state served its intended purpose: communism defeated fascism. The postwar Soviet government failed to adapt to new strategic realities in the nuclear age, however. Soviet scientists invented the ICBM, but their country's military—and more importantly, its centralized economy—was still organized in anticipation of a huge conventional war. The USSR sustained a degree of mobilization readiness in peacetime that Western states achieved only during wars. But these preparations were often divorced from the threat posed by the United States and its allies, and Soviet leaders such as Khrushchev and Mikoian recognized that their country was squandering astronomical resources preparing for the last war.

If the goal of the party-garrison state was to protect the party, and the leaders of the party themselves recognized that they were facing new threats, then why did they fail to adapt the party-garrison state to the realities of the nuclear age, including civil defense? There are several possible explanations. One is that the postwar USSR was not really a "garrison" state but instead something closer to the U.S. "weak contract" state, and that civil defense lost out in the struggle for resources. Another is that the

Soviet regime was simply incapable of the necessary reforms, and that Soviet leaders gave up after a few abortive attempts. An additional possibility is that civil defense was hemmed in by the specific institutional alliances it made to receive the funding it did. The Soviet military was deeply and institutionally invested in the paradigm of large ground forces, and civil defense would be ill advised to challenge it. There is probably substance to all of these explanations, but it seems that the reason that Soviet leaders did not embrace civil defense even as they funded it much more generously than their capitalist rivals was because they were unwilling or unable to truly contemplate the possibility that the USSR could be destroyed by a nuclear war. This obstinacy is reflected by the bizarre, counterproductive secrecy that surrounded the Soviet civil defense program. The USSR refrained from marking its bomb shelters or publicizing emergency plans, leaving many well-educated Soviet citizens unaware that their country even possessed an extensive civil defense effort. From a practical standpoint, secretiveness is a counterproductive feature for a civil defense program, as citizens require thorough knowledge of civil defense preparations for them to be effective. While in a nuclear war such secrecy would sap the ability of civil defense to protect Soviet citizens, in peacetime it had the benefit of keeping civil defense out of sight and out of mind.

Political leaders and ordinary citizens in the United States and the USSR found civil defense disquieting. While some, such as Anastas Mikoian, rejected civil defense because they hoped that superpower rapprochement would end the threat of a nuclear war, others, such as Senator Henry Jackson, did so while taking a confrontational attitude toward the Cold War enemy. In America's open and democratic society, citizens kept civil defense from infringing on their psyches by withholding support for it, keeping civil defense funding at a minimal level for the duration of the Cold War. The USSR's incessant and often senseless inclination for secrecy, meanwhile, allowed the development of a sizable civil defense program that was both ubiquitous and largely invisible. These civil defense efforts gave Soviet leaders hope that their regime would survive a nuclear war in some form, while its low profile kept it from alarming either their citizens or themselves. Unfortunately, marginalizing civil defense did nothing to reduce the possibility of a nuclear exchange, which nearly became a reality at several points during the Cold War. As Representative Sherman observed in 2017, people in both superpowers disliked civil defense because it made the threat of nuclear war feel uncomfortably immediate. Rather than provide reassurance that they possessed some chance of surviving a nuclear war, civil defense preparations reminded them of the possibility of one.

The Cold War ended without a nuclear conflagration, making the wisdom of the superpowers' contrasting civil defense programs difficult to evaluate. The two opponents' civil defense programs represented only a tiny fraction of the costs of strategic nuclear arsenals and did not embolden American or Soviet leaders to think that they could risk nuclear war with impunity. If anything, the weakness of civil defense policy may even have increased the likelihood of a nuclear exchange by reinforcing the illusion that deterrence could not fail. Civil defense officials in the United States and the USSR doggedly pursued the immense resources required to protect their societies from nuclear annihilation, but despite considerably greater Soviet investment, neither country developed a civil defense program that offered citizens much hope of surviving nuclear war, or succeeded in convincing them of the feasibility and desirability of attempting to create such a program.

Notes

Introduction

1. Tsentral'ni derzhavnii arkhiv hromads'kih ob'ednan' Ukraini (Central State Archive of Social Organizations of Ukraine, or TsDAHO), f. 1, op. 24, sp. 4543, ll. 37–38.
2. Mack and Baker, *The Occasion Instant*, 9.
3. Two Russian-language accounts of the USSR's civil defense program exist, but one of these, Fanian's *Grazhdanskaia oborona Moldavskoi SSR*, addresses civil defense only in Soviet Moldova, and the other, Gusev's *Istoricheskie predposylki*, uses archival sources for the period through 1945 only.
4. For instance, the volumes of the *Atomnyi proekt SSSR* document collection published over the past decade make public for the first time items such as the Communist Party of the Soviet Union (CPSU) Presidium's 1953 resolutions ordering the development of civil defense. Riabev, *Atomnyi proekt SSSR*, 2:7:593–600.
5. Kerr, *Civil Defense in the U.S.*; Blanchard, *American Civil Defense 1945–1984*; and Yoshpe, *Our Missing Shield*.
6. Oakes, *The Imaginary War*; Grossman, *Neither Dead nor Red*; and Garrison, *Bracing for Armageddon*.
7. McEnaney, *Civil Defense Begins at Home*; and Rose, *One Nation Underground*.
8. Boyer, *By the Bomb's Early Light*; and Weart, *Nuclear Fear*.
9. Coleman, *The Presidential Recordings of John F. Kennedy*, 6:54.
10. Memorandum of conversation, "Secretary's Meeting with the General Advisory Committee on Arms Control and Disarmament," January 6 [1977], Digital National Security Archive, accessed March 23, 2016, http://nsarchive.gwu.edu/nukevault/ebb521-Irans-Nuclear-Program-1975-vs-2015/07.pdf.
11. Pipes, "Why the Soviet Union Thinks It Could Fight and Win a Nuclear War"; and Gouré, *War Survival in Soviet Strategy*.
12. Gouré, *Vyzhivanie v voine po Sovetskoi strategii*.
13. A mid-1980s attempt to produce a consensus statement on the subject by scientists both supportive and critical of civil defense instead serves as a document of how divided expert opinion on the subject remained as of that date. Dowling and Harrell, *Civil Defense: A Choice of Disasters*.
14. Herman Kahn attributed this phrase to Schelling but noted that he did "not recall inventing it." Kahn, *On Escalation*, 3.
15. Friedberg, *In the Shadow of the Garrison State*.
16. Lasswell, "The Garrison State," 455–68.
17. Friedberg, "Why Didn't the United States Become a Garrison State?," 109–42.

18. The most obvious of these was Stalin's purge of the Soviet General Staff starting in 1936, which severely impaired the Red Army's combat effectiveness and contributed to the disastrous opening phase of the 1941 German invasion.

19. Harrison, "Resource Mobilization for World War II."

20. Jones, *Red Army and Society.*

21. Rowen and Wolf, *The Impoverished Superpower.*

22. Friedberg, "Why Didn't the United States Become a Garrison State?," 113–14.

23. Grossman, *Neither Dead nor Dead*, 8–11. Grossman derives this formulation from Lasswell's later works but admits that he left it "underdeveloped" (109).

24. Grossman, 128.

25. Osipov, "Apokalips vchera."

26. Andriushin, Chernyshev, and Iudrin, *Ukroshchenie iadra*, 181–82.

27. Green and Long, "The MAD Who Wasn't There."

Chapter One

1. Manhattan Engineer District, *A-Bombing of Hiroshima and Nagasaki*, 11.

2. Manhattan Engineer District, 13.

3. United States Strategic Bombing Survey, *United States Strategic Bombing Surveys*, 102.

4. "The Atomic Bomb and Our Cities," 29.

5. *A Visit to Sebastopol a Week After Its Fall*, 29.

6. One eyewitness to the 1863 Siege of Vicksburg noted that "[the city] was well supplied with bomb-proofs, into which whole families might retire when a bombardment was hot." Maury, *Recollections of a Virginian*, 188.

7. *My Cave Life in Vicksburg.*

8. Wells, *The World Set Free.*

9. Weart, *Nuclear Fear*, 125–26. According to literature scholar Paul Brians, the earliest tale of "nuclear holocaust" was Robert Cromie's 1895 book *The Crack of Doom*, in which mad scientists threaten to "undo creation" using atomic technology. See Brians, *Nuclear Holocausts*, 4.

10. Gusev, *Istoricheskie predposylki*, 13–14.

11. United States House of Representatives, *Hearings before Subcommittee No. 1 of the Committee on Military Affairs*, 459.

12. "Over There and Everywhere," 42.

13. Sontag, "The Soviet War Scare of 1926–27," 68–69.

14. Flory, "The Arcos Raid and the Rupture of Anglo-Soviet Relations, 1927."

15. Fischer, *The Soviets in World Affairs*, 2:688.

16. Sontag, "The Soviet War Scare of 1926–27," 71.

17. Kotkin, *Stalin*, 624–25.

18. Cited in Simonov, *Voenno-promyshlennyi kompleks SSSR*, 60.

19. Stalin, "The Tasks of Business Executives."

20. Anokhin, *Oni byli pervymi*, 12–13. In keeping with the Bolsheviks' official policy of the "Dictatorship of the Proletariat," these organizations made defense against gas attacks the task of *only* "laboring people" by excluding "class enemies"

from membership, although the 1926 AVIAKhIM regulations generously allowed "nonworking elements" to donate their labor or money to the worthy tasks of bolstering Soviet air defenses. AVIAKhIM, *Iacheika*, 5.

21. Anokhin, *Oni byli pervymi*, 28–29. See also Leonardov, *Chem grozit voennaia khimiia grazhdanskomu naseleniiu*, for a contemporary example of DOBROKhIM propaganda.

22. Anokhin, *Oni byli pervymi*, 14–15.

23. Anokhin, 16.

24. Velikanova, *Popular Perceptions of Soviet Politics in the 1920s*.

25. Hudson, "The 1927 Soviet War Scare."

26. Simonov, *Voenno-popmyshlennyi kompleks SSSR*.

27. Slepyan, "The Limits of Mobilisation," 853.

28. Both Boris Simonov and Olga Velikanovna assign an instrumental role to the 1927 war scare, but Irina Bystrova argues that the Communist Party did not initiate development of the military-industrial complex until several years later, during the latter part of the first Five-Year Plan. For Bystrova's argument, see Bystrova, *Sovetskii voenno-promyshlennyi kompleks*, 65–69.

29. Leonardov, *Chem grozit voennaia khimiia grazhdanskomu naseleniiu*, 67–70.

30. Quoted in Anokhin, *Oni byli pervymi*, 28.

31. Slepyan, "The Limits of Mobilisation," 856.

32. See Shperk et al., *Inzhnerno-tekhnicheskie sredstva*; and Shperk, *Pravila proektirovaniia ubezhishch v grazhdanskikh zdaniiakh*.

33. Shul'gin, "Obosnovanie trebovanii k zashchitnym svoistvam sooruzhenii GO," 36.

34. "Grazhdanskoi oborone—75 let," 11.

35. Nikonova, "OSOAVIAKhIM kak instrument stalinskoi sotsial'noi mobilizatsii."

36. Anokhin, *Oni byli pervymi*, 21–22. Iosef Unshlikht became Rykov's successor, remaining head of OSOAVIAKhIM only between July 1931 and March 1932. Like Rykov, Unshlikht died a victim of the Great Purges, in 1937.

37. Anokhin, 55–56.

38. Anokhin, 64.

39. In contrast to American complacency, British reluctance to embark on a civil defense effort in the interwar years resulted in considerable part from pessimism about the survivability of air attack even without nuclear weapons. On British attitudes on this subject during the 1930s, see Haapamäki, *The Coming of the Aerial War*.

40. "Averting Death from the Skies," 648–50.

41. MChS Rossii, "Sozdanie i Razvitiia Grazhdanskoi Oborony."

42. Anokhin, *Oni byli pervymi*, 65. Interestingly, OSOAVIAKhIM trained only 880,000 residents after June 22, indicating that its civil defense training took place on a mass scale even during the prewar months.

43. Anokhin, 65. Both Nazi Germany and Imperial Japan neglected civil defense training in the early years of the war, in part owing to institutional squabbling as well as a conviction that enemy bombers would never pose a serious

threat. The increasingly disastrous outcomes of Allied strategic bombing after 1943 forced them to rapidly retool their civil defense efforts, but after the war ended German and Japanese civilians alike widely recalled civil defense as generally ineffective in the face of incendiary and atomic bombings, even though postwar Allied investigators drew the opposite conclusion in their studies of the subject.

44. Anokhin, 68.

45. Narodnyi Komissariat po stroitel'stvu SSSR Tekhnicheskoe upravlenie, *Ukazaniia po prisposobleniiu podvalov sushchestvuiushchikh zdanii pod podval'nye ubezhishcha i ukrytiia PVO.*

46. Beliaev, "Mestnaia protivovozdushnaia oborona," 332.

47. Shul'gin, "Obosnovanie trebovanii k zashchitnym svoistvam sooruzhenii GO," 36.

48. Tooze, *The Wages of Destruction*, 476–85 and 538–49.

49. Beliaev, "Mestnaia protivovozdushnaia oborona," 333.

50. Yoshpe, *Our Missing Shield*, 60.

51. Yoshpe, 61–63.

52. Yoshpe, 63.

53. Yoshpe, 65–66.

54. Yoshpe, 67. Ironically, Douglas, a staunch liberal and supporter of Franklin Roosevelt, had alienated communists with his condemnation of the Soviet invasion of Finland. Despite this, accusations that he was either a communist himself or a fellow traveler persisted into the 1950s. On Douglas's resignation from the communist-dominated Motion Picture Democratic Committee, see Olsen, "The Movie Hearings," 141.

55. Yoshpe, *Our Missing Shield*, 68.

56. Yoshpe, 68.

57. Yoshpe, 68.

58. Yoshpe, 70.

59. Jordan, *Civil Defense before 1950*, 44.

60. Yoshpe, *Our Missing Shield*, 73.

61. Yoshpe, 70–71.

62. Yoshpe, 72. On the status of WWII civil defense legislation in the postwar era, see John R. Steelman to John F. Kennedy, letter, January 22, 1950, NA RG 304, Records of the Office of Civil and Defense Mobilization, MLR 31A, Box 1, Folder E4-2, "Federal-State-Local Relationships." Steelman noted that as of the beginning of 1950, World War II civil defense legislation remained in effect in Florida, Idaho, Michigan, Nevada, and Rhode Island.

63. Craig and Radchenko, *The Atomic Bomb and the Origins of the Cold War*, 95.

64. AVPRF, F. 6, op. 8, p. 7, d. 76, l. 3.

65. AVPRF, F. 6, op. 8, p. 7, d. 76, l. 7.

66. AVPRF, F. 6, op. 8, p. 7, d. 76, l. 15.

67. "The Reserve Officer in Civil Defense," NA RG 397, Records of the Defense Civil Preparedness Agency, MLR 7, Box 15, Folder "The Reserve Officer in Civil Defense."

68. For an important example, see Bradley, *No Place to Hide*. On the history of these efforts, see Boyer, *By the Bomb's Early Light*.

69. Yoshpe, *Our Missing Shield*, 77.

70. Yoshpe, 73.

71. Yoshpe, 79.

72. Yoshpe, 78.

73. Soviet foreign minister Viacheslav Molotov sent a telegram to Washington on February 2, 1946, requesting that Soviet observers be invited to the test that summer. Riabev, *Atomnyi proekt SSSR*, 2:6:90-91.

74. Riabev, 2:6:238-41.

75. Riabev, 2:6:247-48.

76. Riabev, 2:6:350-53.

77. Riabev, 2:6:350-53.

78. Riabev, 2:6:374-75.

79. Riabev, 2:6:402-4.

80. Riabev, 2:6:404.

81. Mikhailov, *Iadernye ispytania SSSR*, 243.

82. Rhodes, *Dark Sun*, 246.

83. Holloway, *Stalin and the Bomb*, 237-42.

84. Norris, "Phone Head Is Chosen to Plan Civil Defense for Atomic War," 9.

85. Yoshpe, *Our Missing Shield*, 97.

86. Tyler, "Civil Defense," 149.

87. Yoshpe, *Our Missing Shield*, 99.

88. Tyler, "Civil Defense," 150.

89. Tyler, 157-58.

90. Quoted in Yoshpe, *Our Missing Shield*, 97-98.

91. Tyler, "Civil Defense," 152.

92. Yoshpe, *Our Missing Shield*, 101-2.

93. On Drew Pearson's campaign against Forrestal, see Ritchie, *Reporting from Washington*, 139-40.

94. Jordan, *Civil Defense before 1950*, argues that Truman sought to avoid creating a civil defense organization altogether. Yoshpe, *Our Missing Shield*, 114.

95. Riabev, *Atomnyi proekt SSSR*, 2:6:642-43.

96. Riabev, 2:6:644-48.

97. Holloway, *Stalin and the Bomb*, 258.

98. Gordin, *Red Cloud at Dawn*, 179-213.

99. John F. Kennedy to Harry S. Truman, letter, October 8, 1949, NA RG 304, Records of the Office of Civil and Defense Mobilization, MLR 1A, box 1, folder E4-1, "Civil Defense, General."

100. Yoshpe, *Our Missing Shield*, 116.

101. John R. Steelman to Harry S. Truman, letter, October 14, 1949, NA RG 304, Records of the Office of Civil and Defense Mobilization, MLR 1A, box 1, folder E4-1, "Civil Defense, General."

102. Yoshpe, *Our Missing Shield*, 117-18.

103. Yoshpe, 120. The dictator would also likely have found novel Symington's statement that "Stalin himself has often asserted, at least once since V-J day, that the countries of capitalism must be destroyed."

104. Symington, "The Importance of Civil Defense Planning," 231–32.

105. Calingaert, "Nuclear Weapons and the Korean War."

106. Friedberg, "Why Didn't the United States Become a Garrison State?"

107. Riabev, *Atomnyi proekt SSSR*, 2:7:134–35.

108. At a January 1951 meeting with officials from the USSR's eastern European satellites, Stalin demanded that they be ready for a war with the United States and its allies in "two or three years." See Cristescu, "Strict Secret de Importantă Deosobită"; English translation available at http://nsarchive.gwu.edu/NSAEBB/NSAEBB14/doc4.htm, accessed January 6, 2018.

109. Riabev, *Atomnyi proekt SSSR*, 2:7:159–61.

110. Anokhin, *Oni byli pervymi*, 73.

111. Anokhin, 76.

112. Anokhin, 77.

113. A 1956 DOSAAF report to the CPSU Central Committee reports continuing progress toward "one of our primary goals of recent years—growing our membership and fulfilling the plan for the collection of membership dues," which trickled up to the all-Union organization. As of that date, the membership of DOSAAF had grown to twenty-four million Soviet citizens. GARF, F. 9552, op. 1, ed. khr. 259, l. 30.

114. According to the manual, "The self-defense group carries out very critical and serious tasks. It is their duty to promptly inform the population of airborne, chemical, and incendiary threats; to administer first aid to the injured; to confirm the fulfillment of preventative antifire measures and the rules of behavior in wartime; to liquidate the damaged areas resulting from air attack; to protect state, cooperative, and personal property; to carry out blackout measures; and to maintain shelters in constant readiness and use them correctly." Perelygin, *Gruppa samozashchity*, 10–11.

115. Perelygin, 11–12.

116. Perelygin, 11.

117. Perelygin, 168. For an example of lax MPVO oversight of DOSAAF civil defense training efforts in the early 1950s, see TsGAMO, F. 6375, op. 1, d. 31, l. 15. In May 1952 Major Sergeev, the MPVO head of the city of Serpukhov, near Moscow, reported to the Moscow oblast civil defense head that he would take measures to correct the inadequacies outlined in a letter sent by Comrade Federovaia, leader of the DOSAAF organization at the "Krasnyi Tekstil'shchik" factory in Serpukhov.

118. Wadsworth, *The Silver Spoon*, 144–45.

119. Wadsworth, 145–47.

120. Yoshpe, *Our Missing Shield*, 125.

121. Wadsworth wrote in 1976 that "naturally, I attempted no reply of any sort: his first accusation was correct in that both of the men *were* important, and for the rest adhering grimly to the political rule that applies to everyone, regardless of family, reputation and all other possible credits: 'Don't ever get into a pissin' match with a skunk.'" Ironically, in subsequent years Wadsworth and Pearson became friends, and Pearson apologized for dismissing Wadsworth "as a worthless relative of worthy people." Wadsworth, *The Silver Spoon*, 156.

122. Yoshpe, *Our Missing Shield*, 161–62.

123. Blair, "Millard F. Caldwell of Florida."

124. The Regional Council for Education announced plans for interstate cooperation among several states to create segregated schools for graduate and professional education in 1948, which African American leaders saw as a means of getting around Supreme Court decisions such as *Gaines v. Canada* 305 (1938). For an example of such a critique, see Johnson, "Why Negroes Are Opposed to Segregated Regional Schools."

125. On the history of the tragic lynching and Caldwell's response, see Davis, "'Whitewash' in Florida."

126. The editorial, "Two Governors on Race Relations," attacked Caldwell for a statement its authors and many others interpreted as an apologia for lynching: "the ordeal of bringing a young and innocent victim of rape into open court and subjecting her to detailed cross-examination by defense counsel could easily be as great an injury as the original crime. This fact probably accounts for a number of killings or lynchings which might otherwise be avoided. Society has not found a solution to this problem." *Collier's* retorted that Caldwell apparently believed that "the mob had saved courts, etc., considerable trouble." The $237,000 was the largest libel award in the history of the United States. The award was reduced at retrial to $100,000, and ultimately *Collier's* settled in 1949 for $50,000. On the libel case, see Davis, "Whitewash," 292–98.

127. Florida became a pivotal battleground in the 1948 presidential election, as with the split in the Florida Democratic Party between the Dixiecrats and the Truman supporters, Republican candidate Thomas E. Dewey also campaigned heavily in the state in hopes that he, too, might win its electoral votes. On the complex politics of the 1948 election in Florida and Caldwell's role in it, see Pleasants, "Claude Pepper, Strom Thurmond, and the 1948 Presidential Election in Florida."

128. African American civil rights activists expressed outrage that Caldwell's "qualifications" consisted largely of his demonstrated aptitude organizing white Southerners to evade increasing federal pressure on civil rights issues. In testimony before the Senate Armed Services Committee, Clarence Mitchell of the National Association for the Advancement of Colored People (NAACP) characterized the appointment of Caldwell as "an insult to colored people" undertaken merely to "give aid and comfort" to the Dixiecrats. "Meet Mr. Caldwell."

129. On the NAACP protest campaign against Caldwell, see Grossman, *Neither Dead nor Red*, 92–102; and McEnaney, *Civil Defense Begins at Home*, 141–46.

130. Yoshpe, *Our Missing Shield*, 161.

131. Wadsworth, *The Silver Spoon*, 157.

132. The Federal Civil Defense Act of 1950 passed the House with only one dissenting vote, and the Senate by voice vote. Yoshpe, *Our Missing Shield*, 154.

133. "Meet Mr. Caldwell," 184.

134. "Caldwell Is Approved," *New York Times*, January 16, 1951, 26; and "Shelters Won't Help, Caldwell Declares," *New York Times*, January 17, 1951, 6.

135. Rabinowitch, "Civil Defense."

136. Riabev, *Atomnyi proekt SSSR*, 2:7:589–92.

Chapter Two

1. "Survey of Public Affairs Aspects of Operation Tryout, August 22, 1953," NA RG 304, Records of the Office of Civil and Defense Mobilization, MLR 1-A, Box 181, Binder "Operation Tryout."
2. "Survey of Public Affairs Aspects of Operation Tryout."
3. "Survey of Public Affairs Aspects of Operation Tryout."
4. "Survey of Public Affairs Aspects of Operation Tryout."
5. "Survey of Public Affairs Aspects of Operation Tryout."
6. "Survey of Public Affairs Aspects of Operation Tryout."
7. See Oakes, *The Imaginary War*; and Garrison, *Bracing for Armageddon*.
8. National Security Resources Board, *United States Civil Defense*.
9. "Proposed Financing Civil Defense Requirements Fiscal Years 1951 through 1954," NA RG 304, Records of the Office of Civil and Defense Mobilization, MLR 1-A, box 178, folder "Budget."
10. Millard Caldwell to Douglas McKay, letter, January 2, 1951, NA RG 304, Records of the Office of Civil and Defense Mobilization, MLR 31A, box 15, folder E4-56, "Bombing Shelters."
11. Albert Cobo to Charles E. Wilson, letter, December 27, 1950, NA RG 304, Records of the Office of Civil and Defense Mobilization, MLR 31A, box 15, folder E4-56, "Bombing Shelters."
12. Millard Caldwell to Douglas McKay, letter, January 2, 1951, and Millard Caldwell to Estes Kefauver, letter, January 4, 1951, NA RG 304, Records of the Office of Civil and Defense Mobilization, MLR 31A, box 15, folder E4-56, "Bombing Shelters."
13. Harry G. Lankford to Leslie Kullenberg, letter, January 26, 1951, NA RG 304, Records of the Office of Civil and Defense Mobilization, MLR 31A, box 15, folder E4-56, "Bombing Shelters."
14. Alfred H. Bergman to Millard Caldwell, letter, January 26, 1951, and Alfred H. Bergman to Colonel Charles Keggan, letter, January 25, 1951, NA RG 304, Records of the Office of Civil and Defense Mobilization, MLR 31A, box 15, folder E4-56, "Bombing Shelters."
15. G. L. Schuyler and Ellery Husted to Leslie Kullenberg, memorandum, December 19, 1950, "Comments on Bomb Shelter Design Submitted by Maryland Concrete Products," NA RG 304, Records of the Office of Civil and Defense Mobilization, MLR 31A, box 15, folder E4-56, "Bombing Shelters."
16. G. L. Schuyler and Emery Husted to Leslie Kullenberg, memorandum, February 8, 1951, "United States Civil Defense, Proposed Revision of," NA RG 304, Records of the Office of Civil and Defense Mobilization, MLR 31A, box 14, folder E4-41, "September 1950 Plan."
17. Schuyler and Husted to Kullenberg, memorandum, February 8, 1951.
18. Millard Caldwell to Albert Cobo, letter, February 28, 1951, NA RG 304, Records of the Office of Civil and Defense Mobilization, MLR 31A, box 15, folder E4-56, "Bombing Shelters."
19. "Civil Defense Budget Is Cut over 50 Percent."

20. Kennedy, "Civil Defense Cut Called Crippling."

21. Table of FY 1951 FCDA Budget Request, NA RG 304, Records of the Office of Civil and Defense Mobilization, MLR 1-A, box 178, folder "Budget." Significantly, neither the House nor the Senate passed the $75 million in shelter funding budgeted by the House Appropriations Committee.

22. "Extract from the House of Representatives Report on Appropriations Committee," NA RG 304, Records of the Office of Civil and Defense Mobilization, MLR 1-A, box 178, folder "Budget."

23. "Extract from the House of Representatives Report on Appropriations Committee."

24. Newsweek Special Report, "Civilians: Vital Link in Defense," 1951, 17, NA RG 397, Records of the Defense Civil Preparedness Agency, MLR 7, box 13, folder "Platform."

25. Millard Caldwell to Frank J. Lausche, letter, April 13, 1951, NA RG 304, Records of the Office of Civil and Defense Mobilization, MLR 1-A, box 178, folder "Budget."

26. Caldwell to Lausche, letter, April 13, 1951.

27. "Wadsworth Praises Cooperation of Film Industry," 5.

28. "Wadsworth Praises Cooperation of Film Industry," 1.

29. The first results of the shelter research effort appeared in print only in late 1951. Federal Civil Defense Administration, *Shelter from Atomic Attack in Existing Buildings, Part I—Method for Determining Shelter Needs and Shelter Areas*. The FCDA circulated the earliest version of this manual at a June 1951 conference, but the final published version came out in April 1952. See "Shelter Program Is Launched at Meeting of State Technicians," 6; and "FCDA Estimates Shelter Available for 2,000,000," 4.

30. Federal Civil Defense Administration, *Shelter from Atomic Attack in Existing Buildings, Part II—Improvement of Shelter Areas*, 7.

31. "Minutes of the Assistant Administrators' Meeting of January 16, 1952," NA RG 304, Records of the Office of Civil and Defense Mobilization, MLR 1-A, box 792, folder "Assistant Administrators' Meetings, 1952."

32. Federal Civil Defense Administration, *Home Shelters for Family Protection in an Atomic Attack*. On the role of atomic testing in the delay of the manual, see John DeChant to Douglas Johnson, letter, April 16, 1953, NA RG 304, Records of the Office of Civil and Defense Mobilization, MLR 1-A, box 792, untitled folder; and memorandum from Paul Wagner, "Home Type Shelters," April 24, 1953, NA RG 304, Records of the Office of Civil and Defense Mobilization, MLR 1-A, box 792, untitled folder.

33. "Monthly Field Report No. 19, November 10, 1952," NA RG 397, Records of the Defense Civil Preparedness Agency, MLR 7, box 11, folder "Monthly Field Reports, 1952–53."

34. "Monthly Field Report No. 21, January 1952," NA RG 397, Records of the Defense Civil Preparedness Agency, MLR 7, box 11, folder "Monthly Field Reports, 1952–53."

35. "Monthly Field Report No. 21, January 1952."

36. "Monthly Field Report No. 18, October 10, 1952," NA RG 397, Records of the Defense Civil Preparedness Agency, MLR 7, box 11, folder "Monthly Field Reports, 1952–53."

37. "Raid Signs Posted in Capitol," *Denver Post*, August 13, 1952.

38. Irving J. Gitlin to James Wadsworth, letter, September 26, 1950, NA RG 304, Records of the Office of Civil and Defense Mobilization, MLR 31A, box 14, folder E4-32, "Television Programs"; John A. De Chant, memorandum, October 13, 1950, NA RG 304, Records of the Office of Civil and Defense Mobilization, MLR 31A, box 14, folder E4-32, "Television Programs."

39. John De Chant to Millard Caldwell, memorandum, January 20, 1951, NA RG 304, Records of the Office of Civil and Defense Mobilization, MLR 31A, box 14, folder E4-32, "Television Programs."

40. Jesse Butcher to Harold L. Goodwin, memorandum, February 13, 1951, NA RG 304, Records of the Office of Civil and Defense Mobilization, MLR 31A, box 14, folder E4-32, "Television Programs." Eleanor Roosevelt proved a particularly amenable interviewer, as her show requested a list of potential questions from the FCDA in advance, which Jesse Butcher of the Audio-Visual Division of the Public Affairs Office gladly provided. Jesse Butcher to Henry Morganthau, letter, February 20, 1951, NA RG 304, Records of the Office of Civil and Defense Mobilization, MLR 31A, box 14, folder, E4-32, "Television Programs."

41. Robert O. Renville to Robert W. Zehring, letter, May 29, 1950, NA RG 304, Records of the Office of Civil and Defense Mobilization, MLR 31A, box 13, folder E4-29, "Survey of Public Opinion."

42. Leslie Kullenberg to James J. Wadsworth, memorandum, December 5, 1950, NA RG 304, Records of the Office of Civil and Defense Mobilization, MLR 31A, box 13, folder E4-29, "Survey of Public Opinion."

43. Janis, "Psychological Problems of A-Bomb Defense," 260.

44. Janis, *Air War and Emotional Stress*, 181.

45. Janis, 234, 237.

46. Janis, 243.

47. Janis, 183.

48. Janis, 250.

49. Robin, *The Making of the Cold War Enemy*, 24.

50. Robin, 59.

51. Robin, 35, 60.

52. Robin, 60–62.

53. Robin, 62–63. Behavioralist Paul Lazerfield coauthored two books on this theme: *The People's Choice*, on the presidential election of 1940, and *Voting*, on the election of 1948. In the former work he argued that "opinion leaders" set the tone for the political behavior of primary groups, and therefore most citizens were unaffected by media messages beseeching them to shift their loyalties.

54. *The Atomic Cafe*, directed and produced by Jayne Loader, Kevin Rafferty, and Pierce Rafferty (The Archives Project, 1982).

55. "Atomic Survival Film Released This Month, First of Series," 7.

56. "Wadsworth Praises Cooperation of Film Industry." The distributor, Castle Films, enjoyed the most advantaged position in the entire arrangement, taking a cut of the revenue while bearing none of the losses if the films proved unpopular.

57. Ken Sitz and Bill Geerhart of the Cold War culture website Conelrad interviewed surviving Archer Productions employees in the early 2000s, including Langlois, Mauer, and Anthony Rizzo. Using these interviews, in addition to a scrapbook about the production and promotion of *Duck and Cover* preserved by Langlois, they compiled an account of the production of the film on which I draw heavily for my discussion. Conelrad, "'Duck and Cover.'"

58. Conelrad, "Atomic Tattoo."

59. Conelrad, "'Duck and Cover.'"

60. Conelrad, "'Atomic Flash.'"

61. Janis, *Air War and Emotional Stress*, 13.

62. Janis, 14.

63. United States Army Medical Department, "What Every Medical Officer Should Know about the Atomic Bomb," 516.

64. Mauer recalled in an interview that originally the monkey was a skunk. Conelrad, "'Atomic Flash.'"

65. Conelrad, "'Atomic Flash.'"

66. Conelrad, "'Atomic Flash.'"

67. Conelrad, "Putting the Jingle in Bert."

68. Jacobs, *The Dragon's Tail*, 102.

69. Archer Productions had no role in the making of the radio adaptation, titled "Bert the Turtle," which was written by Paul Newland and directed by Stephen J. McCormick of the Audio-Visual Division of the FCDA Public Affairs Office; the program nonetheless won first prize at the 1952 annual convention of the Institute for Education by Radio and Television. "FCDA Receives Awards."

70. *Civil Defense Alert* 1, no. 8 (1952): 5.

71. "'Duck and Cover' Introducing Bert the Turtle," NA RG 304, Records of the Office of Civil and Defense Mobilization, MLR 1-A, box 737, folder "Bert the Turtle (Radio)."

72. "'Duck and Cover' Introducing Bert the Turtle."

73. *Duck and Cover*, directed by Anthony Rizzo, produced by Leo M. Langlois (Archer Productions, 1951).

74. *Duck and Cover*.

75. "'Duck and Cover' Introducing Bert the Turtle."

76. *Duck and Cover*.

77. On the Alert America campaign, see Oakes, *The Imaginary War*, 82–83; and Garrison, *Bracing for Armageddon*, 43.

78. Conelrad, "'THE COMMUNIST PARTY LINE.'"

79. Project East River, *Information and Training for Civil Defense*, i.

80. Project East River, 1.

81. Project East River, 8.

82. Project East River, 2.

83. Project East River, 2.
84. Project East River, 6, ix.
85. Project East River, 3.
86. Project East River, 3.
87. Project East River, vii.
88. Project East River, 17.
89. Project East River, vii.
90. Project East River, 15.
91. "Motion Picture Films on Civil Defense," Catalogue PA-MP-1 November 1956, NA RG 397, Records of the Defense Civil Preparedness Agency, MLR 7, Box 36, Folder "Misc Publications PA-MP-1 Catalogue of Motion Picture Films." FCDA FYI # 241 from November 3, 1955, also contained the same recall notice for the ten civil defense instruction films from 1951 to 1952.
92. "Radio Address by Val Peterson, Federal Civil Defense Administrator, Station KIOA Des Moines, for Recording April 30, 1954," NA RG 304, Records of the Office of Civil and Defense Mobilization, MLR 1-A, box 739, folder "Governor Peterson-Speeches."
93. Political scientist Andrew D. Grossman argues that "the main goal of civil defense was to promote an illusion of protection to a select but important political constituency: mostly white, middle-class, suburban America"; see Grossman, *Neither Dead nor Red*, 104. Liberal studies professor Patrick B. Sharp asserts in his *Savage Perils* that "the government had no intention of trying to protect all of its citizens equally from future enemy attacks," (195) blaming Caldwell's influence for the existence of segregated bomb shelters in the Deep South.
94. Wadsworth, *The Silver Spoon*, 157.
95. "Caldwell Wants to Quit: But Civil Defense Head Says Truman Won't Let Him Go."
96. Jim G. Lucas, "FCDA Boss Skips His Own Alert," undated newspaper clipping preserved in NA RG 304, Records of the Office of Civil and Defense Mobilization, MLR 1-A, Box 790, no folder.
97. Wadsworth chaired the regular meetings of the FCDA's assistant administrators—the heads of the FCDA's various divisions—in Caldwell's absence, which by early 1952 appears to have been near constant. On March 5, Caldwell attended the meeting to tell his staff about his hopes that Truman would soon relieve him. For the records of these meetings, see NA RG 304, Records of the Office of Civil and Defense Mobilization, MLR 1-A, box 792, folder "Assistant Administrator's Meetings, 1952," and Box 794, Folder "Asst. Administrator's Meetings Minutes, etc."
98. Wadsworth, *The Silver Spoon*, 174.
99. "Caldwell Resigns Civil Defense Post."
100. Wadsworth, *The Silver Spoon*, 173–75.
101. TsGAMO, f. 7105, op. 1, d. 59, l. 19.
102. TsGAMO, f. 6880, op. 2, d. 736, ll. 1–304.
103. TsGAMO, f. 6880, op. 2, d. 736, ll. 10–11.
104. TsGAMO, f. 6880, op. 2, d. 736, ll. 175–77.
105. TsGAMO, f. 6880, op. 2, d. 737, ll. 631–35.

106. TsGAMO, f. 6880, op. 2, d. 749, ll. 1–2.
107. TsGAMO, f. 7105, op. 1, d. 222, l. 58.
108. TsGAMO, f. 7105, op. 1, d. 222, l. 29.
109. TsGAMO, f. 7105, op. 1, d. 222, l. 59.
110. Riabev, *Atomnyi proekt SSSR*, 2:7:568.
111. Riabev, 2:7:589–92.
112. Vladimirov et al., *Ot MPVO k grazhdanskoi zashchite*, 77.
113. Riabev, *Atomnyi proekt SSSR*, 2:7:593–600.
114. TsDAHO, f. 1, op. 24, sp. 3611, ark. 30.
115. TsDAHO, f. 1, op. 24, sp. 3611, ark. 18ob.
116. TsDAHO, f. 1, op. 24, sp. 3611, ark. 40.
117. TsDAHO, f. 1, op. 24, sp. 3611, ark. 40ob.
118. TsDAHO, f. 1, op. 24, sp. 3611, ark. 38ob.
119. TsDAHO, f. 1, op. 24, sp. 3611, ark. 39.
120. Kissinger, *Nuclear Weapons and Foreign Policy*, 369. The first appearance of a mushroom cloud in a Soviet publication is difficult to date, but no known examples predate 1954. Although the *Pamiatka* enjoyed extremely limited circulation in its first two editions, it is a strong candidate for this honor. Mushroom clouds became common in Soviet publications only the following year.
121. TsDAHO, f. 1, op. 24, sp. 3611, ark. 88ob. The final paragraph differs between the first and third editions of the *Pamiatka*, but the meaning remains essentially similar. TsDAHO, f. 1, op. 24, sp. 3611, ark. 100.
122. Buianov, "Energiia atoma" 3–6; Dorofeev, "Kharakteristika atomnogo vzryva"; Gabrikov, "Sredstva i sposoby protivoatomnoi zashchity"; Naumenko, "Udarnaia volna i svetovoe izluchenie pri atomnom vzryve"; Naumenko, "Pronikaiushchaia radiatsiia i radioaktivnoe zarazhenie pri atomnom vzryve"; and Naumenko, "Udarnaia volna i svetovoe izluchenie pri atomnom vzryve," 10, 12.
123. Quoted in Kissinger, *Nuclear Weapons and Foreign Policy*, 383.
124. Kissinger, 385.
125. A November 30, 1954, report of the Komsomol Central Committee about the military indoctrination of Soviet youth noted that as of that date, DOSAAF had undertaken no measures whatsoever regarding the training of its members in antiatomic defense, and that its leadership was not making any moves to do so. RGASPI, f. M-1, op. 47, d. 385, ll. 9–10.
126. Laksness, *Atomnaia stantsiia*, 245–46.
127. RGANI, f. 5, op. 16, ed. khr. 699, ll. 90–91.
128. Vladimirov et al., *Ot MPVO k grazhdanskoi zashchite*, 252.
129. Naumenko's *Atomnaia energiia i ee ispolzovanie* contains a brief chapter on civil defense against nuclear weapons.
130. GARF, f. 9552, op. 1, ed. khr. 259, l. 29.
131. RGASPI, f. M-1, op. 47, d. 407, ll. 10–11.
132. GARF, f. 9552, op. 1, ed khr. 455, l. 195.
133. GARF, f. 9552, op. 1, ed khr. 455, l. 196.
134. The classified internal casualty estimates used by the MPVO in the late 1950s yield results similar to those of the FCDA in the early 1950s, prior to the introduction

of thermonuclear weapons. The MPVO estimated that in the case of a nuclear attack on a city, 55 percent of its population would become casualties, with one-third of those "irrecoverable." Although crude (small, dense cities would obviously experience a higher proportional casualty rate than larger, more dispersed ones when hit with similar weapons), the estimate that one-sixth of the city's inhabitants would be killed outright is more pessimistic than that used by the FCDA in Operation Tryout. TsGAMO, f. 6880, op. 2, d. 764, l. 60.

135. In June 1957, the DOSAAF Central Committee issued a resolution stipulating stringent measures to improve civil defense training, complaining that in many places courses diverged from regulations, that reports to state and party authorities about progress were of poor quality, and that "many" administrators and managers had blown off civil defense training entirely. See Prezidium Tsentral'nogo Komiteta DOSAAF, *Postanovlenie o sostoianii raboty*, 4.

136. TsGAMO, f. 7105, op. 1, d. 411, l. 43.

137. TsGAMO, f. 7105, op. 1, d. 415, ll. 13–26.

138. TsGAMO, f. 7105, op. 1, d. 411, l. 42.

139. TsGAMO, f. 7105, op. 1, d. 415, l. 27.

140. Gusev, *Istoricheskie predposylki*, 128.

141. Gusev, 128–29.

142. GARF, f. 9552, op. 1, ed khr. 455, l. 197. The agent used in these exercises was chloropicrin, an irritant introduced by the German Army during World War I. To conduct the campaign the Soviet government distributed forty tons of this substance to different parts of the country, in some cases storing it, incongruously, in the facilities of the Grain Ministry.

143. Gouré, *Civil Defense in the Soviet Union*, 111.

144. Sinitsyn et al., *Mestnaia protivovozdushnaia oborona*; and Moskalev, Sinitsyn, and Tertychnyi, *Uchebnoe posobie po MPVO*.

145. Miroshnikov, *Kollektivnye sredstva protivoatomnoi zashchity*, 3.

146. TsGAMO, f. 7105, op. 1, d. 415, l. 37.

147. TsGAMO, f. 7105, op. 1, d. 415, l. 37.

148. Vladimirov et al., *Ot MPVO k grazhdanskoi zashchite*, 135, 153, 168.

149. For instance, the famous Rot Front (Red Front) chocolate factory in Moscow received a "class II" classification, and as a result built heavy bomb shelters for its workers. TsGAMO, f. 6880, op. 2, d. 239, ll. 75–76. Meanwhile, the MPVO classed Factory 383 of the Directorate of the Aviation Industry as a "class III" facility, meaning that, in terms of civil defense planning, the Soviet government treated Rot Front's chocolates as a higher priority than Factory 383's aircraft components. TsGAMO, f. 6880, op. 2, d. 159, ll. 22–23.

150. TsGAMO, f. 6880, op. 2, d. 759, ll. 1–114.

151. For instance, in 1957 the MPVO staff of Moscow's Dzerzhniskii district blasted L. Ia. Shekhmeister, the manager of the Detskaia kniga (Children's Book) printing press in Moscow, after he protested that they were "not objective" in concluding that he had totally disregarded their instructions the previous year. TsGAMO, f. 6880, op. 2, d. 62, ll. 20–21.

152. The MPVO staff of Moscow's Dzerzhinskii district blamed local state authorities for construction delays owing to their constant failure to set firm deadlines for completing the shelters. TsGAMO, f. 6880, op. 2, d. 63, l. 3.

153. TsGAMO, f. 7105, op. 1, d. 411, ll. 32–33; TsGAMO, f. 7105, op. 1, d. 411, ll. 34–37; TsGAMO, f. 7105, op. 1, d. 415, ll. 25–26; TsGAMO, f. 7105, op. 1, d. 415, ll. 31–33.

154. For instance, in 1959 Dzerzhinskii district budgeted 2,693,000 rubles for shelter construction. TsGAMO, f. 6880, op. 2, d. 64, l. 20. That same year Frunze district budgeted 2,468,600 rubles for shelters. TsGAMO, f. 6880, op. 2, d. 762, ll. 41–43. Some areas of the city spent far more: Stalin district planned to spend 6,440,000 rubles on civil defense construction during 1959, and at the end of that year had spent 6,306,200 rubles on completing or modernizing 107 shelters. TsGAMO, f. 6880, op. 2, d. 671, ll. 38–43.

155. Fursenko, *Prezidium TsK KPSS*, 125. This figure suggests that the approximate average level of spending on shelters in the Moscow oblast was similar to that in the USSR as a whole—about ten rubles per urban resident. This could be both because Moscow possessed more shelters that could be upgraded and because the metro system was not funded via civil defense.

156. Tsentral'noe statisticheskoe upravlenie, *Narodnoe khoziaistvo SSSR*, 161.

157. In 1955, the Central Intelligence Agency (CIA) estimated that the overall Soviet defense budget that year totaled about 120 billion rubles. Owing to the methodology used, this estimate probably underestimates labor costs and cannot be directly compared with actual budget figures from archival documents. CIA Office of Research and Reports, "Soviet Defense Expenditures, CIA/SC/RR 22," 2. If this figure is approximately correct, then civil defense, including construction, administration, payroll, and training, probably accounted for between 1 and 2 percent of the USSR's defense spending in the late 1950s. For comparison, during the 1950s the United States spent an average of 0.14 percent of its total defense budget on civil defense. Mitchell, *Civil Defense*, 20.

158. Geist, "Was There a Real 'Mineshaft Gap'?," 18–22.

Chapter Three

1. Riabev, *Atomnyi proekt SSSR*, 3:2:164.

2. Riabev, 3:2:164.

3. Wylie, *Tomorrow!* In 1954, the FCDA relocated from its offices in Gelmarc Towers in Washington to a disused hospital in Battle Creek, Michigan, originally built for the famous Kellogg sanitarium. The move resulted both from a policy stipulating that the government not rent private facilities when suitable government facilities were available and from the belief that Washington would be demolished in a nuclear war and that, as a result, headquartering civil defense there might be inadvisable. The move proved disastrous for the FCDA, as it lost most of its remaining experienced leaders and many needed lower-level personnel because of their disinclination to follow their employer to Michigan. On the move, see "FCDA Moves to Battle Creek—1954," NA RG 397, Records of the Defense

Civil Preparedness Agency, MLR 7, Box 7, Folder "FCDA Moves to Battle Creek—1954."

4. Phillip Wylie to Edward B. Lyman, letter, January 19, 1955, NA RG 396, Records of the Office of Emergency Preparedness, Entry 1009, box 1, folder "Wh-."

5. Edward B. Lyman to Phillip Wylie, letter, February 3, 1955, NA RG 396, Records of the Office of Emergency Preparedness, Entry 1009, box 1, folder "Wh-."

6. Geist, "Was There a Real 'Mineshaft Gap'?," 18–22.

7. "Eisenhower, Dwight D.: Papers as President, 1953–61 (Ann Whitman File) NSC Series," DDEL, box 5, folder "182nd meeting of NSC, January 28, 1954."

8. "A-Bomb Test Lesson."

9. "Statement by Federal Civil Defense Administrator Val Peterson in Support of the FCDA 1954 Budget Request before the House Appropriations Committee on June 4, 1953," NA RG 304, Records of the Office of Civil and Defense Mobilization, MLR 1-A, box 739, folder "Governor Peterson-Speeches."

10. "Monthly Field Report No. 24, April 15, 1953," NA RG 397, Records of the Defense Civil Preparedness Agency, MLR 7, box 11, folder "Monthly Field Reports, 1952–53."

11. A mid to late 1953 draft for "The National Plan for Civil Defense of the United States" included a widespread public shelter program as an essential part of civil defense. "The National Plan for Civil Defense of the United States," NA RG 304, Records of the Office of Civil and Defense Mobilization, MLR 1-A, box 1, folder "I.A.3 'Nat'l Plan for CD of the U.S.' (c. 1953)."

12. United States House of Representatives Subcommittee of the Committee on Government Operations, *Civil Defense for National Survival*, 4:1322.

13. Oakes, *The Imaginary War*, 149.

14. "Eisenhower, Dwight D.: Papers as President, 1953–61 (Ann Whitman File) NSC Series," DDEL, box 5, folder "182nd meeting of NSC, January 28, 1954."

15. United States House of Representatives Subcommittee of the Committee on Government Operations, *Civil Defense for National Survival*, 3:670, 676.

16. United States House of Representatives Subcommittee of the Committee on Government Operations, 4:1313.

17. "Before I go before the Appropriations Committee and ask for large sums of money," explained an exasperated Peterson, "I want the evidence upon which I am proceeding, the foundation of material I bring in to be in the best possible shape." United States House of Representatives Subcommittee of the Committee on Government Operations, 4:1212.

18. United States House of Representatives Subcommittee of the Committee on Government Operations, 4:1214, 1234.

19. United States House of Representatives Subcommittee of the Committee on Government Operations, 4:1320, 1322.

20. United States House of Representatives Subcommittee of the Committee on Government Operations, 4:1227–28.

21. United States House of Representatives Subcommittee of the Committee on Government Operations, 4:1313.

22. Val Peterson to Percival F. Brundage, letter, October 12, 1956, NA RG 396, Records of the Office of Emergency Preparedness, MLR Entry 1009, box 1, folder "-Br-."

23. "Staff Meeting, December 11, 1956," NA RG 396, Records of the Office of Emergency Preparedness, MLR Entry 1035, box 1, folder "BC Staff MTGS."

24. Rose, *One Nation Underground*, 28–29.

25. Allison, "News Roundup," no. 10, 310.

26. Rose, *One Nation Underground*, 29.

27. Cabinet agency status for civil defense had been one of Chet Holifield's persistent demands, and it provided Eisenhower with a token offering to placate congressional civil defense advocates while actually gutting the program. On FCDA and OCDM budgets, see Mitchell, *Civil Defense*, 19–21. Annual appropriations for the FCDA peaked in fiscal year 1957 at $98 million, while appropriations for the OCDM never exceeded $61 million.

28. Security Resources Panel of the Science Advisory Committee, *Deterrence and Survival in the Nuclear Age*, 19–20.

29. Kahn, *Major Implications of a Current Nonmilitary Defense Study*; National Academy of Sciences National Research Council Advisory Committee on Civil Defense, *The Adequacy of Government Research Programs in Non-Military Defense*; and Rockefeller Brothers Fund, *International Security*.

30. Yoshpe, *Our Missing Shield*, 240–41.

31. On the ultimate fate of the Gaither Report recommendations, see Snead, *The Gaither Committee*.

32. Office of Civil and Defense Mobilization, *FCDA Annual Report for 1958*, 7–9.

33. Office of Civil and Defense Mobilization, *The Family Fallout Shelter*.

34. Clymer, "U.S. Homeland Defense in the 1950s," argues that a major objective of the corps was rousing public support for increased spending on air defenses.

35. Project East River, *General Report*.

36. Phillip Wylie to Stuart Symington, letter, September 19, 1950, NA RG 304, Records of the Office of Civil and Defense Mobilization, MLR 31A, box 11, folder E4-2, "Comments & Queries RE Civil Defense—W."

37. *Our Cities Must Fight*, directed by Anthony Rizzo, produced by Leo M. Langlois (Archer Productions, 1951). Written by Ray Mauer, this film, like *Duck and Cover*, appears to draw directly from Wylie's ideas, including some of the same examples and metaphors Wylie utilized in his letters to the FCDA.

38. "Meet the Press, Sunday, March 8, 1953," NA RG 304, Records of the Office of Civil and Defense Mobilization, MLR 1-A, box 739, folder "Governor Peterson-Speeches."

39. "Extract from Gov. Peterson's dialogue on 'Crossfire,' Wed. Eve, Aug. 12, 1953," NA RG 304, Records of the Office of Civil and Defense Mobilization, MLR 1-A, box 739, folder "Governor Peterson-Speeches."

40. "Survive the H-Bomb!," 22.

41. "Radio Address by Val Peterson, Federal Civil Defense Administrator, Station KIOA Des Moines, for Recording April 30, 1954," NA RG 304, Records of the

Office of Civil and Defense Mobilization, MLR 1-A, box 739, folder "Governor Peterson-Speeches."

42. June 1956 FCDA Technical Report TR 27-4 "Operation Exit," NA RG 397, Records of the Defense Civil Preparedness Agency, MLR 7, box 39, folder "FCDA Publications—Technical Report TR 27-4 'Operation Exit.'"

43. Donald W. Mitchell wrote in 1962 that "students of the problem believe that at least a 3- to 6-hour warning would be needed for even partially successful tactical evacuation of most American cities, but that tactical evacuation would lose most of its effectiveness if the warning time was less than 1 hour." Mitchell, *Civil Defense*, 41.

44. "Capital Memo Interview with Val Peterson, Former Governor of Nebraska and Now Head of the Federal Civil Defense Administration," NA RG 304, Records of the Office of Civil and Defense Mobilization, MLR 1-A, box 739, folder "Governor Peterson-Speeches."

45. "4 Wheels to Survival," NA RG 397, Records of the Defense Civil Preparedness Agency, MLR 7, box 31, folder "FCDA Leaflet L-2-8 'Four Wheels to Survival.'"

46. "How Advertising Can Help You Organize a City Civil Defense Evacuation Test," NA RG 397, Records of the Defense Civil Preparedness Agency, MLR 7, box 28, folder "FCDA Kit, Evacuation Advertising."

47. Ringstad, "The Evolution of Civil Defense Film Rhetoric," 105.

48. Mack and Baker, *The Occasion Instant*, 7.

49. Mack and Baker, 39.

50. Mack and Baker, 41.

51. United States Senate Armed Services Committee Subcommittee on Civil Defense, *Civil Defense Program. Part 1 and Appendix*; and United States House of Representatives, *84 H.R. 10660 Reported in Senate*.

52. United States House of Representatives, *Conference Report to Accompany H.R. 10660*, 13.

53. Gusev, *Istoricheskie predposylki*, 127; and TsDAHO, f. 1, op. 24, sp. 3611, ark. 39.

54. TsDAHO, f. 1, op. 24, sp. 4402, ark. 33.

55. TsDAHO, f. 1, op. 24, sp. 3611, ark. 390b.

56. TsGAMO, f. 7105, op. 1, d. 414, ll. 4–5.

57. TsGAMO, f. 7105, op. 1, d. 419, l. 16.

58. TsGAMO, f. 7105, op. 1, d. 427, l. 3.

59. TsGAMO, f. 7105, op. 1, d. 423, l. 46.

60. TsGAMO, f. 7105, op. 1, d. 427, l. 1.

61. Gouré, *Civil Defense in the Soviet Union*, 111.

62. TsGAMO, f. 6880, op. 2, d. 239, l. 57.

63. Seven hundred lucky children from Kirov district's kindergartens and childcare centers would go to the Kurskii Train Station and thence directly to Caucasian towns such as Vorontsovo-Aleksandrovskoe and Novopavlovksia. TsGAMO, f. 6880, op. 2, d. 239, ll. 6–10.

64. TsGAMO, f. 6880, op. 2, d. 239, l. 2.

65. TsGAMO, f. 6880, op. 2, d. 239, ll. 12–13.

66. TsGAMO, f. 6880, op. 2, d. 239, l. 15.

67. TsGAMO, f. 6880, op. 2, d. 239, ll. 15–16.

68. After the Soviet test, Hans Bethe produced an assessment arguing that the USSR's device was probably extremely large and could not scale to a yield much beyond half a megaton. Declassified Soviet documents, however, reveal that the device was close to being deliverable and that Soviet weapons designers developed megaton-range derivatives of it. See Wellerstein and Geist, "The Secret of the Soviet Hydrogen Bomb," 40–47.

69. Wellerstein and Geist, "The Secret of the Soviet Hydrogen Bomb."

70. "Radio Address by Val Peterson, Federal Civil Defense Administrator, Station KIOA Des Moines, for Recording April 30, 1954," NA RG 304, Records of the Office of Civil and Defense Mobilization, MLR 1-A, box 739, folder "Governor Peterson-Speeches."

71. "Radiation Exposure in Recent Weapons Tests," 352.

72. Kunkle and Ristvet, *Castle Bravo*.

73. Lapp, "Civil Defense Faces New Peril," 349–51. On the inability of the FCDA to begin fallout planning owing to security procedures, see Val Peterson's March 1955 congressional testimony. *Hearing before the Subcommittee on Security of the Joint Committee on Atomic Energy Eighty-Fourth Congress First Session on AEC-FCDA Relationship*, 3. This problem was made worse by the fact that the FCDA's move from Washington to Battle Creek, Michigan, resulted in the loss of many FCDA employees with security clearances, further handicapping its efforts to deal with classified material.

74. Lapp, "Civil Defense Faces New Peril," 351.

75. "FCDA Technical Bulletin TB-19-1," NA RG 397, Records of the Defense Civil Preparedness Agency, MLR 7, box 38, folder "FCDA Technical Bulletin TB-19-1 'The Radioactive Fallout Program.'"

76. *Shelter from Atomic Attack in Existing Buildings*, Part II, warned that shelters in fire-risk areas could become "death traps" and urged that those inside them make a hasty exit following a nuclear explosion. Federal Civil Defense Administration, *Shelter from Atomic Attack in Existing Buildings*, Part II, 5.

77. Draft, "Annex 3-National Shelter Program," December 18, 1957, NA RG 304, Records of the Office of Civil and Defense Mobilization, MLR 1-A, box 8, folder "V.C.10.a-5/15/58 Draft, Comments, Revisions."

78. United States House of Representatives Subcommittee of the Committee on Government Operations, *Civil Defense for National Survival*, Part 4, 1269.

79. Yoshpe, *Our Missing Shield*, 291–94.

80. Rose, *One Nation Underground*; Weart, *Nuclear Fear*.

81. As of March 1960, a survey counted a mere 1,565 fallout shelters in the United States. Rose, *One Nation Underground*, 79.

82. Rose, 81.

83. Mitchell, *Civil Defense*, 52.

84. Kahn, *On Thermonuclear War*, 516–18.

85. Central Intelligence Agency, *Civil Defense in the USSR*, 4, 14.

86. Central Intelligence Agency, 14.

87. Central Intelligence Agency, 4.
88. Korionov, *Amerikanskii imperializm*, 231.
89. TsDAHO, f. 1, op. 24, sp. 4402, ark. 166.
90. TsDAHO, f. 1, op. 24, sp. 4402, ark. 170.
91. TsDAHO, f. 1, op. 24, sp. 4402, ark. 170ob.
92. TsDAHO, f. 1, op. 24, sp. 4543, ark. 43.
93. TsDAHO, f. 1, op. 24, sp. 4543, ark. 42.
94. TsDAHO, f. 1, op. 24, sp. 4543, ark. 43. Although not stated directly, the author is likely referring to the Kefauver Committee.
95. TsDAHO, f. 1, op. 24, sp. 4402, ark. 165.
96. Bakanov and Dzharylglasov, *Grazhdanskaia oborona SShA*, 142. The most recent work cited in the work's bibliography is the *FCDA Annual Report for 1955*, published in 1956, and most dated to the Truman administration.
97. Bakanov and Dzharylglasov, 3.
98. Central Intelligence Agency, *Soviet Civil Defense and Air-Raid Shelter Construction*, 1.
99. Committee on Government Operations, *Fifth Report*, 7.
100. Joe Holley, "Leon Gouré, 84; Sovietologist and Civil Defense Expert."
101. Gouré, *Civil Defense in the Soviet Union*. Gouré specifically acknowledged Kahn in the preface to the book.
102. Gouré, ix–x.
103. Gouré, 142–43.
104. Gouré, 149–50.
105. Gouré, 151.
106. Holloway, *Stalin and the Bomb*, 336–40.
107. Mikoian, *Tak bylo*, 7.
108. RGASPI, f. 84, op. 3, d. 265, l. 33.
109. Central Intelligence Agency Office of Research and Reports, *Changing Soviet Civil Defense Concepts*, 1.
110. Gusev, *Istoricheskie predposylki*, 132.
111. Fursenko, *Prezidium TsK KPSS*, 125.
112. Shute, *On the Beach*, 73–79.
113. Frank, *Alas, Babylon*.
114. Miller, *A Canticle for Leibowitz*.
115. Brians, *Nuclear Holocausts*, 45. Exceptions included Wylie's *Tomorrow!*, Judith Merril's *Shadow on the Hearth*, and author Martin Caidin's 1956 novel *The Long Night*, a rather rosy treatment on the theme of civil defense in a city subjected to nuclear attack.
116. Frank, *Alas, Babylon*, 106.
117. Frank, *How to Survive the H-Bomb and Why*. For an assertion that Frank intended his novel as a critique of civil defense, see Sharp, *Savage Perils*, 215–18.
118. Clarkson, *The Last Day*.
119. Brians, *Nuclear Holocausts*, 44.
120. "Alas, Babylon," *Playhouse 90*, directed by Robert Stevens, original airdate April 3, 1960.

121. *On the Beach*, directed and produced by Stanley Kramer (United Artists, 1959). Kramer's adaptation, unlike Shute's novel, never explicitly blames the war on communist aggression.

122. "Gregory Peck Sees His Film in Moscow."

123. Pat Frank died suddenly of acute pancreatitis in October 1964. "Pat Frank, Author and Newsman, Dies."

124. Geist, "Was There a Real 'Mineshaft Gap'?," 18–22.

125. Ivanov, *Energiia podvlastna nam!*

126. Tsatsulin, *Atomnaia krepost'*, 10.

127. Laksness, *Atomnaia stantsiia*.

128. Gakov, *Ull'timatum*, 261–62.

129. For a discussion of censorship of nuclear war imagery in the Soviet media during the 1950s and 1960s, see Peacock, "Contested Innocence," 38–39.

130. Efremov, *Sochineniia*, 3:2:16.

131. Efremov, 3:2:18. Efremov's account of the fate of Zirda bears considerable resemblance to the struggle within the Soviet government between nuclear scientist Andrei Sakharov and the Soviet leadership over atmospheric radiation releases from nuclear weapons testing. Sakharov argued in a 1958 *Atomnaia energiia* article that this radioactivity was causing massive ecological and epidemiological damage. Holloway, "Moral Reasoning and Practical Purpose."

132. Efremov, *Sochineniia*, 3:2:17.

133. Efremov, 3:2:297.

134. Efremov, 3:2:290.

135. Efremov, 3:2:292.

136. Efremov, 3:2:296.

137. Efremov, 3:2:297–98.

138. Strugatskii and Strugatskii, *Obytaemyi ostrov*.

139. For example, in 1955, collective farm workers trumpeted in a report to the CPSU Central Committee that they had bolstered their country's defense capabilities by planting additional corn. RGANI, f. 5, op. 16, d. 709, ll. 10–11.

140. Grushin, *Chetyre zhizni Rossii*, 84. For an extensive discussion of this survey and its significance, see Hale-Dorrell, "For Peace and Friendship of All Countries."

Chapter Four

1. TsDAHO, f. 1, op. 24, sp. 5692, ark. 92.

2. "Memorandum from Secretary of Defense McNamara to President Johnson, 'Recommended FY 1966–1970 Programs,'" 20.

3. On American civil defense during the Cuban Missile Crisis, see Rose, *One Nation Underground*, 193–201; and George, *Awaiting Armageddon*, particularly 42–53, 62–86. On continuity of government and civil defense during the crisis, see Davis, "Continuity of Government Measures."

4. "A Report on National Civil Defense Readiness by Steuart L. Pittman, Assistant Secretary of Defense for Civil Defense to the Committee on Civil Defense and

Post Attack Recovery of the National Governors' Conference, October 27, 1962," NA RG 397, Records of the Defense Civil Preparedness Agency, Records of the Defense Civil Preparedness Agency, MLR A1 37, "Regional Coordination Files, 1963-64," box 4, folder "Governors Conference (Mtgs. & Conferences)."

5. George, *Awaiting Armageddon*, 65–66.

6. Prior to the Cuban Missile Crisis the OCD stipulated a protection factor of 100, meaning that those inside the shelter would receive a maximum of 1/100 the radiation dose of those outside. After the crisis, the OCD lowered this to 40. Yoshpe, *Our Missing Shield*, 348.

7. Office of Civil Defense, *Personal and Family Survival*, 36–37.

8. Barinov, "Inzhenerno-tekhnicheskie meropriiatia GO," 22.

9. Podtelezhnikov, Shchekunov, and Iukhtin, "Povyshat' uroven' inzhenernoi zashchity naseleniia," 24.

10. Joint Committee on Atomic Energy, *Effects of Nuclear Explosions*, 24.

11. Reproduced in Cantelon, Hewlett, and Williams, *The American Atom*, 202.

12. On U.S. nuclear targeting in the mid-1950s, see Kaplan, *The Wizards of Armageddon*, 211–13.

13. For an early example of this definition of "mutual deterrence," see Marseille, "Negotiation from Strength," 16.

14. Kahn, *On Thermonuclear War*, 14–16. According to Kahn, "minimum deterrence" was "coined by some Polaris enthusiasts who argued we needed very little to deter the Soviets," 14.

15. Kahn, 8.

16. Aligica and Weinstein, *The Essential Herman Kahn*, 271.

17. For two accounts of Herman Kahn's life and career, see Ghamari-Tabrizi, *The Worlds of Herman Kahn*; and Bruce-Briggs, *Supergenius*.

18. Kahn, 147.

19. Kahn, 33.

20. Kahn, 16.

21. Kahn, 39.

22. Kahn, 115, 647.

23. Kahn, 647.

24. Wiesner, "Comprehensive Arms-Limitation Systems," 215.

25. Wiesner and York, "National Security and the Nuclear Test Ban," 34–35.

26. "Project Harbor Report of Group A—Strategy and Tactics," 8–9, NA RG 397, Records of the Defense Civil Preparedness Agency, MLR A1 62, box 3, no folder.

27. "Project Harbor Report of Group A—Strategy and Tactics," 8.

28. Recent scholarship indicates that the West German government had little intention to actually acquire its own nuclear weapons, but cultivated the impression that it might in order to extract desired concessions from the United States. Lutsch, "Westbindung or Balance of Power."

29. Fairbanks, "MAD and U.S. Strategy," 138–39.

30. Reproduced in Cantelon, Hewlett, and Williams, *The American Atom*, 207–8.

31. Kaplan, *The Wizards of Armageddon*, 315–16.

32. On McNamara's views regarding the ABM and offensive forces, see Kaplan, *The Wizards of Armageddon*, 320–25; on civil defense, see chap. 4.

33. McNamara used the phrase "assured destruction capability" in a statement before the House Armed Services Committee on February 18, 1965. Coffey, "The Chinese and Ballistic Missile Defense," 18.

34. Rowen, "Introduction," 5.

35. Stone, *"Every Man Should Try,"* 372.

36. Singer, "Deterrence and Shelters," 314.

37. Singer, 315.

38. Dyson, "Thoughts on Bomb Shelters," 15.

39. Dyson, 14.

40. Dyson, 15.

41. Kahn, *Thinking about the Unthinkable*, 91.

42. "Project Harbor Report of Group A—Strategy and Tactics," 20.

43. Tolstikov, *Grazhdanskaia oborona v sovremennoi voine*, 34.

44. On the development of operational arts in Soviet military science, see Glantz, *Soviet Military Operational Art*.

45. Hampe, *Strategie der zivilen Verteidigung*.

46. Khampe, *Strategiia grazhdanskoi oborony*, 5–6.

47. Khampe, 12.

48. Khampe, 125.

49. GARF, f. 9552, op. 1, d. 623a, l. 55, includes a document dated August 25, 1960, on letterhead bearing this title.

50. Sokolevskii, *Voennaia strategiia*, 1st ed., 391–92. This work went through three editions with a variety of additions and substantive changes, but the section on civil defense remained constant through all three. See Sokolevskii, *Voennaia strategiia*, 2nd ed., 395–97; and Sokolevskii, *Voennaia strategiia*, 3rd ed., 400–402.

51. Sokolevskii, *Voennaia strategiia*, 1st ed., 395–96.

52. Sokolevskii, 220.

53. Sokolevskii, 221.

54. Sokolevskii, 229.

55. Sokolevskii, 238.

56. Sokolevskii, 232.

57. Interviews of Soviet military officers after the conclusion of the Cold War indicate that Soviet nuclear doctrine in the 1960s indeed followed that outlined in *Voennaia strategiia*. See Battilega, "Soviet Views of Nuclear Warfare," 151–74.

58. Sokolevskii, 221.

59. John F. Kennedy to Harry S. Truman, letter, October 8, 1949, NA RG 304, Records of the Office of Civil and Defense Mobilization, MLR 1A, box 1, folder E4-1, "Civil Defense, General."

60. Yoshpe, *Our Missing Shield*, 298–99.

61. Yoshpe, 305.

62. Mitchell, *Civil Defense*, 105–6.

63. Mitchell, 106.

64. Mitchell, 106.

65. Mitchell, 105.

66. Yoshpe, *Our Missing Shield*, 305. Steuart L. Pittman later claimed that Kennedy believed in the deterrence value of shelters, but refrained from saying so in his speech for fear of being "provocative." Yoshpe, 308.

67. Mitchell, *Civil Defense*, 107.

68. Yoshpe, *Our Missing Shield*, 320.

69. Yoshpe, 341–42. A decorated Marine veteran of World War II and lawyer, Pittman gained his post on the recommendation of deputy secretary of defense Roswell Gilpatric. "Molder of Civil Defense."

70. Yoshpe, *Our Missing Shield*, 347.

71. Yoshpe, 347.

72. Yoshpe, 371–74.

73. Yoshpe, 344–45.

74. "Memorandum from Secretary of Defense McNamara to President Johnson, 'Recommended FY 1966–1970 Programs for Strategic Offensive Forces, Continental Air and Missile Defense Forces, and Civil Defense,' 3 December 1964," 20.

75. Central Intelligence Agency, "Memorandum of Estimate on Soviet Capabilities for Strategic Attack," 3.

76. Iashin, *Mech' Rossii*, 33.

77. Podvig, *Russian Strategic Nuclear Forces*, 196–205.

78. "Fallout Shelters," 95–108.

79. George, *Awaiting Armageddon*, 33.

80. Melman, *No Place to Hide*, 134–38.

81. Mitchell, *Civil Defense*, 32.

82. Marjorie R. Kruszewski to John F. Kennedy, letter, September 1, 1961, NA RG 397, Records of the Defense Civil Preparedness Agency, MLR A1 57, "Records of Assistant Secretary of Defense for Civil Defense Steuart L. Pittman," box 7, folder "Public Affairs Booklet."

83. "Letters to the Editors," 10.

84. J. F. Johnson to Steuart L. Pittman, letter, February 26, 1963, NA RG 397, Records of the Defense Civil Preparedness Agency, MLR A1 23, box 40, folder "Relationships 5-4 Crank or Anonymous Letters."

85. Yoshpe, *Our Missing Shield*, 362.

86. President Kennedy took Thomas aside at a function for the Brazilian president and asked him to rethink his opposition to the bill. "Memorandum for Mr. Gilpatric," April 30, 1962, NA RG 397, Records of the Defense Civil Preparedness Agency, MLR A1 57, "Records of Assistant Secretary of Defense for Civil Defense Steuart L. Pittman," box 6, folder "SecDef/DepSecDef corres. Aug. '61–Dec. '62."

87. Steuart L. Pittman to Edward J. Hawkins, letter, March 20, 1964, NA RG 397, Records of the Defense Civil Preparedness Agency, MLR A1 57, "Records of Assistant Secretary of Defense for Civil Defense Steuart L. Pittman," box 1, folder "Chronological March 1964."

88. In December 1961, the Federation of American Scientists, despite its general rejection of civil defense on the basis that efforts would be better directed toward

disarmament, admitted that "it is clear that a properly designed fallout shelter program can save at least some people, and in certain situations, most people." Federation of American Scientists, "Civil Defense Shelter Statement," 25.

89. National Academy of Sciences, *Civil Defense*, 17–20.
90. Yoshpe, *Our Missing Shield*, 366–70.
91. Brennan, *Arms Control and Civil Defense*, 28.
92. Brennan, 34.
93. Brennan, 43, 34.
94. Brennan, 34.
95. Brennan, 46.
96. Oskar Morgenstern to Steuart L. Pittman, letter, September 2, 1963, NA RG 397, Records of the Defense Civil Preparedness Agency, MLR A1 23, box 40, folder "Relationships 5-5 Suggestions."
97. "Proposal to explore the possibility and consequences of a US-USSR agreement not to engage in a Civil Defense shelter effort," NA RG 397, Records of the Defense Civil Preparedness Agency, MLR A1 23, box 40, folder "Relationships 5-5 Suggestions." Morgenstern seems not to have been familiar with the findings of either Leon Gouré or the CIA on Soviet shelter construction as of late 1963, despite his participation in Project Harbor.
98. Draft letter to Oskar Morgenstern, J. Romm/Rubinstein/Kelleher/mo/71364, September 17, 1963, NA RG 397, Records of the Defense Civil Preparedness Agency, MLR A1 23, box 40, folder "Relationships 5-5 Suggestions."
99. Draft letter to Oskar Morgenstern, JFDevaney, September 19, 1963, NA RG 397, Records of the Defense Civil Preparedness Agency, MLR A1 23, box 40, folder "Relationships 5-5 Suggestions."
100. Steuart L. Pittman to Oskar Morgenstern, letter, September 30, 1963, NA RG 397, Records of the Defense Civil Preparedness Agency, MLR A1 23, box 40, folder "Relationships 5-5 Suggestions."
101. Steuart L. Pittman to William C. Foster, letter, November 4, 1963, NA RG 397, Records of the Defense Civil Preparedness Agency, MLR A1 57, Records of Assistant Secretary of Defense for Civil Defense Steuart L. Pittman, 1961–64, box 2, folder "Correspondence H.R. 8200 (Congressional)."
102. "Civil Defense during a Period of Detente," NA RG 397, Records of the Defense Civil Preparedness Agency, MLR A1 57, Records of Assistant Secretary of Defense for Civil Defense Steuart L. Pittman, 1961–64, box 2, folder "Correspondence H.R. 8200 (Congressional)."
103. Steuart L. Pittman to Robert S. McNamara, memorandum, December 11, 1963, NA RG 397, Records of Assistant Secretary of Defense for Civil Defense Steuart L. Pittman, MLR A1 57, box 3, folder "Correspondence (Jackson Subcommittee) (Senate Armed Services Committee)."
104. Steuart L. Pittman to Robert S. McNamara, memorandum, January 30, 1964, NA RG 397, Records of Assistant Secretary of Defense for Civil Defense Steuart L. Pittman, MLR A1 57, box 3, folder "Correspondence (Jackson Subcommittee) (Senate Armed Services Committee)."
105. Yoshpe, *Our Missing Shield*, 372.

106. Steuart L. Pittman to Henry M. Jackson, letter, March 4, 1964, NA RG 397, Records of Assistant Secretary of Defense for Civil Defense Steuart L. Pittman, MLR A1 57, Box 3, Folder "Correspondence (Jackson Subcommittee) (Senate Armed Services Committee)."

107. Henry M. Jackson to Steuart L. Pittman, letter, March 4, 1964, NA RG 397, Records of Assistant Secretary of Defense for Civil Defense Steuart L. Pittman, MLR A1 57, Box 1, Folder "Chronological March 1964."

108. On Henry Jackson's support for the ABM, see Kaufmann, *Henry M. Jackson*, 182–85.

109. Kaplan, *The Wizards of Armageddon*, 324.

110. Coleman, *The Presidential Recordings of John F. Kennedy*, 6:54.

111. Yoshpe, *Our Missing Shield*, 387.

112. Originally the OCD envisioned a three- to five-day uninterrupted residence time in community shelters and hoped that power would remain available to help provide ventilation, but by late 1962 it had determined that most shelter inhabitants would need to remain in the shelters for much longer and that it was unreasonable to expect utilities to remain functional even outside blast areas. Without active ventilation in the shelters, temperatures could increase to levels resulting in heatstroke or death. To address this concern the OCD developed human-powered ventilation systems for inclusion in shelter supplies, but because only those items that were developed earlier were purchased for stockpiling in shelters, these ventilation systems never entered serial production. On the background of this decision, see NA RG 397, Records of the Defense Civil Preparedness Agency, MLR A1 33, Box 1, Folders "TM 61-3 Minimum Technical Requirements for Community Group Shelters" and "TM 61-3 Miscellaneous."

113. U.S. General Accounting Office, *Activities and Status of Civil Defense*, 13.

114. Yoshpe, *Our Missing Shield*, 405–9.

115. Bennett, *National Security Policy, 1973–1976*, 547. On the DCPA's budget, see Bennett, 560.

116. Bennett, 547.

117. Bennett, 578.

118. At this point in the meeting, Rockefeller protested Rumsfeld's dismissal of the prospect of a revived shelter program, stating that "there's nothing wrong with shelters" and that "I just built one at my home." Bennett, 574.

119. Bennett, 579.

120. Bennett, 580.

121. Vladimirov, *Ot MPVO k grazhdanskoi zashchite*, 189. Government policy reduced city and oblast MPVO organizations to two officers apiece.

122. See, for instance, *Programma podgotovki lichnogo sostava grazhdanskoi oborony nevoenizirovannykh formirovanii sluzhby transporta i dorog, Utv. 17 ianv. 1963 g*; and *Programma podgotovki serzhantov (komandirov otdelenii) inzhenernykh chastei i uzlov sviazi shtabov grazhdanskoi oborony Utv. 13 dek. 1962 g.*

123. See Ministerstvo zdravookhraneniia SSSR, *Nastavlenie po uchetu*; and *Programmy podgotovki lichnogo sostava grazhdanskoi oborony ob"ektov narodnogo khoziaistva. Utv. 23 iulia 1962 g.*

124. TsDAHO, f. 1, op. 24, sp. 5692, ark. 90.

125. Aksiutin, *Khrushchevskaia "ottepel,'"* 381.

126. Aksiutin, 382.

127. The Soviet public's confusion about the ongoing crisis was fostered by contradictory portrayals of it in official media. See Kozovoi, "Dissonant Voices."

128. Aksiutin, *Khrushchevskaia "ottepel,'"* 360–85. In her *Awaiting Armageddon*, Alice L. George notes that Soviet expatriate journalist Melor Sturua reported in the 1980s that "there was a sense of hysteria about civil defense" during the crisis, but this assessment is difficult to reconcile with the results of Aksiutin's surveys or Kozovoi's account of youth mobilization during it. George, *Awaiting Armageddon*, 65.

129. On this date the CPSU Presidium and Council of Ministers approved the Polozhenie o Grazhdanskoi oborone Soiuza SSR (Regulation Regarding the Civil Defense of the Union of Soviet Socialist Republics).

130. Chuikov's position lacked an exact analog within the structure of the MPVO, but the most senior post within it—the head of the MPVO General Staff—was held by the forgettable Ivan Sheredega until 1959. Sheredega's successor, Oleg Tolstikov, remained head of the USSR Civil Defense General Staff until his retirement in 1970 and was second-in-command to Chuikov after 1961.

131. Kozovoi, "Dissonant Voices," 53. This "dispersal" differed markedly from that advocated by Ralph Lapp in the late 1940s, which had been referred to in Russian by the same word prior to 1961. See Moskalev, *Rassredotochnenie i evakuatsiia naseleniia*.

132. TsDAHO, f. 1, op. 24, sp. 5692, ark. 93. For the regulations governing acceptable use of shelters in peacetime, see Shtab Grazhdanskoi oborony SSSR, *Pravila soderzhaniia i ispol'zovaniia ubezhishch v mirnoe vremia*.

133. TsDAHO, f. 1, op. 24, sp. 5692, ark. 93–94.

134. GARF, f. 9552, op. 1, d. 778, l. 13. Conference reports also noted instances of outright falsification of training statistics. GARF, f. 9552, op. 1, d. 778, l. 18.

135. GARF, f. 9552, op. 1, d. 778, l. 16.

136. GARF, f. 9552, op. 1, d. 921, l. 33.

137. By 1966, Soviet Civil Defense declared that "responsibility for training the general population lies with heads of civil defense of cities, urban districts, rural and village soviets, and interregional civil defense schools," as opposed to DOSAAF. TsDAHO, f. 1, op. 24, sp. 6165, ark. 88.

138. TsDAHO, f. 1, op. 24, sp. 6165, ark. 63.

139. TsDAHO, f. 1, op. 24, sp. 6319, ark. 45.

140. TsDAHO, f. 1, op. 25, sp. 71, ark. 2.

141. As of June 1970 Ukrainian Civil Defense reported that only 23 percent of the 20,591,000 rubles budgeted for construction that year had been spent, a shortfall it attributed to "the poor work of the Republic's construction organizations." TsDAHO, f. 1, op. 25, sp. 388, ark. 135.

142. TsDAHO, f. 1, op. 25, sp. 388, ark. 144.

143. The Ukrainian SSR completed or refurbished 288 shelters with 76,860 spaces in 1970, but it projected that the number of workers requiring shelter would

grow 238,380 from 2,134,720 in 1970 to 2,373,100 in 1971. TsDAHO, f. 1, op. 25, sp. 539, ark. 19–20.

144. Quoted in Garthoff, "BMD and East-West Relations," 295. This is Kosygin's comment as reproduced by *Pravda*, but a recording made by the London Voice of America representative reveals the prime minister's original comment was somewhat different and did not include the portion about "saving human lives."

145. On the failure of the USSR's experimental missile defense for Moscow, the A-35, and the resulting disillusionment of Soviet leaders with ABMs during the 1960s, see Podvig, *Russian Strategic Nuclear Forces*, 413–20.

146. TsDAHO, f. 1, op. 25, sp. 886, ark. 30. The plan to build shelters with spaces for 260,100 people in Ukraine in 1973 is consistent with assertions by Russia's post-Soviet emergency management agency that during the mid-1970s the USSR as a whole built blast shelters with spaces for one million people each year.

147. Gosudarstvennyi Komitet Soveta Ministrov SSSR po Delam Stroitel'stva, *Ukazaniia po proektirovaniiu ubezhishch grazhdanskoi oborony SN 405-70*.

148. TsDAHO, f. 1, op. 25, sp. 692, ark. 41.

149. TsDAHO, f. 1, op. 25, sp. 886, ark. 8. Surprisingly, available documents provide no evidence that Soviet Civil Defense made special preparations to protect the Soviet Party elite.

150. Epishin et al., *Grazhdanskaia oborona*.

151. Egorov, Shliakhov, and Alabin, *Grazhdanskaia oborona*.

152. Oral history of Joanne S. Gailar, interviewed by Stephen H. Stow, February 14, 2003, Center for Oak Ridge Oral History, accessed June 13, 2012, http://cdm16107.contentdm.oclc.org/cdm/singleitem/collection/p15388coll1/id/153.

153. Oral history of Joanne S. Gailar.

154. Gailar, "Seven Warning Signals."

155. Egorov, Shliakhov, and Alabin, *Civil Defense*.

156. Kearny, "Hasty Shelter Construction Studies"; and Kearny, "Construction of Hasty Winter Shelters."

157. Wigner and Gailar, "Will Soviet Civil Defense Undermine SALT?"

158. Wigner and Gailar, "Civil Defense in the Soviet Union," 9–11.

159. Cabage, "End Notes."

160. "City of Oak Ridge Fallout Shelter and Evacuation Map, revised 1/26/73." Author's personal collection.

161. Gouré, *Soviet Civil Defense Revisited, 1966–1969*.

162. Elliot, *RAND in Southeast Asia*, 101–3.

163. Gouré, *Soviet Civil Defense, 1969–1970*, 31.

164. Gouré, 32.

165. The date *MPVO—informatsionnyi sbornik po materialam zarubezhnoi pechati* first appeared remains obscure, as even the holdings of the Russian National Library are incomplete, but likely occurred around 1958. Renamed *Grazhdanskaia oborona—informatsionnyi sbornik po materialam zarubezhnoi pechati* in February 1961, this periodical continued to be published into the post-Soviet era.

166. "Organizatsiia i sostoianie grazhdanskoi oborony v stranakh NATO," 13. At the time, such a law was under consideration in both the state of New York and

nationally, but neither passed. The article also claims the existence of over one million home fallout shelters in the United States.

167. For instance, see "Programma stroitel'stva ubezhishch v SShA," 4–5.

168. "Annotatsiia bibliografiia," 39. The article cited is Byrnes and Underhill, "Shelters and Survival."

169. "Programma stroitel'stva obshchestvennykh ubezhishch v SShA," 9. The article cited is Hagan, "Community Shelters."

170. "Kratkie soobshcheniia."

171. Korzun, *Grazhdanskaia oborona v stranakh NATO*, 4.

172. Korzun, 47.

173. Korzun, 18.

174. Korzun, *Grazhdanskaia oborona v kapitalisticheskikh stranakh*, 11.

175. Korzun, 15.

176. Korzun, 19.

177. Korzun, 45.

178. Korzun, 46.

Chapter Five

1. President's Foreign Intelligence Advisory Board, "The Soviet 'War Scare,'" 69–76.

2. President's Foreign Intelligence Advisory Board, vii.

3. Hoffman, *The Dead Hand*, 60–100.

4. In the 1960s, some observers argued that because nuclear war was obviously an irrational policy choice and that the two superpowers were effectively rational actors, even events such as the Cuban Missile Crisis had little likelihood of escalating to nuclear war. Many scholars considered this view dubious even at the time, and Graham Allison singled it out for derision in his widely influential 1974 book *The Essence of Decision*. In the 1980s and 1990s, scholars uncovered a large number of previously obscure incidents in which the United States mishandled its nuclear arsenal in ways that ran a constant risk of accidents. For instance, see Sagan, *The Limits of Safety*. In the early 1990s, new information came to light about Soviet nuclear activity during the Cuban Missile Crisis that revealed not only that the United States failed to assess Soviet capabilities and intentions accurately, but also that if the United States had invaded Cuba, as seemed likely at some points in October 1962, the Soviet forces on the island would have attacked the U.S. forces using tactical nuclear weapons. See Mikoyan, *The Soviet Cuban Missile Crisis*.

5. Quoted in Pipes, "Why the Soviet Union Thinks It Could Fight and Win a Nuclear War," 1.

6. Friedberg, "A History of U.S. Strategic 'Doctrine,'" 56.

7. Erickson, "The Soviet View of Deterrence," 249.

8. Hines, Mishulovich, and Shull, *Soviet Intentions*, 2:145.

9. "Voenno-politicheskie i voenno-strategicheskie kontseptsii SShA," 345–46.

10. Kahn, *Ob eskalatsii*, 23.

11. Kissinger, *Iadernoe oruzhie i vneshniaia politika*; and Brodie, *Strategiia v vek raketnogo oruzhiia*.

12. Sheidina, *SShA: "Fabriki mysli,"* 74.

13. Sheidina, 185.

14. Mozzhorin, *Tak eto bylo*, 167–68.

15. Hines, Mishulovich, and Shull, *Soviet Intentions*, 1:22–47; and Podvig, *Russian Strategic Nuclear Forces*, 50–54.

16. Dvorkin and Produkin, *Povest' o 4 TsNII MO*, 46–63.

17. Podtelezhnikov, Shchekunov, and Iukhtin, "Povyshat' uroven' inzhenernoi zashchity naseleniia," 24.

18. Altunin, "O teorii grazhdanskoi oborony," 33.

19. Altunin, 38.

20. A February 1972 report by the General Inspectorate and the Central Political Directorate of the Soviet Army and Navy on the results of their investigation of the status of civil defense preparations in Soviet Ukraine provides figures only on shelters meeting the then-current engineering requirements, suggesting that Soviet civil defense disregarded older shelters from the 1950s and earlier that could not be upgraded when tabulating shelter availability. TsDAHO, f. 1, op. 25, sp. 692, ark. 41.

21. TsDAHO, f. 1, op. 25, sp. 692, ark. 40.

22. Instructions to begin civil defense planning for surprise attack appeared in a May 26, 1973, order from the head of Soviet civil defense—that is, General Altunin. TsDAHO, f. 1, op. 25, sp. 886, ark. 7.

23. TsDAHO, f. 1, op. 25, sp. 1083, ark. 11–12.

24. TsDAHO, f. 1, op. 24, sp. 6165, ark. 810b–82.

25. TsDAHO, f. 1, op. 24, sp. 6165, ark. 85ob.

26. TsDAHO, f. 1, op. 24, sp. 6165, ark. 64–65.

27. Head of the Ukrainian Civil Defense General Staff colonel general V. Chizh reported progress in these fields in a 1972 report to the Ukrainian SSR Communist Party Central Committee. TsDAHO, f. 1, op. 25, sp. 692, ark. 23–27.

28. TsDAHO, f. 1, op. 25, sp. 692, ark. 40.

29. Shtab Grazhdanskoi oborony SSSR Nauchno-Metodicheskii Tsentr, *Lektsii po grazhdanskoi oborone*, 87–88.

30. Perminov and Gorbunov, "Kompleksnye pokaznye," 22–23.

31. According to 1973 Soviet civil defense regulations, the distance evacuees would travel from their homes depended on which of three groups the government assigned their city to on the basis of its presumed importance to enemy strategic planners. Evacuees from cities of the "1st group" would travel at least forty kilometers, the "2nd group" thirty, the "3rd group" twenty-five, and those living near "targets of special importance" twenty kilometers. TsDAHO, f. 1, op. 25, sp. 886, ark. 9.

32. Epishin et al., *Grazhdanskaia oborona*, 59.

33. Gouré, *Soviet Civil Defense 1969–1970*, 31–32.

34. Yoshpe, *Our Missing Shield*, 406.

35. Defense Civil Preparedness Agency, *Protection in the Nuclear Age*, 49–56.

36. Yoshpe, *Our Missing Shield*, 430.

37. Yoshpe, 432.
38. Yoshpe, 419.
39. Yoshpe, 438.
40. Yoshpe, 420–21.
41. Yoshpe, 422–24.
42. Yoshpe, 446–53.
43. Nitze, "Ensuring Security in the Era of Détente," 207.
44. Broyles, Wigner, and Drell, "Civil Defense in Nuclear War," 56.
45. Broyles, Wigner, and Drell. This claim about inadequate shelter ventilation, which Joanne Gailar, Eugene Wigner, and Cresson Kearney characterized as "the most serious flaw in the whole Soviet Civil Defense Planning," received considerable attention from Americans debating the significance of the Soviet civil defense program during the 1970s and 1980s. As it turns out, both sides of the debate were wrong, and the figure attracting the American researchers' attention was just one of many misprints or misstatements in the civil defense manuals they translated, and did not reflect Soviet civil defense planning accurately. *Grazhdanskaia oborona—informatsionnyi sbornik po materialam zarubezhnoi pechati* published numerous articles in the early 1960s about Western shelter living experiments, including the increased ventilation requirements required in less-temperate climates. The Soviet shelter construction regulations of the 1970s took these considerations into account, but the oversimplified summary of shelter design in the popular manuals glossed over the issue, leading to widespread confusion in the West. For these regulations, see Gosudarstvennyi Komitet Soveta Ministrov SSSR po Delam Stroitel'stva, *Ukazaniia po proektirovaniiu ubezhishch grazhdanskoi oborony SN 405-70*, 39–41. Ironically, Drell was absolutely correct in his assertion that "selective quotations from civil defense manuals are not reliable guides to the effectiveness of a civil defense program" (56)—Soviet civil defense, in this instance, was *more* effective than implied by the translated manuals.
46. Gouré, *War Survival in Soviet Strategy*, 1.
47. Gouré, 2, 5, 18.
48. Gouré, 3.
49. Pipes, "Why the Soviet Union Thinks It Could Fight and Win a Nuclear War," 1–34.
50. "Memorandum of conversation, 'Secretary's Meeting with the General Advisory Committee on Arms Control and Disarmament,'" Digital National Security Archive, January 6 [1977], accessed March 23, 2016, http://nsarchive.gwu.edu/nukevault/ebb521-Irans-Nuclear-Program-1975-vs-2015/07.pdf.
51. Cyrus Vance's hopes to approach the USSR for civil defense negotiations is mentioned in the summary of a February 15, 1978, conversation between Samuel P. Huntington and secretary of defense Harold Brown. "PRM 32," National Security Archive, Civil Defense/Emergency Management Collection (Rumbarger Donation), box 10, folder "DoD Review of CD Program (PRM 32)."
52. "Alternative U.S. Civil Defense Programs, November 21, 1977," National Security Archive, Civil Defense/Emergency Management Collection (Rumbarger Donation), box 10, folder "DoD (PA&E) review of CD program '77–78."

53. "Alternative U.S. Civil Defense Programs, November 21, 1977."

54. Central Intelligence Agency, *Soviet Civil Defense*, 1.

55. Central Intelligence Agency, 4.

56. See Geist, "Was There a Real 'Mineshaft Gap'?," 26.

57. "PRC Meeting 8-3-78," National Security Archive, Civil Defense/Emergency Management Collection (Rumbarger Donation), box 10, folder "DoD Review of CD Program (PRM 32)."

58. "PRC Meeting 8-3-78."

59. "PRC Meeting 8-18-78," National Security Archive, Civil Defense/Emergency Management Collection (Rumbarger Donation), box 10, folder "DoD Review of CD Program (PRM 32)."

60. Bradsher, "Civil Defense Move Followed a Failure," 9.

61. Yoshpe, *Our Missing Shield*, 479–80.

62. In January 1979 Paul Warnke reiterated his hope that the SALT process would include limits on civil defense in the future, despite the unwillingness of Soviet negotiators to discuss it. "Civil Defense Won't Alter U.S.-Soviet Strategic Balance, Warnke Says." Queried in congressional testimony as to whether the United States might need a civil defense program to strengthen its negotiating position and facilitate this goal, Warnke replied, "I really have never been an advocate of the bargaining chip theory. I think that spending money on things so you can later give them away is an imprudent expenditure of funds." U.S. Senate Committee on Banking, Housing, and Urban Development, *Second Session*, 20.

63. Bureau of Public Affairs Office of Public Information, "Special Report No. 47: Soviet Civil Defense," September 1978, NA RG 59, Records of the Department of State, Bureau of Public Affairs Office of Public Communications Records Relating to Major Publications, 1949–1990, box 8, folder "Special Report #47 'Soviet Civil Defense 1978.'"

64. "An Analysis of Civil Defense in Nuclear War," National Security Archive, Civil Defense/Emergency Management Collection (Rumbarger Donation), box 10, folder "ACDA Position on CD."

65. "An Analysis of Civil Defense in Nuclear War."

66. Harold Brown to George M. Seignious, photocopy of letter, date illegible, National Security Archive, Civil Defense/Emergency Management Collection (Rumbarger Donation), box 11, folder "Civil Defense—Carter Administration."

67. Downey, "The Misguided Concept," 44.

68. Cavers, "That Carter Evacuation Plan," 15–19.

69. Kincade, "Carter and Civil Defense."

70. Cavers, "That Carter Evacuation Plan," 15.

71. Yoshpe, *Our Missing Shield*, 494–95.

72. Arbatov, "The Dangers of a New Cold War," 37. Arbatov may have made this statement earnestly, but no examined documents from Soviet civil defense, internal or external, mention any plans envisioning a war between the Soviet Union and a non-Western power such as China.

73. Gouré, *Vyzhivanie v voine po Sovetskoi strategii*, 3–4.

74. Quoted in Yoshpe, *Our Missing Shield*, 456.

75. "Notes of Meetings at the Soviet Embassy and at The Old Executive Office Building Washington D.C. March 6, 1980," National Archives Record Group 383, Records of the Arms Control and Disarmament Agency, MLR 4, box 4, folder "Physicians for Social Responsibility Effects of Nuclear War."

76. Frolov, "Grazhdanskaia oborona SShA."

77. Giuffrida, *National Survival—Racial Imperative*. This work attracted considerable attention at Giuffrida's nomination hearings, in which he explained that the argument of the paper was not that such measures would be desirable but that better race relations both within the military and among society at large would be desirable. U.S. Senate Committee on Governmental Affairs, *First Session on Nomination of Louis O. Giuffrida*.

78. Chardy, "Reagan Aides." According to Chardy, the exercise in question, "Rex-84," elicited prompt protest from attorney general William Smith, who disapproved of the proposed martial law measures. To alleviate the controversy, the White House took the fateful step of transferring North from his position as NSC FEMA liaison to international covert operations, where he subsequently found himself at the center of the Iran-Contra scandal. The outlines of North's FEMA involvement fell under public scrutiny along with the revelation of Iran-Contra. This account remains unsubstantiated and, like much of FEMA's continuity-of-government planning, provides fodder for conspiracy theorists.

79. "Nomination of Louis O. Giuffrida to Be Director of the Federal Emergency Management Agency," Ronald Reagan Presidential Library, accessed January 7, 2018, http://www.reagan.utexas.edu/archives/speeches/1981/22481c.htm.

80. Margasak, "Emergency Agency Probe Continues."

81. Kurtz, "FEMA Chief."

82. "House Finds Misconduct at U.S. Emergency Agency."

83. Blanchard, *American Civil Defense*, 25.

84. "National Security Decision Directive Number 26 (Unclassified Version)," NA RG 311, Records of the Federal Emergency Management Agency, MLR 18 UD-UP, Box 1, Folder "NSDD-26." FEMA's budget request for fiscal year 1983 planned for a renewed shelter survey and the restart of shelter marking and stocking after a ten-year hiatus. Neither FEMA nor its critics, however, spent much time discussing this aspect of the program, and in order to be fully effective it would have required measures akin to the Shelter Incentive Program that Steuart L. Pittman championed.

85. Scheer, "Civil Defense Program to Be Revived." Jones understandably attempted to deny this comment after the fact, but Scheer taped the interview. Scheer made Jones's comments the centerpiece of his 1982 book *With Enough Shovels*.

86. "Speech Presented by Marilyn J. Braun to the House Sub-Committee on Environment, Energy, and Natural Resources, April 22, 1982," National Security Archive, Civil Defense/FEMA Collection (Dyke Donation), box 2, folder "FEMA—Crisis Relocation."

87. Weiss, "Evacuation Plan."

88. Hirshon, "Cambridge Nuclear Attack Booklet."

89. Garrison, *Bracing for Armageddon*, 166; and Thompson, "Debate Widens."

90. This figure is somewhat low because FEMA refused to count cases that remained legally ambiguous, such as New York City and Greensboro, where Braun refused to participate in CRP out of her personal conviction rather than on the orders of the local government. "Report on Calls to Regions, June 10–11, to Obtain Updated Information on Local Negative Actions Concerning CRP," NA RG 311, Records of the Federal Emergency Management Agency, MLR 18 UD-UP, box 1, folder "Crisis Relocation."

91. "The Nuclear Threat to Marin County: A Prevention and Source Document," photocopy in NA RG 311, Records of the Federal Emergency Management Agency, MLR 18 UD-UP, box 1, folder "News Clippings."

92. Louis O. Giuffrida to Edwin Meese, memorandum, August 11, 1982, NA RG 311, Records of the Federal Emergency Management Agency, MLR 18 UD-UP, box 1, folder "Meese, Edwin on CD."

93. Jim Holton for CD Council members, memorandum, August 13, 1982, NA RG 311, Records of the Federal Emergency Management Agency, MLR 18 UD-UP, box 1, folder "Public Affairs/Holton"; and "The Day After, Screenplay by David Hume, revised 8/10/82," NA RG 311, Records of the Federal Emergency Management Agency, MLR 18 UD-UP, box 1, folder "The Day After."

94. *The Day After*, directed by Nicholas Meyer, produced by Robert Papazian (ABC Circle Films, 1983).

95. One April 1982 *New York Times* editorial suggested that those responsible for the civil defense program be fired. Apparently some in FEMA concurred; on April 6 Frank S. Salcedo, FEMA Civil Security Division chief, wrote a memorandum to Giuffrida arguing that the only way to salvage the civil defense program would be to make a visible change in leadership and a "change in attitude." Salcedo asserted that "civil defense is necessary but should be approached now in a more modest but realistic and skillful manner." Frank Salcedo to Louis O. Giuffrida, memorandum, April 6, 1982, NA RG 311, Records of the Federal Emergency Management Agency, MLR 18 UD-UP, box 2, folder "CD Management."

96. "Media Strategy Paper," NA RG 311, Records of the Federal Emergency Management Agency, MLR 18 UD-UP, box 1, folder "Public Affairs/Holton."

97. Originally published as a series of articles in the *New Yorker* in early 1982, *The Fate of the Earth* appeared in book form later that year. The *New York Times* cited Peter Scharfman, the director of the 1979 Office of Technology Assessment study on the effects of nuclear war, as saying that he took "serious exception" to what Schell had written. Phillip M. Boffey, "Contemplating the Heart of Nuclear Darkness," *New York Times*, March 28, 1982, photocopy in NA RG 311, Records of the Federal Emergency Management Agency, MLR 18 UD-UP, box 1, folder "News Clippings."

98. Jennifer Leaning to all chapter contacts and the Board of Directors, memorandum, December 7, 1982, National Security Archive, Civil Defense/FEMA Collection (Dyke Donation), box 2, folder "FEMA—Crisis Relocation."

99. Leaning and Keys, *The Counterfeit Ark*.

100. Dyke donated his papers to the National Security Archive, where they are preserved as National Security Archive, Civil Defense/FEMA Collection (Dyke Donation).

101. "Nuclear War/Civil Defense Conference, February 16–17, 1985," National Security Archive, Civil Defense/FEMA Collection (Dyke Donation), box 2, folder "FEMA—Crisis Relocation." The conference numbered nineteen participants, including Jennifer Leaning of PSR and representatives of Common Cause, Nuclear Free America, and the Federation of American Scientists.

102. Peter Dyke to all network members, memorandum, March 6, 1985, National Security Archive, Civil Defense/FEMA Collection (Dyke Donation), box 2, folder "FEMA—Crisis Relocation."

103. In an April 28, 1982, op-ed in the *Washington Post*, New York representative Donald J. Mitchell, one of the strongest supporters of civil defense in Congress, asserted that in a nuclear war the USSR would suffer the deaths of fifteen million and that with the CRP policy U.S. casualties would be similar. Mitchell circulated the op-ed as a letter to other members of Congress to persuade them to vote for FEMA's budget request. Donald J. Mitchell, "In Defense of Civil Defense," NA RG 311, Records of the Federal Emergency Management Agency, MLR 18 UD-UP, box 1, folder "Congressional Items."

104. Reed, "Coast-to-Coast Protests."

105. Solomon and Marston, *The Medical Implications of Nuclear War*, 555.

106. In the early 1980s Sagan asked fellow symposium participant and nuclear weapons effects expert Harold Brode to collaborate on his research about nuclear winter. Brode regarded the apocalyptic claims of Sagan and his collaborators as overblown and later described their efforts as the "nuclear winter doomsday hooha." Eden, *Whole World on Fire*, 241.

107. Dowling and Harrell, *Civil Defense*, ix–x.

108. *Info-Ray* 27, no. 3 (1982): 1, photocopy in NA RG 311, Records of the Federal Emergency Management Agency, MLR 18 UD-UP, box 1, folder "News Clippings."

109. Teller, "Civil Defense Is Crucial," A19.

110. Jim Holton to Bennett Lewis, memorandum, June 4, 1982, NA RG 311, Records of the Federal Emergency Management Agency, MLR 18 UD-UP, box 1, folder "Public Affairs/Holton."

111. "New Gallup Survey Results on Civil Defense Announced," NA RG 311, Records of the Federal Emergency Management Agency, MLR 18 UD-UP, box 1, folder "News Clippings."

112. Blanchard, *American Civil Defense*, 22–23.

113. The records of the FEMA Civil Defense Council meeting of September 1, 1982, attest to the discussion between different decision makers in the agency about how to attempt to maintain forward momentum on CRP without the hoped-for increase in funding. The inclusion of options such as charging the salaries of civil defense researchers to other areas of the FEMA budget make the question of how the agency ultimately acted extremely difficult to ascertain. "CD Council Meeting 9/1/82," photocopy in NA RG 311, Records of the Federal Emergency Management Agency, MLR 18 UD-UP, box 2, folder "Agenda for CD Council Meetings."

114. Louis O. Giuffrida to Edwin Meese, memorandum, May 11, 1982, NA RG 311, Records of the Federal Emergency Management Agency, MLR 18 UD-UP, box 1, folder "Meese, Edwin on CD." Senator Patrick J. Leahy of Vermont wrote a letter to

FEMA on this topic, to which FEMA general counsel George Jett replied equivocally. George Jett to Patrick Leahy, letter, August 6, 1982, photocopy in NA RG 311, Records of the Federal Emergency Management Agency, MLR 18 UD-UP, box 2, folder "Agenda for CD Council Meetings."

115. "Talking Points Subject: Support of Civil Defense Objectives by State and Local Jurisdictions," NA RG 311, Records of the Federal Emergency Management Agency, MLR 18 UD-UP, box 1, folder "State and Local Support of CD Objectives."

116. Blanchard, *American Civil Defense*, 23.

117. Marilyn J. Braun to James L. Proffitt, W. E. Swing, R. L. Powell, and Charles W. Porter, memorandum, June 6, 1983, National Security Archive, Civil Defense/FEMA Collection (Dyke Donation), box 2, folder "FEMA—Crisis Relocation."

118. Boyd, "A Disaster Agency's Image Disaster."

119. Blanchard, *American Civil Defense*, 23–24.

120. John H. Pickett to Jerry Stephens, letter, October 15, 1982, National Security Archive, Civil Defense/Emergency Management Collection (Rumbarger Donation), box 11, folder "FEMA/Office of Public Affairs Civil Defense Program 1982."

121. Steuart L. Pittman to Louis O. Giuffrida, letter, July 29, 1982, National Security Archive, Civil Defense/Emergency Management Collection (Rumbarger Donation), box 11, folder "FEMA/Office of Public Affairs Civil Defense Program 1982."

122. FEMA's claims for the program wavered, sometimes utilizing the 80 percent survival figure while at other times making the more modest claim that the program would "double" the number of Americans surviving nuclear attack.

123. "Charges made in 'Defense Monitor' on Proposed Civil Defense Program vs. Facts," NA RG 311, Records of the Federal Emergency Management Agency, MLR 18 UD-UP, box 2, folder "Budget Items."

124. Garrison, *Bracing for Armageddon*, 16.

125. Garrison, 175–76.

126. "Civil Defense Relocation Plan Said to Be Dropped."

127. Becton, *Becton*, 179–89.

128. U.S. Senate Committee on Governmental Affairs, *Hearings on the Nominations of Julius W. Becton, Jr.*, 69.

129. Quoted in Hiatt, "U.S. War-Survival Plan Favors Officials."

130. Cushman, "U.S. Report Declares Civil Defense in Poor Shape and Getting Worse." The actual civil defense appropriation for fiscal year 1987 totaled $139 million.

131. Hiatt, "States Pushed to Improve Nuclear War Readiness."

132. Turner, "2 States Defy."

133. Center for Defense Information, "Soviet Civil Defense."

134. U.S. Senate Subcommittee on Arms Control, Oceans, International Operations, and the Environment, *United States and Soviet Civil Defense Programs*, 28.

135. U.S. Senate Subcommittee on Arms Control, Oceans, International Operations, and the Environment, 34. Gayler's "qualified Russian observers" included prominent Soviet oncologist Nikolai Blokhin and economist Nikolai Inozemtsev, figures well connected with Western advocates of reduced tension between the superpowers, but not privy to information about Soviet civil defense efforts.

136. U.S. Senate Subcommittee on Arms Control, Oceans, International Operations, and the Environment, 28.

137. U.S. Senate Subcommittee on Arms Control, Oceans, International Operations, and the Environment, 32. Wigner and Gouré believed that in a crisis this course of action would lack credibility, in part because the Soviet Union could respond in kind and retarget its forces to maximize American casualties, with or without relocation, but also because of the implausibility that the president would make blatant threats to commit mass murder even in a tense international crisis.

138. Leaning and Keys, *The Counterfeit Ark*, 59.

139. National Security Archive, "Permanent Operational Assignment to Uncover NATO Preparations for a Nuclear Missile Attack on the USSR."

140. Burns, "Russians, Too, Joke."

141. Lown, *Prescription for Survival*, 154–61.

142. Unbeknownst to Lown, Soviet civil defense had anticipated this problem and developed extensive technical means to overcome it, dictating that blast shelters include provisions to maintain a livable atmosphere and temperature without any reliance on external air to allow them to survive firestorms. These measures included insulation, bottled oxygen, carbon dioxide scrubbers, and refrigeration systems.

143. "Soviet Physicians Comment on the Threat of Nuclear War."

144. Lown, *Prescription for Survival*, 155–67.

145. Legchaev, *Iadernoe oruzhie*, 43.

146. Published in English as Aleksandrov and Stanchikov, "Numerical Simulation."

147. Skeptical of a series of studies on the opinions of American and Soviet youth on nuclear war undertaken by Eric Chivian of the IPPNW, Mikhail Galperin, Robert R. Holt, and Polly Howells conducted their own study of the subject. Galperin, a Soviet expatriate himself, expected that he would find that Soviet youth believed the messages of civil defense propaganda, only to be surprised when his findings confirmed Chivian's. "These results directly contradict the senior author's memories of the attitudinal climate in the Soviet Union when he attended school there in the 1960s and early 1970s," wrote Galperin, concluding that "we can only hypothesize that Soviet information policy has changed on this issue in the last 12 years, and (since all of our subjects left the USSR before 1984) before the Gorbachev reforms." Galperin, Holt, and Howells, "What Soviet Emigré Adolescents Think about Nuclear War," 9–10.

148. *Izvestiia*, June 4, 1987, 7.

149. Rosenberg, ". . . And Turner Launches a Counterattack on WTBS."

150. Founded in 1980, the OISM later became notorious as a center of global warming denialism, attempting to collect signatures of scientists doubting that carbon dioxide pollution was causing climate change.

151. Oregon Institute of Science and Medicine, "Soviet Civil Defense," six VHS cassettes (author's personal collection). The OISM also produced video adaptations of Cresson Kearny's *Nuclear War Survival Skills* and "Facts about Nuclear War as Explained to School Children by Dr. Jane Orient," in which Dr. Orient lectures a group of bored-looking adolescents about the Soviet military threat and civil defense measures.

152. Ing, *The Chernobyl Syndrome*, 2.

153. Austin, *The Guardians*, 16.

154. Leaning and Keyes, *The Counterfeit Ark*, 17.

155. Barkenbus and Weinberg, "Moving to Defenses through the Defense-Protected Build-Down (DPB)," 24–25.

156. Weinberg, "Speculations on a Defense-Dominated World," 105.

157. Chester, "The Role of Civil Defense—1986," 183. Chester took note of the fact that "passive defense has hardly been mentioned in the debate" surrounding Reagan's SDI program.

158. Dyson, *Weapons and Hope*.

159. Schell, *The Abolition*, 138.

160. Gromyko, *Novoe myshlenie v iadernyi vek*.

161. Podvig, "Did Star Wars Help End the Cold War?"; and Podvig, *Russian Strategic Nuclear Forces*, 230–32.

162. Dowling and Harrell, *Civil Defense*, 119–22.

163. Potter and Kerner, "The Soviet Military's Performance at Chernobyl," 1039.

164. Geist, "Political Fallout."

165. Gouré, *Status of Soviet Civil Defense*, 1.

166. Pry, *Strategic Nuclear Balance*, 2:223.

167. For the reform regulations, see *Organizatsionno-metodicheskie ukazaniia*.

168. For examples of Soviet civil defense manuals omitting or downplaying nuclear warfare, see Shubin, *Grazhdanskai oborona*; and Kozhbakhteev, *Znai i umei*.

169. For instance, see Krutskikh, *Memuary*.

170. The MChS resulted from the post-Soviet merger of GO with the State Commission for Emergency Situations (GKChS), an emergency management agency founded in mid-1989. On the history of the GKChS, see Elie, "Late Soviet Responses to Disasters."

171. Shoigu joked about the popularity of his ministry in a 2009 press conference. "It's really too bad that the MChS is the most popular, and not, say, the Ministry of Culture—it means that they need to change something in the conservatories, so there were fewer accidents and catastrophes." Baltspetspobezhopasnost', "MChS imeet vysokii uroven' populiarnosti strane."

172. Wilson, "FEMA Asks $20 Million for Fallout Shelters."

173. "Optimism Increases on Surviving Atom War."

174. Jennifer Leaning, "Star Wars Revives Civil Defense."

175. Robert Ehrlich and Ruth H. Howes reported in 1987 that "whether or not this ominous connotation may seem far-fetched, Soviet civilians and officials have reported it in individual conversations." Dowling and Harrell, *Civil Defense*, 159.

176. Dowling and Harrell, 114–19.

Conclusion

1. "Kiselev: Rossia sposbna prevratit' SShA v radioaktivnyi pepel'."

2. Elie, "Late Soviet Responses to Disasters."

3. "Rogozin: Do kontsa Noiabria kabmin primet programmu obespecheniia radiatsionnoi bezopasnosti."

4. "Ekspert rasskazal o plane spaseniia rossian v sluchae iadernoi voiny."

5. "V Moskve polnost'iu podgotovili."

6. RosOtvet, a noncommercial service that makes inquiries to Russian government organs, formally requested that the MChS post the locations of bomb shelters in Moscow and St. Petersburg on the internet, only to be told this was impossible because this information is a state secret. "Adresa bomboubezhishch v Moskve i Peterburge." Citizens have tagged known Moscow bomb shelter sites on Wikimapia. "Ubezhishche grazhdanskoi oborony v gorode Moskva."

7. Payton, "Russia Launches Massive Nuclear War Training Exercise with '40 Million People.'" An English-language version of the official MChS description of the exercise can be found at "Large-Scale All-Russian Civil Defense Drill to Take Place from 4 to 7 October."

8. Ramm, "Gubernatorov, FSB"; and Ramm and Kaledina, "Minoborony poluchila pravo."

9. "Putin: 'Briatsat' atomnym oruzhiem—poslednoe delo."

10. "Evgenii Federov: 'Dmitrii Kiselev uchastvuet v zagovore protiv Rossii."

11. Mills, "West Coast Lawmakers Sound Alarm on North Korea."

12. Zimmerman, "North Korea Tensions Have Hawaii Pols Revisiting Emergency Attack Plans."

13. Bush, "Planning for Nuclear Attack."

14. Gouré, *War Survival in Soviet Strategy*, 18.

15. "Alternative U.S. Civil Defense Programs, November 21, 1977," National Security Archive, Civil Defense/Emergency Management Collection (Rumbarger Donation), box 10, folder "DoD (PA&E) review of CD program '77–78."

16. The 1973 shelter construction plan for the Ukrainian SSR provides concrete figures for shelter construction costs at the height of Soviet civil defense efforts during the mid-1970s. The most expensive category of these shelters—freestanding, single-purpose shelters—cost on average 232 rubles per shelter space. Soviet civil defense also developed blast shelter space more economically via creative use of existing structures. Equipping mines and other existing underground structures as shelters cost an average of 143 rubles per space. Presumably shelters incorporated in new construction cost less than the freestanding shelters, but these costs were paid by the organizations responsible for these projects and not civil defense. TsDAHO, f. 1, op. 25, sp. 886, ark. 30. Presuming that Soviet civil defense could construct blast shelters at an average cost of 200 rubles per shelter space, construction for 175 million Soviet citizens living in urban areas would cost a total of 35 billion rubles. The investment of 5 billion rubles per year, less than 10 percent of the USSR's likely annual defense expenditures under Brezhnev, would have been sufficient to complete such a system in seven years.

17. For an insightful recent account of how infighting within the CPSU led Mikhail Gorbachev and his allies to intentionally dismantle the traditional bases of communist power, see Miller, *The Struggle to Save the Soviet Economy*.

Bibliography

Primary Sources

Russia
Central State Archive of Moscow Oblast' (TsGAMO)
Foreign Policy Archive of the Russian Federation, Moscow (AVPRF)
Russian State Archive of Contemporary History, Moscow (RGANI)
Russian State Archive of Socio-Political History, Moscow (RGASPI)
State Archive of the Russian Federation (GARF)

Ukraine
Central State Archive of Social Organizations of Ukraine, Kiev (TsDAHO)
    Fond 1

United States
Dwight D. Eisenhower Library (DDEL), Abilene, Kansas
National Archives (NA), College Park, Maryland
    Record Group 304, Records of the Office of Civil and Defense Mobilization
    Record Group 396, Records of the Office of Emergency Preparedness
    Record Group 397, Records of the Defense Civil Preparedness Agency
National Security Archive, Washington, D.C.

Published Materials

"A-Bomb Test Lesson: Dig a Trench." *San Francisco Chronicle*, March 20, 1953.
"Adresa bomboubezhishch v Moskve i Peterburge." *RosOtvet*, October 20, 2016. Accessed April 21, 2017, http://rosotvet.ru/adresa-bomboubezhishh-v-moskve-i-peterburge/.
Aksiutin, Iurii. *Khrushchevskaia "ottepel'" i obshchestvennye nastroeniia v SSSR v 1953–1964gg.* 2nd ed. Moscow: ROSSPEN, 2010.
Aleksandrov, V. V., and G. L. Stanchikov. "Numerical Simulation of the Climatic Consequences of a Nuclear War." *USSR Computational Mathematical Physics* 24 (1984): 87–90.
Aligica, Paul Dragod, and Kenneth R. Weinstein, eds. *The Essential Herman Kahn: In Defense of Thinking.* Lanham, MD: Lexington Books, 2009.
Allison, Helen C. "News Roundup." *Bulletin of the Atomic Scientists* 13, no. 4 (1957): 147–49.
———. "News Roundup." *Bulletin of the Atomic Scientists* 13, no. 10 (1957): 309–12.

Altunin, A. T. "O teorii grazhdanskoi oborony." *Voennaia mysl'* 56, no. 2 (1974): 30–40.

Andriushin, I. A., A. K. Chernyshev, and Iu. A. Iudrin. *Ukroshchenie iadra: Stranitsy istorii iadernogo oruzhiia i iadernoi infrastraktury SSSR*. Sarov: "Krasnyi Oktiabr'," 2003.

"Annotatsiia bibliografiia." *Grazhdanskaia oborona—informatsionnyi sbornik po materialam zarubezhnoi pechati* 2, no. 6 (1962): 39.

Anokhin, Aleksei. *Oni byli pervymi: (Ocherk o rukovoditeliakh oboronnogo Obshchestva)*. Moscow: Magistr-PRO, 2000.

Arbatov, Georgi. "The Dangers of a New Cold War." *Bulletin of the Atomic Scientists* 33, no. 3 (1977): 33–40.

"The Atomic Bomb and Our Cities." *Bulletin of the Atomic Scientists* 2, nos. 3–4 (1946): 29–30.

"Atomic Survival Film Released This Month, First of Series." *Civil Defense Alert* 1, no. 1 (1951): 7.

Austin, Richard. *The Guardians*. New York: Jove Books, 1985.

"Averting Death from the Skies." *Popular Mechanics* 75, no. 5 (1941): 648–50.

AVIAKhIM. *Iacheika obshchestva druzei aviatsionnoi i khimicheskoi oborony i promyshlennosti. (Polozhenie i instruktsiia)*. Moscow: Tipografiia Upravleniia Delami Soveta Narodnykh Komissarov SSSR, 1926.

Bakanov, R. A., and S. Dzharylglasov. *Grazhdanskaia oborona SShA*. Moscow: Medgiz, 1959.

Baltspetspobezhopasnost'. "MChS imeet vysokii uroven' populiarnosti strane," September 27, 2011. Accessed June 12, 2018, http://srobspb.ru/m/20570/mchs_imeet_wysokiy_uroweny_populyarnosti_w_st-rane.html.

Barinov, A. "Inzhenerno-tekhnicheskie meropriiatia GO." *Grazhdanskaia zashchita* 41, no. 10 (2007): 20–24.

Barkenbus, Jack N., and Alvin M. Weinberg, eds. "Moving to Defenses through the Defense-Protected Build-Down (DPB)." In *Strategic Defenses and Arms Control*, edited by Jack N. Barkenbus and Alvin M. Weinberg, 23–65. New York: Paragon House, 1988.

———, eds. *Strategic Defenses and Arms Control*. New York: Paragon House, 1988.

Battilega, John A. "Soviet Views of Nuclear Warfare: The Post–Cold War Interviews." In *Getting Mad: Nuclear Mutual Assured Destruction, Its Origins and Practice*, edited by Henry D. Sokolski, 151–74. Carlisle, PA: Strategic Studies Institute, 2004.

Becton, Julius. *Becton: Autobiography of a Soldier and Public Servant*. Annapolis, MD: Naval Institute Press, 2008.

Beliaev, A. N. "Mestnaia protivovozdushnaia oborona strany v gody Velikoi otechestvennoi voiny." *Istoricheskie zapiski* 102 (1978): 327–59.

Bennett, M. Todd, ed. *National Security Policy, 1973–1976*. Vol. 35 of *Foreign Relations of the United States, 1969–1976*. Washington, DC: Government Printing Office, 2014.

Blair, William G. "Millard F. Caldwell of Florida; Legislator, Governor, Justice." *New York Times*, October 25, 1984, B22.

Blanchard, B. Wayne. *American Civil Defense 1945–1984: The Evolution of Programs and Policies*. Emmitsburg, MD: Federal Emergency Management Agency, 1985.

Boyd, Gerald M. "A Disaster Agency's Image Disaster." *New York Times*, January 6, 1984, A12.

Boyer, Paul. *By the Bomb's Early Light: American Thought and Culture at the Dawn of the Atomic Age*. New York: Pantheon Books, 1985.

Bradley, David. *No Place to Hide*. Boston: Little, Brown, 1948.

Bradsher, Henry S. "Civil Defense Move Followed a Failure." *Washington Star*, November 16, 1978, 9.

Brennan, Donald G., ed. *Arms Control and Civil Defense*. Harmon-on-Hudson, NY: Hudson Institute, 1963.

Brians, Paul. *Nuclear Holocausts: Atomic War in Fiction, 1895–1984*. Kent, OH: Kent State University Press, 1984.

Brodie, Bernard. *Strategiia v vek raketnogo oruzhiia*. Moscow: Voennoe izdatel'stvo, 1961.

Broyles, A. P., E. P. Wigner, and S. D. Drell. "Civil Defense in Nuclear War—a Debate." *Physics Today* 29, no. 4 (1976): 44–47, 50, 52, 53, 55–57.

Bruce-Briggs, B. *Supergenius: The Mega-Worlds of Herman Kahn*. Idaville, PA: North American Press, 2005.

Buianov, A. "Atomnaia tekhnika shestoi piatiletki." *Voennye znaniia* 9, no. 6 (1956): 2–3.

———. "Energiia atoma." *Voennye znaniia* 7, no. 3 (1954): 17.

———. "Energiia atoma." *Voennye znaniia* 7, no. 4 (1954): 18–19.

———. "Energiia atoma." *Voennye znaniia* 7, no. 5 (1954): 18–19.

———. "Energiia atoma." *Voennye znaniia* 7, no. 6 (1954): 20–21.

Burns, John F. "Russians, Too, Joke Sadly on Atom-War Survival," *New York Times*, June 11, 1982, A2.

Bush, Evan. "Planning for Nuclear Attack: Lawmakers Want to Undo 1984 Ban on 'Preparing for the Worst.'" *Seattle Times*, May 9, 2017. Accessed June 28, 2017, http://www.seattletimes.com/seattle-news/bill-would-remove-prohibition-on-planning-for-nuclear-attack/.

Byrnes, A., and G. Underhill. "Shelters and Survival." *New Republic* 146, no. 3 (1962): 3–40.

Bystrova, Irina. *Sovetskii voenno-promyshlennyi kompleks: Problemy stanovlenie i razvitiia (1930–1980e gody)*. Moscow: Institut Rossiiskoi istorii RAN, 2006.

Cabage, Bill. "End Notes," July 2000. Accessed June 12, 2018, http://www.ornl.gov/info/reporter/no17/lnjuly_00.htm.

Caidin, Martin. *The Long Night*. New York: Dodd, Mead, 1956.

"Caldwell Is Approved." *New York Times*, January 16, 1951, 26.

"Caldwell Resigns Civil Defense Post." *New York Times*, November 8, 1952, 30.

"Caldwell Wants to Quit: But Civil Defense Head Says Truman Won't Let Him Go." *New York Times*, February 14, 1952, 14.

Calingaert, Daniel. "Nuclear Weapons and the Korean War." *Journal of Strategic Studies* 11, no. 2 (1988): 177–202.

Cantelon, Philip L., Richard G. Hewlett, and Robert C. Williams, eds. *The American Atom: A Documentary History of Nuclear Policies from the Discovery of Fission to the Present*. 2nd ed. Philadelphia: University of Pennsylvania Press, 1991.

Cavers, David F. "That Carter Evacuation Plan." *Bulletin of the Atomic Scientists* 35, no. 4 (1979): 15–19.

Center for Defense Information. "Soviet Civil Defense," *Defense Monitor* 11, no. 5 (1982): 6.

Central Intelligence Agency. "Memorandum of Estimate on Soviet Capabilities for Strategic Attack, Issued 18 October 1963." January 10, 1964, 3. Accessed January 8, 2018, https://www.cia.gov/library/readingroom/docs/CIA-RDP82R00025R000400030007-2.pdf.

——. *National Intelligence Estimate NIE-60: Civil Defense in the USSR*. Langley, VA: Central Intelligence Agency, 1952.

——. *NI-78-10003: Soviet Civil Defense*. Langley, VA: Central Intelligence Agency, 1978.

——. *Soviet Civil Defense and Air-Raid Shelter Construction*. Langley, VA: Central Intelligence Agency, 1958.

Central Intelligence Agency Office of Research and Reports. *Changing Soviet Civil Defense Concepts, CIA/RR CB 62-56*. Langley, VA: Central Intelligence Agency, 1962.

——. "Soviet Defense Expenditures, CIA/SC/RR 22." Langley, VA: Central Intelligence Agency, 1955.

Chardy, Alfonso. "Reagan Aides and the Secret Government." *Miami Herald*, July 5, 1987, 1.

Chester, Conrad. "The Role of Civil Defense—1986." In *Strategic Defenses and Arms Control*, edited by Jack N. Barkenbus and Alvin M. Weinberg, 166–88. New York: Paragon House, 1988.

"Civil Defense Budget Is Cut over 50 Percent." *Washington Post*, April 7, 1951.

"Civil Defense Relocation Plan Said to Be Dropped." *New York Times*, March 4, 1985, A9.

"Civil Defense Won't Alter U.S.-Soviet Strategic Balance, Warnke Says." *Aerospace Daily*, July 11, 1979, 55.

Clarkson, Helen. *The Last Day: A Novel of the Day after Tomorrow*. New York: Dodd, 1959.

Clymer, Kenton. "U.S. Homeland Defense in the 1950s: The Origins of the Ground Observer Corps." *Journal of Military History* 75 (2011): 835–59.

Coffey, J. I. "The Chinese and Ballistic Missile Defense." *Bulletin of the Atomic Scientists* 21, no. 10 (1965): 17–19.

Coleman, David, ed. *The Presidential Recordings of John F. Kennedy*. Vol. 6, *The Winds of Change*. New York: W. W. Norton, 2016.

Committee on Government Operations. *Fifth Report by the Committee on Government Operations: Civil Defense in Western Europe and the Soviet Union*. Washington, DC: GPO, 1959.

Conelrad. "'Atomic Flash': The Birth of Bert." Accessed April 13, 2012, http://conelrad.com/duckandcover/cover.php?turtle=01a.

———. "Atomic Tattoo." Accessed April 12, 2012, http://www.conelrad.com/atomicsecrets/secrets.php?secrets=11.
———. "'THE COMMUNIST PARTY LINE': Critics of Bert and the Fall of Archer." Accessed April 13, 2012, http://conelrad.com/duckandcover/cover.php?turtle=01c.
———. "Duck and Cover: The Citizen Kane of Civil Defense." Accessed April 13, 2012, http://www.conelrad.com/duckandcover/.
———. "Putting the Jingle in Bert: Post Production." Accessed April 13, 2012, http://conelrad.com/duckandcover/cover.php?turtle=01b.
Craig, Campbell, and Sergey Radchenko. *The Atomic Bomb and the Origins of the Cold War.* New Haven, CT: Yale University Press, 2008.
Cristescu, C. "Strict Secret de Importantă Deosobită—Stalin decide înarmerea României." *Magazin istoric* 29, no. 10 (1995): 15–23.
Cromie, Robert. *The Crack of Doom.* London: Digby, Long, 1895.
Cushman, John H. "U.S. Report Declares Civil Defense in Poor Shape and Getting Worse." *New York Times,* July 9, 1986, A20.
Davis, Jack E. "'Whitewash' in Florida: The Lynching of Jesse James Payne and Its Aftermath." *Florida Historical Quarterly* 68, no. 3 (1990): 277–98.
Davis, Tracy C. "Continuity of Government Measures for Civil Defense during the Cuban Missile Crisis." In *The Atomic Bomb and American Society: New Perspectives,* edited by Rosemary B. Mariner and G. Kurt Piehler, 153–84. Knoxville: University of Tennessee Press, 2009.
Defense Civil Preparedness Agency. *Protection in the Nuclear Age.* Washington, DC: GPO, 1977.
Dorofeev, A. "Kharakteristika atomnogo vzryva." *Voennye znaniia* 7, no. 8 (1954): 19–20.
Dowling, John, and Evans M. Harrell, eds. *Civil Defense: A Choice of Disasters.* New York: American Institute of Physics, 1987.
Downey, Thomas J. "The Misguided Concept." *Worldview* 22, no. 1 (1979): 44.
Dvorkin, Vladimir, and Aleksei Produkin. *Povest' o 4 TsNII MO i iadernoi sderzhivanii.* Iubeleinyi: PSTM, 2009.
Dyson, Freeman J. "Thoughts on Bomb Shelters." *Bulletin of the Atomic Scientists* 18, no. 3 (1962): 14–15.
———. *Weapons and Hope.* New York: Harper and Row, 1984.
Eden, Lynn. *Whole World on Fire: Organizations, Knowledge, and Nuclear Weapons Devastation.* Ithaca, NY: Cornell University Press, 2006.
Efremov, Ivan. *Sochineniia.* Moscow: "Molodaia gvardiia," 1976.
Egorov, P. T., I. A. Shliakhov, and N. I. Alabin. *Civil Defense.* Washington, DC: National Technical Informaton Service, 1973.
———. *Grazhdanskaia oborona.* 3rd ed. Moscow: Vyshaia shkola, 1977.
"Ekspert rasskazal o plane spaseniia rossian v sluchae iadernoi voiny." *NTV,* October 9, 2016. Accessed April 21, 2017, http://www.ntv.ru/novosti/1670699/.
Elie, Mark. "Late Soviet Responses to Disasters, 1989–1991: A New Approach to Crisis Management or the Acme of Soviet Technocratic Thinking?" *Soviet and Post-Soviet Review* 40, no. 2 (2013): 214–38.

Elliott, Mai. *RAND in Southeast Asia: A History of the Vietnam War Era*. Santa Monica, CA: RAND, 2010.

Epishin, M. T., F. I. Urvanov, A. F. Dubrovnik, and N. S. Tarasov. *Grazhdanskaia oborona: Uchebnoe posobie dliia provedeniia zaniatii po programme vseobshchego obiazatel'nogo minimuma znanii naseleniia*. 2nd ed. Moscow: Izdatel'stvo "Sovetskaia Rossiia," 1977.

Erickson, John. "The Soviet View of Deterrence: A General Survey." *Survival* 24, no. 6 (1982): 242–51.

"Evgenii Federov: 'Dmitrii Kiselev uchastvuet v zagovore protiv Rossii." *BFM.ru*, February 20, 2017. Accessed June 28, 2017. https://www.bfm.ru/news/347200.

Fairbanks, Charles H. "MAD and U.S. Strategy." In *Getting Mad: Nuclear Mutual Assured Destruction, Its Origins and Practice*, edited by Henry D. Sokolski, 137–47. Carlisle, PA: Strategic Studies Institute, 2004.

"Fallout Shelters." *Life*, September 15, 1961, 95–108.

Fanian, D. S. *Grazhdanskaia oborona Moldavskoi SSR*. Kishinev: Shtiintsa, 1989.

"FCDA Estimates Shelter Available for 2,000,000." *Civil Defense Alert* 1, no. 11 (1952): 4.

"FCDA Receives Awards for Radio, TV Programs." *Civil Defense Alert* 1, no. 12 (1952): 8.

Federal Civil Defense Administration. *Home Shelters for Family Protection in an Atomic Attack*. Washington, DC: GPO, 1953.

———. *Shelter from Atomic Attack in Existing Buildings*. Parts I–II. Washington, DC: GPO, 1952.

Federation of American Scientists. "Civil Defense Shelter Statement." *Bulletin of the Atomic Scientists* 17, no. 2 (1962): 25–28.

Fischer, Louis. *The Soviets in World Affairs*. 2 vols. Princeton, NJ: Princeton University Press, 1951.

Flory, Harriette. "The Arcos Raid and the Rupture of Anglo-Soviet Relations, 1927." *Journal of Contemporary History* 12, no. 4 (October 1977): 707–23.

Frank, Pat. *Alas, Babylon*. New York: Bantam Pathfinder, 1960.

———. *How to Survive the H-Bomb and Why*. New York: Lippincott, 1962.

Friedberg, Aaron. "A History of U.S. Strategic 'Doctrine'—1945 to 1981." In *The Strategic Imperative: New Policies for American Security*, edited by Samuel P. Huntington, 53–99. New York: Ballinger, 1982.

———. *In the Shadow of the Garrison State: America's Anti-Statism and Its Cold War Grand Strategy*. Princeton, NJ: Princeton University Press, 2000.

———. "Why Didn't the United States Become a Garrison State?" *International Security* 16, no. 4 (Spring 1992): 109–42.

Frolov, V. S. "Grazhdanskaia oborona SShA." *SShA: Ekonomika, politika, ideologiia* 11, no. 3 (1980): 121–27.

Fursenko, A. A., ed. *Prezidium TsK KPSS 1954–1964 Postanovleniia, 1959–1964*. Vol. 3. Moscow: ROSSPEN, 2008.

Gabrikov, F. "Sredstva i sposoby protivoatomnoi zashchity." *Voennye znaniia* 7, no. 9 (1954): 18–19.

Gailar, Joanne S. "Seven Warning Signals: A Review of Soviet Civil Defense." *Bulletin of the Atomic Scientists* 25, no. 10 (1969): 18–22.

Gakov, Vladimir. *Ul'timatum: Iadernaia voina i bez"iadernykh mir v fantaziiakh i real'nosti*. Moscow: Izdatel'stvo politicheskoi literatury, 1989.

Galperin, Mikhail, Robert R. Holt, and Polly Howells. "What Soviet Emigré Adolescents Think about Nuclear War." *Political Psychology* 9, no. 1 (1988): 1–12.

Garrison, Dee. *Bracing for Armageddon: Why Civil Defense Never Worked*. New York: Oxford University Press, 2006.

Garthoff, Raymond L. "BMD and East-West Relations." In *Ballistic Missile Defense*, edited by Ashton B. Carter and David N. Schwartz, 275–329. Washington, DC: Brookings Institution, 1984.

Geist, Edward. "Political Fallout: The Failure of Emergency Management at Chernobyl." *Slavic Review* 74, no. 1 (Spring 2015): 104–26.

———. "Was There a Real 'Mineshaft Gap'? Bomb Shelters in the USSR, 1945–62." *Journal of Cold War Studies* 14, no. 2 (2012): 3–28.

George, Alice L. *Awaiting Armageddon: How Americans Faced the Cuban Missile Crisis*. Chapel Hill: University of North Carolina Press, 2003.

Ghamari-Tabrizi, Sharon. *The Worlds of Herman Kahn: The Intuitive Science of Thermonuclear War*. Cambridge, MA: Harvard University Press, 2005.

Giuffrida, Louis O. *National Survival—Racial Imperative*. Carlisle, PA: U.S. Army War College, 1970.

Glantz, David M. *Soviet Military Operational Art: In Pursuit of Deep Battle*. New York: Routledge, 1991.

Glasstone, Samuel, and Phillip J. Dolan, eds. *Effects of Nuclear Weapons*. 3rd ed. Washington, DC: U.S. Dept. of Defense, 1977.

Gordin, Michael. *Red Cloud at Dawn*. New York: Farrar, Straus and Giroux, 2009.

Gosudarstvennyi Komitet Soveta Ministrov SSSR po Delam Stroitel'stva. *Ukazaniia po proektirovaniiu ubezhishch grazhdanskoi oborony SN 405-70*. Moscow: Stroiizdat, 1970.

Gouré, Leon. "Another Interpretation." *Bulletin of the Atomic Scientists* 34, no. 4 (1978): 48–51.

———. *Civil Defense in the Soviet Union*. Berkeley: University of California Press, 1962.

———. *Soviet Civil Defense 1969-1970*. Coral Gables, FL: Miami University Center for Advanced International Studies, 1971.

———. *Soviet Civil Defense Revisited, 1966-1969*. Santa Monica, CA: RAND Corporation, 1969.

———. *The Status of Soviet Civil Defense in the Light of the Chernobyl Reactor Accident and Other Recent Disasters*. Arlington, VA: SAIC, 1989.

———. *Vyzhivanie v voine po Sovetskoi strategii: Grazhdanskaia oborona SSSR*. Moscow: Progress, 1978.

———. *War Survival in Soviet Strategy: Soviet Civil Defense*. Coral Gables, FL: Center for Advanced International Studies, 1976.

"Grazhdanskoi oborone—75 let." *Grazhdanskaia zashchita* 41, no. 10 (2007): 11.

Green, Brendan R., and Austin Long. "The MAD Who Wasn't There: Soviet Reactions to the Late Cold War Nuclear Balance." *Security Studies* 26, no. 4 (2017): 606–41.

"Gregory Peck Sees His Film in Moscow." *New York Times*, December 18, 1959, 34.

Gromyko, Anatolii. *Novoe myshlenie v iadernyi vek*. Moscow: Mezhdunarodye otnosheniia, 1984.

Grossman, Andrew D. *Neither Dead nor Red: Civilian Defense and American Political Development during the Early Cold War*. New York: Routledge, 2001.

Grushin, B. A. *Chetyre zhizni Rossii v zerkale obshchestvennogo mneniia. Zhizn' 1-ia: Epokha Khrushcheva*. Moscow: Progress-Traditsiia, 2001.

Gusev, A. V. *Istoricheskie predposylki sozdaniia i razvitiia sistemy Mestnoi PVO SSSR (1918–1961 gg.)*. Kostroma: KGTU, 2009.

Haapamäki, Michele. *The Coming of the Aerial War: Culture and the Fear of Airborne Attack in Inter-War Britain*. London: I. B. Tauris, 2014.

Hagan, Roger. "Community Shelters." *Nation* 194, no. 8 (1962): 160–67.

Hale-Dorrell, Aaron. "For Peace and Friendship of All Countries: Soviet Citizens' Opinions of Peace during the Cold War, May 1960." MA thesis, University of North Carolina at Chapel Hill, 2009.

Hampe, Erich. *Strategie der zivilen Verteidigung*. Frankfurt a. M.: R. Eisenschmidt Verlag, 1956.

Harrison, Mark. "Resource Mobilization for World War II: The USA, UK, USSR, and Germany, 1938–1945." *Economic History Review* 41, no. 2 (1988), 171–92.

Hearing before the Subcommittee on Security of the Joint Committee on Atomic Energy Eighty-Fourth Congress First Session on AEC-FCDA Relationship. Washington, DC: GPO, 1954.

Hiatt, Fred. "States Pushed to Improve Nuclear War Readiness: U.S. Puts Condition on Civil-Defense Funds." *Washington Post*, July 10, 1986, A4.

———. "U.S. War-Survival Plan Favors Officials: Agency Proposes Bomb Shelters for Officeholders, Land Records." *Washington Post*, May 10, 1986, A1.

Hines, John G., Ellis Mishulovich, and John F. Shull, eds. *Soviet Intentions 1965–1985*. Vol. 1, *An Analytical Comparison of U.S.-Soviet Assessments during the Cold War*. McLean, VA: BDM, 1995.

———. *Soviet Intentions 1965–1985*. Vol. 2, *Soviet Post-Cold War Testimonial Evidence*. McLean, VA: BDM, 1995.

Hirshon, Paul. "Cambridge Nuclear Attack Booklet Is a Hit." *Boston Globe*, September 17, 1981, 19.

Hoffman, David. *The Dead Hand: The Untold Story of the Cold War Arms Race and Its Dangerous Legacy*. New York: Doubleday, 2009.

Holley, Joe. "Leon Gouré, 84; Sovietologist and Civil Defense Expert." *Washington Post*, April 5, 2007. Accessed June 12, 2012, http://www.washingtonpost.com/wp-dyn/content/article/2007/04/04/AR2007040402621.html.

Holloway, David. "Moral Reasoning and Practical Purpose." In *Andrei Sakharov: The Conscience of Humanity*, edited by Sidney D. Drell and George P. Shultz, 115–30. Stanford, CA: Hoover Institution Press, 2016.

———. *Stalin and the Bomb: The Soviet Union and Atomic Energy, 1939–1956.* New Haven, CT: Yale University Press, 1994.
"House Finds Misconduct at U.S. Emergency Agency." *New York Times,* July 26, 1985, A9.
Hudson, Hugh D. "The 1927 Soviet War Scare: The Foreign Affairs-Domestic Policy Nexus Revisited." *Soviet and Post-Soviet Review* 39, no. 2 (2012): 145–65.
Iashin, Iu. A., ed. *Mech' Rossii: Oruzhie raketno-iadernogo udara.* Moscow: MGTU, 2009.
Ing, Dean. *The Chernobyl Syndrome and How to Survive It.* New York: Baen, 1988.
Ivanov, Valentin. *Energiia podvlastna nam!* Moscow: Trudrezervizdat, 1951.
Jacobs, Robert A. *The Dragon's Tail: Americans Face the Atomic Age.* Amherst: University of Massachusetts Press, 2010.
Janis, Irving L. *Air War and Emotional Stress: Psychological Studies of Bombing and Civilian Defense.* New York: McGraw Hill, 1951.
———. "Psychological Problems of A-Bomb Defense." *Bulletin of the Atomic Scientists* 6, nos. 8–9 (1950): 256–62.
Johnson, Chas H. "Why Negroes Are Opposed to Segregated Regional Schools." *Journal of Negro Education* 18, no. 1 (Winter 1949): 1–8.
Joint Committee on Atomic Energy. *Effects of Nuclear Explosions on Weather and Health and Construction of New AEC Office Building, April 15, 1955.* Washington, DC: GPO, 1955.
Jones, Ellen. *Red Army and Society: A Sociology of the Soviet Military.* Boston: Allen & Unwin, 1985.
Jordan, Nehemiah. *Civil Defense before 1950: The Roots of Public Law 920.* Washington, DC: Institute for Defense Analysis, 1966.
Kahn, Herman. *Major Implications of a Current Nonmilitary Defense Study.* Santa Monica, CA: RAND, 1958.
———. *Ob eskalatsii. Sokrashchennyi perevod s angliiskogo.* Moscow: Voennoe izdatel'stvo, 1966.
———. *On Escalation: Metaphors and Scenarios.* New York: Praeger, 1965.
———. *On Thermonuclear War.* Princeton, NJ: Princeton University Press, 1961.
———. *Thinking about the Unthinkable.* New York: Horizon Press, 1962.
Kaplan, Fred. *The Wizards of Armageddon.* Stanford, CA: Stanford University Press, 1983.
Kaufmann, Robert G. *Henry M. Jackson: A Life in Politics.* Seattle: University of Washington Press, 2000.
Kearny, C. H. "Hasty Shelter Construction Studies." In *Civil Defense Research Project: Annual Progress Report, March 1970–March 1971,* ORNL-4784, 78–89. Oak Ridge, TN: Oak Ridge National Laboratory, 1972.
———. "Construction of Hasty Winter Shelters." In *Civil Defense Research Project: Annual Progress Report, March 1971–March 1972.*
Kennedy, Paul P. "Civil Defense Cut Called Crippling." *New York Times,* April 8, 1951, 20.
Kerr, Thomas J. *Civil Defense in the U.S.: Bandaid for a Holocaust?* Boulder, CO: Westview Press, 1983.

Khampe, Erikh. *Strategiia grazhdanskoi oborony*. Translated by M. A. Dubianskoi. Moscow: Izdatel'stvo inostrannoi literatury, 1958.

Kincade, William H. "Carter and Civil Defense." *Christian Science Monitor*, December 6, 1978, 26.

"Kiselev: Rossia sposobna prevratit' SShA v radioaktivnyi pepel'." *Novaia Gazeta*, March 16, 2014. Accessed April 21, 2017, https://www.novayagazeta.ru/news/2014/03/17/98050-kiselev-rossiya-sposobna-prevratit-ssha-v-radioaktivnyy-pepel.

Kissinger, Henry. *Iadernoe oruzhie i vneshniaia politika. Sokrashchennyi perevod s angliiskogo*. Moscow: Izdatel'stvo inostrannoi literatury, 1959.

———. *Nuclear Weapons and Foreign Policy*. New York: Harper, 1957.

Knefler, Joe. "Tale Explores World Doomed by Radiation." *Los Angeles Times*, November 22, 1959, E7.

Korionov, V. *Amerikanskii imperializm-zleishchii vrag narodov*. Moscow: Gospolitizdat, 1952.

Korzun, L. I. *Grazhdanskaia oborona v kapitalisticheskikh stranakh*. Moscow: Chekhovskii Poligrafkombinat, 1970.

———. *Grazhdanskaia oborona v stranakh NATO*. Moscow: Znanie, 1969.

Kotkin, Stephen. *Stalin: Paradoxes of Power, 1878–1928*. New York: Penguin, 2014.

Kozhbakhteev, V. M. *Znai i umei: Pamiatka dlia naseleniia*. 2nd ed. Moscow: Voenizdat, 1991.

Kozovoi, Andrei. "Dissonant Voices: Soviet Youth Mobilization and the Cuban Missile Crisis." *Journal of Cold War Studies* 16, no. 3 (Summer 2014): 29–61.

"Kratkie soobshcheniia." *Grazhdanskaia oborona—informatsionnyi sbornik po materialam zarubezhnoi pechati* 2, no. 9 (1962): 24–25.

Krutskikh, D. A. *Memuary*. Moscow: Izdatel'svo Moskovskogo gosudarstvennogo universiteta lesa, 2001.

Kunkle, Thomas, and Byron Ristvet. *Castle Bravo: Fifty Years of Legends and Lore*. Kirtland AFB: Defense Threat Reduction Information and Analysis Center, 2013.

Kurtz, Howard. "FEMA Chief, 6 Aides Defy Hill Subpeona." *Washington Post*, December 13, 1984, 1.

Laksness, Kh. K. *Atomnaia stantsiia*. Translated by N. Krymovoi. Moscow: Izdatel'stvo Inostrannoi Literatury, 1954.

Lapp, Ralph E. "Civil Defense Faces New Peril." *Bulletin of the Atomic Scientists* 10, no. 9 (1954): 349–51.

"Large-Scale All-Russian Civil Defense Drill to Take Place from 4 to 7 October." *EMERCOM of Russia*. Accessed April 21, 2017, http://en.mchs.ru/mass_media/news/item/32915549/.

Lasswell, Harold. "The Garrison State." *American Journal of Sociology* 46, no. 4 (January 1941): 455–68.

Leaning, Jennifer. "Star Wars Revives Civil Defense." *Bulletin of the Atomic Scientists* 43, no. 4 (1987): 42–46.

Leaning, Jennifer, and Langley Keys, eds. *The Counterfeit Ark: Crisis Relocation for Nuclear War*. New York: Ballinger, 1984.

Legchaev, V. Ia. *Iadernoe oruzhie—ugroza biosfere i zhizni na zemle.* Smolensk: Uprpoligrafizdat, 1983.
Leonardov, B. *Chem grozit voennaia khimiia grazhdanskomu naseleniiu.* Moscow: Gosudarstvennoe voennoe izdatel'stvo, 1925.
"Letters to the Editors." *Life*, October 6, 1961, 10.
Lown, Bernard. *Prescription for Survival: A Doctor's Journey to End Nuclear Madness.* San Francisco: Berret-Koehler, 2008.
Lutsch, Andreas. "Westbindung or Balance of Power. The Federal Republic of Germany's Nuclear Policy between the NPT and NATO's Dual Track Decision (1962–1979)." PhD diss., University of Mainz, 2014.
Mack, Raymond W., and George W. Baker. *The Occasion Instant: The Structure of Social Responses to Unanticipated Air Raid Warnings.* Washington, DC: National Academy of Sciences National Research Council, 1961.
Manhattan Engineer District. *A-Bombing of Hiroshima and Nagasaki.* Whitefish, MT: Kessinger Publishing, 2004.
Margasak, Larry. "Emergency Agency Probe Continues." *Free Lance-Star*, August 2, 1984, 19.
Marseille, Walter W. "Negotiation from Strength." *Bulletin of the Atomic Scientists* 11, no. 1 (1955): 13–18.
Maury, Dabney Herndon. *Recollections of a Virginian in the Mexican, Indian, and Civil Wars.* New York: Charles Scribner's Sons, 1894.
Maxim, Hiram Stevens. *Airships in Peace and War.* London: J. Lane, 1910.
McEnaney, Laura. *Civil Defense Begins at Home: Militarization Meets Everyday Life in the Fifties.* Princeton, NJ: Princeton University Press, 2000.
MChS Rossii. "Sozdanie i Razvitiia Grazhdanskoi Oborony." 2014. Accessed January 6, 2018, http://www.mchs.gov.ru/upload/site1/document_file/hyASWsz8EL.pdf.
"Meet Mr. Caldwell." *Crisis* 58, no. 3 (1951): 183–84.
Melman, Seymour, ed. *No Place to Hide: Fallout Shelters—Fact and Fiction.* New York: Grove Press, 1962.
"Memorandum from Secretary of Defense McNamara to President Johnson, 'Recommended FY 1966–1970 Programs for Strategic Offensive Forces, Continental Air and Missile Defense Forces, and Civil Defense,' 3 December 1964." National Security Archive Electronic Briefing Book No. 275. Accessed March 12, 2013, http://www.gwu.edu/%7Ensarchiv/nukevault/ebb275/20.pdf.
Merril, Judith. *Shadow on the Hearth.* Garden City, NY: Doubleday, 1950.
Mikhailov, Viktor N. *Iadernye ispytania SSSR: Obshchie kharakteristiki, tseli, organizatsiia iadernykh ispytanii SSSR.* Moscow: Izdat, 1997.
Mikoian, Anastas. *Tak bylo.* Moscow: VAGRIUS, 1999.
Mikoyan, Sergo. *The Soviet Cuban Missile Crisis: Castro, Mikoyan, Kennedy, Khrushchev, and the Missiles of November.* Stanford, CA: Stanford University Press, 2012.
Miller, Chris. *The Struggle to Save the Soviet Economy: Mikhail Gorbachev and the Collapse of the USSR.* Chapel Hill: University of North Carolina Press, 2017.

Miller, Walter M. *A Canticle for Leibowitz*. New York: Bantam Pathfinder, 1960.
Mills, Curt. "West Coast Lawmakers Sound Alarm on North Korea." *U.S. News and World Report*, February 10, 2017. Accessed June 28, 2017, https://www.usnews.com/news/world/articles/2017-02-10/california-lawmakers-sound-alarm-on-north-korean-nukes.
Ministerstvo zdravokhraneniia SSSR. *Nastavlenie po uchetu i otchetnosti meditsinskoi sluzhby grazhdanskoi oborony. Utv. 2/VIII 1962 g.* Moscow: Medgiz, 1962.
Miroshnikov, I. *Kollektivnye sredstva protivoatomnoi zashchity*. Moscow: Izdatel'stvo DOSAAF, 1957.
Mitchell, Donald W. *Civil Defense: Planning for Survival and Recovery*. Washington, DC: Industrial College of the Armed Forces, 1962.
"Molder of Civil Defense: Steuart Lansing Pittman." *New York Times*, October 30, 1961, 17.
Moskalev, M. D. *Rassredotochnenie i evakuatsiia naseleniia*. Moscow: Izdatel'stvo DOSAAF, 1960.
Moskalev, V. D., V. P. Sinitsyn, and A. S. Tertychnyi. *Uchebnoe posobie po MPVO*. Moscow: Izdatel'stvo DOSAAF, 1955.
Mozzhorin, Iu. A. *Tak eto bylo: Memuary Iu. A. Mozzhorina*. Moscow: ZAO "Mezhdunarodnaia Programma Obrazovaniia," 2000.
My Cave Life in Vicksburg with Letters of Trial and Travel. New York: D. Appleton, 1864.
Narodnyi Komissariat po stroitel'stvu SSSR Tekhnicheskoe upravlenie. *Ukazaniia po prisposobleniiu podvalov sushchestvuiushchikh zdanii pod podval'nye ubezhishcha i ukrytiia PVO*. Moscow: Gosudarstvennoe Izdatel'stvo stroitel'noi literatury, 1941.
National Academy of Sciences. *Civil Defense: Project Harbor Summary Report*. Washington, DC: National Academy of Sciences, 1964.
National Academy of Sciences National Research Council Advisory Committee on Civil Defense. *The Adequacy of Government Research Programs in Non-Military Defense*. Washington, DC: National Academy of Sciences—National Research Council, 1958.
National Security Archive. "Permanent Operational Assignment to Uncover NATO Preparations for a Nuclear Missile Attack on the USSR—February 2, 1983." Accessed May 19, 2014, http://www2.gwu.edu/~nsarchiv/NSAEBB/NSAEBB426/docs/9.Permanent%20Operational%20assignment%20to%20uncover%20NATO%20preparations%20for%20a%20nuclear%20missile%20attack%20on%20the%20USSR-February%202,%201983.pdf.
National Security Resources Board. *Damage from Atomic Explosions and the Design of Protective Structures*. Washington, DC: GPO, 1950.
———. *United States Civil Defense*. Washington, DC: GPO, 1950.
Naumenko, I. *Atomnaia energiia i ee ispolzovanie*. Moscow: Izdatel'stvo DOSAAF, 1955.
———. "Pronikaiushchaia radiatsiia i radioaktivnoe zarazhenie pri atomnom vzryve." *Voennye znaniia* 7, no. 11 (1954): 20.

———. "Pronikaiushchaia radiatsiia i radioaktivnoe zarazhenie pri atomnom vzryve." *Voennye znaniia* 7, no. 12 (1954): 22.
———. "Udarnaia volna i svetovoe izluchenie pri atomnom vzryve." *Voennye znaniia* 7, no. 10 (1954): 18–19.
Nikonova, O. Iu. "OSOAVIAKhIM kak instrument stalinskoi sotsial'noi mobilizatsii." *Rossiiskaia istoriia* 55, no. 1 (2012): 90–104.
Nitze, Paul. "Ensuring Security in the Era of Detenté." *Foreign Affairs* 54, no. 2 (1976): 207–32.
Norris, John G. "Phone Head Is Chosen to Plan Civil Defense for Atomic War." *Washington Post*, March 6, 1949, 9.
Oak Ridge National Laboratory. *Civil Defense Research Project: Annual Progress Report, March 1970–March 1971*, ORNL-4679. Oak Ridge, TN: ORNL, 1971.
———. *Civil Defense Research Project: Annual Progress Report, March 1971–March 1972*, ORNL-4784. Oak Ridge, TN: ORNL, 1972.
Oakes, Guy. *The Imaginary War: Civil Defense and American Cold War Culture*. New York: Oxford University Press, 1994.
Office of Civil Defense. *In Time of Emergency: A Citizen's Handbook on Nuclear Attack, Natural Disasters*. Washington, DC: GPO, 1968.
———. *Personal and Family Survival*. Washington, DC: GPO, 1966.
Office of Civil and Defense Mobilization. *The Family Fallout Shelter*. Washington, DC: GPO, 1958.
———. *FCDA Annual Report for 1958*. Washington, DC: GPO, 1959.
Olsen, Sidney. "The Movie Hearings." *Life* 23, no. 21 (1947): 141.
"Optimism Increases on Surviving Atom War." *New York Times*, June 4, 1987, A23.
"Organizatsiia i sostoianie grazhdanskoi oborony v stranakh NATO." *Grazhdanskaia oborona—informatsionnyi sbornik po materialam zarubezhnoi pechati* 2, no. 1 (1962): 10–18.
Organizatsionno-metodicheskie ukazaniia po podgotovke Grazhdanskoi oborony na 1989 god. Moscow: Tipografiia VtsK GO SSSR, 1988.
Osipov, Sergei. "Apokalips vchera. Kak SShA i SSSR stroili bomboubezhishche 'drug ot druga.'" *Argumenty i fakty*, August 12, 2017. Accessed January 6, 2018, http://www.aif.ru/society/safety/apokalipsis_vchera_kak_ssha_i_sssr_stroili _bomboubezhishcha_drug_ot_druga.
"Over There and Everywhere." *U.S. Air Service* 3, no. 4 (1920): 38.
"Pat Frank, Author and Newsman, Dies," *Washington Post, Times-Herald*, October 13, 1964, B5.
Payton, Matt. "Russia Launches Massive Nuclear War Training Exercise with '40 Million People.'" *Independent*, October 5, 2016. Accessed April 21, 2017, http://www.independent.co.uk/news/world/europe/russia-nuclear-weapon -training-attack-radiation-moscow-vladimir-putin-a7345461.html.
Peacock, Margaret. "Contested Innocence: Images of the Child during the Cold War." PhD diss., University of Texas at Austin, 2008.
Perelygin, N. S. *Gruppa samozashchity*. Moscow: Voennoe Izdatel'stvo, 1950.
Perminov, S., and P. Gorbunov. "Kompleksnye pokaznye." *Voennye znaniia* 27, no. 1 (1975): 22–23.

Pipes, Richard. "Why the Soviet Union Thinks It Could Fight and Win a Nuclear War." *Commentary* 64, no. 1 (1977): 1–34.

Pleasants, Julian M. "Claude Pepper, Strom Thurmond, and the 1948 Presidential Election in Florida." *Florida Historical Quarterly* 76, no. 4 (1998): 439–73.

Podtelezhnikov, A., V. Shchekunov, and A. Iukhtin. "Povyshat' uroven inzhenernoi zashchity naseleniia." *Grazhdanskaia zashchita* 42, no. 10 (2008): 24–25.

Podvig, Pavel. "Did Star Wars Help End the Cold War? Soviet Response to the SDI Program." *Science and Global Security* 25, no. 1 (Spring 2017): 3–27.

———. *Russian Strategic Nuclear Forces*. Cambridge, MA: MIT University Press, 2001.

Potter, William, and Lucy Kerner. "The Soviet Military's Performance at Chernobyl." *Soviet Studies* 43, no. 6 (1991): 1027–47.

President's Foreign Intelligence Advisory Board. "The Soviet 'War Scare.'" February 15, 1990. Accessed January 7, 2018, https://nsarchive2.gwu.edu/nukevault/ebb533-The-Able-Archer-War-Scare-Declassified-PFIAB-Report-Released/2012-0238-MR.pdf.

Prezidium Tsentral'nogo Komiteta DOSAAF. *Postanovlenie o sostoianii raboty po obucheniiu naseleniia PVO v organizatsiiakh DOSAAF*. Moscow: Izdatel'stvo DOSAAF, 1957.

Programma podgotovki lichnogo sostava grazhdanskoi oborony nevoenizirovannykh formirovanii sluzhby transporta i dorog, Utv. 17 ianv. 1963 g. Minsk: Voennoe izdatel'stvo, 1963.

Programma podgotovki lichnogo sostava grazhdanskoi oborony ob"ektov narodnogo khoziaistva. Utv. 23 iiulia 1962 g. Moscow: Voenizdat, 1962.

Programma podgotovki serzhantov (komandirov otdelenii) inzhenernykh chastei i uzlov sviazi shtabov grazhdanskoi oborony Utv. 13 dek. 1962 g. Moscow: Voennoe izdatel'stvo, 1962.

"Programma stroitel'stva ubezhishch v SShA." *Grazhdanskaia oborona—informatsionnyi sbornik po materialam zarubezhnoi pechati* 2, no. 9 (1962): 9.

Project East River. *General Report: Part 1 Report of Project East River*. New York: Associated Universities, 1952.

———. *Information and Training for Civil Defense: Part 9 of the Report of Project East River*. New York: Associated Universities, 1952.

Pry, Peter Vincent. *The Strategic Nuclear Balance*. 2 vols. New York: Crane Russak, 1990.

"Putin: 'briatsat' atomnym oruzhiem—poslednoe delo." *TASS*, October 27, 2016. Accessed June 28, 2017, http://tass.ru/politika/3740162.

Rabinowitch, Eugene. "Civil Defense: The Long-Range View." *Bulletin of the Atomic Scientists* 6, nos. 8–9 (1950): 226–30.

"Radiation Exposure in Recent Weapons Tests." *Bulletin of the Atomic Scientists* 10, no. 9 (1954): 352.

Ramm, Aleksei. "Gubernatorov, FSB i politsiiu v sluchae voiny·podchiniat voennym." *Izvestia*, October 11, 2016. Accessed April 21, 2017, http://izvestia.ru/news/637442.

Ramm, Aleksei, and Anna Kaledina. "Minoborony poluchila pravo zabirat' chastnye pekarnye i avtoservisy." *Izvestia*, October 18, 2016. Accessed April 21, 2017, http://izvestia.ru/news/638470.

Reed, Michael. "Coast-to-Coast Protests Greet Reagan's Civil Defense Buildup." *National Journal*, March 27, 1982, 554–56.

Rhodes, Richard. *Dark Sun: The Making of the Hydrogen Bomb*. New York: Touchstone, 1995.

Riabev, L. D., ed. *Atomnaia bomba 1945–54*. Book 6, Vol. 2 of *Atomnyi proekt SSSR: Dokumenty i materialy*. Moscow: Fizmatlit, 2006.

———, ed. *Atomnaia bomba 1945–54*. Book 7, Vol. 2 of *Atomnyi proekt SSSR: Dokumenty i materialy*. Moscow: Fizmatlit, 2007.

———, ed. *Vodorodnaia bomba 1945–56*. Book 2, Vol. 3 of *Atomnyi proekt SSSR: Dokumenty i materialy*. Moscow: Fizmatlit, 2009.

Ringstad, Arnold. "The Evolution of Civil Defense Film Rhetoric." *Journal of Cold War Studies* 14, no. 4 (Fall 2012): 93–121.

Ritchie, Donald A. *Reporting from Washington: The History of the Washington Press Corps*. Oxford: Oxford University Press, 2005.

Robin, Ron. *The Making of the Cold War Enemy: Culture and Politics in the Military-Industrial Complex*. Princeton, NJ: Princeton University Press, 2001.

Rockefeller Brothers Fund. *International Security: The Military Aspect*. Panel II of the Special Studies Project. New York: Rockefeller Brothers Fund, 1958.

"Rogozin: Do kontsa Noiabria kabmin primet programmu obespecheniia radiatsionnoi bezopasnosti." *TASS*, October 30, 2015. Accessed April 21, 2017, http://tass.ru/politika/2393170.

Rose, Kenneth D. *One Nation Underground: The Fallout Shelter in American Culture*. New York: New York University Press, 2004.

Rosenberg, Howard. ". . . And Turner Launches a Counterattack on WTBS." *Los Angeles Times*, February 13, 1987. Accessed January 7, 2018, http://articles.latimes.com/1987-02-13/entertainment/ca-2080_1_ted-turner.

Rowen, Henry S. Introduction to *Getting Mad: Nuclear Mutual Assured Destruction, Its Origins and Practice*. Edited by Henry D. Sokolski, 1–12. Carlisle, PA: Strategic Studies Institute, 2004.

Rowen, Henry, and Charles Wolf, eds. *The Impoverished Superpower: Perestroika and the Burden of Soviet Military Spending*. San Francisco: Institute for Contemporary Studies, 1990.

Sagan, Scott. *The Limits of Safety: Organizations, Accidents, and Nuclear Weapons*. Princeton, NJ: Princeton University Press, 1993.

Scheer, Robert. "Civil Defense Program to Be Revived: Reagan Seeks to Counter Possible Attack by Soviets." *Los Angeles Times*, January 15, 1982, 22.

———. *With Enough Shovels: Reagan, Bush, and Nuclear War*. New York: Random House, 1982.

Schell, Jonathan. *The Abolition*. New York: Knopf, 1984.

———. *The Fate of the Earth*. New York: Knopf, 1982.

Security Resources Panel of the Science Advisory Committee. *Deterrence and Survival in the Nuclear Age*. Washington, DC: Office of Defense Mobilization, 1957.

Sharp, Patrick B. *Savage Perils: Racial Frontiers and Nuclear Apocalypse in American Culture*. Norman: University of Oklahoma Press, 2007.
Sheidina, I. L. *SShA: "Fabriki mysli" na sluzhbe strategii*. Moscow: Nauka, 1973.
"Shelter Program Is Launched at Meeting of State Technicians." *Civil Defense Alert* 1, no. 4 (1951): 6.
Shperk, V. F. *Pravila proektirovaniia ubezhishch v grazhdanskikh zdaniiakh*. Moscow: Tipografiia VIA RKKA, 1931.
Shperk, V. F., N. I. Shmakov, A. I. Pangsen, and M. P. Vorob'ev. *Inzhnerno-tekhnicheskie sredstva PVO*. Leningrad: Tsentral'naia Tipografiia Narkomvoentorga, 1929.
Shtab Grazhdanskoi oborony SSSR. *Pravila soderzhaniia i ispol'zovaniia ubezhishch v mirnoe vremia*. Moscow: Grazhdanskaia oborona SSSR, 1962.
Shtab Grazhdanskoi oborony SSSR Nauchno-Metodicheskii Tsentr. *Lektsii po grazhdanskoi oborone*. Moscow: Izdatel'stvo DOSAAF, 1969.
Shubin, E. P., ed. *Grazhdanskaia oborona*. Moscow: Prosveshchenie, 1991.
Shul'gin, V. "Obosnovanie trebovanii k zashchitnym svoistvam sooruzhenii GO." *Grazhdanskaia zashchita* 41, no. 8 (2007): 36–38.
Shute, Nevil. *On the Beach*. New York: Ballantine Books, 1974.
Simonov, N. S. *Voenno-promyshlennyi kompleks SSSR v 1920-50 e gody: Tempy ekonomicheskogo rosta, struktura, organizatsiia proizvodstva i upravlenie*. Moscow: ROSSPEN, 1996.
Singer, J. David. "Deterrence and Shelters." *Bulletin of the Atomic Scientists* 17, no. 8 (1961): 310–14.
Sinitsyn, V. P., N. F. Malov, M. N. Mandrazhitskii, and V. D. Borkhunova. *Mestnaia protivovozdushnaia oborona*. Moscow: Gosudarstvennoe Uchebno-Pedagogicheskoe Izdatel'stvo, 1955.
Slepyan, Kenneth D. "The Limits of Mobilisation: Party, State and the 1927 Civil Defence Campaign." *Europe-Asia Studies* 45, no. 5 (1993): 851–68.
Snead, David. *The Gaither Committee, Eisenhower, and the Cold War*. Columbus: Ohio State University Press, 1999.
Sokolevskii, V. D., ed. *Voennaia strategiia*. Moscow: Voenizdat, 1962.
———. *Voennaia strategiia*. 2nd ed. Moscow: Voenizdat, 1963.
———. *Voennaia strategiia*. 3rd ed. Moscow: Voenizdat, 1968.
Solomon, Frederick, and Marston, Robert Q., eds. *The Medical Implications of Nuclear War*. Washington, DC: National Academies Press, 1986.
Sontag, John P. "The Soviet War Scare of 1926–27." *Russian Review* 34, no. 1 (January 1975): 66–77.
"Soviet Physicians Comment on the Threat of Nuclear War." *Congressional Record*, August 3, 1982, E3631–E3632.
Sovremennye Soedinennye Shtaty Ameriki: Entsiklopedicheskii spravochnik. Moscow: Izdatel'stvo politicheskoi literatury, 1988.
Stalin, J. V. "The Tasks of Business Executives." *Pravda*, February 5, 1931.
Stone, Jeremy. *"Every Man Should Try": Adventures of a Public Interest Activist*. New York: Public Affairs, 1999.

Strugatskii, Boris, and Arkadii Strugatskii. *Obytaemyi ostrov*. Moscow: Detskaia literatura, 1971.
"Survive the H-Bomb!" *Newsweek*, August 31, 1953, 22.
Symington, W. Stuart. "The Importance of Civil Defense Planning." *Bulletin of the Atomic Scientists* 6, nos. 8–9 (1950): 231–32.
Teller, Edward. "Civil Defense Is Crucial." *New York Times*, January 3, 1984, A19.
Thompson, Marcia. "Debate Widens on Nuclear Blast Topic." *Louisville Times/ Lafeyette News*, July 7, 1982, 6–7.
Tolstikov, O. V. *Grazhdanskaia oborona v sovremennoi voine*. Moscow: Izdatel'stvo DOSAAF, 1962.
Tooze, Adam. *The Wages of Destruction:The Making and Breaking of the Nazi Economy*. New York: Viking, 2007.
Tsatsulin, Ivan. *Atomnaia krepost'*. Moscow: Voennoe ivdatel'stvo, 1958.
Tsentral'noe statisticheskoe upravlenie. *Narodnoe khoziaistvo SSSR: Statisticheskii sbornik*. Moscow: Gosstatizdat, 1956.
Turner, Wallace. "2 States Defy U.S. over Nuclear Attack Planning." *New York Times*, March 31, 1987.
"Two Governors on Race Relations." *Collier's*, February 23, 1946, 94.
Tyler, Leon Gardiner. "Civil Defense: The Impact of the Planning Years, 1945–1950." PhD diss., Duke University, 1967.
"Ubezhishche grazhdanskoi oborony v gorode Moskva." *Wikimapia*. Accessed April 21, 2017, http://moscow.wikimapia.org/tag/44690/.
United States Army Medical Department. "What Every Medical Officer Should Know about the Atomic Bomb." *Bulletin of the United States Army Medical Department* 8, no. 6 (1948): 504–17.
United States House of Representatives. *84 H.R. 10660 Reported in Senate*. Washington, DC: GPO, 1956.
———. *Conference Report to Accompany H.R. 10660*. Washington, DC: GPO, 1956.
———. *Hearings before Subcommittee No. 1 of the Committee on Military Affairs, March 25, 1920–April 2, 1920*. Washington, DC: Government Printing Office, 1920.
United States House of Representatives Subcommittee of the Committee on Government Operations. *Civil Defense for National Survival*. Parts 3–4. Washington, DC: Government Printing Office, 1956.
United States Senate Armed Services Committee Subcommittee on Civil Defense. *Civil Defense Program. Part 1 and Appendix*. Washington, DC: GPO, 1955.
United States Strategic Bombing Survey. *United States Strategic Bombing Surveys*. Maxwell Air Force Base, AL: Air University Press, 1987.
U.S. General Accounting Office. *Activities and Status of Civil Defense in the United States*. Washington, DC: Government Printing Office, 1971.
U.S. Senate Committee on Banking, Housing, and Urban Development. *Second Session on Oversight of the Role of Civil Defense in the U.S.-Soviet Strategic Balance, the Effectiveness of Existing Soviet and United States Programs, the Feasibility of Passive Defenses for the Survival of the Population and Economy, January 8, 1979*. Washington, DC: GPO, 1979.

U.S. Senate Committee on Governmental Affairs. *First Session on Nomination of Louis O. Giuffrida to Be Director of the Federal Emergency Management Agency, May 6, 1981*. Washington, DC: GPO, 1981.

———. *Hearings on the Nominations of Julius W. Becton, Jr., James P. McNeil, and William R. Barton, October 23, 1985*. Washington, DC: GPO, 1985.

U.S. Senate Subcommittee on Arms Control, Oceans, International Operations, and the Environment. *United States and Soviet Civil Defense Programs*. Washington, DC: GPO, 1982.

"V Moskve polnost'iu podgotovili podzemnye ukrytie dlia evakuatsiia naseleniia." *RIA Novosti*, September 29, 2016. Accessed April 21, 2017, https://ria.ru/moscow/20160929/1478130933.html.

Velikanova, Olga. *Popular Perceptions of Soviet Politics in the 1920s: Disenchantment of the Dreamers*. Basingstoke: Palgrave Macmillan, 2013.

A Visit to Sebastopol a Week After Its Fall, by an Officer of the Anglo-Turkish Contingent. London: Smith, Elder, 1856.

Vladimirov, V. A., N. N. Dolgin, and F. G. Melanichev. *Ot MPVO k grazhdanskoi zashchite. Stranitsy iz istorii MPVO-GO- PSChS sub"ektov Rossiiskoi Federatsii*. Moscow: In-oktavo, 2004.

"Voenno-politicheskie i voenno-strategicheskie kontseptsii SshA." *Sovremennye Soedinennye Shtaty Ameriki: Entsiklopedicheskii spravochnik*, 345–46. Moscow: Izdatel'stvo politicheskoi literatury, 1988.

Wadsworth, James J. *The Silver Spoon: An Autobiography of James J. Wadsworth*. Geneva, NY: W. F. Humphrey, 1980.

"Wadsworth Praises Cooperation of Film Industry." *Civil Defense Alert* 1, no. 2 (1951): 5.

Weart, Spencer R. *Nuclear Fear: A History of Images*. Cambridge, MA: Harvard University Press, 1988.

Weinberg, Alvin. "Speculations on a Defense-Dominated World." In *Strategic Defenses and Arms Control*, edited by Jack N. Barkenbus and Alvin M. Weinberg, 89–110. New York: Paragon House, 1988.

Weiss, Kenneth. "Evacuation Plan Described as Disastrous Itself." *Montgomery County Journal*, July 8, 1982, A1.

Wellerstein, Alex, and Edward Geist. "The Secret of the Soviet Hydrogen Bomb." *Physics Today* 70 no. 4 (2017): 40–47.

Wells, H. G. *The World Set Free: A Story of Mankind*. New York: E. P. Dutton, 1914.

Wiesner, Jerome B. "Comprehensive Arms-Limitation Systems." In *Arms Control, Disarmament, and National Security*, edited by Donald G. Brennan, 198–233. New York: George Braziller, 1961.

Wiesner, Jerome B., and Herbert F. York. "National Security and the Nuclear Test Ban." *Scientific American* 211, no. 4 (October, 1964): 27–35.

Wigner, Eugene, and Joanne Gailar. "Civil Defense in the Soviet Union." *Foresight* 1, no. 3 (1974): 9–11.

———. "Will Soviet Civil Defense Undermine SALT?" *Human Events*, July 8, 1972, 9.

Wilson, George C. "FEMA Asks $20 Million for Fallout Shelters." *Washington Post*, March 21, 1987, A6.

Wylie, Phillip. *Tomorrow!* New York: Rinehart, 1954.
———. *Triumph.* Garden City, NY: Doubleday, 1963.
Yoshpe, Harry B. *Our Missing Shield: The U.S. Civil Defense Program in Historical Perspective.* Washington, DC: GPO, 1981.
Zimmerman, Malia. "North Korea Tensions Have Hawaii Pols Revisiting Emergency Attack Plans." *Fox News*, April 17, 2017. Accessed June 28, 2017, http://www.foxnews.com/politics/2017/04/17/north-korea-tensions-have-hawaii-pols-revisiting-emergency-attack-plans.html.

Index

Page numbers in italics signify graphics.

1927 war scare, 22, 25, 241, 257n28
1983 war scare, 189–90, 226–27, 241.
 See also Operation "RYAN"
2016 war scare, 240–42

Able Archer, 189
ABM Treaty, 6, 179, 207
agitation, 12, 14, 19, 242, 243, 249–50
Air War and Emotional Stress (1951 book), 65
Aksiutin, Iurii, 174
Alas, Babylon (1959 novel), 129–31, 274n117
Alert America campaign, 75
Altunin, Boris, 196, 198, 210, 211, 235
American Imperialism: The Bitterest Enemy of the Peoples (1952 book), 122
Amerika (1987 miniseries), 230
Andromeda Nebula (1957 novel), 134
Andropov, Yuri, 189, 226, 241
antiballistic missile (ABM), 5, 6, 146, 148–50, 171, 178–79, 192, 207, 280n108
antinuclear movements, 69, 163, 211, 214–15, 217–18, 224, 226–27, 233. *See also* civil defense protest movement
Archer Productions, 69–73, 75, 108, 265n69
ARCOS affair, 22, 24
Armenian earthquake, 235–36, 248
arms control, 7, 141, 145–47, 187, 192–93, 201–3, 206, 211; and civil defense, 166–70, 232–33
Arms Control and Disarmament Agency (ACDA), 166–69, 192, 204–9

assured destruction, 15, 149–50, 192–93, 202, 277n33
assured retaliation, 193
atomic bomb. *See* nuclear weapons
Atomic Cafe (1982 film), 69
Atomic Energy Commission (AEC), 57, 62, 96, 117, 118
Atomnaia krepost' (1958 novel), 132
Atómstöðin (1948 novel), 86, 132
AVIAKhIM, 24, 256–57n20

Becton, Francis, 224, 225
Beers, Barnet, 33–34, 39, 43, 48, 50, 52
behavioralism, 67–68; *The American Soldier* (1949 book), 67; influence on U.S. civil defense, 74
Beria, Lavrenti, 35–37, 44–45, 52, 82–83, 97, 194
Berlin Crisis (1948), 43
Berlin Crisis (1961), 153, 162–64, 189
Bikini Atoll, 34–36, 117–18
biological weapons and warfare, 24, 27, 30, 53, 69, 90–91
blackout procedures, 31, 45, 84, 260n114
blast shelters, 29, 33, 186–88, 196–99, 213, 223, 227–28, 237, 244–45, 282n146; DCPA proposal, 204; different from fallout shelters, 119, 184; effectiveness in Hiroshima and Nagasaki, 17–19; effectiveness in WWII, 18–19, 29; Eisenhower-era proposal, 100, 102–7, 245; FCDA proposals, 55–62, 105–6; Russian, 241; Soviet, 79–82, 90–94, 176–80,

blast shelters (cont.)
  208; Soviet, cost of, 269n155,
  269n157, 293n16; Truman-era
  proposal, 55–61, 245
blat, 93
Block, Herbert, *50, 61, 109*
Boston, 63
Braun, Marilyn J., 214–15, 221, 288n90
Brennan, Donald, 150, 166
Brezhnev, Leonid, 15, 174, 191, 195–96, 226–28, 234, 247
Brodie, Bernard, 195
Brown, Harold K., 204, 206, 208–9, 219
Bukharin, Nikolai, 22, 24, 27
Bulganin, Nikolai, 52, 83
Bulletin of the Atomic Scientists, 18, 51, 65, 118, 151, 209, 210
Bush, George H. W., 224, 309

Caldwell, Millard P., 112, 245; governor of Florida, 49; head of FCDA, 49–51, 57–61, 266n97; racial controversy, 49, 51, 78, 261n126, 261n128, 266n93; resignation, 79; role in 1948 presidential election, 49, 261n127
California, 1, 100, 102, 112, 125, 141, 143, 163, 212, 216
Calonius, Lars, 72–73
Cambridge, Massachusetts, 215–16, 221
Cannon, Clarence, 62, 164
A Canticle for Leibowitz (1959 novel), 129–30
Carter, Jimmy, 173, 203–4, 207–10
Castle Bravo, 102
Caucasus, 115–16
Central Intelligence Agency (CIA), 121–25, 128, 167, 203, 206–7, 218, 235, 269n157, 279n97
Chazov, Evgenii, 228–29
chemical weapons, 23–24, 26–28, 53, 90–91
Chernobyl, 191, 234–36, 244, 248
Chester, Conrad, 232, 292n157
children, 68–75, 110, 114, 116, 122, 180, 272n63, 291n147

Chuikov, Vasilii, 175–78, 197, 281n130
civil defense, definition, 2; economic arguments against, 5–6, 100, 127–28, 245; nineteenth-century antecedents, 20–21; origin of name, 34; strategic arguments against, 146, 151–52, 206–8; in Switzerland, 120, 225, 239; technical controversy about, 7, 202, 208, 219–20, 228–29, 245; in United Kingdom, 27–28, 30, 34, 257n39. *See also* civil defense, Soviet Union; civil defense, United States
civil defense, Russia. *See* Ministry of Extreme Situations
civil defense, Soviet Union: budgets, 15, 18, 82, 93–94, 128–29, 178–80, 269n154, 281n141, 293n16; at Chernobyl, 234–35; relationship to Soviet nuclear strategy, 153–57, 210–11; and surprise attack, 196–97; temporary dissolution, 127–29; U.S. interpretations of, 121–22, 125–27, 181–84, 199–200, 202–3, 235–36. *See also* Grazhdanskaia Oborona; Mestnaia Protivovozdushnaia Oborona
civil defense, United States: budgets, 57, 59–60, 102–4, 159–61, 164, 172–73, 201, 210, 214, 216, 218, 220–21, 224, 245; post-Cold War, 242–43, 248; relationship to U.S. nuclear strategy, 203–8, 213–14; Soviet interpretations of, 122–24, 183–86, 211, 226–27; in World War II, 30–32. *See also* Defense Civil Preparedness Agency; Federal Civil Defense Administration; Federal Emergency Management Agency; Office of Civil and Defense Mobilization; Office of Civil Defense; Office of Civilian Defense
Civil Defense: A Choice of Disasters (1987 book), 219
Civil Defense Act of 1950, 51, 56–57, 60, 261n132

Civil Defense Alert (magazine), 62, 69, 73
Civil Defense and Arms Control, 166–67, 169
Civil Defense in the Soviet Union (1962 book), 126–27
Civil Defense of the USA (1960 book), 124, 127
civil defense protest movement, 123, 218
Civil Defense Research Group (ORNL), 202, 232
Clarkson, Helen, 130
cobalt bomb, 129, 216
Communist Party of the Soviet Union (CPSU), 11, 82, 122, 136, 153, 174, 228, 233, 250, 293n17
community shelter program, 139, 157–64; assumptions about Soviet attack, 161–62; design assumptions, 159–60, 280n112; estimated effectiveness, 159–61; shelter marking, 139, 159, 172, 214, 287n84; shelter stocking, 139, 159, 287n84; shelter survey, 139, 159, 172, 222, 287n84
computers, 159–60, 181, 204
continuity of government, 2, 4, 212, 222, 225
The Counterfeit Ark: Crisis Relocation for Nuclear War (1984 book), 218
counterforce, 147–51, 162, 169, 200, 205, 231, 235, 237; de facto U.S. policy, 193; defined, 143–44; relationship to civil defense, 150–51, 169; in Soviet strategy, 195–96. *See also* NUTS
countervalue, 143–46, 148–50, 196, 205, 231, 237. *See also* MAD
Crimean War, 20
Crisis Relocation Program (CRP), 190, 192, 200–204, 211–26, 231, 238, 288n90, 289n103; local opposition, 215–16, 221, 225. *See also* Evacuation: strategic
Cuban Missile Crisis, 6, 138, 139, 174–75, 189, 241, 247, 275n3, 276n6, 283n4

The Day After (1983 film), 216–17, 230
Dead Man's Letters (1986 film), 230
Defense Civil Preparedness Agency (DCPA), 173, 182, 200–201, 204, 206, 209
détente, 169, 190, 201–4, 248
deterrence, 142–48, 150, 193–94, 239; civil defense as contributor to deterrence, 77, 158, 213, 231–33; civil defense as impediment to deterrence, 151–52, 167
DOBROKhIM, 23–24
Doctor Strangelove (1964 film), 131, 144
Doomsday Machine, 121, 144
DOSAAF, 46–47, 85–91, 129, 176–77, 198, 260n113, 267n125, 268n135, 281n137
DOSARM, 45–46
Drell, Sidney, 202, 285n45
drills, 24, 27, 45, 70, 241; duck and cover, 71; evacuation, 110, 122
Duck and Cover (1951 film), 68–76, 78, 117, 122, 265n57
Dulles, John Foster, 79, 105, 136, 142
Dyke, Peter, 218, 288n100
Dyson, Freeman, 151–52, 233
Dzerzhinskii, Felix, 23

Efremov, Ivan, 133–35
Eisenhower, Dwight, 53, 79, 153; Federal Highways Act of 1956, 112–13; opposition to civil defense, 13, 100–101, 104–5, 136
emergency management, 2, 201, 208–9, 212, 214, 218, 221–22, 240
Energiia podvlastna nam! (1951 novel), 132
Estonia, 88
evacuation: drills, 110, 114; post-attack, 106; strategic, 107, 110, 123, 182, 187, 190, 199–200, 206, 213–14, 217–18, 220–22, 224, 238, 244, 284n31; tactical, 13, 100, 106–7, 109–11, 124, 127, 137, 272n43; types, 106

Index   317

fallout, 95–99, 102, 116–18, 130; poor understanding of in early 1950s, 117–18. *See also* fallout shelters
Fallout Protection (1961 booklet), 163
fallout shelters, 13, 16, 273n81, 282–83n166; community, 137–41, 146, 151, 157–65, 169, 172, 175, 177, 180, 182, 184–85, 187; differences from blast shelters, 55–56, 119; first proposed, 119; home, 99, 102, 105–6, 119–21, 127, 137; neglected in CRP, 222, 278n66; Soviet, 140, 176, 196–98. *See also* community shelter program; Shelter Incentive Program
Fate of the Earth (1982 book), 217, 233, 288n97
Federal Civil Defense Administration (FCDA), 13, 20, 79, 94–95, 135–37, 187, 244–46, 271n2; established, 50; hopes for how civil defense would work, 53–55, 98–99; merged with Office of Defense Mobilization, 104; moved to Battle Creek, 269n3, 273n73; origins in NSRB, 47–49; public communications strategy, 61–78, 135; shelter development plans, 54–60, 100–106; Soviet perceptions of, 123–27; tactical evacuation, 106–13
Federal Emergency Management Agency (FEMA), 190, 203, 237, 248, 287n78, 288n95, 289n113, 290n122; and CRP, 212–25; established, 209; and peacetime emergency management, 190, 212, 217–18
Federal Highway Act of 1956, 113
Finland, 28, 258n54
fire, 119, 180, 273n76, 291n142
First Main Directorate, 35, 41
First World War, 21
Ford, Gerald, 173–74
Forrestal, James, 39–40
Frank, Pat, 129–31, 275n123
Friedberg, Aaron, 10, 193
Frunze district, Moscow, 80–81, 91–93, 269n154

Gailar, Joanne, 181–83, 208
Gaither Report, 104–5, 159
Garrison, Dee, 140, 223
Garrison state, 8–10, 14, 20, 40, 42–43, 52, 55, 89, 93, 141, 146; defined, 9. *See also* party-garrison state
Germany, 9, 21–22, 27, 32, 40, 65, 147, 154, 184–85, 257n43
Giuffrida, Louis O., 212–13, 217, 222, 224, 287n77; racial controversy, 212
Gorbachev, Mikhail, 131, 191, 229, 233–35
Gordievskii, Oleg, 227
Gosplan, 36, 37
Gouré, Leon, 125–27; early life, 125–26; role in Vietnam War, 183; studies of Soviet civil defense, 126–27, 182–83, 199–200, 230, 235–36, 244, 248
Grazhdanskaia Oborona (Soviet civil defense organization), 89, 174–80, 196–99, 210–11, 234–36, 281n137. *See also* civil defense, Soviet Union
Grechko, Andrei, 195
Gromyko, Anatolii, 229–30, 233
Ground Observers Corps (GOC), 108
The Guardians (1985 novel), 231

Hampe, Erich, 153–55
Hebert, F. Edward, 164–65, 168, 170
Hiroshima, 4, 71, 85, 119, 129; shelters, 17–18; Soviet observers, 32–33
Hitler, Adolf, 9, 28, 30, 39–40, 125, 132, 185
Hoegh, Leo, 104–5
Hopley, Russell J., 39–41, 43
Hudson Institute, 144, 150, 166, 232

Integrated Emergency Management Systems (IEMS), 221
Intermediate Nuclear Forces (INF) Treaty, 233
International Physicians for the Prevention of Nuclear War (IPPNW), 227–28, 291n147
Ivanov, Boris, 234
Ivy Mike, 101, 117

Jackson, Henry "Scoop", 5, 170–72, 252, 280n108
Janis, Irving L., 65–67, 71
Johnson, Lyndon, B., 149, 160, 170–72, 183
Jones, T. K., 214, 287n85

Kahn, Herman: adequate civil defense program, 121; argument against countervalue targeting, 143–45, 147–50; early life, 143; Soviet views of, 185–86, 195; views on strategic implications of civil defense, 121, 126, 152, 158, 199–200
Kazakhstan, 41, 95, 117
Kearny, Cresson, 182, 291n151
Kennedy, John F.: early advocate of civil defense, 42, 64; impact of death on civil defense program, 171–72; support of fallout shelters, 6, 16, 64, 121, 130, 139, 148, 157–58, 161–62, 164, 170, 184, 187
KGB, 226–27, 235
Khrushchev, Nikita, 9, 99, 136, 138, 153–54, 191, 229, 247, 251; cancels Soviet civil defense program, 127–29
Kiev, 88, 125, 177, 198, 235
Kiselev, Dmitrii, 240–42
Kissinger, Henry, 6, 195, 203
Knowledge Society, 87, 228–29
Korean War, 43–44, 64
Korzun, Lev, 185–86
Kramer, Stanley, 131

La Guardia, Fiarello, 30–32
Laird, Melvyn, 173, 200
Landis, James M., 31–32
Lapp, Ralph, 64, 104, 118, 281n131
Larsen, Paul J., 42, 47–48
Lasswell, Harold, 9–10
The Last Day: A Novel of the Day After Tomorrow (1959 novel), 130
Laxness, Halldor, 86–87, 132
Leaning, Jennifer, 218, 221, 231, 237
Leningrad, 30, 46, 88

Life (magazine), 162
Lown, Bernard, 228
Lucky Dragon, 117–18

MAD (Mutual Assured Destruction), 15, 150, 192–94, 202, 231–33. *See also* countervalue; nuclear strategy
Malenkov, Georgii, 36, 52, 83, 86, 97, 127, 129, 131
Malyshev, Viacheslav, 52, 83, 97
massive retaliation, 136, 141–42, 144, 148
McNamara, Robert S.: and cancellation of SIP, 164, 170–72; favorable views of civil defense, 156–58, 160–61; strategic outlook, 15, 148–50, 193, 277n33
The Medical Implications of Nuclear War (1986 book), 219
Meese, Edwin, 212, 217
Merril, Judith, 274n115
Meshcheriakov, M. G., 34, 35, 52
Mestnaia Protivovozdushnaia Oborona (MPVO), 19, 26–30, 45, 47, 80–95, 97, 113–19, 123–25, 135–37, 153–54, 184; abolition, 129; assumptions about nuclear attack, 267–68n134; foundation, 26; transfer to MVD, 28; in WWII, 28–30. *See also* civil defense, Soviet Union
Michigan Survey Research Center, 64–65
Mikoian, Anastas, 14–15, 127–28, 131, 136, 175, 194, 251–52
military-industrial complex, 25, 257n28
Miller, Walter, 129–30
Ministry of Extreme Situations (MChS), 236, 240–41, 248, 292nn170–71
Ministry of Medium Machine-Building, 52, 97
missiles, 161–62, 179, 242–43; advocated by Gaither Report, 105; anticipated by FCDA, 100, 110; impact on civil defense, 16, 55, 94; Soviet interpretations of strategic importance, 153, 155–57, 191, 193; as survivable retaliatory force, 142–43, 149

Molotov, Viacheslav, 28, 42
Morgenstern, Oskar, 167–68, 279n97
Moscow (city), 28–30, 80, 88, 91–92, 94, 115–16, 197, 241
Moscow (oblast), 115–16, 198, 269n155

Nagasaki, 17–18, 71, 85; Soviet observers, 32–33; tunnel shelters, 18
National Academy of Sciences, 105, 165
National Association for the Advancement of Colored People (NAACP), 49, 51, 78, 261n128
National Security Council (NSC), 101–5, 136, 173, 212–13, 287n78
National Security Resources Board (NSRB), 39–44, 47–48, 50–51, 57–58, 64–65, 124
New Orleans, 63, 110
"New Thinking", 233, 235
New York (state), 73, 120
New York City, 21, 28, 31, 58, 72, 110, 123, 162, 216, 288n90
Nitze, Paul, 201, 204, 212
Noel Gayler, 226
North, Oliver, 212
North Atlantic Treaty Organization (NATO), 105, 125, 141, 147–48, 184–85, 189
NSDD-26, 213–14, 226, 237
NSDD-259, 237
nuclear blackmail, 144–45, 151, 182, 186, 192, 199–200, 233, 291n137
nuclear proliferation, 147–48
nuclear strategy, 6–7, 187, 190–203, 231–34, 238, 244; relationship to civil defense, 140–57; Soviet, 153–57; U.S., 141–52. *See also* counterforce; countervalue
nuclear war: anticipated fatalities in, 138, 156, 160–61, 180, 182, 208, 237, 289n103, 290n122; civil defense officials' conception of, 53–56, 66, 84–86, 94, 97, 103, 137, 159, 197, 237; ecological effects of, 7, 97–98, 129, 228–29, 275n131, 288n97, 289n106;

likelihood of, 76–77, 148, 151, 253; portrayal in official propaganda, 68–78, 84–86, 91, 228–29; portrayal in popular culture, 4, 86, 129–36, 216–17, 231, 249; possibility of victory in, 55, 94–95, 131, 156, 180, 182, 189–90, 203, 214, 239, 248; relationship to civil defense, 2, 4–8, 154, 192–96, 199, 211, 244–49; Soviet attitudes toward, 4, 14–15, 86–87, 97, 180, 252–53; Stalin's attitudes toward, 19–20, 34–38, 41–45; survivability of, 55, 97, 127, 156, 214, 225, 278–79n88. *See also* nuclear strategy; nuclear weapons
nuclear weapons: availability of, 96; effects, 11, 35, 38, 43–45, 52, 55, 62, 77, 84, 91, 129, 180, 218–19; fission, 94–97; fusion, 96–99, 101–2, 107; tests, 36, 38, 41, 62, 94. *See also* nuclear war
nuclear winter, 219, 229, 246, 289n106
NUTS (Nuclear Utilization Target Selection), 150, 231. *See also* counterforce; nuclear strategy

Oak Ridge, Tennessee, 182–83
Oak Ridge National Laboratory, 181, 202
Obshchestvo druzei Vozdushnogo Flota (ODVF), 23–24
Obytaemyi ostrov (1971 novel), 135
Office of Civil and Defense Mobilization (OCDM), 99, 104, 112, 119, 127, 157, 244, 271n27
Office of Civil Defense (OCD), 139, 141, 144, 148, 150, 152, 157, 159–60, 162–65, 167–73, 182, 184, 212, 244, 276n6, 280n112
Office of Civilian Defense, 19, 31, 34, 39, 249
On Escalation (1965 book), 186, 195, 255
On the Beach (1957 novel), 129–31, 133, 135
On Thermonuclear War (1960 book), 121, 144–45

Operation Alert, 123
Operation Crossroads, 34–35
Operation "RYAN", 226–27
Oregon Institute of Science and Medicine (OISM), 230, 291n150
OSOAVIAKhIM, 24–29, 45–46, 249, 257n42
Our Cities Must Fight (1951 film), 70, 108, 271n37

Pamiatka naseleniiu po zashchite ot atomnogo oruzhiia, 84–87
party-garrison state: damaged by Khrushchev's reforms, 191–92; defined, 9; differences from garrison state, 9–11; ill-adapted to nuclear arms race, 38, 55, 93, 95, 99, 113, 154–56, 178, 246–47; possible post-Soviet revival, 242; relationship to CPSU, 52, 250–51; role of civil defense in, 19, 22–28, 136–38, 140, 178, 187, 194, 238; undermined by Gorbachev, 229
PD-41, 203, 207, 209, 213, 219
peaceful coexistence, 131, 135–36, 153, 176
peacetime draft, 44
Pearson, Drew, 48, 260n121
Peck, Gregory, 131
Peterson, Val: as federal civil defense administrator, 54, 100–104, 108–10, 112, 117–18, 136, 270n17; governor of Nebraska, 100; made ambassador to Denmark, 104; mocks *Duck and Cover*, 78, 117
Philadelphia, 63
Physicians for Social Responsibility (PSR), 211, 215, 217–18, 231, 289n101
Pipes, Richard, 203–4, 248
Pittman, Steuart L., 7, 139, 141, 150, 159, 164–72, 184, 209, 219, 222, 278n69
Podol'sk, 90–92, 94, 114–16
poison gas. *See* chemical weapons
Politburo, 4, 82, 179, 191. *See also* Presidium

Presidium, 82–83, 86–90, 93, 122, 127–29, 136–37, 174–75. *See also* Politburo
primary groups, 67, 68; in *Duck and Cover*, 74
Project East River. *See Report of Project East River*
Project Harbor Study, 165, 181
propaganda: civil-defense ill-adapted for, 243; distinct from agitation, 12–14; Soviet, 19, 22, 25–27, 45, 47, 87–89, 91, 115, 122–23, 126, 135, 176–77, 180, 183, 198–99, 229, 249, 291n147; U.S., 55–56, 60–61, 64, 66–70, 75–77, 80, 108, 110–12, 249–50
Proxmire, William, 225
Pry, Peter, 235–36
public education campaigns: 1956–58, 90–91, 268n135; Soviet, 1955–56, 87–88; U.S., 1951–53, 174, 236
public opinion surveys, 5; in Soviet Union, 136, 229, 291n147; in U.S., 64–66, 77, 220, 223
Puchkov, Vladimir, 240
Putin, Vladimir, 240–42

Rabinowitch, Eugene, 51
racism, 120, 212; and FCDA policy, 78, 266n93
radiation, 275n131; after atomic bombings of Japan, 33; from fallout, 98, 102, 117–19, 130, 159–60; fears of, 77, 219, 229–30; protection against, 35, 55, 111, 139, 159–60, 180, 198
radio, 39, 48, 54, 66, 68, 73, 75, 78, 86, 110, 117, 152, 180
radioactivity, 103, 133, 235, 275n131
radiological warfare, 124
RAND Corporation, 65, 67, 104–5, 125–26, 143–45, 183
rassredotochnenie (dispersal), 175, 281n131
Reagan, Ronald, 189, 212–13, 215, 218, 223–24, 231–32

Index   321

Report of Project East River, 76–78, 108
Rockefeller, Nelson P., 105, 120–21, 164, 173, 280n118
Rogozin, Dmitrii, 241
Rongelap, 117–18
Roosevelt, Eleanor, 31, 64, 264n40
Roosevelt, Franklin Delano, 30
Rose, Kenneth D., 120
Rukovodstvo po podgotovke krupnykh naselennykh punktov i ob"ektov narodnogo khoziaistva k zashchite ot vozdeistviiakh atomnogo oruzhiia, 83–87, 91, 113
Rumsfeld, Donald, 173, 201, 280n118
Rybakov, Viacheslav, 230
Rykov, Aleksei, 24, 26

Sagan, Carl, 219, 289n106
San Francisco, 110, 216, 221
Scheer, Robert, 214, 287n85
Schell, Jonathan, 217, 233
Schelling, Thomas, 8
Schlesinger, James R., 193, 201
schools, 35, 37, 63, 69–70, 72, 93, 176, 229
Second World War: British civil defense in, 27–28, 34; German civil defense in, 154; Japanese civil defense in, 17–18; as nuclear war, 7; Soviet civil defense in, 28–30, 114, 249; U.S. civil defense in, 30–32, 39, 52, 249
Shelter Incentive Program, 159, 165, 170–73, 287n84
shelters, 2, 5, 14–21, 27–28, 241; gas shelters, 29; improvised, 29, 182, 198; ventilation, 172, 180, 280n112, 285n45, 291n142. *See also* blast shelters; fallout shelters
Shoigu, Sergei, 236, 240, 292n171
Shute, Nevil, 129–35
Singer, J. David, 151
sirens, 12, 17, 56, 115; false alarms, 1, 2, 112
Special Committee under the Council of Ministers, 36–37, 82–83

Stalin, Joseph, 9, 12, 14, 19–29, 33–39, 52, 55, 242–43, 256n18, 260n108; death, 82; refusal to permit civil defense against nuclear weapons, 41–45, 247; skepticism about military utility of nuclear weapons, 19–20, 34–38
Stanford Research Institute, 103, 159
Steelman, John, 41–42, 64
Stone, Jeremy, 166
Strategic Arms Limitation Talks Treaty (SALT), 182, 192, 204, 208, 210, 286n62; Soviet refusal to negotiate about civil defense, 207
Strategic Arms Reduction Treaty (START), 233
Strategic Defense Initiative (SDI), 223–24, 231–34, 237, 292n157
Strategic Rocket Forces, 155
Strugatskii, Arkadii, 135
Strugatskii, Boris, 135, 230
Survival Under Atomic Attack (1950 booklet), 64, 72
Survival Under Atomic Attack (1951 film), 69–70, 72
survivalism, 230
Symington, W. Stuart, 43–44, 47–48, 65, 108, 259n103

"Team B", 203
television: antinuclear campaigners appear on Soviet, 227–28; broadcasts of civil defense propaganda, 66, 73, 180, 240, 242; growth of, 70, 191; popular portrayals of civil defense on, 131, 217, 230; U.S. civil defense officials appear on, 64, 78, 216
Teller, Edward, 192, 220
Thinking about the Unthinkable (1962 book), 152, 277
Thomas, Albert, 164, 278n86
Tirana, Brandyl, 210, 219
Tolstikov, Oleg, 152, 281n130
Tomorrow! (1954 novel), 98, 135

Truman, Harry: announces Soviet A-bomb test, 41–42; appointment of Millard Caldwell as civil defense administrator, 48–49; establishes FCDA, 50; Hesitation to authorize civil defense program, 40–41, 43, 52, 157, 243; re-election, 49, 261n127; refusal to accept Caldwell's resignation, 78–79
Tsygichko, Vitalii, 194

Ukraine, 1–2, 138, 175, 179–80, 197, 284n20
United Kingdom, 22, 25, 28, 30, 147
United States Air Force, 1, 108, 142, 153
United States Civil Defense (1950 book), 44, 47, 51
United States Congress, 250; demands for civil defense, 13, 102–5, 113, 187, 209–11, 271n27, 289n103; hostile to civil defense spending, 6, 12, 16, 43, 55, 59–61, 63, 72, 76, 78, 95, 100, 139, 141, 159, 162, 164–65, 170, 172–73, 187, 216, 218, 220, 222, 225, 246; insistence on state and local control of civil defense, 39, 44; investigates alleged corruption in FEMA, 213; passes Civil Defense Act of 1950, 51
United States Strategic Bombing Survey (USSBS), 17–18, 33
Universal Military Training (UMT), 44
U.S. Civil War, 20
U.S. Department of Defense (DOD), 40, 138, 158–61, 172, 193, 204–9, 211, 217, 245
U.S. Department of State, 147, 204, 206–7
U.S. House of Representatives, 165, 169, 214, 220, 242; Appropriations Committee, 59–60, 62, 136, 164, 220–21
U.S. Senate, 51, 123, 165, 169–70, 220, 226

Vance, Cyrus, 204, 285n51
Vannikov, Boris, 35–38, 45, 52
Villella, Fred J., 213
Voennaia mysl' (journal), 196
Voennaia Strategiia (1962 book), 154–57
Voennye znaniia (magazine), 86–87, 189
Vorobev, Serafim, 234
Voroshilov, Kliment, 23–24, 27

Wadsworth, James, J., 47–48, 50, 61, 64–65, 69, 78–79, 260n121, 266n97
War Survival in Soviet Strategy (1976 book), 202, 210
warning time, 91, 106, 109–10, 125, 197, 272n43
Warnke, Paul, 192–93, 286n62
Washington (state), 110, 225, 243
Washington, D.C., 49, 63, 78, 112, 161–62, 269n3
weak contract state: cause of contradictory policies, 60, 99, 105, 113, 137, 139, 141, 171, 187, 190, 220, 222, 238; contrast with garrison state, 8–9, 136, 238, 246, 251; defined, 10; relationship to civil defense, 38, 44, 55, 113, 139, 141, 170, 192, 246, 250
Weinberg, Alvin, 232–33
Welles, Orson, 108
Wells, H. G., 21
Wiesner, Jerome, 146, 150
Wigner, Eugene, 165, 181–83, 192, 202, 208, 226, 291n137
Winchell, Walter, 39–40, 43
Winter War, 28
The World Set Free (1914 novel), 21
Wylie, Philip, 98, 108, 129–31, 135, 209

York, Herbert F., 146
Young, Stephen, 164, 170

www.ingramcontent.com/pod-product-compliance
Lightning Source LLC
Chambersburg PA
CBHW051208300426
44116CB00006B/472